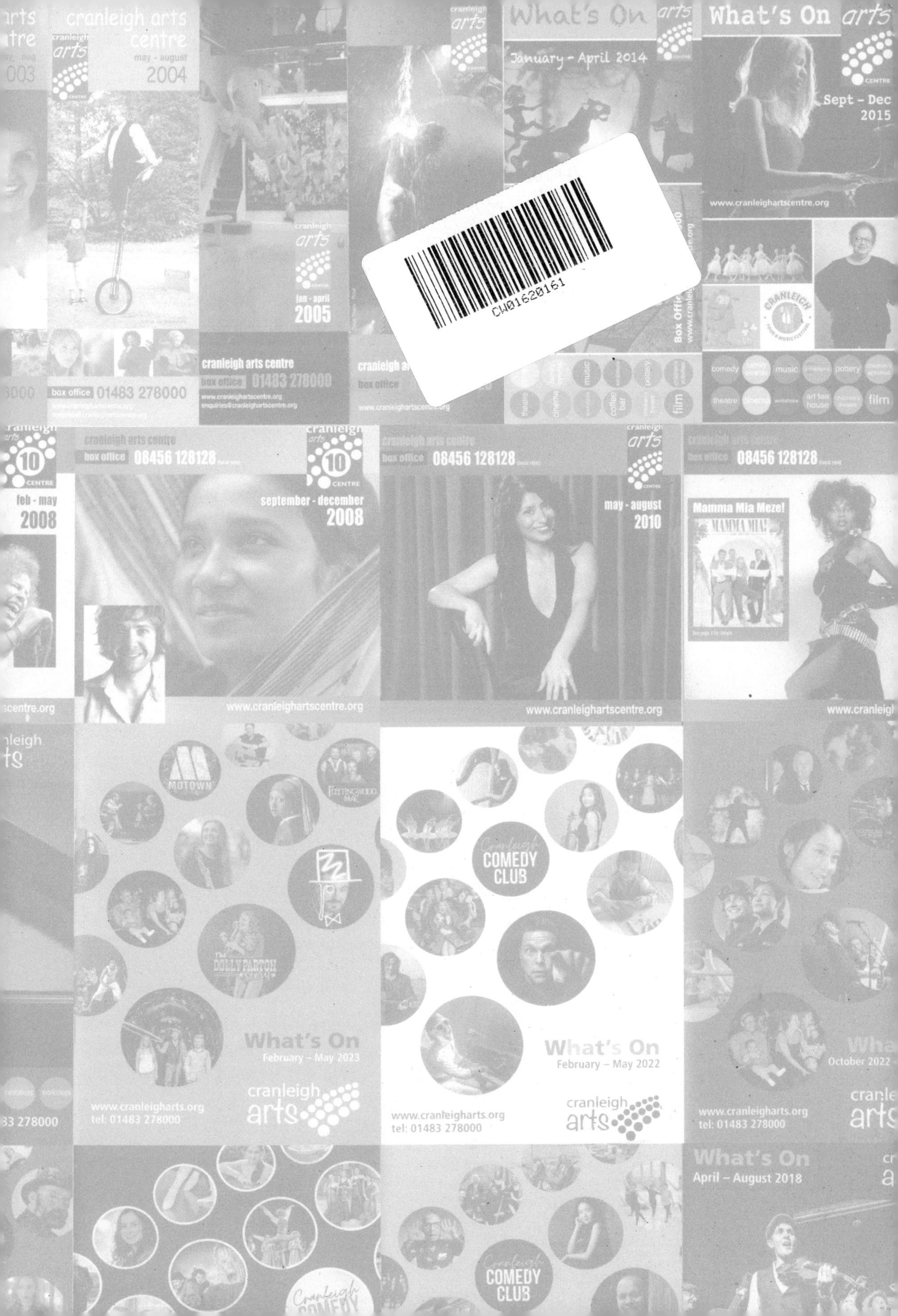
cranleigh arts centre
may - august
2004
box office 01483 278000
jan - april
2005
cranleigh arts centre
box office 01483 278000
www.cranleighartscentre.org
What's On
January - April 2014
What's On
Sept - Dec
2015
www.cranleighartscentre.org
comedy
music
pottery
theatre
cinema
film
coffee bar
feb - may
2008
cranleigh arts centre
box office 08456 128128
september - december
2008
www.cranleighartscentre.org
box office 08456 128128
may - august
2010
www.cranleighartscentre.org
box office 08456 128128
Mamma Mia Meze!
MOTOWN
The DOLLY PARTON STORY
What's On
February – May 2023
www.cranleigharts.org
tel: 01483 278000
cranleigh arts
Cranleigh COMEDY CLUB
What's On
February – May 2022
www.cranleigharts.org
tel: 01483 278000
cranleigh arts
October 2022
www.cranleigharts.org
tel: 01483 278000
What's On
April – August 2018
Cranleigh COMEDY CLUB

Cranleigh Arts

50 YEARS AT THE HEART OF THE COMMUNITY

Clive Wouters

Quacks Books

First Published in Great Britain in 2024

7 Grape Lane, Petergate, York YO1 7HU
Tel: +44 (0)1904 635967
Email: info@quacks.info
Website: radiusonline.info
Quacks Books is an imprint of Radius Publishing Ltd

A CIP catalogue record for this book is available from the British Library.

ISBN: 978-1-912728-93-0

Set on a page size of 176 x 250mm printed on offset one hundred gsm chosen for its sustainability.

Dedicated to all those
who have kept the vision alive
and value the arts.

Contents

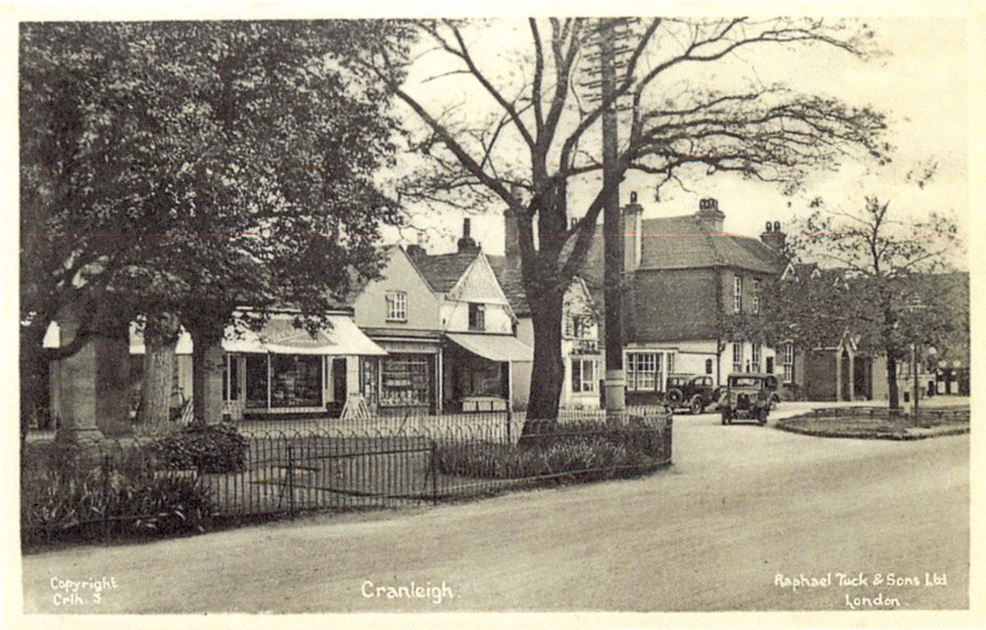

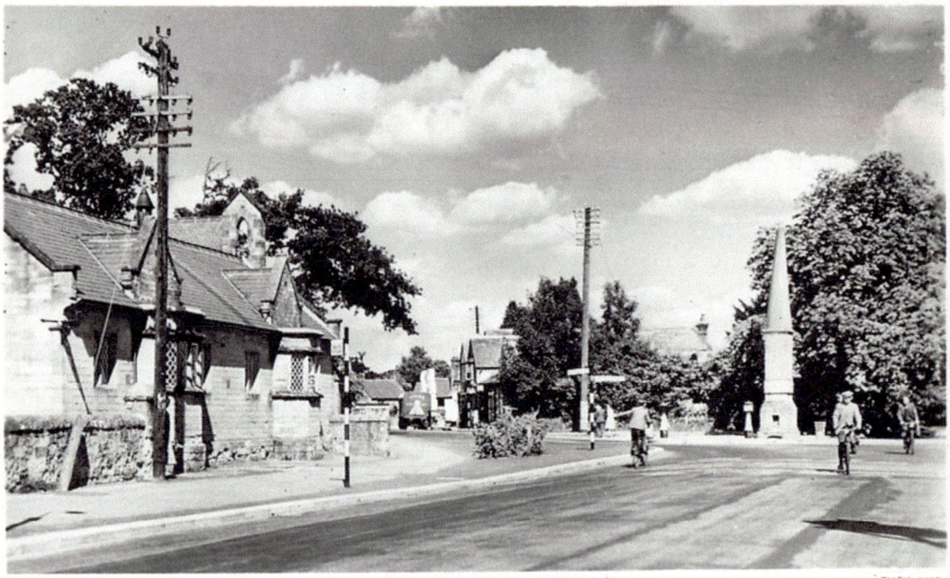

CL 4 HIGH STREET AND OBELISK, CRANLEIGH A TUCK CARD

Chapter One

Introduction

Cranleigh has always had a strong sense of its own identity and particular strengths as a village. The main features of its church, distinguished school, memorial hall, public houses and its long high street, lined with maples from the village green to the obelisk marking the toll road, all serve to give it its charm and vibrancy. Its inhabitants have been variously: farm labourers and their gentry, professional folk and retirees, home counties commuters, as well as the providers of all the crafts and services a community needs: butcher, fishmonger, general stores, post office and banks.

For almost the last fifty years another key part of the character of the village has been the Cranleigh Arts Centre. Created by the people of Cranleigh, for the people of Cranleigh, it has evolved and grown over the years to serve the cultural needs of the village. It has weathered vicissitudes of funding and creative differences, but through the vision and passion of key people, and the energy and support of an army of volunteers, it has played a significant role in making Cranleigh the valued and loved place it is today.

South East Arts Association said in 1989 that *"Cranleigh Arts Centre could provide a model case study of a village school conversion and is likely to prove of national importance"*. But besides the bricks and mortar, this is the also the story of how people can create and deliver a vision, and how that necessarily has to change as the community it belongs to changes. Every arts centre is different, but the problems they face are universal. How do we engage people? What do people want? What do we put on? How can we plan for the future? How do we finance it? The limiting issues and coping strategies seem to have come round in a cycle, often driven by external factors. Boom and bust, lean years and plentiful have to be managed for both survival and evolution. Change has been a constant.

This account aims to be a record of the efforts of those involved and their achievements, an examination of the process of engaging a local community in the arts, and an acknowledgement of the wider changing context in which the arts has had to operate.

The fact that Cranleigh Arts has survived and is thriving after fifty years is both instructive and a cause for celebration.

Chapter Two

Serving the community in the 1970s

From the grass roots comes ambition

Coming together

The need for a communal space for the arts is identified within the local groups in Cranleigh

Post-war Britain, from the Festival of Britain onwards, saw an increase in groups and activities relating to the arts, as more leisure time and income, together with the expansion and exposure to the arts in the sixties and seventies, led to a demand for participation. Cranleigh was no exception. The seeds of a village arts centre were sown initially by Howard Pickersgill, Art Director at Cranleigh School, who wrote to *The Surrey Advertiser* 9th April 1971.

Cranleigh Need for an Arts Centre

Sir,

I wonder if I might seek the hospitality of your columns to put before your readers the idea of an 'Arts Centre for Cranleigh'.

I have known Cranleigh for 20 years ever since I started 'Painting for Pleasure' classes in the Surrey County Council Evening Institute with the eager support of the Principal, Denis Thorpe, I have found a constant and growing interest in the arts in the community.

In the fifties we ran very successful exhibitions of painting, first in Ambulance Rooms and then in the Practical Block of Glebelands School. By successful, I refer to the volume of work shown, its standard, and the great public interest it aroused.

Coming back to Cranleigh four years ago, to take up my present work, I was very interested to see that exhibitions were being revived; largely thanks to the energy and enthusiasm of Joy Atwell and Gwen Viney. This exhibition was received with great acclaim and resulted in the formation, almost by...

...spontaneous combustion, of an Arts and Crafts Society. This Society has recently put on a third annual show for two days instead of the previous one and this attracted the interest of yet greater number of viewers and made increased sales.

Is it not time now, in view of this interest, to consider whether the community is not asking for an Arts Centre situated in the middle of the village offering opportunity for space, liaison and publicity to other societies than the Arts and Crafts Society, such as the Literary Society, the Choral Society, the Cranleigh Players and so on.

It would be interesting to know to what service the local Council plan to put the old Church of England Primary School. It would seem to me to be ideally suited to the kind of purpose I have suggested.

I would be very interested to know what support there would be for such a scheme and I would be grateful if your readers would write either to the paper or directly to me.

Howard Pickersgill, *Director of Art. The Art School. Cranleigh School*

A letter in support was published on 23rd April.

Arts Centre in Cranleigh

Sir,

In support of the proposal put forward by Mr Pickersgill in his letter of April 9th, may I say that Cranleigh Players have for some time been seeking accommodation in the village suitable for holding meetings and rehearsals. We find that having to rely on the good offices of members making their houses and outbuildings available for rehearsals and storage puts limitations on our activities as a dramatic society. The availability of premises as envisaged by Mr Pickersgill would enable my society to extend considerably in the field of dramatics.

The old Church of England School mentioned has now been let; we unfortunately were unable to obtain part of this building. In the event of similar premises being available my society would be very interested in joint occupation with other organisations.

Elizabeth Vivian, *Hon Sec.*

The Arts and Crafts Society, whose membership included Mrs Jill Pickersgill, geared up for action as reported in *The Surrey Daily Advertiser* on 30th April.

> *"The Arts and Crafts Society is to organise a survey in Cranleigh on Saturday to get views of the general public on the possibility of opening an Arts Centre in Cranleigh. It is visualised as a village community effort and the aims of such a Centre would be to enrich the area culturally and socially, and liaison between other societies founded in the arts would be encouraged. There would be facilities for the practise of crafts and exhibitions of work by outside artists. Premises would need to be found, but the first task would be to find out if support for this kind of venture would be forthcoming. Members gave their signatures to the Hon Sec, Mrs B Steele, in support."*

By 1st October the ball was rolling as reported again in *The Surrey Daily Advertiser*.

> *"Members of interested groups and societies met at Cranleigh School on Monday to discuss the financial aspects of setting up an arts centre in Cranleigh.*
> *Societies represented included the Camera Club, the Cranleigh Arts and Crafts Junior Society, the Literary Society, the Choral Society and the Cranleigh Players.*
> *It now seems most likely that an early start will be made with this venture. Further negotiations are taking place and it is hoped to make an announcement shortly.*
> *A working party is to be set up consisting of two members of each interested society who will investigate financial details and report back to their various groups."*

Who were the main participants?

Why the different groups wanted to be involved

The oldest was the Cranleigh Players, established for 25 years, who had a strong local reputation. They presented musical evenings such as 'Old Time Music Hall' and an annual pantomime, as well as straight plays, and had some success in local drama competitions. They regularly had a float in the annual Carnival parade, often winning first prize. Jane Shean remembers being dressed as a puffin on a pile of stones for the 'Goodnight, Mrs Puffin' float in 1966 and nearly being pitched into the crowd when it went over a bump just in front of the judges. Another outstanding production was 'The Crucible'. Other notable events were a Passion Play in St Nicholas Church, 'Ring Round the Moon' in 1971 and 'The Passing of the Third Floor Back' in 1972. The reviewer at the time declared that they *"had emerged as more than just an amateur company"*. Hiring the village hall had become too expensive as the electricity used was charged at peak rate and all the technical equipment had to be specially rigged and derigged each time. They also had a large stock of costumes, props and scenery to store which they had moved about using various old barns, even a chicken shed. They had tried other local halls but needed a base and a clubroom now they were so successful. Presently they were rehearsing in the loft of a disused stable. Their Chairman was Peggy Martin and their main director/producer was Betty Webb. Malcolm Beeson, newly moved to Cranleigh, became their technical wizard, building his own transistorised dimmer racks from drawings in an electronics magazine. Jon and Val Hewitt were also active members.

The Camera Club had been going for fifteen years under Reg Monk and had grown to thirty plus members but, meeting in the St John's Ambulance building, they also lacked the facilities to enable continuity for their activities.

The Cranleigh Arts and Crafts Society was founded by Joy Atwell and Sam Maynard in 1968 and had begun in 1969 to hold increasingly successful annual exhibitions in the Village Hall, but wanted somewhere to meet monthly for demonstrations and talks. A local craft potter as well as local artists were in this group and identified a need for studio space as well as an exhibition space. They had about one hundred members.

In 1971 the Literary Society, under the leadership of Matt Moor, instigated the Cranleigh Awards for Poetry and Prose. This expanded in 1972 with the sponsorship of *The Surrey Advertiser* into a much bigger affair. Nationally recognised poet Edwin Brock judged the poetry, while the prose fell to the Editor, Mr J Penycate. There were 1,684 entries in total, including from 107 schools within a 20 mile radius of Cranleigh.

Cranleigh also supported a Subscription Concert series at Cranleigh School, which had the London Mozart Players as regular performers.

A sense of how these groups were beginning to develop ways of working together comes from the last paragraph of an article on the Fourth Annual Arts and Crafts Society Exhibition.

> *"A link up of the arts was provided on Saturday evening by the Cranleigh Players and members of the Literary Society when a diversion from viewing to listening was given in a lively and entertaining poetry session."*

First Steps

An umbrella organisation is established to forward the common purpose to raise funds for an arts building for everyone

In order to enter into agreements for land or property rental or purchase or to submit bids for funding a Trust needed to be formed. The Players being the highest profile group and the most used to this sort of thing were at the fore and put forward

Malcolm Beeson to lead the operation and he subsequently became the founding Chairman and first Director of what was to be called the Cranleigh Arts and Leisure Trust (CALT). Publicity and fundraising commenced through 1973 to get the wider community involved from the considerable membership base of the organisations. A prospectus was drawn up and plans considered for what an arts centre building might look like. By November 1973 at the Players' Xmas Fayre people were invited to *"view the new Arts Centre plans"*.

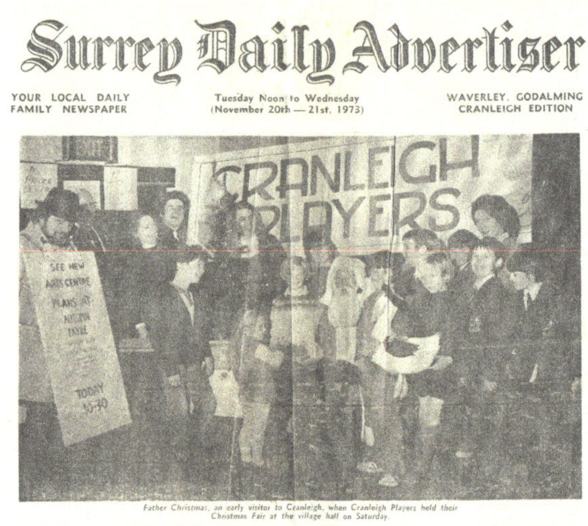

Surrey Daily Advertiser

YOUR LOCAL DAILY FAMILY NEWSPAPER

Tuesday Noon to Wednesday (November 20th — 21st, 1973)

WAVERLEY, GODALMING CRANLEIGH EDITION

Father Christmas, an early visitor to Cranleigh, when Cranleigh Players held their Christmas Fair at the village hall on Saturday.

In June 1973, Jack Wagg, Clerk to Hambledon Rural District Council, was able to come up with a possible site. The railway line through Cranleigh from Guildford had been closed in 1965 by Dr Beeching, the only cut in Surrey, and there was a portion of that land, now ceded to Hambledon and the Parish council, that could be available. It lay off Knowle Lane, behind Starbucks, the printers, adjoining Warrens Yard, which is broadly behind where Marks and Spencer's is now. Planning permission was applied for to erect a temporary building with access from Knowle Lane. It then transpired that outline plans for a possible relief road, talked about for some years, might slice through part of the railway site which complicated matters. There was also some continued interest in the old village school building, which had gradually been wound down since the opening of the new school, Glebelands, in 1959. Some use had continued for a few years as pupils and classes were transferred, but it was now deteriorating. However it had just partly been let to a table tennis club and the two wings to local artists. When the District Council turned down the initial plan put to them for the railway site as too grandiose, discussion and consultation continued at length about both spaces.

There was however a sense of urgency to Jack Wagg's suggestions due to the impending absorption of Hambledon District Council into Waverley Borough Council in the up-coming Local Government reorganisation, which had led to a clearing of desks and a desire to tidy up the assets and finances. Also there was a fear that the new authority might just shelve the project as it got to grips with its new portfolios, although the designated Chief Executive, Jack Wagg, would provide continuity between the two administrations. The plans for the railway site were revised and made more acceptable, but then news came that the village school might be made available after all.

For the formal structure of the Cranleigh Arts and Leisure Trust it was proposed to have a constitution with an elected committee alongside the appointment of trustees, who had legal oversight of it. They were to be: Marc van Hasselt, Headmaster of Cranleigh School; Anthony Young, Parish Councillor and master at Cranleigh School; and William Narraway, local professional portrait artist and President of the Arts and Crafts Society (who was replaced after his death in 1980 by Peter Levy). On 9th March 1974 the Trust deed was signed and a constitution agreed at an inaugural public meeting on 19th June at Glebelands School attended by 40 people. This would be further ratified at the AGM in June 1975 and subsequently in 1977 and 1978. The trust would own the land for an arts centre, erect such buildings as necessary, administer funds and allow it to be enjoyed by the people of Cranleigh and other villages for education and recreation.

> *"The objects of the Trust shall be to foster and promote the maintenance of artistic taste and knowledge, understanding and appreciation of the arts and in the interests of social welfare facilitating other leisure time activities (apart from sport) for the inhabitants and district with the object of improving the conditions of life particularly by the establishment of the Cranleigh Arts and Leisure Centre."*

The public meeting was well reported in *The Surrey Advertiser*. First the constitution was read. Mr F Everington, a local solicitor who gave his services voluntarily, had advised on this, and would go on to help with the ongoing changes and applications. Its approval was another necessary precursor to being able to apply for grants to raise the £100,000 cost of building the planned Arts and Leisure Centre on the leased railway land, for which planning applications had already been made. Doubt was expressed by Mr R Jinman that once a building had been acquired then even more money would be needed for staff to run it. How true that was to become in 1998. This would also be the start of a perennial battle between capital and operational expenditure down to the present day. The founder societies were guaranteed representation on the committee and an annual subscription of 25p per society member would be levied. Two bank accounts would be needed to separate building fund money from day to day costs and it was noted that already fundraising had started, putting the trustee fund at £750.

The costs of the plans broke down as follows:

for a main hall 21m by 10m, with stage, lighting and fundamentals would be £45,000;

art studios, craft workshops and offices in three groups of buildings would be £16,500; photography workshop 9m by 5m £11,000;
music practice and store rooms £14-15,000.
Each society would have its own lockable area and the car park could be used as a buffer against possible encroachment on the site by the relief road. It could be started by building a workshop/meeting room for £11,000. Mr Pickersgill suggested aiming for a simplified multi-purpose main hall for £25,000.
These plans were all approved by the meeting and a management committee elected consisting of Dr Malcolm Beeson, Chairman; Mrs Nancy Horne, Secretary; Mr D Coles, Treasurer; Mr K Soden-Barton, Asst Treasurer; Mr R Atwell; Mrs J Blower; Mr L Field; Mr J Hewitt; Mr R Monk; Mr D Newson; Mr H Pickersgill; Mr W Tucker.

The ambition

How to make the theory a reality by getting local support

The Cranleigh Arts and Leisure Trust's ambition to build an arts centre fitted with the recent improvements to Cranleigh that had come with the Stockland Square development created from the old railway station (1966), the new Post Office (1959) and the new Leisure Centre (1964). In 1961 the population was about 6,000 but there were considerable developments on the north and east sides of the village in the 1960s: Park Mead (1964/5), Overford Drive (1965), Hitherwood (1965/6), Cranleigh Mead Wimpey (1966/7), Summerlands and Nuthatch (1967/8). Thus by 1971 it had risen to approximately 10,000. This influx of young families, attracted by the sense of community that Cranleigh had, wanted to get involved in the life of the village and in social and cultural activities. They were a ready source of members for the partner societies and ready volunteers for projects in the village.

In the 1975/6 prospectus, which was used to sell the idea of a new arts centre to the people of Cranleigh, the local literary giant, novelist, essayist and critic Frank Swinnerton wrote a Foreword. He had lived in the village for fifty years and had celebrated it in his book of observations, 'Reflections from a Village'. He penned a glowing piece extolling Cranleigh's rural bliss and friendliness and noting many newcomers since 1923.

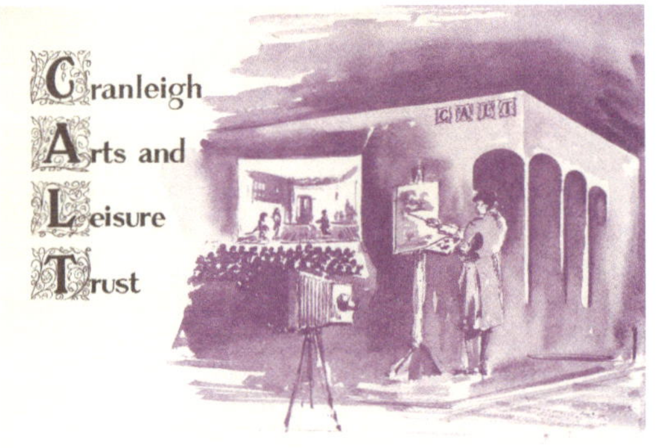

"And the friendliness of old Cranleigh has embraced the expanding population most remarkably. It has stimulated far wider interests than we knew in former days and the coordination of those interests demands a Centre for social and artistic activity. That is the justification, if justification were needed, for the grand scheme of CALT. If you would know more, read on!"

The Prospectus had a profile of the village, a history of the initiative, details of the three founding societies and plans for the building of an arts centre. The use of the old village school as an arts centre is described as *"a landmark in the evolution of CALT and will serve as its headquarters for the foreseeable future. It will provide a cultural and social meeting place not only for the CALT societies individually but for integrated CALT activities and for other societies also: the realisation of many villagers' dreams"*. It also described the railway land and the ambition to have purpose-built accommodation there, with drawings. It concluded with more endorsements including from David Shepherd, the wildlife artist, Oscar Quitak and Andree Melly, professional actors who also ran a health food shop in the High Street, Michael More-Molyneux, who would become Surrey's Lord Lieutenant, and other local worthies.

Fundraising went into overdrive. The three groups raised £1,000 by raffles, shows, collections and sales and Hambledon added £5,000 as a farewell present before becoming Waverley on 1st April 1974. A big initiative was launched the following year. A concert with a soloist and the London Schubert Orchestra was presented on 10th May 1975 at Cranleigh School, but few tickets were sold which led to red faces all round. An organ recital by Martin White in St Nicholas Church was a sell-out however. It seems Classical music was unpredictable even then. In July there was a stall at the Cranleigh Show to raise the profile and a Hallowe'en Fayre fundraiser in October in the Village Hall. This featured a painted Covent Garden back-drop and members in medieval costume, courtesy of the Players, running craft, food,

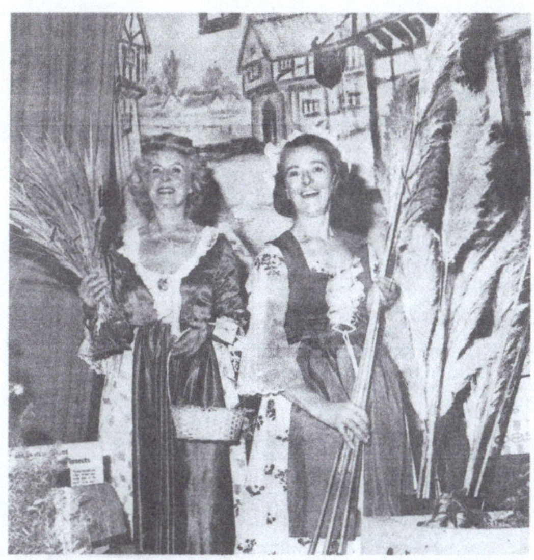

Back in medieval times

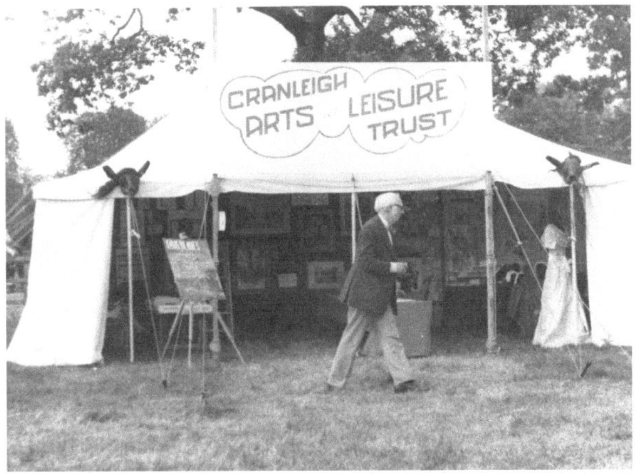

garden and gift stalls and of course – a raffle. The Arts and Crafts Society sold handmade gifts, the Camera Club showed slides and there were games and competitions. This included the first artistic competition to design a Christmas card, which was offered to all readers of all ages of the *Surrey Daily Advertiser*. The winners were announced at the Hallowe'en Fayre with the idea to produce the winners' cards and sell them to raise funds. 110 entries were received and displayed and voted on by attendees. This has since over the years evolved into a series of open competitions in various areas to engage with and celebrate Cranleigh's artistic community.

Waverley Council was now reassessing the old village school building as the current leases were due to expire, and seemed to support the idea of it being leased as a base to CALT. The Leisure and Culture committee took over management of the building from the Finance and Lands committee and set up a working party in early 1975, which included Cranleigh councillors Mr Trevor Williams and Mr John Wiskar, who reported back to the Parish Council on progress: Mr Wiskar said that a space was also needed for the Junior Brass Band, who might also be included; the Rev E F Johnson, who was added to the working party as Parish Council representative, said that when the old school was sold to the council by the Church Commissioners it was meant to benefit the community, with a particular request that it be used as a day centre for old people. There were two site meetings in May and June, with CALT represented by Dr Beeson and Vice-Chairman David Newson presenting their ideas. However it was decided that the Cranleigh Pottery and the Cranleigh Art School would have their leases of the East and West wings renewed for six and seven years respectively, which left just the middle section to be decided, the table tennis group having given notice they were moving to the Recreation Centre. By now the Surrey Institute of Further Education had thrown their hat in the ring too. Reporting this to the Parish Council in June there was discussion of possible extensions to the buildings.

> *"Mr Williams said he thought this would be very difficult and costly in view of the old and damp condition of the building. The Chairman, Mr P Levy, said that in his opinion there would be a riot if the school were to be extended and it was unanimously agreed that the Parish Council would object if this were proposed."*

Finding a Home

The Old Village School building becomes the most practical solution and best model for a community arts centre

By the first AGM in June 1975 Malcolm Beeson was able to announce that the recommendation had been made by the working party to Waverley to let CALT lease the building and put in place their plans to transform it into a cultural centre. He said that the acquisition of the building would give new direction to the trust but it would continue to strive for a purpose-built Arts and Leisure Centre on the site it had chosen off Knowle Lane. The operational expenditure of rent and running costs would be covered by fundraising by the societies using the building in the evening and by hiring out the space to groups such as Adult Education during the day. The two wings would continue to be occupied by an artist, Peter Oliver, who ran a school of painting and a potter, Donald Marsh, but the trust could have the rest.

So the Cranleigh Arts Centre came into being, to be added to incrementally over time as availability of space and funds allowed. The constitution was amended unanimously to allow other societies or individuals with an interest in the arts to be affiliated with the trust. Mr Trevor Williams immediately became the trust's first affiliated member. Dr Beeson was re-elected Chairman; Mr Jon Hewitt, vice-chairman; Mr Les Field, Treasurer; Mrs N Horne, Secretary; Mrs J Blower; Mrs D Savedra; Rev E F Johnson; Mr R Atwell; Mr E Odell Foster; Mr R Monk and Mr S Maynard to the committee.

At first it was a bare rental arrangement. The condition of the building was very poor. Although the outside walls were sound, inside the floorboards were riddled with dry rot, the plaster needed repair, there were no furnishings, no heating and only temporary lighting. Toilet and cloakroom facilities in the rear building were adequate, having been recently improved. There was space for a small kitchen and also a heating boiler in this rear section, which contained a long corridor and additional spaces. The most useful room was the central one nearest the road (now the Crane Room), which would be the performance/meeting space, seating about 90. There were plans for the installation of lighting, a false ceiling and a moveable stage. This was in addition to the new flooring, plastering and heating required for the whole main building. Outside was no better. In February 1976 *The Surrey Advertiser* reported that as the entrance from the car park was unlit there had been accidents to people using the building at night due to the low wall. The Art and Crafts Society said they put candles in bottles for their members to come and go by. A spokesman for CALT said they could do nothing until the lease had been signed. In July 1976 Malcolm Beeson was writing to Waverley asking for a structural survey

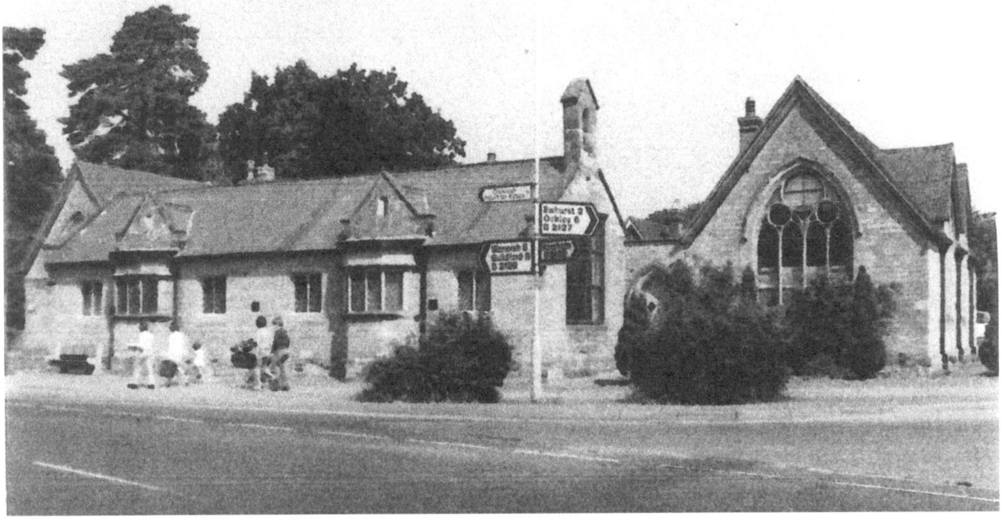

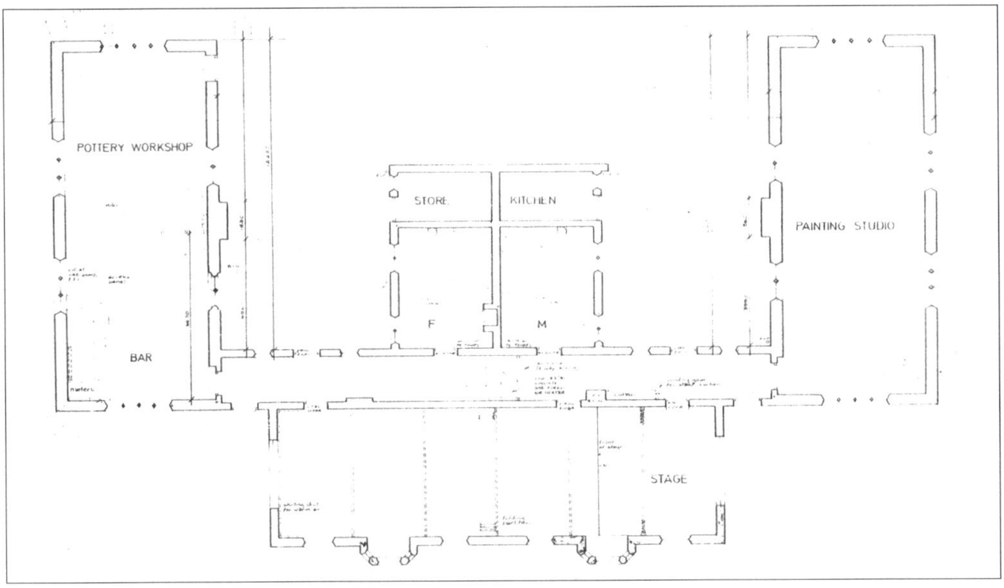

before they would agree to taking on full responsibility for the building. Negotiations over the lease centred on how much of the damp and rotten windows Waverley would put right.

Part of the campaign of banging the drum for the Arts Centre was an article in *The Surrey County Magazine* by Judith Doyle in March 1976 which was a call to arms and a celebration of what had been achieved. She drew on the material in the Prospectus and her own visit to see the old school building at Christmas 1975 noting, *"a certain amount of imagination was needed to visualise the inside as it will appear when the transformation is complete"*. She outlined the plans and costs that had been drawn up and the difficulties encountered along the way. She wrote of the societies that had come together and the trustees who had been appointed. She concluded:

> *"The Cranleigh Arts Centre project has valuable lessons for the rest of Surrey as it demonstrates a compromise between what every community would like – e.g. an expensive purpose built centre – with what almost any community could afford. There must be many communities where a village school, or similar building, is finally declared redundant because of rebuilding or reorganisation. ... Old school buildings tend to be particularly suitable for arts Centres as they are often sited in the middle of the village or town. WE'D LIKE TO WISH GOOD FORTUNE TO THE CRANLEIGH ARTS CENTRE. MAY IT NOT ONLY PROSPER BUT GIVE A LEAD TO SIMILAR SCHEMES IN SURREY COMMUNITIES WHERE THERE IS A DEARTH OF FACILITIES AT THE MOMENT. THE COST IS LOW AND THE POSSIBILITIES ARE GREAT." (Her caps.)*

To which the Editor added: *"It is wholly regrettable that Surrey County Council do not make provision, in conjunction with Local Councils, for Arts Centres out of the rates – but Cranleigh's example will surely inspire many similar projects."*

Dilys Savedra, Head of Adult Education for Surrey County Council, based at Glebelands School, wanted to expand classes in Cranleigh and had agreement from Waverley to use the School for a nominal rent. They already used the West wing for some classes – Painting for Pleasure with Pat Harvey (1974/5). Ann Horrocks joined her to do pottery classes, and there were other classes with Cynthia Sixsmith, Liz Hoad and John Kidd. These people overlapped with the CALT ambitions for the building too. Ann's husband Jon, Mike Savedra and David Weaver did much renovation work, creating concrete work places for pottery and putting in a false ceiling. There was an annual exhibition by the Adult Education classes. Ann had the inspiration to organise the Arts Centre around a coffee bar plus exhibition space, after visiting the New Brewery Arts Centre in Cirencester and started, with Jill Newcomb, Head of Careers with Guildford Borough Council, a weekly exhibition of local artists on a Saturday, with coffee available. They insisted on round tables to encourage socialising.

Adult Education was the main user, but the member groups used it too. By 1976 a regular Theatre Group began to meet at the Centre, which culminated in a mime performance of 'Don Quixote'. Adult Education expanded into embroidery and upholstery; there was even badminton! Brian Hemingway and Edie Goodfellow started the Cranleigh Film Society with regular showings in the large room, now equipped for studio performances. Once they had a Public Performance Licence, having met fire regulations, there was also support from South East Arts Association who added Cranleigh to their list of small scale tour venues, including 'Under Milk Wood' in October 1977, and a one man show about Lewis Carroll called 'Crocodiles in Cream' with Clive Wouters in March 1978. By this time Cranleigh History and Archaeological Society and Cranleigh Film Society had joined as member organisations. Cranleigh School of Ballet were signed in with classes too. Keeping the building looked after was difficult with so many people using it and the Chairman had to write a stern letter to the member groups asking them to *"follow the rules"*! Dilys Savedra more often than not, with other volunteers, did the locking up at the end of the day. Eventually she became de facto Centre manager in combination with her Adult Education role.

Teething troubles settling in

It becomes clear that having a building is both a blessing and a problem as the financial and logistical difficulties are revealed

After the AGM in 1977 a new Treasurer was appointed who ran a rule over the accounts, as they do. Malcolm Beeson reported to the Trustees in September that *"This gives us a clearer picture of our Centre running costs etc. and will be invaluable for forward planning. But ... there is a marked deterioration in our cash balance"*. He explains that there are two accounts: one for a building fund controlled by the trustees and the other for current expenditure, controlled by the management committee. That had now been split into 'project', 'admin' and 'running costs and income'. He went on, *"The most encouraging fact to emerge from these latest figures is that the Arts Centre is now paying its way. However CALT itself is still struggling to make good a large deficit, caused mainly by the losses on the promotional Schubert concert and the Prospectus"*. There had been an unexpected rates demand and significant expenditure on the building. He hoped that the Trustees would agree to suspend the minimum contingency fund retention in their reserves account in order to pay immediate expenses. Against this there was £2,000 expected soon when the railway land lease was relinquished. They agreed and the work went ahead. By Jan 1978 the replastering of the main long wall and bays in the main room was completed for £355 and new skirting boards and timber cladding of doorways were installed for £360. This battle of juggling reserves against urgent expenditure needed to keep the building operational was to continue for the next fifty years!

A local architect, Mr Leadrum, had been part of the team creating the railway site project and he was also advising on how the old school could be brought up to scratch. In August 1977 Malcolm Beeson wrote to the Beecham Group Charity

Appeals Committee to ask for financial assistance for a grant of £10k – £50k and outlining the Trust's achievements and ambitions.

> *"The Trust intends to promote the interests of the Arts in the area by two means: By the establishment of an Arts Centre and by the creation of further local societies with artistic interests. This latter objective has already been achieved in part by the formation, at the instigation of the Trust, of a Film Society ...[and] ... a local Archaeological Society. We have been granted a long-term lease on the former village school and have over the past two years spent £6,000 on the renovation of this 100 year old building."*

The work done was listed as:

1. Replaced the rotten wooden floor with concrete.
2. Built a stage.
3. Installed central heating.
4. Replastered some walls.
5. Exposed the local stone of other walls and dressed them.
6. Completely rewired.
7. Installed stage lighting.
8. Installed emergency lighting.
9. Installed exhibition lighting.
10. Installed a 12' cinema screen.
11. Provided chairs and tables.

> *"The two outer wings are currently occupied by commercial artists but will come under control of the Trust within a few years. We will also have the option of infilling the area between the wings. We plan to do this as soon as possible in order to provide further meeting rooms and badly needed storage space. We also hope to provide a larger auditorium and plans for this are being drawn up by Waverley District Council. The Arts Centre is in use almost continuously, both during the day and in the evenings. It is constantly mentioned in the local papers and has been featured in The Surrey County Magazine."*

Despite being an employee of Beechams, after a delay, in May 1978 he was refused. It was necessary to be registered as a charity so negotiations started with the Charity Commission in 1976/7. The details required included the Constitution, which had been agreed at the AGM in 1975, and Minutes and Accounts. However various changes in wording and additional clarification and clauses needed to be added. So letters went back and forth. The then Chairman, Mr E Odell Foster, dealt with this and subsequently when he stood down Malcolm Beeson took it up, finally finishing the application by May 1978. But they were still not happy and two extra EGMs were needed in June to approve the final wording as Waverley, when drafting the lease, had also wanted changes.

As CALT's plans became more realised they argued that, having poured so much time and money into the Village School on behalf of the Council, they wanted more security and ownership. Thus a longer lease for twenty-one years was drafted in 1977. They would surrender the lease they had taken on the railway land and bid for the school. This went back and forth between the lawyers as major and minor points were resolved. Malcolm Beeson reports to the Trustees: *"We are still fighting with them over the lease but are putting the pressure on them now." "We are fed up with their tardiness and bullying approach."* (Jan 1978). There was concern over the roof and damp-proofing, which Waverley conceded responsibility for, and in return CALT accepted two Council nominees to the management committee. CALT were offered the rest of the building as it might became available (April). However by August: *"We are back to square one".* Drafts seemed littered with errors. The copy sent in June had 36 or more errors, so could not sensibly be signed by the trustees, one of whom had even been omitted in one draft! The Council's solicitor admitted, *"I am appalled at the number of errors which have managed to creep into this lease and I congratulate you on the assiduity with which you have discovered them. I am afraid that there are probably yet more corrections which have escaped detection".* Finally, on 2nd October 1978 the lease was signed with Waverley Borough Council for the central part of the building with an option to add the two wings as they came available, which they did in due course. Surrey County Council Adult Education Centre were allowed to be the main hirers giving some guaranteed income. The rolling nature of these discussions led to some ambiguity when the first rent review took place later on. Ironically the value added to the building by the Trust led the District Valuer to suggest commercial rents under pressure from Waverley, which as a charity they were ill placed to afford. That led to quite a battle in the 1980s.

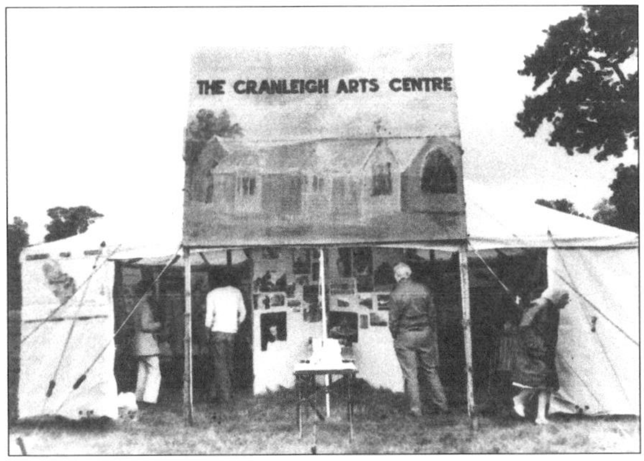

Discussions in May and June 1978 show that some divisions were starting to open up as to how to use the space in the Arts Centre. While the development of the central meeting and performance space was proceeding well, the best use of the East and West wings was debated. The Arts and Crafts Society wanted regular access, the Adult Education Institute had been promised space and a reception area was also needed. The acting Chairman Jon Hewitt writes that he *"is certain that a meeting of all interested parties can be arranged after the new Management Committee has met".*

All the societies were written to in May 1978,

> *"to remind all users of the Arts Centre that a rigid set of rules exist governing the use of the Centre .. drawn up and agreed by a committee comprising representatives from all founder societies. The purpose of the rules is to ensure the efficient running of the Centre with the minimum of expense. I trust you will comply ... and thus demonstrate your respect both for those who made the Centre the worthy 'home' it is today for so many groups and also for other users."*

The Players came in for special censure for removing tables to the Village Hall and not returning them, leaving heaters and other equipment on, using the space outside booked times, leaving scenery behind and being anti-social to other users. They were warned that future bookings might be prejudiced. Malcolm Beeson concluded,

> *"I hope most sincerely that teething troubles such as these will not be allowed to prejudice the unity and cooperation on which the acquisition and develop-ment of the Arts Centre has been and always must be based."*

Celebration

In 1978 the Opening Arts Festival shows the potential of the new enterprise. The great and the good rally round

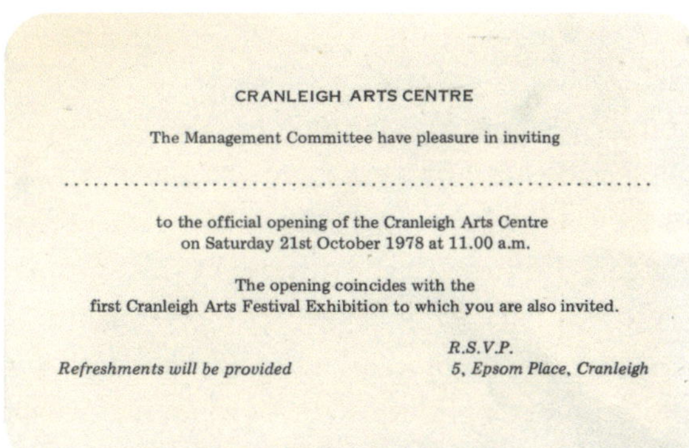

CRANLEIGH ARTS CENTRE

The Management Committee have pleasure in inviting

....

to the official opening of the Cranleigh Arts Centre
on Saturday 21st October 1978 at 11.00 a.m.

The opening coincides with the
first Cranleigh Arts Festival Exhibition to which you are also invited.

Refreshments will be provided

R.S.V.P.
5, Epsom Place, Cranleigh

To mark the official opening of the new Arts Centre in October 1978 there was a week-long Arts Festival. Jack Wagg, now joined as Press Officer, said,

> *"The hard work of members has created the nucleus of a Centre for artistic endeavour and display. This first phase is complete. Much remains to be developed if the buildings are eventually to fulfil the community art needs of Cranleigh, but the first real step forward is to be celebrated in a festival which will show the public something of all the activities of the several societies involved."*

It appears that the Management Committee had felt that the *"Councillors and/or officers of Waverley had shown a lack of thought"* towards CALT but Jack Wagg spoke to Kathy Callow (presumably a Councillor) who assured him that *"no disrespect was intended and that it would not happen again".* He recommended that invitations be sent to the Chairman and Vice-Chairman of Waverley and to the Chairman and Vice-Chairman of the Leisure and Culture Committee, plus the five members for Cranleigh, to help smooth things over. This was typical of his insight and approach.

Things began on the morning of Saturday 21st when the Godalming Fleur de Lys Morris Dancers danced up the High Street from Stocklund Square to the Arts Centre. Then it was formally opened by William Talbot, chairman of West Surrey College of Art, who appealed for close links and exchange visits between the two and to take advantage of the expertise open to artists and photographers at Farnham. Issuing a word of warning Mr Talbot said villagers should not be too serious and pompous about their use of the building. *"It's here to have fun with."* Paying tribute to the hard work which had gone into the renovation he said it was a credit to everyone connected with it. *"In the 1980s there will be many more leisure hours available and Cranleigh will be in the lead."* There was also the welcome return of Claude Blogg, former headmaster of the Church of England school, who said it was like going home. Although now confined to a wheelchair he said he was delighted to have been able to attend. *"It is wonderful that the school is going to be used for education and the efforts of the people connected with the trust are enormous and they should be congratulated for their work."* At the reception there was an exhibition of the different crafts supplied by the societies in the trust.

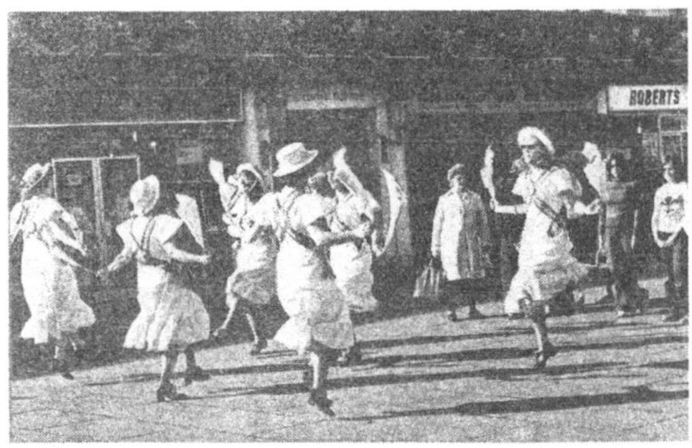

Dancing heralds

On Saturday evening Peter Corey, Linda Jamiec, Renny Krupinski and Nick Burnell performed in a Festival Revue with supper. More than 40 villagers enjoyed mime, comedy and music. *"A gem of an evening – the time just flew by with some of the best comedy I have seen for a very long time, simply performed,"* said Jon Hewitt to *The Surrey Advertiser*. They were actors from the Redgrave Theatre, Farnham and were part of a link forged through South East Arts who had provided touring theatre shows already.

On Sunday Peter Corey was back leading an all-day theatre workshop which was attended by 40 children between the ages of 6 and 13.

Mr Martin White gave an organ recital at St Nicholas Church including the debut of a sonata by Venetian Giovanni Pescetti, only recently discovered.

On Tuesday there was 'An Evening of Light Entertainment' which co-compere Malcolm Beeson said he hoped will *"emphasise that light entertainment at its best demands as much skill in performance and presentation as do more rigid art forms"*. It comprised of:
Company – five female and three male vocalists in Carpenters type music.
Duo – local jazz musicians Pat Dey and Ted Edwards, who worked at Beechams in the daytime but had musical aspirations, on guitar and bass.
Jonathan Sandall – Horsham Young Musician winner – who played Debussy, Gossec and Boru on Flute.

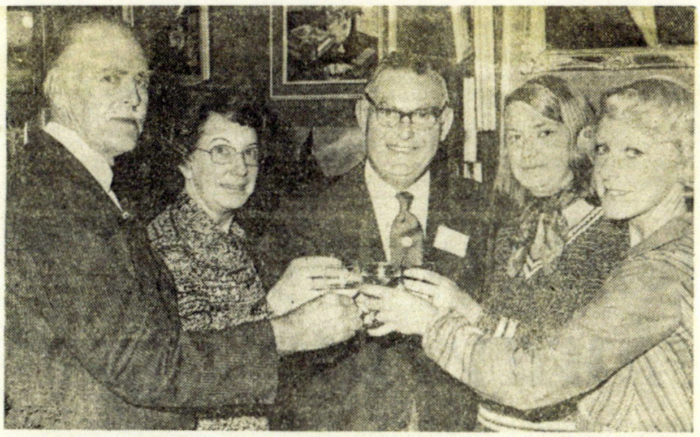

Left to right, chairman of the Art and Craft Society, Mr. Edward Odell-Foster; secretary of the Film Society, Mrs. Cicely Archer; chairman of Cranleigh Camera Club, Mr. Reginald Monk; secretary of the Cranleigh History and Archaeological Society, Mrs. Judie english; chairman of the Cranleigh Players, Mrs. Shirley Dubbins.

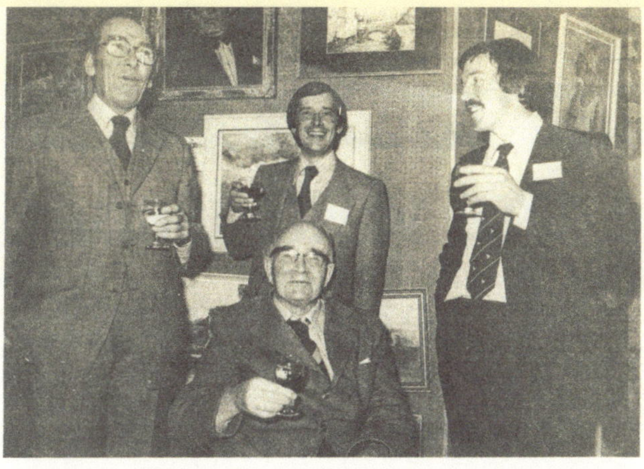

ENJOYING not only the paintings on display but a glass of wine too, are four of the men who made the Arts Centre possible. At its opening on Saturday are, from left to right, William Talbot, chairman of the Board of Governors at West Surrey College of Art, Richard Whitehead, and John Hewitt, chairman and vice-chairman of the Cranleigh Arts and Leisure Trust committee and seated, Claude Blogg, fourth and last headmaster of Cranleigh school until 1967 where the Arts Centre now thrives.

The second half starred Oscar Quitak and Andree Melly, familiar to Cranleigh residents as they ran 'Nuts' health food shop but were professional actors too. Andree was a regular panellist on TV's 'What's My Line' and her husband Oscar was an established West End and Shakespearean actor, often in film and TV. They revived two short plays from 'Mixed Doubles' a look at married life: 'Countdown' written for them by Alan Ayckbourn and 'Permanence' by Fay Weldon, which they had successfully performed in the West End. A reviewer commented: *"In both the truisms for every married couple in the audience rang home. They laughed not only at the marvellous characters portrayed by Andree and Oscar but at situations and statements that were strangely familiar".*

Also advertised for the week were a film 'The Clockmaker of St Paul' a dark French oeuvre by Bertrand Tavernier; The Canterbury Clerks – light-hearted songs through the ages; pottery for children; Elgar and Purcell performed by Cranleigh School Chapel String Ensemble and one act plays by local drama groups.

The local press reviewer was enthusiastic:

> *"If the hugely successful Festival is to continue every year, as the organisers hope, then they had better enlarge the 90 seat theatre. Cosy enough, with cleverly positioned spotlights, once the word gets around, more people will want to enjoy the entertainment on offer. Those who already have consider themselves fortunate that the years of waiting for an Arts Centre are over."*

At the following Management meeting it seemed that whilst the Festival had made a loss of £22, about 600 people had visited the Centre. Good footfall by any measure.

Moving forward

Jack Wagg gets more involved and the team settle in to consolidate the building and its activities. The Second Arts Festival in 1979

A key player by this stage was Jack Wagg, a Bramley resident, who put his political skill behind the project. Initially having been involved as Chief Clerk to Hambledon District Council, he had encouraged CALT to be properly set up and managed in order to facilitate progress and steered the initial negotiations. Since Jack took over as Chief Clerk to Hambledon in 1961 it had gained a reputation as an innovative local authority. Blunden Court, Bramley, was one of the first sheltered housing schemes in the country, featured on a special BBC programme. Leisure facilities were opened, including the Cranleigh Swimming Pool and Frensham Country Park established. In 1972 he was clerk to the committee formed to undertake the reorganisation of local authorities. Combining Hambledon, Farnham, Godalming and Haslemere into Waverley was not easy. In 1974 he was made the first Chief Executive of Waverley and so brought continuity to the process and he continued his interest in the Centre. He worked tirelessly, often in difficult circumstances, to achieve a high quality service for all Waverley ratepayers. He also set up the twinning of Waverley with Mayen-Koblenz. When he retired in 1978 he joined CALT as Press Officer for the opening and quickly moved to develop a vision for the Arts Centre.

In November he was elected Vice Chairman and became involved in fundraising, liaison with Waverley, and working with Malcolm Beeson on legal matters.

From 20th to 27th Oct 1979 there was a Second Arts Festival. For this considerable work had been done to prepare the building. Reg Monk gave the interior and exterior doors a facelift, banishing forever the 'Corporation' green. A bar had been constructed by Geoff Dubbins, Dilys and Mike Savedra, and there was a new bar area, refreshed by Reg Lawrence and Jack Wagg. The Arts and Crafts Society's Sam Maynard painted a large mural on the outside rear wall which was much admired and proclaimed its ambitions.

It was opened by David Howell MP, Energy Secretary, on the Saturday. To get a drink at the bar patrons had to buy a Festival mug. He was presented with one by Malcolm Beeson's seven year old daughter, Sandra, which featured in a picture in *The West Sussex County Times*. He urged more support for the arts but while government might encourage the arts it shouldn't pay for it. *"If artistic endeavour is to flourish, the main impulse and contribution must come from the people and that is what we see here today in Cranleigh."*

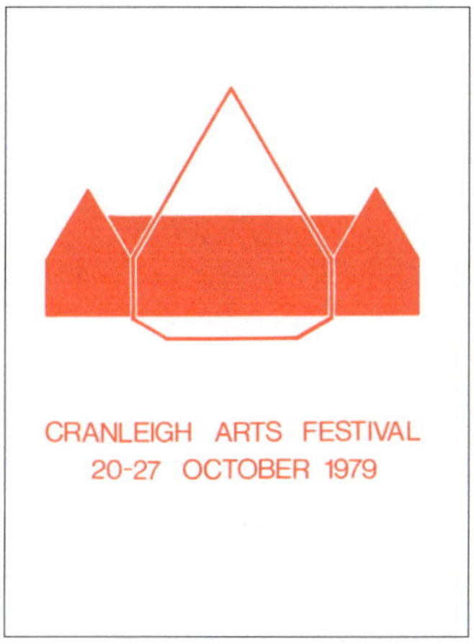

THE ADVERTISER, OCTOBER 26, 1979

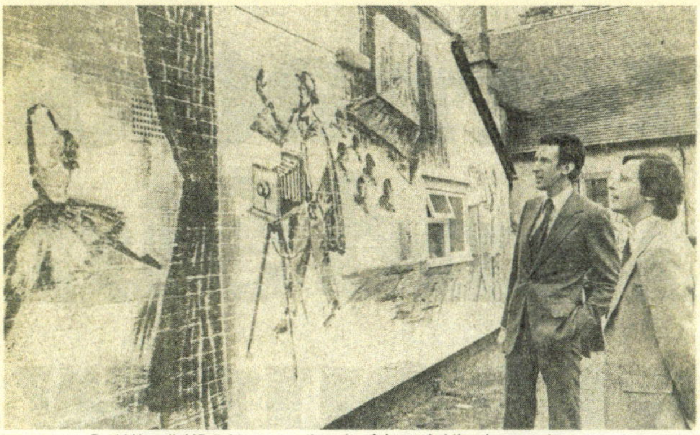

David Howell, MP (left), surveys the colourful mural at the playground entrance.

Sunday 21st had something for everyone with a Village Trail, an Exhibition and a Piano Recital by Andrew Wilson.

Monday 22nd: a talk by Antony Hopkins CBE, composer and the regular presenter of BBC Radio 3 programme 'Talking About Music', who commented that this was the first time he had performed in a stationary DC10!

Tuesday 23rd: Children's entertainment Pulling Strings and then a Marionette Production

Wednesday 24th: A sold out Junior Drama workshop and evening film 'The Lacemaker'.

Thursday 25th: A junior arts and crafts workshop.

'An Evening of light entertainment' which was composed of a mix of amateur and professional performers:
Two plus one – Duo (Pat Dey and Ted Edwards) plus Janice Niemann, who was a local professionally trained classical singer. *"Together they played favourite numbers with dexterity and expertise. .... Her singing was both beautiful and sensitive with a quality rarely found in today's pop world."*
Song and Dance – Sally Kingston, Billy Deamer, Tony Papas. Members of Second Generation. *"In their brightly coloured tracksuits .. (they).. gave a performance of dancing that was polished, energetic and amazingly well managed on such a small stage."*
'Man and Beast' Anthology. Oscar Quitak and Andree Melly with Sally Bazely
The reviewer said that *"the whole performance was a sheer delight from beginning to end".*
Friday 26th: J C Mole's Amazing Jazz Band; Organ Music for Pleasure in St Nicholas Church.
Saturday 27th: lunchtime: Brenda and Ian Longman - Folk
Afternoon: David Kossoff, a children's show.
Evening: David Kossoff's one man show 'A Funny Kind of Evening' which had sold out three weeks in advance. Kossoff was a regular on children's TV with his retelling of bible stories as well as a celebrated film and television actor. A reviewer wrote: *"Mr Kossoff had the audience in the palm of his hand as he switched from hilarity to sadness and back to hilarity. His reference to this being the first time he had performed in 'an upholstered shoe box' nearly brought the house down".* Both he, and Antony Hopkins, on his night, mingled informally with the audience in the bar afterwards. Leo Smith, the bar manager and licensee, said he'd enjoyed the whole thing – even if he never got out from behind the bar to see any of it!

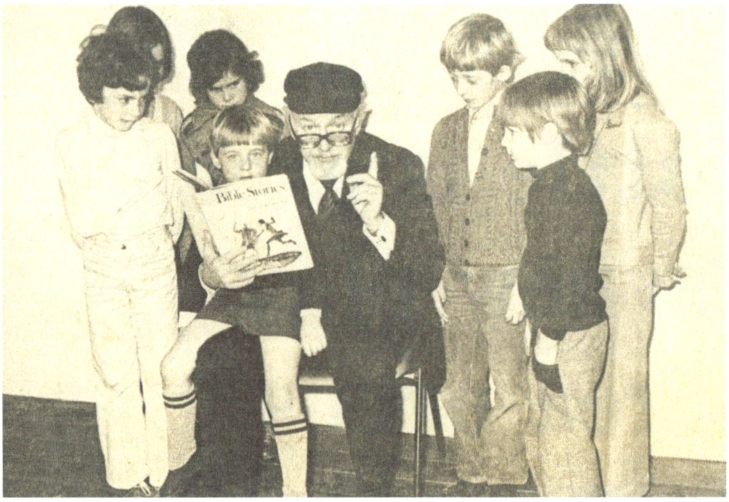

There had been a subcommittee to organise this and a long list of business support was included on the back of the programme including several banks, the Postmaster, Cranleigh Motor Company, Crosby and Co., David Mann and Sons Ltd, DBS

Cranleigh Ltd, Cosco Ltd, the local councils and the Shere Potter. It seems as if not only the people but the businesses of Cranleigh were starting to get behind the Arts Centre project, which was reflected in a growing self-confidence. The quality of performer it attracted showed it would be taken seriously. Sponsorship amounted to £415 and with bar profits an overall profit of £100 was banked. The eclectic artistic mix of the Festivals was to be the blueprint for subsequent programming.

Where to next?

How would the organisation develop from this initial success? Can the ambitions of the different societies be reconciled?

The organisation began to develop out from the management committee of approximately seventeen members. There was a Constitution sub-committee which comprised the founder societies. There was a Bar committee set up in September 1979 and, as the creative ball started rolling, in December 1979 an Events Committee was added to co-ordinate the public events staged at the Centre. They first met in early 1980 and by the third meeting in April Jack Wagg was in the Chair.

Through 1979 thoughts turned to how the building could be expanded to fulfil the aspirations intended for the railway site, now relinquished. The societies were canvassed and a panel including the local authority's architects was convened, together with a quantity surveyor Mr M Edwards, who was also Chairman of the Farnham Maltings. The differing priorities were exposed with P English suggesting that *"most societies thought that the new extension would be of no benefit to them"*. On 26th November a meeting was held with all interested parties to review the plans as drawn up. In the light of the critical comments about the current 'shoebox', the proposal was for a 'theatre in the round' space that could double as an exhibition Hall. Some concerns were raised. The seating capacity was regarded as too low and upped to 220. Apprehension was expressed about the Auditorium being sunk 6ft, in view of the wet soil round the Centre. That could be overcome said the architects. Retractable seating, which had been on a wish list for a long time was also added. Costing was £130,00 potentially doubling in two years' time with 2% inflation. At the end of the meeting it was agreed that the architects should apply for outline planning permission to get the ball rolling at least.

CALT had achieved its initial aims and found a dedicated space for the arts in Cranleigh. It was successfully attracting a range of groups and classes to use the facilities. It was providing an exhibition space for artists and a studio space for performers both amateur and professional. Inevitably there was a tension between the different sectional interests of the founding groups who had brought this into being. They had a loyalty to their members and not necessarily to the Arts Centre as a project. Jack Wagg, co-opted onto the Committee from November 1978, became a pivotal figure on all the aspects of the management of the CALT project: publicity, fundraising and the programme. He was adept at paperwork and committees. In March 1980 he became Chairman of the Management Committee on the resignation of Richard Whitehead. His engagement with Waverley and the ongoing discussions about the development of the building became the impetus for Jack Wagg's overarching vision – the Master Plan – which would be the focus and guide for the next stage of development and for it to evolve from CALT into Cranleigh Arts Centre Ltd. from the start of the 1980s.

Chapter Three

Consolidation, evolution and the 'Master Plan' in the 1980s

Building a structure

The inspiration

The context of the evolution of the Arts Centre under the leadership of Jack Wagg

The Arts Centre had been created by the local community as Britain moved out of the recession of the early 1970s and achieved some growth and financial optimism. However the political climate became more unstable and another oil crisis brought inflation and the 'winter of discontent' for James Callaghan, the Labour Prime Minister. The start of the 1980s saw Margaret Thatcher and the Conservative party holding the reins, but it was a while before confidence returned and inflation came down again. Towards the end of this period the 'Lawson boom' of 1987 brought down unemployment, but economic change had led to the closure of heavy industry, a reduction of trade union power, privatisation and the 'big bang' in the City. Britain became a net importer of goods for the first time. Civil unrest broke out in a series of riots across the country as the social results of these changes had an impact.

In the South East, and in leafy Cranleigh, the effects were not profound but still felt. The Centre's Newsletters of the time ring with optimism for the future as the community comes together: *"such enterprises are undertaken not merely in our own interests but also on behalf of future generations of Cranleighans. As Cranleigh has grown .. so must its Arts Centre grow".* (Chairman 1982) However in 'the deteriorating financial climate' expanding the membership and raising money become a priority. *"No one who understands and values the benefits for the days and years ahead can hold back from finding more cash, which is the fuel of all our activities."* (Chairman 1983) The Centre benefits from the Government initiative to get people into work when it takes on young trainees of the Manpower Services Commission Youth Training Service (YTS) in 1983, who work for two years enlarging the building. In the second half of the decade there is more money in subsidy available as the economy picks up, which allows the programme to expand and there is money for the first time for a paid member of staff. Although there were fears that another recession might be on the way.

It had taken four years of generating enthusiasm and activity around the idea of an arts centre, and mobilising the interested parties, to create an organisation to deliver that idea and settle on a building in which to operate. Two successful Arts Festivals had shown that there was an appetite for this and when societies acted together they could have quite an impact. Inevitably there were sectional interests, particularly as decisions had to be made about sharing access, storage, installations and responsibilities. As the decade began and Jack Wagg assumed the Chairmanship he knew from his experience what he thought needed to be done. He was not a member of one of the founder societies but had mucked in from the early days, running the bar and raffles, and established his credentials as a grafter, but also as a political operator in the wider local context. He had bought the chairs and tables for the coffee bar himself, because he knew that it would bring people in. His 'vision', as it came to be known, steered the growth of Cranleigh Arts through the 1980s, as it tries to make the transition towards a professionally-run, aspirational community arts centre rather than a shared venue serving disparate but related arts groups.

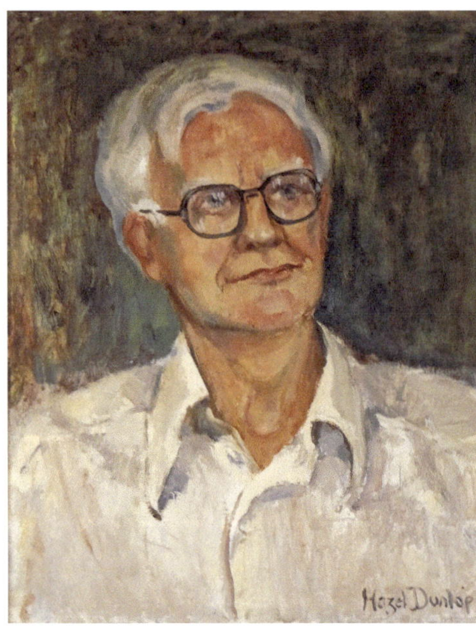

He was a man who usually got his own way and said of himself, *"I'm considered a bit of a dictator"*. He was amiable but not perhaps overtly charismatic and wanted the Centre to be for the community, not a private members club. The changes he brought in didn't please everyone, but he had the support of a loyal band of volunteers and the majority of members at AGMs to sustain the direction of travel. The strategic choices he made proved to be the right ones in the end, despite the criticisms and divisions at the time. There are four strands to what he did: engage the right people in the right structure; raise money; develop and expand an inclusive programme; build a centre to be proud of. Although he died in 1997, a year before the re-opening of the extended building, his contribution is acknowledged in the Jack Wagg Auditorium, the multi-purpose hall that he had envisioned within the thriving expanded Centre.

Improving the Building

Great efforts are made to ensure that the building is fit for purpose but getting agreement was not easy

From the beginning a purpose-built building had been planned for the railway land, after initially erecting some portable workshops and stores. With additional land from the Parish Council there would be room for a larger permanent building, which was to have a stage/exhibition hall with bar and reception on the ground floor and workshops and committee rooms/offices above. In the prospectus there were outline plans to this effect.

> *"These plans represent the material requirements of the proposed Centre. To maximise the utilisation of the available space each internal unit has been designed to fulfil several potential functions. For example part of the Main Hall may also serve as a stage, so that using this area it will be possible to promote both stage productions and exhibitions. CALT intends to strive for a purpose-built Arts Centre. Such a centre would ease the accommodation problems for many local organisations."*

Once the railway land had been surrendered in October 1978 and the old school leased instead, thoughts were pursued as to how that building could be adapted to satisfy CALT's requirements. The Management Committee had considered 'Quo Vadis' at its meeting in February 1979, agreeing that more space was needed to house the societies and expand activities. Although during the lease discussions there had been early horror from the parish council at the prospect of developing the existing structure, outline planning permission was applied for in November 1979 to expand on the site and fill in the space between the two wings. This was granted in March 1980. Now detail had to be put into exactly what could be achieved. The outline from 1975 and the ideas from 1979 needed to be worked up more thoroughly and translated into action. Wagg's 'vision' was to design the end point and work back. It would be a long process taking almost twenty years to complete, but with the different parts identified they could then each be built, when resources permitted, moving towards the end goal.

In the January 1980 Newsletter Chairman Richard Whitehead wrote that the Management Committee had been considering an extension and had met with architects and surveyors who had costed it. *"I should stress however that this planning application does not mean we have agreed to the Centre expansion. Apart from the initial cost, which will probably rise to £180,000/£200,000 within two years, the running costs would be approximately £10,00/£15,000 each year and such a step needs careful consideration. If anyone has any views on the extension I hope they will write to me."* In March he adds: *"no reaction received ... presumably no one wants it!"* At the June AGM Jack Wagg, now Chairman, suggests raked seating in the main performance space and a public meeting is arranged with an expert where drawings and a model were submitted. Reaction was not altogether favourable. The Chairman writes in *Vision* for Nov/Dec:

> *"Clearly members are looking at this question from a personal interest point of view. This is a great danger as we have a number of important ideas and proposals and it is important that each proposal should be examined on the basis of its contribution towards the greatest benefit to our Community Arts activities in general."*

This was to be the model for his leadership going forward and the first skirmish in his battle for improvement. The raked seating eventually gets installed in 1990

The application for outline planning permission for extending the building was worked on in 1979 and1980. Nick Galpin, who had been involved in the process, describes this in the May/June/July 1981 edition of *Vision*.

> *"A simple balsa wood model of the scheme is at Godalming. These drawings and the model were given a thorough inspection by members of CALT in November 1979. ... These drawings were also exhibited in the Cranleigh Library for some time, at the Cranleigh Show in 1980 and at a 'Welcome to Cranleigh' meeting at the Village Hall last year. A lot of water has gone under the bridge since 1979 and our thoughts have begun to alter a little since these drawings were done."*

He suggests a Building Committee be formed to list the objectives and prepare a 'brief' for the architect.

> *"It should be done thoughtfully and carefully by people with experience in every branch of the arts. Give as much information to the architect as you can with confidence at this stage, relating to every task that the total building and site has to fulfil. Not an easy job. May God help those whose task it will be."*

The Management Meeting in April 1981 had identified that three strong leaders were needed. For the Events Committee, for the proposed Buildings Committee and a Fundraising Organiser. Jon Horrocks, who had chaired the Events Committee for a year, took on the task of leading the Building Committee. At that meeting the Waverley architect, Michael McLellan, attended to unpick the parking problem. The proposed extension would mean the loss of parking spaces which Waverley objected to, but by narrowing the bays a compromise was reached. In a later lease the Arts Centre took control of the whole space at the rear. Once CALT had become

Cranleigh Arts Centre Ltd at the start of 1982, the Council of Management in February set up the Building Group under Jon's Chairmanship and appointed Arthur Gomez as architect. Young and ambitious, he had worked successfully with Jack Wagg on a number of projects for Waverley. Things moved quickly. He was briefed and he had plans available in July for presentation to an EGM in September. Nick Galpin had submitted an interesting alternative idea, to remove an historic old barn from Godalming and install it as the Main Hall, but this was politely rejected.

A full explanation of the process was written up by Jon Horrocks in the August/September *Vision*. He explains as follows.

> *"Our written brief was short and functional. It listed in general terms the present uses of the Arts Centre and its principal users. It expected these uses and users to continue in the future and that the list would gradually grow. It emphasised that ... daily running will continue to be on a voluntary basis and on a small budget."*

He had to allow for staged development, as money became available and that each completed section be immediately usable. The work should also allow daily activities to continue with as little interference as possible. The wish list was for a Main Hall, storage and an office. He concluded: *"Of course it is going to take a long time to finish and details will no doubt change before we get there. ... Here at least is a worthy and practical place to begin".*

The reports of the EGM by the Editor of *Vision* and by the Chairman say that the proposals were *"received with acclaim"*, and *"a bit of Cranleigh history in the making"*. The Editor notes that *"positive responses from the member societies will ensure that we achieve our aim to provide a multi-purpose building that can satisfactorily accommodate whatever activities and interests we or our grandchildren can dream up".* But also hints at some concerns,

> *"There were those at the meeting who worried about growth. Growth is inevitable. As Cranleigh has grown, not only in size but in breadth of interests, so must its Arts Centre grow. Most of us, as always, worried about money; but finance for the scheme will more easily be arranged by a flourishing, expanding community than it would be by a moribund, inward-looking assembly growing daily more distant from any potential new membership."*

Anne White concludes by praising the architect,

> *"...whose imaginative and sympathetic approach to the work was generous and impressive. When at last everyone has made her/his views known, it is to be hoped that we shall remember one important point: we must not foist upon Cranleigh a hall designed by a committee, but confidently accept the final, considered decisions of the professional."*

Jack Wagg under Chairman's Notes adds:

> *"...every viewpoint will be carefully considered ... but nothing will hold up the overall concept. The first stage will be commenced early in 1983. We have no other choice as our financial stability depends on creating greater viability which only extra space can achieve. ... I am absolutely convinced that only the early implementation of our broad proposals will satisfy the majority of Societies and their active membership. I am equally sure that nothing less will satisfy Jill Delamere, the forthright young Drama member, whose cry from the heart for working space to practise her art stirred most of us at the meeting. I conclude remembering the words of Founder Member and Benefactor Jon Hewitt when he reminded the meeting that the faint-hearted would have stopped the creation of the Arts Centre seven years ago, but the farsighted pressed on then as the community will expect of us now."*

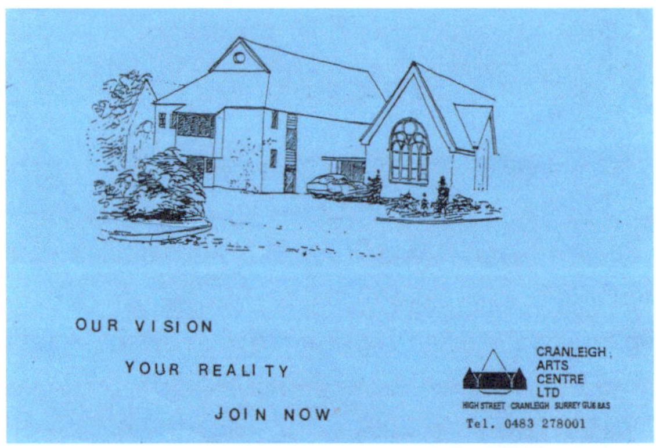

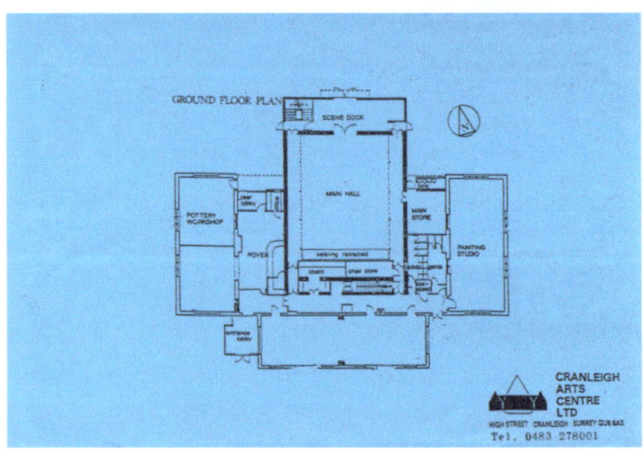

The development plans were given a boost by the news in November that Peter Oliver was giving up the Studio and that the Arts Centre could take possession of the East Wing. A public meeting was held to discuss the best use for it and it was the wish of the Management that it should be given over to painting and craft under the auspices of Sam Maynard of the Arts and Crafts Society and the Adult Education service. There were financial implications and a burst of fundraising was launched to improve and fit it out ready for a launch in January 1983 with new lighting and gas heating. Painting for Pleasure, a Life Class, two days of Adult Education classes, a regular craft workshop and painting classes on two other days quickly filled the week and could generate income.

Starting to build – buy a brick!

YTS apprentices start to make the vision a reality but not without problems

Another key factor in early 1983 was discussion about the engagement of the Manpower Services Commission and its Youth Training Scheme, organised through Surrey Voluntary Services Council. Eventually it was agreed that trainees would work on Phase 1 of the extension plans. They needed a caravan installed for storage and teaching purposes in an area behind the Centre which led to an adjustment of the car park space, which took some time to set up. Six trainees worked at a time under a supervisor. *"Chris Meads, the local supervisor for MSC and his trainees have proved themselves good workers and colleagues with the interests of our project at heart".* They started in October 1983 and continued through to early 1986, having built a new foyer and coffee bar onto the West wing and new toilets onto the East wing. *"The work has gone ahead without hindrance to the day to day use of the Centre and relationships continue to be happy and fruitful."* By the halfway stage 26 school-leavers had found permanent jobs following the training. Under the scheme the labour was free and just required the steady provision of materials; a cost of £5,000 in the early months of 1984. This did put some strain on the finances and cashflow. People could buy a brick for £1 and were encouraged to help fundraise, including in one case a sponsored parachute jump by Jane White, the Cranleigh reporter on *The Surrey Mail*; the Chairman even sold off some of his goldfish!

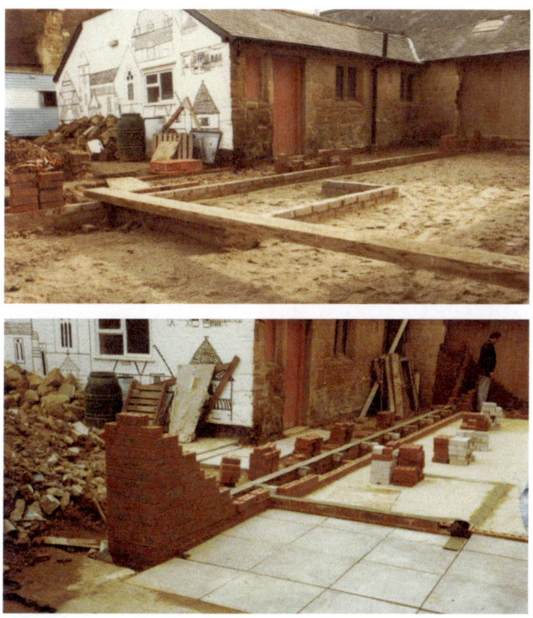

laying the base for the new foyer

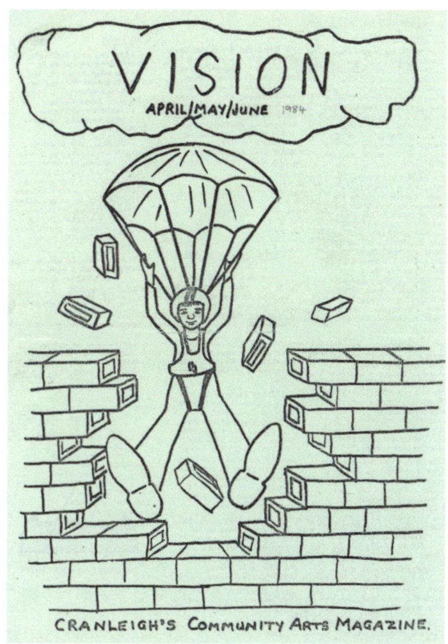

Jon Horrocks reported in *Vision*:

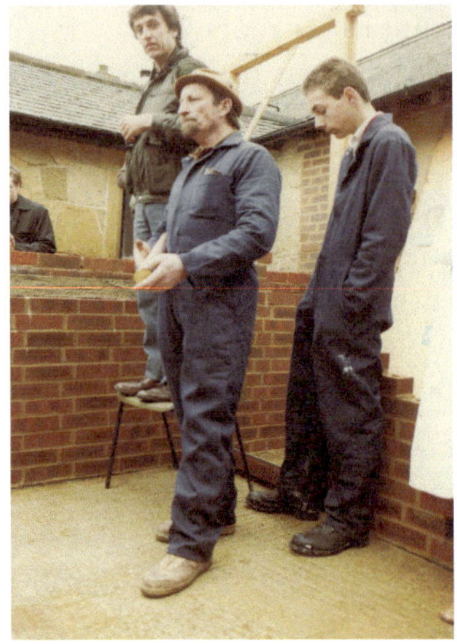

Mr Meads with two YTS trainees

"Our new foyer project is a complete building from the foundations to the fittings and as such it fulfils most of the requirements for onsite training which is the primary concern of the MSC. On our part we must be content to accept that construction will proceed at a rate determined by the needs of training a new generation. Those of you who pass the site from day to day may have met Mr Meads ... and will perhaps have had some conversation with him. If so you will have found that he is expansive and knowledgeable and moreover is fully conscious of our slender resources. ... Keen observers will not have failed to notice that for two months we seem to have been knocking down more than we have been building up. ... Large gaps in the walls of both corridor and the Bar Gallery make our world very dusty and draughty. ... As I write the foundations are appearing – laid on a hard ironstone stratum which lies some eighteen inches below the ground on which the old school was built. This geological feature which appears elsewhere in Cranleigh has saved us considerable expense in the foundations. I expect to see the concrete base laid and the brickwork begin to rise for the 11 inch cavity wall which must for a long time defend us from the outside world."

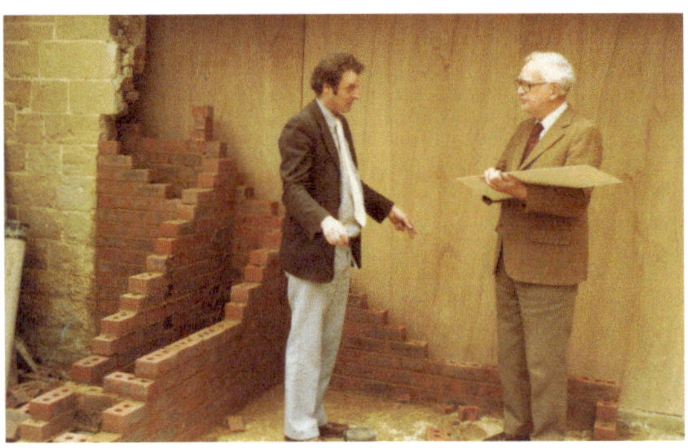

In March the Mayor of Waverley, Frank Cordier, presided over a ceremony to bury a time capsule containing a history of the Centre and its benefactors in the foundations of Phase 1, *"so that in the centuries ahead the people of Cranleigh may know how the Cranleigh Community Arts Centre of the eighties came into being"*. Jack Wagg listed the many benefactors and organisations who had helped to get to this stage *"I believe it is important to know the breadth of interest in this joint community project"*. The canister contained a message for the next century villagers which hoped that they would develop its efforts *"that one day Cranleigh will become a true home for art and craft, learning and pleasure"*.

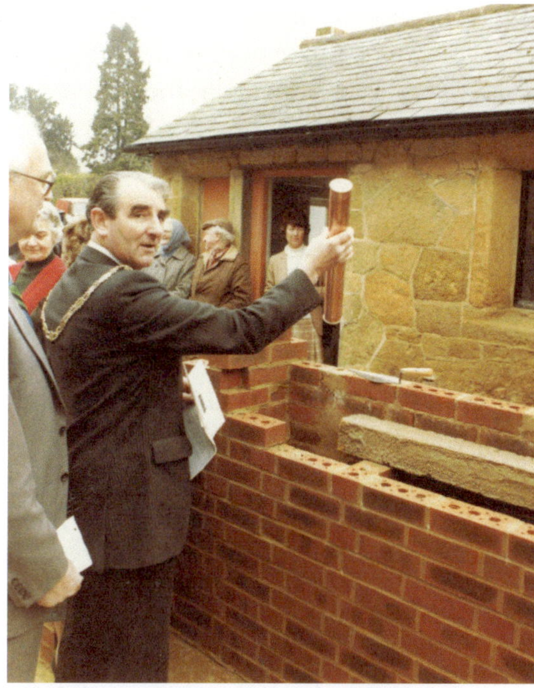

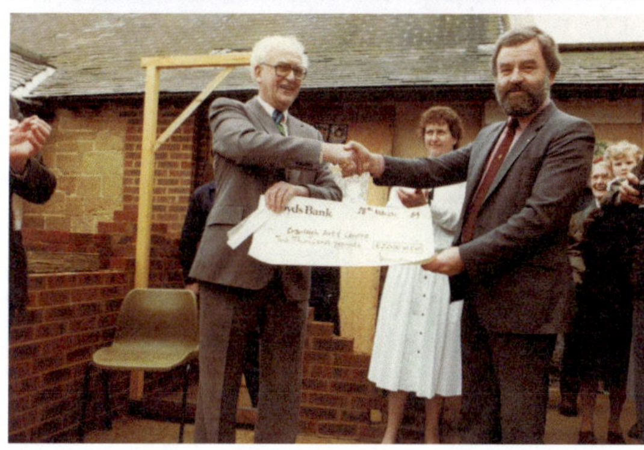

Appeals for money went up a gear too, leading to some local push-back. An application to the Arts Council of Great Britain for a grant of 25% of costs was refused, but TV South Charitable Trust came in with £2,000 and South East Arts Association was able to help with the cost of roofing materials. An application to the Parish Council provoked local debate with headlines in *The Cranleigh Times* in February 1984: **'No Cash for Arts Centre Demand'** and **'Arts Under Fire'**. Parish Councillors Peter English and Peter Levy, who both had previously been connected to the Arts Centre, said, *"the Centre should be made to stand on its own feet and not receive taxpayers' money"*. (Mr English) called the ambitious scheme to extend the Centre *"a white elephant which would eventually have to be taken over by Waverley Council"*. Mr Levy, who had spearheaded the saving of the village hospital and had been refused council money, said that no one was against the (arts) activities, but that they should not be subsidised and this would set a precedent. Jack Wagg defended the value and success of Cranleigh Arts Centre to the village in the press and spoke at the council meeting. They eventually agreed a grant of £200.

The work continued through 1984 with Phase 1, the new coffee bar and foyer, completed in March 1985. The opening was a social event with a meal, barbershop quartet and cabaret. This was celebrated by a poem in *Vision* which concluded,

"When we put on our coats and got into our cars
And faced the night outside,
We looked back to the extension and said,
We will call it 'Jack Wagg's pride'."

The YTS team then began Phase 2 on the other side to create new toilets and storage. As the scheme was due to be wound up there was a push to get as much completed as possible, but the boys had it finished in February 1986. While the shell may have been there it took the next few years to complete the fitting out, tiling, electrics and plumbing, which all had to be done by volunteers and with limited funds. Buying a brick may have some appeal but buying fittings for the disabled toilet less so.

Their departure coincided with the signing of the new 99 year lease from Waverley. *"Cranleigh Arts Centre is now yours for life!"* declared Jack Wagg in the newsletter. This assuaged the fears of critics who suggested that it was futile to invest in improvements to the Centre when Waverley could repossess it in the future.

> *"We shall be paying a full rent and sustaining our independence requiring tight housekeeping to balance the books. ... We have a collective responsibility to maximise the use of the Centre facilities and our income. We propose to be more vigorous in seeking suitable lettings of rooms not required internally. ... We shall also be injecting more attractions into the Foyer Coffee Bar, such as the Poetry Evening."*

In his Report to the AGM in June 1986 he says that this has been a year to remember for its progress and that we are *"happy and confident that we have established a secure base from which an expanding and lively community arts movement can flourish in Cranleigh for very many years to come."*

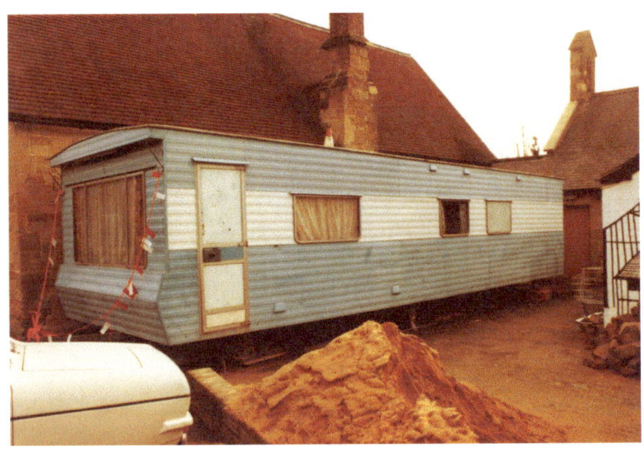

It took years and some neighbours' complaints before the caravan used by the YTS was removed and the site tidied up, with a view to erecting a temporary classroom for Pottery, while an extension was built as 'phase 3'. The new lease had included the car park land and so space was now available for this. The car park was to be a mixed blessing and continues to be so. In Autumn 1987 the Chairman writes:

> *"We are now in the middle of a drive to keep our Car Park available to Centre users – it will be a struggle to keep the invaders out. You can all help by explaining the fact that we are paying a substantial rent for our premises which includes the car park and as a charity we are not able to subsidise parking for the public and fulfil our duty to look after Arts Centre users as best we can."*

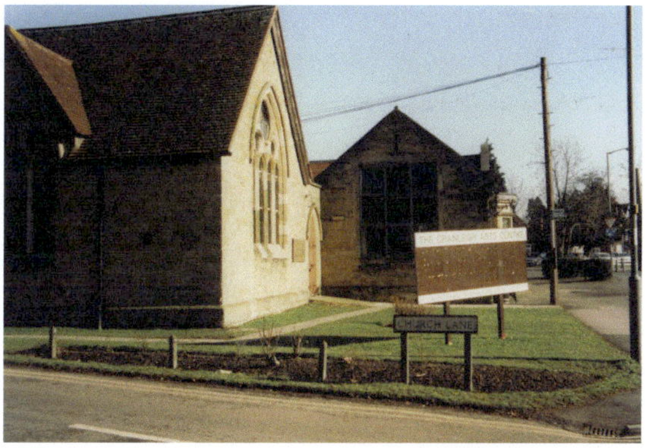

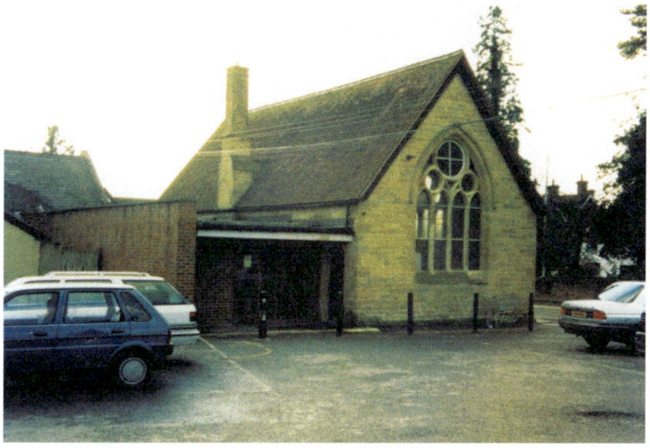

Management meeting minutes record various attempts to leaflet cars and tackle this but with little effect. Vandalism is also an ongoing issue at night with broken windows, as well as people stealing toilet paper!

So the building was becoming fit for purpose but was a growing financial liability and hard to maintain. Some of the residents of Cranleigh didn't value it as highly as the dedicated artists who had taken it over. Without sufficient space inside or outside from which to make money, unlike Farnham Maltings for example, and with a full repairing lease from Waverley, it would always be a drag on resources.

Improving the Organisation – the membership

How the Arts Centre engaged with those who used it, the change of status to a charitable Limited Company and the subsequent falling out with members

A sense of the wind of change blowing was not only in the bricks and mortar but can be had from the way in which CALT projected itself. A newsletter had been produced by Charles Hard since 1975 which went to all members and contained reports from the four societies (the Film Society had been added) a diary and a letter from the Chairman. In October 1979 the Arts and Crafts Society started its own newsletter *Scope*: *"a more adventurous publication to supplement the informative CALT Newsletter, which some of us manage to get around to reading if it doesn't get pushed under last week's newspapers!"* so wrote editor, Betty Steele.

So in September 1980 *"prompted to join in some friendly and cooperative rivalry"* the CALT newsletter became *VISION*, an A5 booklet with a new editor Anne White, a publisher by trade. She wrote:

"The development of the Arts Centre passes through a crucial period, your efforts, your opinions and your voice will be roused by VISION for it is coming into

existence to inform and to activate. Its pages will be open to you, your societies and to all friends of the Arts Centre."

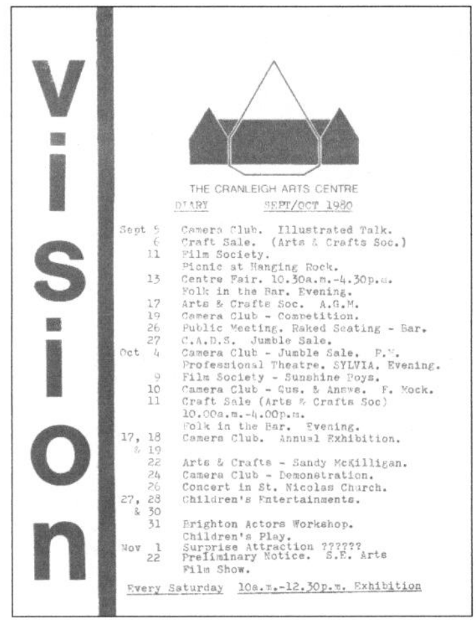

Vision

THE CRANLEIGH ARTS CENTRE

DIARY SEPT/OCT 1980

Sept 5 Camera Club. Illustrated Talk.
6 Craft Sale. (Arts & Crafts Soc.)
11 Film Society.
Picnic at Hanging Rock.
13 Centre Fair. 10.30a.m.-4.30p.m.
Folk in the Bar. Evening.
17 Arts & Crafts Soc. A.G.M.
19 Camera Club - Competition.
26 Public Meeting. Raked Seating - Bar.
27 C.A.D.S. Jumble Sale.
Oct 4 Camera Club - Jumble Sale. P.M.
Professional Theatre. SYLVIA. Evening.
9 Film Society - Sunshine Boys.
10 Camera Club - Qus. & Answs. F. Mock.
11 Craft Sale (Arts & Crafts Soc)
10.00a.m.-4.00p.m.
Folk in the Bar. Evening.
17, 18 & 19 Camera Club. Annual Exhibition.
22 Arts & Crafts - Sandy McKilligan.
24 Camera Club - Demonstration.
26 Concert in St. Nicolas Church.
27, 28 & 30 Children's Entertainments.
31 Brighton Actors Workshop.
Children's Play.
Nov 1 Surprise Attraction ??????
22 Preliminary Notice. S.E. Arts
Film Show.

Every Saturday 10a.m.-12.30p.m. Exhibition

It was also a response to criticism that communication between the management, members and the societies had become poor, as expressed at the June 1980 AGM. As well as an editorial leader, *Vision* contained an expanded Chairman's Notes and a full list of contact details for the Committee and the Society Representatives. It is promoting upcoming events and activities more strongly and noting the energy in all areas. This may have been galvanised by the Management Committee having delegated the programme to an Events Committee formed earlier in the year. Whereas under the Arts and Crafts Society entry it merely says 'For all news read *Scope*' there is the addition of material from the newly affiliated History and Archaeological Society and the Cranleigh Amateur Dramatic Club (CADS), rising phoenix-like from the ashes of the Players. A big success is the Saturday Mini-art Exhibition. *"The tempo at the Centre is stepping up, now the doors are open every Saturday morning with at least 50 new and old friends popping in to see the exhibition, for a chat over coffee or to offer to help."* This was another part of helping the exchange of ideas and trying to develop a common cause. By the end of the eighties the now *New Vision* had almost become the Centre brochure with pictures and adverts for events.

As described in Chapter 2 the original structure of the organisation was that there were three trustees with a trust director, who had overall responsibility, oversight and held the purse strings and delegated all practical management to a Committee composed of elected officers and representatives of each of the affiliated societies, who reported back and answered to the annual AGM. The constitution, as amended to comply with requests from Waverley and the Charity Commission, also required representatives from Waverley and the Parish Council to attend. As the majority sub-lessee Adult Education were also represented; their leader, Dilys Savedra, took on the role of Centre Manager and main keyholder.

It is clear from the Minutes of the Management Committee that once Jack Wagg joined in September 1978 his input is significant and appreciated. He expedites the signing of the lease, discusses insurance with Waverley, contributes to the success of the opening and is on the fundraising sub-committee. In February 1979 he is presenting architects' drawings for the enlargement of the Centre. In April he is grappling with the rates assessment and bar licence application. In the autumn he is part of a working party to decorate the building before the 2nd Festival, and running a regular coffee morning with Adult Education to raise money. He puts forward ideas for retractable seating and is on the newly formed Events Committee, which is galvanised by his discussions with South East Arts Productions. But his next proposal is more radical.

The move to become a Limited Company

The next step in evolving the management and containing liability

In February 1980 at the Management Committee meeting, following the death of trustee William Narraway in November, the Trustees had approached Mr Peter Levy.

> *"A discussion followed on the various activities of the Trustees and CJW (Jack Wagg) suggested that as an alternative to dispense with the need to have trustees, a company limited by guarantee might be formed which would reduce any liability at present falling on the Committee."*

It was agreed that the Chairman, Richard Whitehead, should approach their solicitor to find out what that entailed and report back. At the next meeting in March due to pressure of work he resigned and Jack Wagg was voted in as Chairman. He then steered the transition to a new identity but provoked a serious split in the ranks. He would need all his political skills to achieve Limited Company status as he was convinced that this evolution was necessary for both organisational and financial reasons. It is ironic in the light of how it ultimately affected them that the liability issue had first been raised by Nancy Horne when Secretary, who was also a member of the Arts and Crafts Society.

In November 1980 the Management Committee agreed to task a solicitor to draw up a draft of the Company Limited by Guarantee papers. In the Jan/Feb 1981 *Vision* the Chairman writes in anticipation:

> *"So far as Cranleigh Arts Centre is concerned we are into the year of decision. Fundamental matters have to be decided and concerted efforts made to work together in unity and goodwill to implement these decisions. Let us remember that a community arts centre has to serve a wide band of the residents of all ages with their diverse views and aspirations. ... Activities and membership must grow if we are to remain viable in the deteriorating financial climate. Our affiliated Societies are no longer making a significant contribution to the cost of running the Centre. One way or another our income must increase – it is for the membership to decide how this is to be achieved."*

By the March/April edition he is praising the collaborative work done by society members and asking how that mutuality could be enhanced for the 400 membership. May/June/July brought a riposte by Dilys Savedra to a previous attack on the Management committee for not getting things done. Having listed a lot of hands-on activities done by individual committee members, she concluded: *"The reaction it gets from the large membership can be summed up: complete inertia, general apathy, fierce resistance to change, insularity within societies, lack of interest in events".* Since she worked closely with Jack Wagg, it may be assumed his view was not dissimilar. His Chairman's notes strike a more positive note inviting readers to the AGM.

> *"The AGM is important with its scheduled discussion on the proposal to convert our organisation to a Company Limited by Guarantees, a change which will open the way for the future. The debate must soon be concluded on the proposal to create more space for our activities. Come to the AGM, give a clear signal that we are going forward in happy and enthusiastic cooperation, then celebrate it with a drink in the Bar."*

Schism

A microcosm of village politics

The Arts and Crafts Society (A&CS) had the largest membership (140+) and through their subscriptions contributed a significant sum annually. In the new constitution they wanted a proportionate increase in representation on the Management Committee, which was rejected. The earlier raked seating consultation had not gone down well with those who attended, some not seeing the need, others wanting the money spent elsewhere. Six letters and an editorial in their magazine *Scope* Jan/Feb 1981 fanned the flames, although some balance was maintained by the Editor, Betty Steele, a long-time supporter of the Arts Centre and who also served on the Events Committee. One member, Phyl Cartwright, said she was withholding her subscription to CALT and was *"profoundly disturbed by the manner in which the proposal ... has been presented. Pertinent questions were brusquely brushed aside and it was stated that voting would be by chequebook only".* The Arts and Crafts members felt they were the majority and that 'a minority interest' was being served by a 'highly expensive scheme'. Promises of a vote, 'for or against' and 'now it will be up to you' did not materialise and hearing 'the decision would be made by the Arts Centre Management Committee' left them feeling disenfranchised. These feelings came to a head when the Company Limited by Guarantee proposal was put to the AGM in June.

On 10 June the Arts and Crafts Society held an EGM and voted to disaffiliate from CALT. Geoffrey Howard, their Chairman, explained in *Scope*,

> *"The object of forming a Company is to safeguard individual members against any financial liability which may arise and your Committee agrees with this change. ... However the Articles of the new company insist that each and every member of the associated societies must legally be a member of the Company. As a considerable number of our Arts and Crafts Society members do not wish to join the Company this excludes the Society as a whole from Company Association. However there are very many members who will wish to join .. and this they can do as individuals. I personally will certainly wish to join."*

The Editor comments *"Responses from members so far have ranged from apathy to anger and a good deal of puzzlement in between. The person who has had to bear the brunt of the reaction has been Geoffrey Howard, who has done so with patience and fortitude who must have wished at times he had gone on his holidays or was not so accessible to us all in the centre of the village."* Jack Wagg also attracted the flak. He wrote to Geoffrey Howard on 1st June, *"I am becoming increasingly perturbed by the number of your members who have felt it necessary to approach me with their worries over the current debate and the way a few are conducting it. I feel the developments are unhealthy and dangerous".* He suggests he should attend the EGM *"so that we can talk and listen to each other".* This was declined.

Over three A4 pages of the next *Scope* are given to letters on the topic which give insight to how the debate went. It seems the A&CS Committee had finally voted 7-5 to disaffiliate and put this to the EGM meeting. Wilfred Colverson proposed the motion arguing,

> *"In such circumstances the members should back up the Committee they have elected to act on their behalf; to fail to do so would be tantamount to a vote of no confidence. To continue an unprofitable and vexatious relationship with the Trust would place an unacceptable strain upon our representatives and it might be impossible to find office-bearers willing to undertake such a burden and possibly even members willing to serve on the Society's committee. Furthermore the Trust's inflexibility in insisting that all Society members must become fully paid up members of CALT would mean a loss of nearly a third of the Society's members. ... CALT appears to have developed into a monolithic structure contemptuous of the needs of its constituent societies and bent on pursuing extravagant schemes for its own aggrandisement. The Society must treasure its independence."*

Pat Harby and Jennifer Hunter argued for compromise, a rethink or a recount.

> *"Surely if an Arts Centre cannot present an image of community nothing can. A community is shared responsibility, openness to new ideas and suggestions, it should be a place where people care and protect one another and where closed*

minds, pettiness and power struggle are laid aside for higher ideals and values. Sadly this doesn't seem to be happening."

There are fears that the Society will not survive on its own or that there will be a split and two arts groups will then compete. Edward Odell Foster tried to sum it up. He was an elder statesman having been a past Chairman and committee member of both CALT and the Arts and Crafts Society. He says that those charged with liaison and representation had found it increasingly difficult and frustrating:

> *"These members have included some of our oldest and most hard-working. In recent months it has become increasingly apparent that because of this we were in imminent danger of losing them ... The loss of these long-standing, knowledgeable and hard-working committee members could well have placed the whole Society in jeopardy. This was Morton's Fork for your committee. Either we faced antagonising many of our members by recommending disaffiliation or the Committee disintegrated with perhaps little prospect of a strong new body being formed in the foreseeable future. ... But to the committee fell the task of action and one can only deal with actualities in such circumstances; in the extreme case rioters may be misguided but one still has to deal with the riot."*

He concluded:

> *"Could I here suggest what I believe to be one of the keys to the situation on both sides – just two words – sensitivity and diplomacy."*

So in the end, ignoring what any village politics may have contributed, for the Society it was about potentially losing significant valuable older members thus creating an existential threat, so pragmatism prevailed.

The crucial vote

Jack gets his way and the change is made which signals the move towards broader membership and loosens the ties to societies

At the CALT AGM later in the month Jack Wagg had to propose it to his members. In his text for the speech one can sense that he knows he has to work to win the crowd over. It is typed in red with pauses and emphases marked. Is there also a touch of moral blackmail?

> *"We have before us an important yet simple and straightforward resolution. It ought to be capable of examination and decision in a happy family atmosphere...*

...without interference by outside influences or contention. However I must refer to the recent decision of the Arts and Crafts Society which could influence some members here tonight in the attitude they take. The Arts and Crafts Society has opted out of the new Company from its inception. It is my conviction that what happened on 10th June is neither (of) short or long significance for Cranleigh Arts Centre which will remain the venue and activity centre for all enthusiastic and unselfish supporters of the arts. However I am delighted to hear from the Chairman of the Arts and Crafts Society, Geoffrey Howard, that there is scope for discussion to bring the A&CS back into the fold. I am pleased to give my personal undertaking that it would be my endeavour to get all A&CS members back as Centre members on terms fair to all at the earliest possible moment.

"So let us turn to the motion and ask ourselves – are we prepared to convert our organisation to a Company Limited by Guarantee with IDENTICAL OBJECTIVES AS HAS THE EXISTING TRUST ? REPEAT. *If it is so simple and so limited why do we want to do it? Almost since the formation of the Trust the committee has been advised and made fully aware of the financial dangers to committee members working under the existing constitution. This awareness has been reinforced by events in other voluntary organisations."*

He continues to explain about consulting solicitors, mentioning Howard Pickersgill, and that the necessary papers have been approved by the Inland Revenue and the Charity Commission, and that the Articles of Association are fixed at this stage but variable in future should it be wished.

"Once the Company has taken over the Committee members would no longer be in danger of substantial personal financial liability but they like every other member would be liable to contribute £1 in the event of a financial collapse. So you are being asked to be ready if the worst happened to throw £1 into the kitty instead of the committee members collectively being liable to find an undefined sum of money. If the Centre is to continue to provide a service comparable with the present for all age groups then we need to give the committee members this protection. To fail to do so is to take a callous attitude towards Committee members and their families.

> *"Finally I consider this is a matter of confidence in the committee. I put it to you that each one of you has a moral obligation to support your committee. Give them the backing to which they are entitled and then I am sure they will continue to strive in the development of this Centre and for all who wish to participate in the arts."*

The vote was carried. He wrote in *Vision* for Aug/Sept 1981,

> *"The Annual Meeting has given a clear indication that the proposal to manage our affairs through a Company Limited by Guarantee is overwhelmingly supported. The meeting could have almost been a celebration but for the news that the Arts and Crafts Society would stay out of the new Company. ... I should like to stress that everyone interested in the arts and crafts will always be welcome at the great variety of public events at the Centre."*

A different view was given by Wilfred Colverson in *Scope*.

> *"The Chairman's statement that in his view the Society's decision would have no significant effect on CALT's future presumably fairly represented his attitude to the Society. His boast that he would soon persuade the bulk of the Arts and Crafts members to return to the fold hardly carried conviction nor did his repeated presentation of CALT as such a happy family. The whole conduct of the meeting seemed designed to gloss over the real issues, the few questions were sidestepped and the one attempt, by one of CALT's most respected trustees, to amend the proposed constitution was brushed aside."*

Presumably it was not the first difficult meeting Jack had chaired to eventually get his way.

Discussions continued to try to find a solution as recommended by Edward Odell Foster. So in December another EGM was held by the Arts and Crafts Society which reversed their decision. It had been confirmed that, contrary to previous opinion, membership of the new company would be a matter for individual decision and it was not obligatory for all A&CS members to join. There had been other constitutional matters in dispute but as this was the main bone of contention cordial relations could be resumed. Moving forward the Arts and Crafts Society were to use the Centre on preferential terms, key players remained on the Events Committee and the storm subsided. As there remained a per capita levy, which was slow to be paid, some Arts and Crafts Society members were critical of CALT's finances and budgeting and disputed their liability for it. By the time of the Second AGM of the new Company in June 1984 the Chairman reported:

> *"It was regretted that the Arts and Crafts Society had decided not to be affiliated to the Arts Centre Ltd; nevertheless this had not created a startling situation because the Society was still using the Centre and individual members were still contributing in many ways to the activities of the Centre."*

In February 1986 The Chairman reports he *"met the Chairman of the Society as part of our policy to create a greater understanding between both organisations. It is evident that real problems still exist mainly with the older members of the A&CS which date back to the original break away. At present there is no intention to make amends and reaffiliate with CAC Ltd".* Eventually they would retreat to the newly built Band Room and the Village Hall as the relationship evolved again. Some meetings are returning to the Centre currently.

What do we learn from this battle?

Internal change is as difficult to deal with as external changes

This case study, with its extensive quotations, serves to illustrate the village dynamic. There is a strong sense of ownership within the village community leading understandably to many small sectional groups pursuing their interests and wanting to operate in their own way. Tall poppy syndrome is at work too, with a concern, sadly amplified today by social media, that some people or organisations get too big for their boots and are resented or resisted, even if their wish is to improve the community they live in. The battle clearly shows Jack's methods and his passion for the future direction of the Arts Centre. It shows a microcosm of the interplay of the Centre and the community. The difficulties of making changes and building in accountability continue to appear as the organisation has to evolve.

With the AGM's approval the paperwork could be signed and the assets and management of CALT were transferred to Cranleigh Arts Centre Ltd. The process had been efficiently steered by the Chairman and Committee, three of whom, Dilys Savedra (Centre Manager), Reg Monk (Founder Member/Camera Club) and Reg Lawrence (Treasurer) said they would no longer serve if the motion was not passed, pulling the same tactic on this meeting as the Arts and Crafts Society committee members had on theirs. Registration was however delayed by a civil servants' strike as the name had to be approved by the Department of Trade and Industry. In January 1982 it was approved and the first Council of Management meeting was held on 15th February, with the CALT management committee members moving over to the new company. Its first AGM was held in the following year on 23rd April 1983. The disaffiliation of the Arts and Crafts Society led to further loosening of the groups from the structure of management. The push towards an individual membership, who elected the Management Committee at the AGM, albeit comprised often of key players from the core societies, evolved through the 1980s. Various amendments were made to the Articles at subsequent AGMs to change the quorum numbers, the co-option details and to tidy up anomalies, such as an age limit of 70 on Committee members due to the Companies Act 1948, the drawing of lots for who retires in rotation and definitions of membership. Since amendments to the Articles required Dept of Trade approval (although this was later removed) the Secretary, Ron Phelps, was kept busy initially. Trying to keep a register of voting members was difficult. As societies like the Drama Group expired and new ones emerged like the Bridge Club, the Music Listening Group and the Film Society, the affiliated societies changed. By 1990 there were seven elected members, four appointees/co-opted, three local councillors and only three society representatives. This enabled the Council of Management to be more representative of those who supported the Centre directly and perhaps removed some of the factional interest lobbying which had been the danger in the early eighties.

Improving the Organisation – the administration

Enter the consultant

Apart from structural changes to the membership evolving during the eighties, as the scale of activities increased, it became clear by 1987 that some administrative changes were needed too. At this time Betty Steele had resigned as Publicity Officer with no replacement on the horizon. As fundraising was crucial with building work ongoing a suggestion was made to engage a professional fundraiser but pro tem a sub-committee was formed. Another step change would happen in the year October 1987 to October 1988 which was driven by both financial and personnel imperatives. Whilst the members of the Management Committee, the Building Group and the Events Committee did much of the heavy lifting, both practically and figuratively, Jack Wagg reported to the Committee in July that,

> *"his position was almost full time and South East Arts had offered the services of a consultant to advise on a management structure. This may result in a structure where staff may be paid or purely voluntary as at present. There are not many totally unsupported Arts Centres and the results of the consultant's report will be discussed at a future management meeting."*

The report by Hilary Renwick, an independent consultant, was commissioned by South East Arts on behalf of Cranleigh Arts Centre and was an important stock-take of what had been achieved and how practically the organisation could move forward. She spent a day on site *"looking at the entire operation of the building, to suggest ways in which the Centre could make better use of its resources and expand and develop its existing programme"*. Her notes are summative and hope to *"represent an objective overview of the Centre and make a useful contribution to the planning of the building"*. She notes the rapid expansion of the village, its affluence and preponderance of younger (25-40) commuters, who might prefer metropolitan culture. But *"there are dozens of local societies representing a wide range of interests, many of which have creative or cultural aims. … the Arts Centre acts as the coordinating body and focus for local arts activity."* She makes four or five main points under the headings of: building, artistic activity, staff and management and finance.

Under building she approves of its development: the placing of the proposed auditorium at the rear away from traffic noise, the recent benefit of the car park, the staging of the building work as money becomes available and concludes it *"has a reputation for being friendly and welcoming, the coffee bar is popular and the studio and pottery room are in good use. The performing space* (the infamous 'shoebox') *is of limited use because of its dimensions, the quality of the floor and its uncomfortable seating. It is hard to see how the building in its present state could be more intensively used, given the entirely voluntary staffing arrangements. Neither is there the storage space or equipment to enable a swift and frequent change of use for various spaces"*.

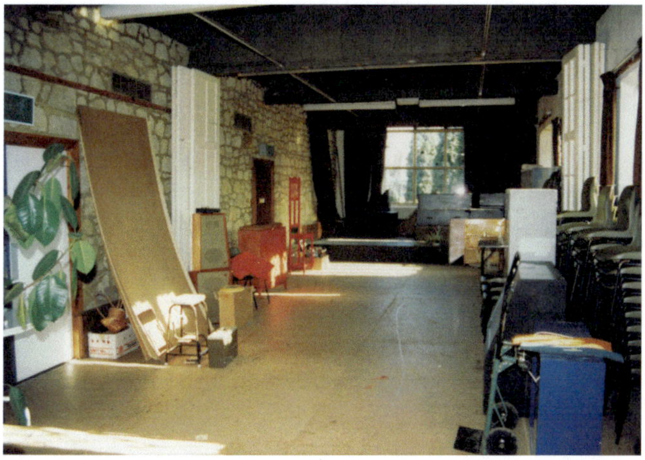

Under artistic activity she notes *"the organisation has not become a passive minder of space … and has maintained and developed a programme which is admirably responsive to local needs."* She praises the mutually beneficial relationship with Adult Education and *"work with and for children is one of the Centre's greatest strengths … a children's Saturday Club should be considered"*. However she says, *"The Centre needs to give concerted attention to publicity, at present it is underselling itself"*. She suggests a new logo should be used on all communications; the Newsletter should be improved; market research should inform event planning and audience targeting; and publicity should be properly budgeted at the start of the year aiming to increase year on year.

Under staff and management she is blunt.

> *"I do not believe that the Arts Centre can do more than 'tread water' artistically and administratively unless the means are found to employ a paid worker, preferably on a full time basis. The building has a hard working, motivated and enthusiastic band of volunteers who have subsidised the running costs, got the building up on its feet and created a very good atmosphere. However the building needs an administrative focus. … a sustained and reliable presence."*

She explains that this could open up wider community outreach, more professional programming and better coordination. She attaches a job description but has the caveat that while a need for a cleaner/caretaker had been expressed, to use such an appointee in that role would be *"a waste of their expensive expertise"*. The person should report to the Council and attend all subcommittees.

Under finance she sees the opportunities the new worker could make to increasing Coffee Bar and Bar income. She recommends that people with arts and fundraising experience be co-opted to the Council to *"assist the long-term financial and artistic planning which will be essential for revenue support from Waverley and/or South East Arts"*. She notes *"a reluctance to court possible political interference, but no further support will be available from South East Arts without a matching commitment from the Council (Waverley)."* She advises, *"The Council of Management should be wary of fundraisers, as they can cost a lot of money. The advent of a worker should give the Council more time to go out and actively fundraise for the building works. … More determined publicity should raise income and the right worker should be able to tap into other funding sources, trust funds, other local authority monies, e.g. playschemes and Social Services."*

At the Council of Management meetings in November and December 1987 the ideas were chewed over. South East Arts required more information if a grant was to be forthcoming, so nudging them towards more future planning. A change of roles was decided between Dilys Savedra, the Adult Education Organiser, Vice Chair and longstanding titular Centre Manager for ten years and Rosemary Dubois, who had served on the Events Committee and had been running the successful children's programme and theatre trips amongst other activities. Mrs Savedra would

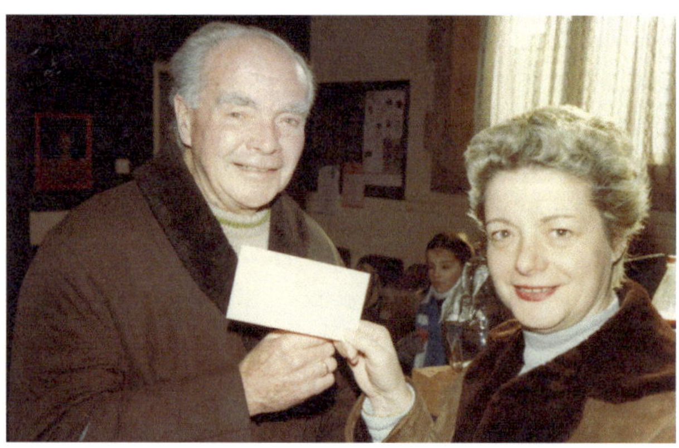

Dilys Savedra with Treasurer Reg Lawrence

be Bookings Manager and Vice Chairman, while Mrs Dubois would take the title of Centre Manager. This seemed to start to move towards the recommendations Hilary was making. At the December meeting inevitably the debate was over the problems rather than solutions and although some initiatives were under way such as finding a fundraiser and new committee members, the idea of a new logo was rejected along with resistance to expanding the hospitality provision. The Chairman kicked it into the long grass saying no decisions could be taken until March going into the new financial year and grant provision was known.

By April 1988 after lobbying and meetings South East Arts agreed *"to pay £2,000 for the current financial year to enable the Centre to employ a part-time Administration / Secretary / Receptionist for 15 hours a week for 33 weeks"*. Their representative would help with recruitment and would have a seat on the Committee going forward. Dilys Savedra meanwhile advised that she had been promoted within Adult Education and would be leaving Surrey CC in the autumn. The Secretary, Anne Hull, started in June and, thanks to a substantial gift from Harry Secombe, who had just become the first Patron, she was provided with a phone, desk and photocopier. Waverley had come up with £1,000 for building improvements, as did the Parish Council for £300. The Chairman could subsequently report in *New Vision* (which now regularly featured the architect's picture of the proposed new building on its front cover) of Summer 1988, *"I feel entitled to say that the past year has seen official support grow by leaps and bounds"*. In prospect of a grant by Waverley of £5,000 for two years an appraisal building development document would be drawn up for future yearly planning. In September the Chairman believed that *"a new mood of cooperation was developing between S.E. Arts/the local authority/arts societies"*. This was reinforced in his optimistic notes to members in *New Vision*. In December David and Basia Weaver, the in-house artists, submitted a new logo design which was accepted.

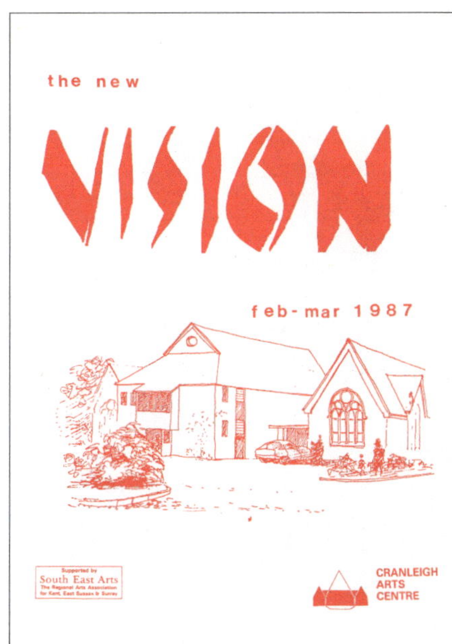

The move towards changes to the organisational structure had been started and thought turned now to the programme and lettings. With the Bookings Manager Dilys Savedra moving on, this had all largely fallen to Rosemary Dubois as Centre Manager. It was clear that to increase revenue this part of the operation had to be cleverly managed. The Events Committee had served well for ten years and reported to the Management Committee, but, with the increase of South East Arts involvement and subsidy, professional bookings were tending to go through Rosemary as well. The Management Committee had called a joint meeting in Sept 1988 *"to discuss ways of widening the scope of events, possibly with increased funding"*. It appears from the Discussion Notes that there were some frustrations on both sides. It was suggested that these meetings should happen once a year, however that was postponed in 1989, and by December the Council of Management had drawn up a restructuring plan which dissolved the Events Committee and centralised programming within the Secretariat in 1990. This led to more walkouts, with further criticism of the management and its style and intentions, as we shall see. The growing pains would continue.

Chapter Four

Delivering the Mission in the 1980s

Managing the programme and the finances

Developing the Programme

The operation of the Events Committee

> *"Besides its role as a coordinating and managerial body acting on behalf of the three constituent societies, CALT is also tentatively searching for ways of furthering local appreciation of the Arts. ... In this way CALT is coming to represent a cultural nucleus for a large part of Waverley District."*

So said the original prospectus in 1975 and such aspirations were reshaped and enshrined in the Constitution approved by the Charity Commission in 1977 which said:

> *"The objects of the Trust shall be to foster and promote the maintenance of artistic taste and knowledge, understanding and appreciation of the arts and in the interests of social welfare facilitating other leisure-time activities (apart from sport) for the inhabitants of Cranleigh and district with the object of improving their conditions of life particularly by the establishment of the Cranleigh Arts and Leisure Centre."*

These were subsequently endorsed with minor amendments in 1982 and 1996 to the Charity Commission. Eventually, riffing on the BBC's motto to *"inform, educate, entertain the people"*, a shorthand was developed for marketing and PR purposes of ***'To enrich, entertain & inspire our community…'***.

The evolution from just being a venue for the affiliated societies to being the hub of local artistic and cultural provision was driven by two circumstances, the ownership of a building that needed to be used and improved if it was to fulfil its function, and the need for revenue to maintain the building and support its activities. The Limited Company status made its legal and financial operation more secure and the changes to membership opened up community ownership of the project. What had to develop also was what happened within its walls, for whom and to what profit.

The two opening Festivals in 1978 and 1979 showed that by working together a good week of diverse quality programming and participation could create a buzz in the village and, if not making a profit, could break even when the community and its businesses got behind it. A sub-committee had coordinated these and so the suggestion was made by the Chairman, Richard Whitehead, at the Management meeting of November 1979, that they should continue to run all public events in the Centre, *"being aware of the regulations"*. This was further discussed in December when it was agreed to form an Events Committee for this purpose and *"The Chairman felt that several positions should be filled by able people who were not necessarily members of the Management Committee"*. In January 1980 this was established, comprising Reg Lawrence (Treasurer), Dilys Savedra (Centre Manager), Jack Wagg (Publicity/legal/fundraising), Leo Smith (Bar), Geoff Dubbins (Players) and Mrs L Whitehead, to ensure that the public events led by different interest groups were coordinated. The committee was amended to include Jon Horrocks, who was Chairman for a long while, and Mike Savedra (Building) and Sam Maynard (Arts and Crafts Soc.). Fundraising was also part of the brief and they added Phil Green, Chris Green, Betty Steele and Christine Gumbrell. In the first year membership changed a little, but regulars subsequently included Alan Steer, Brenda Stone, Corrie Ahearn, Liz Hoad, Basia Weaver and Ann Horrocks.

In March *"CJW (Jack Wagg) reported that no decisions had been reached at the first meeting of the Events Committee but another meeting would be held ... Topics of discussion included Festival '80 and possibilities of raising money."* So income generation had come onto the agenda quite soon. By April 1980 Jack Wagg is CALT Chairman and reports back on the Events Committee under ten headings – various changes of personnel and proposals for events and fundraising, as well as some building maintenance issues. So it had quickly developed into a key part of the Centre's organisation with the Chairman in attendance. As the year went on they organised a fundraising fair, co-ordinated public events such as film showings, exhibitions and visiting theatre from South East Arts, and a party at Christmas.

The Minutes reflect a dedicated group of people who are fizzing with ideas and keen to reach out and connect with both potential performers and groups and the audience of Cranleigh. The Chairmanship is taken on by Jon Horrocks, and when he moves to direct the Building Group it tends to rotate around a small group. Alan Steer, Peter Hoad and John Hurst in the early part of the decade and Basia Weaver, Rosemary Dubois, Jill Newcomb, Ann Horrocks, Jane Stevens, Betty Steele, Mary Holmes and Liz Hoad in the latter. These names are constant through this period and month on month they co-ordinated and organised the events that brought people in. An example of this can be seen in *Vision* of Sept/Oct 1980 where they write:

> *"When the Events Committee was emerging during the spring the idea of opening the Arts Centre Bar for coffee with a mini arts exhibition every Saturday morning was suggested. Would it work, who would come, let's try it and find out. A date was fixed for mid-May and held to – a modest start with a few photographs quickly developed into substantial exciting exhibitions. Every morning .. the Bar has thronged with enthusiastic supporters of these one person shows of painting, pottery, design, photography, weaving etc. All have been of a high standard, contrasting and stimulating."*

Mention is then made of Corrie Ahearn and Liz Hoad, who both go on to make significant contributions. *"Just two of the people involved in Saturday mornings at the Centre. By the end of the year 50 exhibitors will have shown their work, more than 20 members will have helped with coffee and some 50/60 visitors will have come each week – quite a lot of people – will you have been one of them?"* Ann Horrocks, an Adult Education tutor and wife of Events Chairman Jon, was a prime mover in all this.

South East Arts Association had been supportive from the start and Bob Henry, their Drama Director, came and met the committee in July 1980. His input on budgeting, touring, booking productions, other venues and marketing was informative and this became a continuing and sustaining relationship. At that meeting it was decided to put on a Children's Week rather than a third Festival in October. This commitment to children, perhaps reflecting the fact that many had young families, also became an ongoing feature of their planning.

Each represented Society had something to offer. The Arts and Crafts Society led with the Saturday Exhibitions/Coffee mornings and monthly Craft Markets. For bigger events they came together. The Players were expert at Jumble Sales and running social events, such as a Pickwickian evening for New Year or a 1920s event. The History and Archaeology Society supplied a bric-a-brac stall. The Camera Club took care of decorations and raffles. Non-affiliates like the Adult Education Group and Folk Club also contributed on a regular basis. The social element of bringing people together was important either as an audience for films, plays or demonstrations, as collaborators in fundraising events like the 'Fayres', or as practitioners and performers; this was the glue that made people commit time and energy to the project. Audrey Norman, Editor, wrote in Aug/Sept 1985 *Vision*,

> *"Every time there is an occasion to come together there is such a feeling of friendliness and fellowship ... the folks who take on the many voluntary tasks around the Centre are worth their weight in gold. I liken it to a ship with the ratings doing their humble but necessary duties with 'Captain Jack Wagg' at the helm."*

So there was a direction of travel. 'Captain Jack' regularly attended the meetings through 1980-1983. The Minutes of the Executive Committee in February 1983 record under Item: Events Committee Report: *"Time was against considering this item fully. The Chairman however detected possible defects in lines of communication and would discuss remedies with the Committee."* In April we read: *"Peter Hoad is prepared to be group leader and is enthusiastic. The Group should take care not to make arrangements unless there is adequate organisation at the Centre for the event involved. The Chairman will continue to report on behalf of the Group."* So Captain Jack was keeping a close eye on the crew.

In 1984 Rosemary Dubois was asked to join the committee. She had previously been to art classes with Ann Horrocks and would become a key player in the development of the Arts Centre. She quickly became one of the main programme planners with a special interest in children's theatre and also ran the theatre trips, which were popular with members. Due to workload Jack Wagg pulled back from attending meetings so communication with the Management Committee was via the Events Chairman, Peter Hoad and others, who reported back and forth. The building hire rates were set by the Management Committee and it was left to Dilys Savedra to fit in the Adult Education classes and extra bookings. She refused a potential booking from a right wing group as inappropriate and banned another after some ructions over how they had left the facilities. The Events Committee, like every Programmer to follow, had to juggle with the ticketing of booked events and the suitability and profitability of what they were offered. At times events happened offsite, as with some music recitals and a remarkable Danish choir at St Nicholas church, but the object was really to get people through the doors of the Centre.

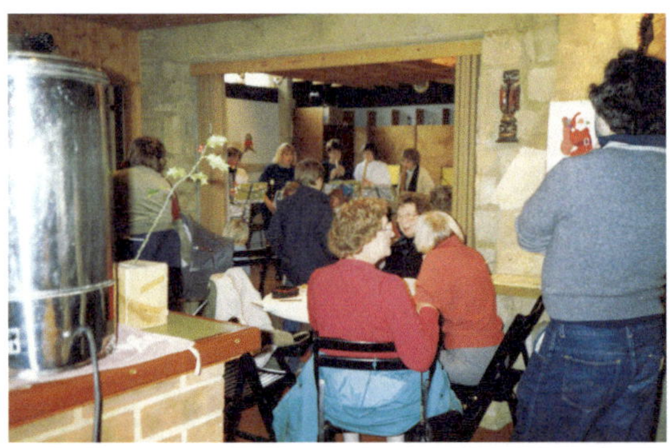

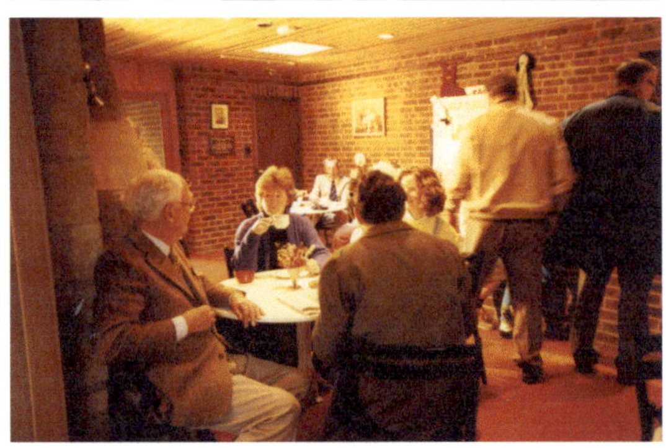

Coffee bar looking towards gallery.
Coffee bar looking towards car park.

Putting it all together

What did the programme look like? Are there too many chiefs?

If we sample the programme at different times we can see how it developed over this period. In

November 1979 it was almost exclusively events for the Film Society, Camera Club, and Arts and Crafts Society, three or four each, with one special event, a visiting professional play. By November the following year regular exhibitions had been introduced and in addition to Arts and Crafts, Camera and Film Clubs, there was a regular Folk Club and the Archaeological Society with one monthly meeting each and the Drama group with weekly meetings. Special events were a Raku open-air firing party, South East Arts Film show and an Arts and Crafts Christmas Sale. In 1982 November was similar with the addition of a Bonfire Party and a Flute Concert.

By 1985 we find Studio and Painting Workshop features in addition to Arts and Crafts, the Drama group meets weekly, the Film Society offers a film, the Craft Market is there still and two newcomers are the Music Listening Group and the Bridge Club. There was a touring theatre production in October and the Guildford and District RSPB seem to be regular bookers. Each summer at this time there were extensive children's activities, so events were often either project based or socially inspired. In November 1987 the same societies were represented in Diary, with a special evening from The Pickwick Players (later cancelled) and a 1940s Evening. There is a possible Poetry Group starting. Alongside all these are the Adult Education classes which included life drawing and an attempt to provide drama classes, since the demise of Cranleigh Amateur Dramatic Society. Putting events together with a theme is tried this month with Birds, which brings together the RSPB, an art exhibition and a concert. They tried to have something on each Saturday. The professional events usually needed a subsidy which came out of a grant from South East Arts. In 1988 the Crane Club was launched for the first and third Thursday evenings to provide Folk and Jazz. However the model did not change very much, perhaps limited by the focus and interests of the small group involved. Almost every event seemed to be organised by a different committee member and it took ages to get responses from people. They did have successes, often dependent on the efficiency of the publicity drive for a particular offering, but some good ideas or approaches are recorded in the minutes as falling by the wayside or not able to be pursued.

> *"Julian Lloyd Webber's offer was turned down because it was too costly."* April 1980.
>
> *"The Folk Group cannot be formally affiliated to the Centre since they have no constitution."* Sept 1980.
>
> *"An informal meeting to discuss the future of Music in the Arts Centre: however little has resulted to date, because of a lack of similar musical tastes."* Feb 1981.
>
> *"The Committee decided to have fewer events through the autumn as the 1982/3 programme was not very well supported."* March 1983.

Things do settle though and even take a quirky turn when in March 1989 when it is proposed that a tea party and a film be put on to celebrate the completion of the ladies' loos!

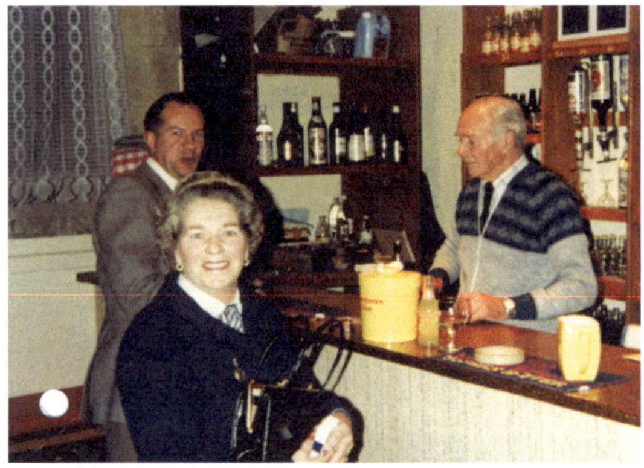

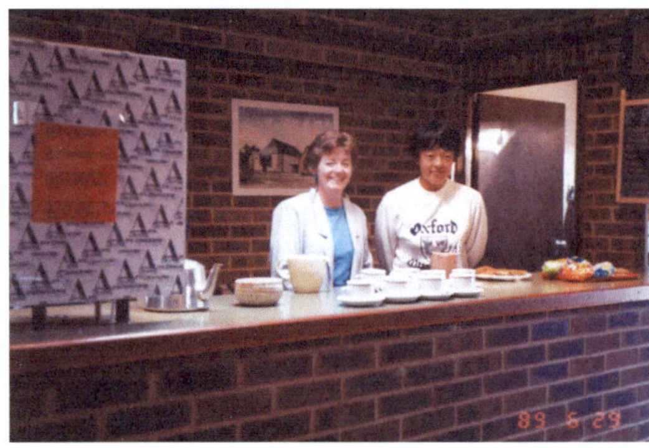

The original bar in the Gallery
The new coffee bar once the foyer was built

The clash of the Committees

Let's talk about who does what

Cracks in this structure start to appear in 1987, when John Hurst (Bridge Club representative from July 1986), takes over the Chairmanship of the Events Committee in December 1986. At the Management Meeting in April he had passed on a complaint about the state of the Centre including the toilets, which had provoked discussion. In May he asks for a budget out of grant allocations to work from. In July he hopes for new members for the Events Committee. In October he raises Publicity as an issue, with the resignation of Betty Steele, he makes a proposal for a professional fundraiser and he also queries fundraising strategy. Clearly a man on a mission. At the December executive meeting Betty Steele acts in his absence and presents two proposals regarding distribution of tickets on commission and the right form for the engagement of artists. The Chairman appears to dismiss both. John Hurst writes to him at once.

> *"Dear Jack,*
> *I have received a report of the Management Committee meeting ... which unfortunately I was unable to attend.*
> *From my informant it is obvious that you have criticisms of the Events Committee and me as Chairman. It is obvious that the chairman of this committee must have the confidence of the chairman of the management committee and when this ceases to be the case, resignations are called for. With regret, I therefore offer my resignation to take effect immediately...*

> *...When I was asked to consider chairing the Events Committee I did so on the understanding that I was not prepared to act as a 'dogsbody' but would try to instil a little order into the committee's deliberations. Generally the committee members are hard working and very enthusiastic and if they are not given encouragement I fear you may lose more members.*
> *As the Events Committee is most important and decisions reached are often contrary to your own ideas I wonder if you should consider being an active member or even taking the Chair.*
> *Needless to say I wish the Arts Centre continued success and for the time being will remain a member of the Management committee."*

Jack writes back:

> *"Dear John,*
> *I find it difficult to understand what kind of report you received to persuade you to write your letter of the 10th.*
> *I certainly raised two items of criticism of the Events subcommittee which [I'm] sure any one of us is entitled to do particularly when one is in the position of having to pick up the pieces.*
> *One of the items was I understand raised when Jane Stevens was in the chair and the other had been tried before your time without success.*
> *If you feel you must give up then this must be for you to decide, whether you do or not I should like to thank you for what you have done over the past months."*

At the next Management meeting (at which John Hurst was also absent) Jack expressed his thanks publicly and Hurst continued to represent the Bridge Club on the management committee for another three years. But Jack could see there was a problem with this model. He did attend the next Events Committee meeting where it was agreed that Betty Steele, who had been an elected committee member of the Arts Centre since the beginning, would report back and forth. Betty Steele was a staunch member of the Arts and Crafts Society, editing their newsletter *Scope*, which had fielded much of the breakaway criticism. She must have been upset by the schism but continued to be very loyal and hardworking for Cranleigh Arts. Since Rosemary Dubois was now Centre Manager she would liaise back and forth too.

Aware that its members were a diminishing band of stalwarts in March 1988 the committee asked the Management Committee to constitutionally require each affiliated society to send representatives to serve on the Events Committee. It isn't clear whether the message got through. It certainly seemed that better communication was necessary so the Management Committee suggested a joint meeting with the Events Committee to *"discuss ways of widening the scope of events, possibly with increased funding"*. Chris Dubois, who had been co-opted to the Management Committee in February 1987 and had proved a useful addition, volunteered to open the meeting in September 1988; Jane Stevens would do so for the Events Committee. Seventeen people attended what seems from the notes to have been a positive meeting. Chris asked what input the events committee needed from management and what their policy was for booking events. Jane replied that the group each had their specialisms but worked as a team and felt overstretched. Some events had to be taken on trust when booked and she queried whether success should be measured by quality, quantity or income. The ensuing discussion ranged over desirable improvements to facilities, regularity of programming, the merits of different types of music and drama and the need for more support with Front of House management.

> *"The Chairman (Jack Wagg) in closing the meeting, said that the Council of Management had found it most useful for appreciating the problems of the Events Committee. Perhaps it should be repeated from time to time and could include tutors and voluntary helpers."*

In June 1989 John Hurst suggested another meeting to which "*the Chairman agreed in principle but said that there should be clearly defined topics for discussion. The Autumn would be a better time*". In October the Events Committee didn't think there was a need for a joint meeting until next year.

Shaking up the structure for delivery

Jack Wagg makes more organisational change

However there were radical changes afoot to restructure. In December *"the Chairman outlined a proposal for future changes in the structure of the Council of Management, the frequency of meetings and the involvement of members of the Events Committee. The purpose of these proposals was to make best use of human resources and to encourage longer-term planning."* At the January 1990 Council meeting a memorandum was presented by the Chairman and Secretary. The logic was to enable those who had the time and commitment to get on with the day to day running of the Centre to do so, whilst keeping engaged through reporting or consultation those who constitutionally were responsible for the Centre and who had relevant expertise or who wanted to contribute but with less time available. In essence it was to streamline the delivery by centralising and delegating decision-making to a small group. *"The Executive Committee will be the power house of the Centre and care will be needed to ensure that we achieve the balance available to take necessary action in respect to management and construction."* The minutes record:

> *"Considerable discussion followed on whether and how the proposed structure would lead to the improvements suggested in the memorandum and also whether change was really needed. Miss Newcomb asked what would happen to the Events Committee. The Chairman said that the committee was never formally constituted but had developed over a number of years from people with a common interest in various aspects of events and exhibitions."*

This was not strictly true. It continued:

> *"In the proposed structure the Events Committee as such would disappear, but the various members would still be involved through the Council of Management, the Consultative Forum and ad hoc working groups set up for various purposes."*

This was an olive branch, yes, but would that really happen in practice? The motion to adopt in principle was put to the vote and passed 5-4 with one abstention and the Chairman not voting. The Captain had set his course.

The next task was to set out how delegated powers should be delineated. It was to be a revision of past practices and a formalising of how things worked now, as Jack explained in the next memorandum.

> *"The development of the Arts Centre has been underway for 12 years. During the second half of this period in particular we made substantial progress both as to extension of the premises and also in its use for recreation, entertainment and learning. We have reached the current stage by the recruitment of a variety of volunteers, some of whom had considerable experience and practical know-how, whilst others relied on zeal and goodwill. In addition there has been a constant shortage of money. In order to maintain progress, diverse practices and substantial risks have been taken and fortunately optimism has paid off. We could not have moved forward so successfully if we had stuck to traditional and constitutional practices. However with the substantial increase in cash flow ... it becomes unfair to the officers to operate in this way."*
>
> *"The day to day management centres on the Coffee Bar where the Centre Manager, The Administrative Secretary/Receptionist and the Chairman meet daily bringing into partnership as many volunteers as can be persuaded to participate. When the Centre Manager was invited to accept this voluntary role, it was agreed there should be a partnership between the Centre Manager and the Chairman –*

each standing in for the other. The pressures on both parties have increased considerably but continue to work happily. The Hon Secretary has offered to take up some of the workload and we shall undoubtedly take up his offer. The Admin Secretary/Receptionist is a key link between the officers and the public, but we shall need to explore the possibility of increasing her hours."

The interpersonal relationship between Jack (Chairman), Rosemary Dubois (Centre Manager), Anne Hull (Administrative Secretary/Receptionist) and Geoff Goodfellow (Hon. Secretary) was obviously very strong. He suggested Reg Monk (Building maintenance expert), Harry Stadler (Treasurer) and Jill Newcomb be added as members of the Executive.

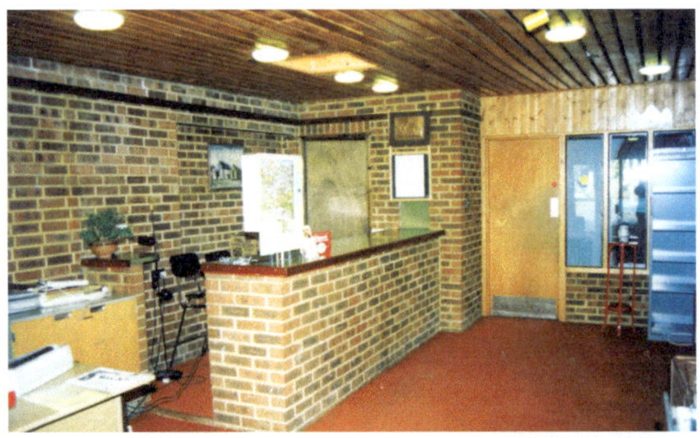

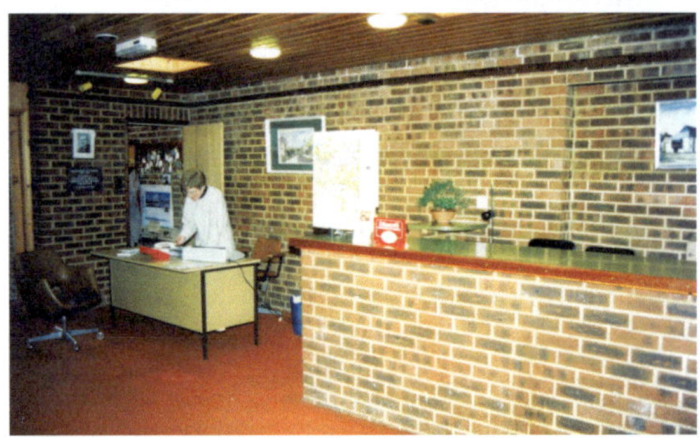

Anne Hull at her desk in reception

Discussions continued through February on the restructuring of the management into a three tier model: Executive Committee, Full Council and a Full Council plus all comers Consultative Forum. It was amended and approved at the March meeting. The Minutes record:

"Members expressed concern that the proposed disbanding of the Events Committee could lead to a loss of voluntary effort in putting forward future proposals and staging events, even though ... the frequency of the Consultative forum (had been increased) to three times a year." ... "The Chairman said that new proposals were intended to bring about better mutual understanding between the Council of Management and members making up the existing Events Committee. The lack of an elected Chairman of the latter had caused difficulties in communication between the two, particularly regarding long-term planning and costing of events. He reminded the meeting that the Events Committee was not formally constituted and that the proposed close liaison between producers of the three different types of events and the Executive Committee and the Council of Management should lead to improved coordination. He would write a letter to the Events Committee members introducing the proposed changes."

The motion was proposed by John Hurst, who had perhaps seen it coming, and adopted unanimously, subject to a review once a year on the efficiency of the system. The Chairman reported to the July 1990 AGM.

> *"Our organisation is being reshaped to meet the needs of the workers. Firstly we have a small Executive Team ... to sustain the tempo on all urgent management decisions. Secondly the Council of Management ... keeping policy on line for long term operations. ... Finally we shall be organising a whole series of consultative forums. So there is going to be a genuine opportunity for everyone to play an ongoing and exciting part. ... I close this report with a special acknowledgement of the important voluntary input of so many members and friends who are upholding the best traditions of community enterprise."*

Push-back against organisational change

Admin or artists? The dangers of alienating willing volunteers by centralisation

The last meeting of the Events Committee was on 24th May 1990, which the Chairman attended. Its responsibilities were redistributed to genre producers as listed in Autumn 1990 *Vision* as: Exhibition organiser: Jill Newcomb (although she gave it up shortly after); Music Events: Betty Steele; Poetry/Literature: Jane Stevens; Professional Drama: Rosemary Dubois. They did not go without a fight, however. On 29th May Basia Weaver wrote to the Chairman and Committee of Management to make a formal protest.

> *"Any institutional change is bound to generate uncertainty and some disappointment, but if handled well it should also generate enthusiasm and encourage continuing commitment whether to a greater or lesser degree.*
> *Whilst acknowledging the need for change in the management structure and quite accepting that my own involvement will no longer be required, I am appalled at the way the Events Committee has been treated in the process.*
> *After over ten years as the Events Committee, generating Events, Exhibitions, ideas, enthusiasm, loyalty, commitment, private and public funds, time, skills labour, fun and food; all bound together by a generous community spirit; we were informed that we were not an OFFICIAL Events Committee! So we were TOLD and not consulted of our demise! And it was not made clear who is now redundant or who will be asked to continue in their present role within the inner or outer layer of the new structure....*

> *...Is it any wonder, that after such a corporate slap in the face the Events Committee members feel so aggrieved and that our enthusiasm has been very seriously dampened if not obliterated.*
> *On the way to a bigger and brighter future, the alienation of a long standing group of committed volunteers was totally unnecessary."*

Her husband David Weaver, who like Basia had given endless hours in service to Cranleigh Arts, recalls:

> *"There was a meeting when Jack told everybody that they weren't needed any longer. That was it. You can go now. It appears to have been as blunt as that. Certainly Basia and Ann (Horrocks) were absolutely livid. Not for themselves so much but because all the other people who volunteered and put in time, not a word of thanks to anybody, just said all right you can go now. Bang."*

Jill Newcomb couldn't attend the following Management meeting on 12th June but wrote in similar vein:

> *"I know that Basia Weaver's letter reflected the feelings of every member of the Events Committee, with the exception of Rosemary. I am therefore concerned that unless your reply is both understanding and conciliatory that the Arts Centre will lose the support of 8 or 9 members including some of its most creative members, and a large proportion of those who have been prepared to give time and thought to Arts Centre activities. They are not likely to feel enthusiastic about the somewhat condescending suggestion that there are lots of jobs they could do, and their attitude to attending the AGM could well depend on your letter.*
> *"You are correct in saying that information about the proposed changes were given at several Events Committee meetings, though this was by its nature limited and changing. However opinions of these experienced people was not sought and their attempts at making positive responses (e.g. that a members club which could also act as ideas generator might be formed, and that a New Year's Eve Party - a possible fundraiser – be held) were roughly dealt with.*
> *"I think I can speak for them as well as myself in saying that our admiration and shared pride in the philosophy and achievements of the Centre and for your own immeasurable part in this is unchanged, but it is at risk of being completely overlaid by recent hurts."*

Jack sends her a short reply: *"It appears that a group of members and others have decided to put me in the dock and therefore I prefer to deal with the matter guided by my conscience. I am distressed to learn that some members are regarded as superior to others".*

The Chairman defended himself at the Council Meeting to which the letters were addressed, stressing again *"that nobody was being made or considered redundant under the new structure. There was never enough voluntary effort for the many and varied activities in the Centre".* After considerable discussion it was agreed that the Chairman would write a conciliatory letter expressing the appreciation of the Council of Management to all those who had been on the Events Committee. He did so, briefly explaining the process and consultation, saying it was provisional for twelve months, and asking for support for the upcoming Secombe Arts Festival *"bearing in mind that the future of the Pottery and the Gallery depend on the success of this event. In so far as our decisions have been misunderstood by failure on our part, we do of course apologise and look forward to the continued support of all members, new and old".* He concludes with *"best thanks".* He was being a bit disingenuous claiming that the Events Committee was not formally constituted, as it had been set up by the Management Committee, under the previous Chairman in January 1980, with him as a founder member. But as he said privately to Rosemary Dubois of the changes, *"We need admin not artists".*

Another staunch member of the Events Committee, Betty Steele, who organised the Music gave notice in July that she would step down at the end of the year. She wrote explaining,

> *"I am finding that running a home and a full time business does not leave enough time to put in the work necessary to organise an event, particularly as now there is no longer any 'back-up' in the form of the Events Committee, essential in the past for all the small jobs shared out and the general support given in so many ways. This is not to deny the great help and support given, as always, by Rosemary and Chris Dubois but there is a limit to what one can ask them to do."*

She continues to discuss the recent music event which played to only 20 people and wonders why. She suggests improving publicity and presentation. *"Perhaps we might start with the Management Committee and ask why they do not attend these events."* Jack's pencilled draft reply reads,

> *"We are passing through a difficult period because too many members are not prepared to join together to work for community activities. Members of the Council of management are in general as bad as anyone. The objective is to correct this weakness. ... Finally no one should believe they are not wanted – this has never been suggested. We need people to work together in their little groups."*

However this is heavily scored out and a briefer more neutral acknowledgement sent instead, but it gives a sense of what he might have been feeling. This change is a good example of how he worked both with and against people to realise his vision, not only for the building, but for the organisation that had to run it. He knew that it needed to move towards a more professional model of management.

Later in 1995 looking back on his decade as Chairman he reflected:

> *"Soon the battle of ideas began: should we be content with the minimum and provide only for the then middle-class, middle-aged membership or should we plan for the best possible Community Arts Centre for all ages and groups. After substantial arguments, heartaches and some resignations, the progressive view carried the day."*

At the AGM in July 1990 he sold the reorganisation idea to members that it was *"to meet the needs of the workers"* and that the four-monthly all-comers forums would *"be a genuine opportunity for everyone to play an ongoing and exciting part"*, to be reviewed in twelve months. However at the AGM in 1991in the discussion *"a number of those present felt that the new structure referred to at the previous AGM was not working well. Members were not being as actively involved as previously and the amount of information being given to the ordinary members about developments in the Centre was very limited."* In reply

> *"The Chairman agreed that the arrangements for open discussion meetings had not been successful but it was hoped that a series of such meetings as the one proposed in the autumn to discuss aspects of fundraising would improve the situation. Regarding information dissemination, all members received 'Vision' and the Secretary, Anne Hull, was available every day to provide information. Lack of funds and volunteer effort militated against a regular individual system of notification."*

In a Waverley Policy Report of 1989 it records *"There are no fulltime staff but 250 members and 30 volunteers are involved in the running, converting and organising events throughout the year"*. The Chairman was not for turning, but the perceived space between the Executive, the core volunteers and the wider artistic community could seem a chasm at times.

Some returned to the fold, but others didn't and in a small community that matters. What underlies this episode, which has been examined in depth, is that it is an example of the universal split between the creatives and the administrators, both are needed, but each thinks the other doesn't really understand what they do. When all these people do it voluntarily, from a passion, then egos are bruised and it can become a power struggle, as it may have been here. It was also about the difficulties of effecting change and growing the organisation's ability to deliver its aims. Communication was also a problem as the organisation moved from a collective to being more hierarchical. Anxiety from volunteers and supporters in the face of change was to happen again and again. However as money began to flow in and the facilities improved in line with its ambitions, Cranleigh Arts needed to become more professional and accountable in its structures.

Managing the Money

The work of the Treasurers

There have been a number of distinguished Treasurers over the life of Cranleigh Arts. It is an unenviable task as money has always been short, keeping track of it is difficult in a volunteer organisation, and having a legal responsibility to outside authorities, including the annual AGMs, the Charity Commission and sponsoring authorities. In this period Reg Lawrence (1977-85), Tony Stevens (1986-88), and Harry Stadler (1989-99) were all praised and thanked for their ability to do this. The economic background to the '70s and '80s was a rocky one with inflation peaking at over 25% in 1974. A brave time to start an arts centre! It had halved by 1978 but rose again in 1980. However economic growth was boosted by low interest rates and cuts to income tax which helped to increase consumer spending and a boom in the housing market. In the southeast particularly this promoted a big boost to consumer confidence reflected in the optimism towards the future of the Arts Centre and its growth too. The bubble would burst in the recession of 1991-92 making money much harder to get again.

Where did it come from?

Operating on a shoestring

At first income was limited to annual subscriptions from affiliated societies on a per capita basis, lettings from hires to those societies and to others, and from events held, either specifically for fundraising or presentations open to the public. To give an idea of what these amounted to in 1978: hiring for societies was set at £1.25 for the first 30 sessions a year; in 1979 this was increased to £2, with outside organisations paying £5. Once the bar and coffee bar were up and running these became regular earners. Folk evenings, for example, could bring in between £25 and £40 profits on the bar. This was at a time when they were paying out £875 for stage curtains, £200 in rent to Waverley, £140 on Calor gas heaters. There was some previous capital raised which was held in the Trustees account amounting to £2000, but that would not last long. Special fundraising events were held such as an Autumn Fair in 1980 which brought all the societies together working collaboratively and netted £400. The motivation was that building improvement could be done from this source of money and not have to put hire rates or subscriptions up. These continued to be regular events ringing the changes between fairs, flea markets, socials, 'film and meal' deals, tabletop sales and special concerts.

Favours were pulled in to keep running costs down; Jack Wagg initially arranged for duplicating to be done at the Waverley offices rather than having to buy a machine, although this added to the time and energy required to get it done. One Committee member was able through his business to get electrical work done as a favour. At social parties willing volunteers provided the food and for the festive punch a raffle was arranged to raise the £20 cost of it. Posters could be silkscreened or drawn by the resident artists, usually Basia Weaver.

At the start of the eighties the booked events were costing £50-£100 with tickets at £1 or less for children; but by 1984 they were paying £260 for the poet Brian Patten and tickets had risen to £4 / £5 non-members. A look at 1987 finds Masque Dance Theatre performing for £150, tickets £2 and Pickwick Players Theatre for £300, tickets £3. A week long Watercolour Exhibition brought in £340 and the bar made profits of £1,600 in three months. By 1988 South East Arts had committed a grant to support losses on productions: so 'Tess of the D'Urbervilles' cost £250, but tickets could be offered at £2.50 adults, £1.50 for young people, non-members £3. (It makes a loss of £42.) In 1989 Snap Theatre Company present 'A Taste of Honey' for £500. £250 is given by South East Arts so Cranleigh Arts is liable for £250. It sells for £3 and 57 people attend. (So a loss of about £100.) This was the pattern seen in the minutes: small gains, low prices to get people in, and a difficulty to make any substantial money from the programme. Audience numbers were capped at about 90 on rather uncomfortable seating until the rake is put in. Average attendance was 48 in 1980 and seemingly not much greater at the end of the decade. The audience seemed loyal but the limitations were the capacity of the venue – bar or auditorium, and the difficulties of effective publicity, both generating the material and broadcasting it.

Membership support

How to jolly up the troops

Once individual membership was an option, after the transition to Limited Company status, the widening of potential members and donors was part of the 'sell'.

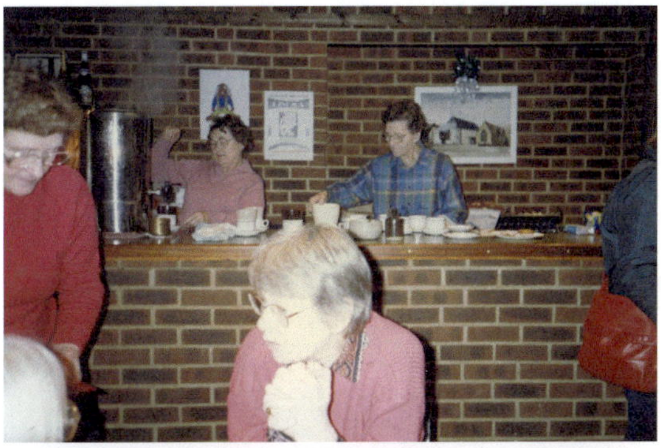

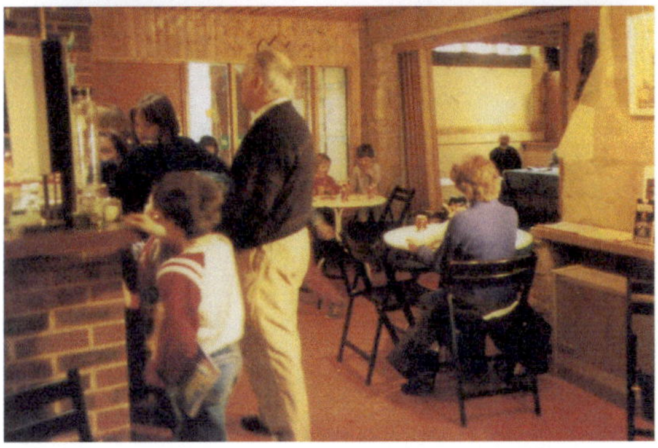

Discounted tickets, social events and a sense of arts participation, education and ownership were features of the newsletters' content. **'Join us and celebrate the arts in Cranleigh'** was the message, but that came with a responsibility to contribute. There is variety, value for money and a good vibe – if you have paid your sub! *"See you in the coffee bar – only Mum will give you a cheaper cup!"* The Coffee bar was a consistent high income source, beloved of Jack Wagg, and profits went directly into the Building Fund.

Subscriptions seemed to be resistant to increase. Support for the Centre remained good but it seemed hard to boost the numbers overall. The rift with the Arts and Crafts Society led to a drop in their group membership contribution, but some increase in individuals joining.

Sample Membership data:

Year	Total	A&C Soc	Camera Club	Film Soc	CADS	History/ Archaeology Soc	Individual
1980/1	328	224	34	23	14	15	18
1981/2	302	168	32	35	21	13	33
1982/3	265	203	30	?	?	13	18

However Income from Subscriptions barely rises:
1979/80: £174.
1980/81: £207.
1983/84: £183.
1987/88: £360.
Leading to an optimistic 1990/91: Projected: £633

Fundraising
From rattling a bucket to high profile galas

Complaints were made that from Jack Wagg's arrival and assumption of the Chairmanship money became the main focus of attention. It is true that the newsletters have a constant petition for everyone to make their contribution. In October/November 1981 he writes *"if you are frustrated or inconvenienced whilst at the Centre ... please don't grumble – help solve the problem by giving a little cash and raising some more. Money doesn't solve every problem but it helps!"*. The same issue carries an article by Jon Hewitt, former acting-Chairman, who is now back in the area as fundraising organiser. He argues that fundraising is a corporate activity for which everyone is responsible. The availability of Grant money for substantial improvements is also linked to running costs being met by small but committed member donations.

> *"It is essential that every member of the Arts Centre makes exceptional efforts to raise money from within and around the community of Cranleigh. In order for the Arts Centre to flourish expansion is essential. ... It is of paramount importance that a strong Centre based funding programme is planned and implemented. ... Each project will be allocated a principal method of fundraising. Each fundraising activity will be given its own financial target and reason. ... It has been said before that the Arts Centre will live or die by what is put into it by the people of Cranleigh. I only ask you to think carefully and evaluate how much effort is required and whether you are doing your share."* Echoes of JFK here?

Once the plans for the development of the building are accepted in 1982 and the YTS scheme gets going to create Phases One and Two the appeals become constant and the persuasion veers from *"if you use the Centre, don't be selfish, contribute"* to *"give us your money, now!"*. Even an interest free loan scheme is introduced in order to provide working capital for expenditure. There is a levy on members of £2.50 in 1982/3 when £1,000 is needed quickly for the East Wing upgrade when Peter Oliver finally moves out. Some were slow to pay so the Chairman writes – *"I must remind those who made a major issue of protecting the East Wing as an Arts Studio that the management has done its bit, the Studio has been secured. But the bill must be paid."* Do we sense a bit of a dig at the Arts and Crafts lobby who had been a bit difficult? In a later newsletter he writes *"Already since we first occupied the school buildings we have raised and spent over £13,000 and now we need as much again for the next leap forward."* The value of that today allowing for inflation is about £75,000; quite an achievement, but in the end much, much more would be needed, nearer £2,000,000, as we shall see.

There was also a PR story to manage. If you cry *"we are short of cash"* too often then the public think that you are in crisis. In 1985, when there was a push to get the YTS building additions completed before the scheme ended, the local paper carried the headline **'Cranleigh youth training project under threat'**. There was a press briefing on Phase Two from Jon Horrocks but the quotes seem alarmist.

> *"The Arts Centre does not have enough resources to carry on building. ... We are living from month to month. ... Phase Two which has only just started will cost £8,000 but the Centre's funds are down to a few hundred pounds. ... We are running along the breadline. But if we can keep a few hundred in hand we can carry on."*

This followed an appeal to members for donations, interest free loans or four year covenanted donations, which had tax advantages. It had some effect as the materials were provided until the boys left in December. However the Chairman had to write reassuringly to the membership in the newsletter: *"While the boys are still with us we must speed up the delivery of materials for their use. So larger scale fundraising is imperative"*. But: *"Please scotch any rumours you hear that we have a crisis on our hands. We are on course and the scheme will continue"*.

Arts Council funding

South East Arts continues its support

Through this period grant income increased as the Arts Centre established itself and, under Jack Wagg, looked outward more. As we have seen, South East Arts, the regional arm of the Arts Council, was a supporter from the early days, seeing its potential as a touring venue and providing guarantees against loss or subsidies for individual theatre bookings, as part of its regional network of Arts organisations. In 1984 it produced a brochure **'This is your Arts Centre...'** which featured pictures and statistics from its forty Centres across the region, Kent, East Sussex and Surrey, but gave individual Centres two pages of their own material and branding. It posed and answered questions such as: *"What is your Arts Centre? Why is your Arts Centre so special? Who is the Arts Centre for? Who pays for the Arts Centre? What does the Arts Centre do for the Local Economy?"*. They paid for the Renwick Report, which highlighted the growing success of the Arts Centre, but also the need for organisational support. In response they make a change from Project funding to Revenue funding. From Summer 1988 South East Arts allocated an annual £2,000 for the part-time Secretary thus supporting the day to day management. This artistic endorsement of being a 'strategic client' helped to raise the profile and sell the Arts

Centre locally. In the South East Arts Regional Plan 1989 they wrote,

> *"Cranleigh Arts Centre could provide a model case study of a village school conversion and is likely to prove of national importance..."*

Ask the landlords

The relationship with Waverley – give with one hand, take with the other?

At that time South East Arts could not support buildings, so Waverley Borough Council and the Cranleigh Parish Council had to be tapped for development and maintenance funding. It took most of this period for Jack Wagg to persuade his former colleagues to commit serious money. There were ongoing wrangles about the rateable value and what rent should be paid and the changes to the lease went back and forth as additional estate was added. Despite Jack's claims in 1986 that *"the Centre is yours for life"* it wasn't until late 1989 that it was finally signed.

The original lease in 1978 was for 21 years and with the annual rent fixed at £200 for the first seven years. In February 1982 when the longer 99 year lease was starting to be negotiated the District Valuer proposed £1,650 reviewed every five years. A leap which was impossible for the Company. Jack writes, *"This is a complete misunderstanding of the history of this matter"*. But the Council seem to want to charge a 'commercial market' rent. Nothing has happened so in July 1984 he writes to get the support of Mrs Margot Gordon, the Chair of the Leisure and Culture Committee, as *"my discussions have been less than progressive"*. He suggests a rent of £1,450 and offers to buy the freehold. This falls on deaf ears at Waverley and he gets a back rent demand in November for £2,500. He rejects this as impossible to find, *"I have become very frustrated at the inexplicable lack of progress"*. The Company is invited to apply for a grant of £2,000 from them to cover the shortfall. He applies and submits a long letter of justification which details the facts of the matter as he sees them. There has been little support from Waverley to date, having received only £975 in the last ten years. He compares Cranleigh Arts with the Redgrave Theatre, Farnham which has a minimal rent and a £26,000 grant. He says again that there has been previously no suggestion of a commercial lease or rent. Cranleigh Arts revenue is set as high as the market will bear. He lists the many and varied activities at the Centre and underlines the community nature of them. The grant is given but goes back in rent – from one pocket to another for Waverley!

The discussions continue through 1985 with the East Wing now added to the lease. Finally in February 1986 the District Valuer proposes a rent of £1,800 which is accepted, with the agreement that Cranleigh Arts will not seek further grant aid. The draft lease is drawn up again, but then negotiations begin over the car park. By

July 1989 an amended lease is agreed, to commence on 1st November 1989, but there have to be additions of the rights of way of the neighbours so it isn't finally completely signed off until March 1990. Quite why it took so long was explained by the Borough Planning Manager as due to *"the tardiness of the Council's external solicitors"*. Confusion over when exactly the lease started doesn't help, as no bills for rent were sent and preferring not to backdate the bills to 1986 they waive that. The battle would be replayed in 1995 when the rent is next reviewed and Harry Stadler has to argue the case all over again. Inevitably the Council officers and the Councillors each have their own agenda and problems. But at this time, to judge from the records, their support seems rather begrudging, perhaps resentful of this rival upstart to the artistic centre of Farnham in the west and of Jack's gamekeeper turned poacher tactics.

However as this decade goes on they begin to see what an asset the Arts Centre could be, perhaps influenced by South East Arts' commitment. The Leisure Strategy plan for Waverley into the 1990s tabled in 1989 makes three proposals for Cranleigh Arts Centre:

2.13 In future years an allocation of grant aid support should be made on a three year basis.

2.14 In order to assist in the development of the performance hall project, and improvements to the arts facilities within the complex, provision should be made in the capital programme.

2.15 To offer encouragement to succeed in promotion and marketing, so that Cranleigh Arts Centre becomes a centre of excellence.

It is also noted that Adult Education run 19 classes with 400 students at the Centre; 5,000 people use it annually.

But at the AGM in July 1990 there was concern that the bigger arts picture was changing. It is recorded:

> *"The Chairman said that Waverley Borough Council was now much more financially supportive than in the past (e.g. revenue would be inflation linked), but because of changes in Central Government policies (following the Wilding Report on national and regional arts bodies) the annual contribution from South East Arts would probably be reduced in the future. Ms Charmian Stowell (SE Arts) regretfully confirmed the Chairman's opinion and said that small Arts Centres, such as Cranleigh, would probably suffer more, even though she personally considered that small centres are the bedrock of a wide range of national arts activities and promotions. In answer to a question she felt that Cranleigh's policy of slow but steady evolution to be the correct one."*

The Parish Council

Finding support close to home

Each year Jack would also apply to the Cranleigh Parish Council for support. In 1984 with the major building push starting he writes a long explanatory letter to them.

> *"It is now very desirable that we should receive prominent local support and to this end I write this letter for consideration of the Parish Council as the representative body of Cranleigh. My Council of management asks me to invite the Parish Council to take the lead by making a substantial contribution to our building fund and thus guarantee the programme of building on our important community project."*

He receives £200 which is repeated in subsequent years. But in 1987 the Parish Council take the Centre to task for complaints from neighbours and he replies that they are doing all they can to secure and make the temporary buildings visually acceptable.

> *"We are ongoing victims of vandalism. Many windows and the glass door to the new extension have been smashed, the site-builders' mobile hut has been broken into three times, its windows smashed and now grotesquely paint sprayed. Further adults dump supermarket trolleys and other obnoxious rubbish on the site. All this diverts attention and effort from the important positive task we have set ourselves supported by the Parish Council."*

He concludes that if substantial funds can be given then it will all be quickly completed and cleared up. They increase their donation to £300. In 1988 he is in a stronger position with Harry Secombe as Patron and Waverley finally committing to £500 biannually.

Enter a Patron

The effect of having a big name involved

From 1988 the involvement of Sir Harry Secombe and the commitment of funds from Waverley, South East Arts and the Parish Council allowed a gear change in financial health. The celebrity pulling power of the new Patron and the community authority endorsement and support meant that the ambitions of the Chairman and the executive could more likely be realised. Two things come from this: the possibility or need for a professional fundraiser and 'a Big Event'. A Fundraising campaign is explored in 1990 with David Greer. This was both to raise the funds for the Pottery

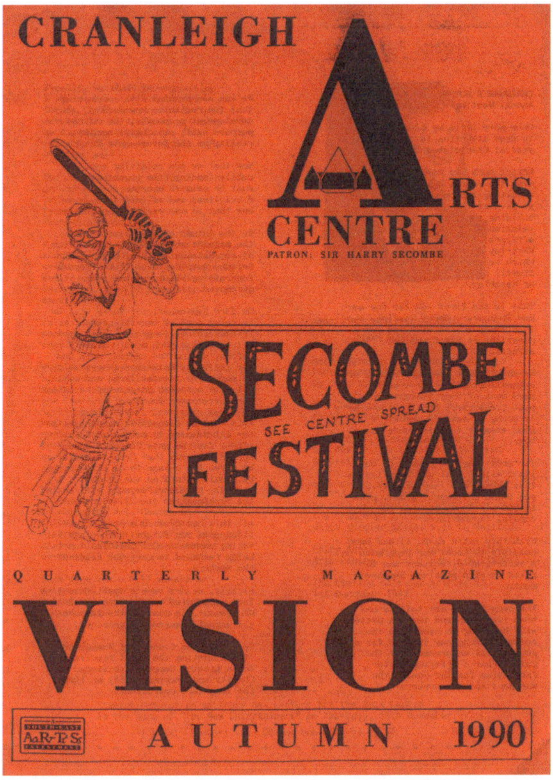

£1.00 £1.00

CRANLEIGH CRICKET GROUND

SECOMBE FESTIVAL

SECOMBE ALL STARS v CRANLEIGH

SUNDAY 23rd SEPTEMBER 1990 1 day match

SECOMBE ALL STARS	SCORE	AUTOGRAPHS
Sir Harry Secombe (Capt.)		
Richard Kershaw		
Richard Stilgoe		
Charles Collingwood		
Roy Castle		
Neil Durden Smith		
Graham Roope		
Christopher Martin-Jenkins		
Roy Virgin		
Bill Frindall		
Mike Denness		
Keiran Prendeville		

CRANLEIGH 1st XI
Paul Bedford (Capt.)
Matthew Barnes
Clem Williams
Glenn Thompson
David Newbery
Justin Weller
Mark Turrell
Robin Underwood
Gary Longhurst
Adrian Erricker
Conrad Cheeseman

PLAY BEGINS AT 2.00 p.m.
There will be a Tea Interval

Commentary:
Christopher Martin-Jenkins

Umpires:
Tony Stillwell
John Rowbottom

Scorers:
Matthew Callard
Ben Morrison Smith

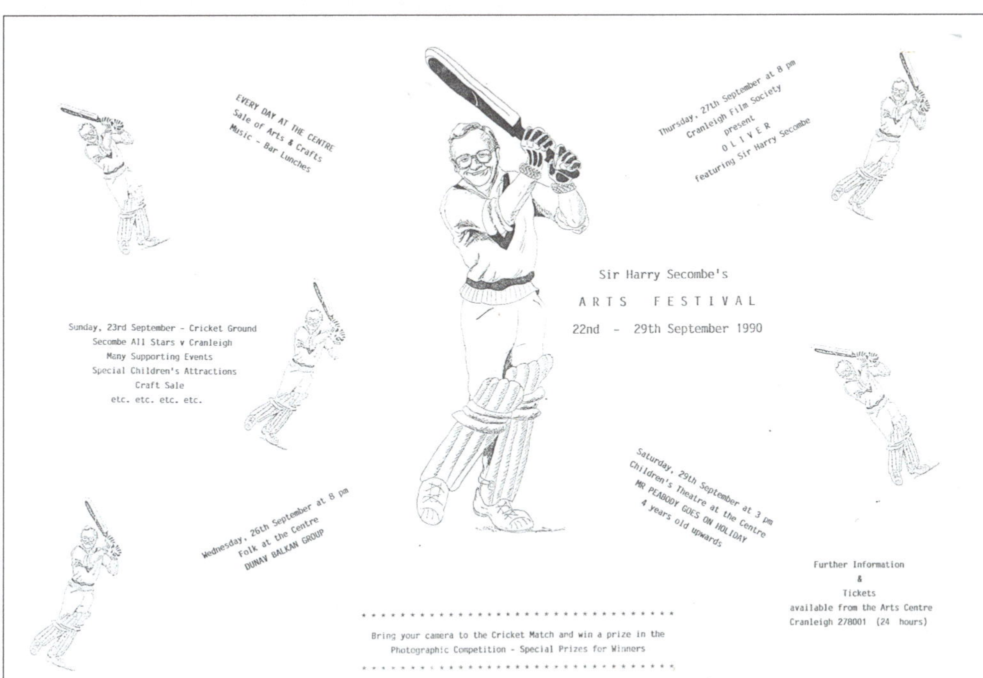

extension in the short term, but also for the long term capital project of the main hall. He reports back with a long list of targets, strategies which highlight the need for multiple approaches, and suggests improving PR and record keeping. He proposes a budget of £10,000 plus his fee of c.£3000 for six months' work. This is rejected as unworkable financially and the idea is kicked into the long grass.

However the staging of a grand Fundraising Week in September 1990 using Harry Secombe's contacts to include a Concert and a Celebrity Cricket Match is set in train. The Cricket Match is successfully achieved but the Concert, which was to be at Cranleigh School, then changed to the Prep School Hall, foundered. The organising sub-committee of seven included the Chairman, the Centre Manager, the Secretary and Jon Hewitt, all busy people. Big names were lined up by the Producer, Brigadier Gerald Landy, who organised Harry's fundraiser concerts for the Army Benevolent Fund. After doing the sums Sir Harry's PA wrote to Rosemary Dubois.

> *"It is clear that a very large team, which you do not have, is needed to raise money from advertising and sponsorship in order to support the actual concert returns. We did not realise that you would only have 3 or 4 people working part-time on this aspect and were under the impression that all your members would be involved. As you know from your own experience, local fundraising is very difficult and you say that you are unlikely to raise much from the programme etc. In view of this it is not fair to ask artists of the calibre Gerald Landy has approached to present a concert from which there would be little or no return to the Arts Centre Fund, once all the expenses have been met. The cost of such a 'bill' would be between £10,000 and £15,000 if paid for, and it is insane to 'use' all this valuable time for no return. So it is with great regret that I have to tell you that Sir Harry and Brigadier Landy are withdrawing from the Concert on September 30th."*

A celebrity lunch was also shelved. The Concert was staged successfully, if slightly more low-key, a year later and the Cricket match became the centrepiece of a week of activities more focussed on the Arts Centre. It showed those at the helm that ambitious fundraising projects are difficult to pull off with limited resources. You need money to speculate to accumulate – not easy when you make no profits.

Income Streams
A collection of snapshots

Tracking statistics across this decade is made difficult as the value of the pound almost halves due to inflation. The equivalent value of £1 in 1980 becomes £1.89 in 1990 so income and expenditure shown in the annual accounts cannot be taken at face value for comparison. Turnover in 1979/80 is £2,800; in 1990 it is £17,300. That balancing the books and keeping track of it all, after the difficulties at the beginning, is clearly on the Treasurers' minds, as reflected in the comments in their reports to the Committee. Between the projected budget for 1979/80 and 1980/81 they build in a 50% increase to expenditure, but income is only increased by 10%. Certain costs, as today, are more volatile; the cost of heating and lighting triples in this decade. The way income and expenditure were apportioned and the separate accounts being run for different parts of the operation also vary, which also makes comparison difficult. Eventually there are two main accounts: one for building development and one for running costs. Income for the building came from fundraising events, donations, loans, grants and hospitality (coffee bar). For the building fund the Coffee Bar and exhibition income was a steady earner rising to £5,502 in 1990/91. Running costs came from subscriptions, productions and lettings.

As the buildings are improved and enlarged lettings' income is more profitably developed:

1979/80:	£1,541
1980/81:	£2,243
1985/86:	£4,860
1989/90:	£7,233
1990/91:	£9,814

Where this came from can be deduced from an analysis of the sessions booked in 1982:

Associated Societies:	120
Adult Education:	591
Others: Artists, Folk, Young Farmers, etc:	124

So income was heavily dependent on the Adult Education contribution in this period, which was to be a problem later when they were reorganised in the 1990s and suffered cutbacks.

The bank (Lloyds) did allow an overdraft facility to ease cash flow, but most years saw the accounts balance. They even allowed a £24,000 bank loan in 1991 for building work, but by then grants had been guaranteed from Waverley and South

East Arts and the Arts Centre was seen as a well-run going concern.

People are a financial resource too. Volunteers, from the start of Cranleigh Arts, have saved the Centre thousands of pounds and continue to do so today. In 1988 there were 27 volunteers who together were averaging 80 hours per week in catering, maintenance, secretarial, accounts, Front of House, Membership admin, publicity and exhibitions. If the part-time paid secretary was on £2,000, then they were worth four times that to the organisation.

In his AGM address in July 1990 Jack Wagg reflected positively on what had been achieved. There were now close links with South East Arts and Waverley, reflected in both revenue and capital support; the remaining building development proposals *"will become a reality in the foreseeable future"*; we have *"magnificent help and inspiration from our Patron, Harry Secombe"*; and *"our organisation is being reshaped to meet the needs of the workers"*. He concluded,

> *"We must all hope and believe that a "Beeching" will not reappear to cause the Arts Centre to follow the Cranleigh Railway Station to oblivion – if we keep up our constructive tempo surely no one will dare. I am sure there will always be determined members who will defend and strengthen the Arts Centre against all comers."*

Chapter Five

The Vision achieved – the 1990s

Raising the money and the roof!

How the aspirations for the building were brought to fruition in the course of the decade. However, due to the scale of the project, sourcing the money was to be difficult.

The decade of the 1990s saw the evolution of the Arts Centre in three distinct areas: building, programme and management. The vision for the development of the building was to be achieved and it was to become a flexible and lively venue that expanded its activities in line with its mission. It acquired a new leadership team that was able to raise the money that this needed and who ensured that its ambitions were taken seriously. With this, prompted by the grant applications and external scrutiny which that involved, there needed to be a professionalism of approach that has characterised it ever since, but which has sometimes been a problem to sustain and to keep connected to the grassroots ethos of its original founders.

The fortunes of the arts are inevitably bound up with the current economic climate and so it was in this period. The eighties boom, which was particularly reflected in the South East, had created the bubble of optimism that had led to the progress we have seen so far. However the recession of the early 1990s made this much harder to sustain. In the expanding community of Cranleigh the newly built house prices were falling. Interest rates had been very high but they began to fall along with inflation. However the building and maintenance costs went up and the availability of users' income for discretionary spending on arts activities went down. The cliff edge would come in 1992 when economic confidence took a knock.

The first project planned for 1991 was to build a new pottery on the East Wing, which would free the West Wing to become an enlarged Gallery and Front of House/Bar space. The Council minutes show Chairman Jack Wagg pushing this through, with a bank loan and a builder standing by, despite some disquiet from some members at doing this in the current climate. This was completed in the summer. £3,000 from a concert in November by Patron Harry Secombe helped to rebuild the funds. A new entrance porch was proposed for the next phase, but as a building of historic interest it was deemed it might be costly to achieve something that would pass the planners' strictures. Meanwhile a new face at the Council is Waverley's Arts and Museums Officer Carol Sacha, who had been appointed after an Arts Council Audit suggestion to Waverley. She has many ideas for local sources of funding, and suggested applying, in line with the Council's Arts Strategy 1989, to The National Foundation for Sport and the Arts (FSA), who wanted to support 'large scale aspirations'. The FSA had been set up by the pools companies to feed back some of their profits into community projects.

So an application was put in for a grant of £400,000 in order to complete a major part of the rebuilding – the addition of a new hall at the rear. David Howell, the local MP, who had opened the second Festival in 1979, was persuaded to write his endorsement, along with the patron, Sir Harry Secombe. This however was rejected in November 1992 as there was a requirement of match funding by the local authority, which had not been included. But Cranleigh Arts was invited to reapply.

Jack's potty about new facility

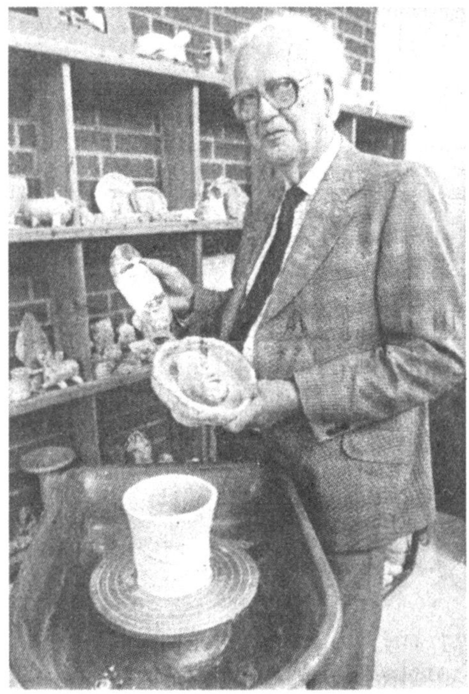

CRANLEIGH Arts Centre manager Jack Wagg among the pots which have been created in Cıanleigh Arts Centre's new pottery.

Enthusiastically the ball was kept rolling by a front page headline in *The Surrey Advertiser* of Friday 4th December 1992: **'Small theatre project 'exciting'...'**. It went on: *"A new small-scale theatre could soon be coming to Cranleigh. It may not be a grand state-of-the-art entertainments complex but for Cranleigh it is felt to be long overdue."* The reporter, Lisa Raynsford, goes on to summarise the changes made so far and that long-time planning permission had been approved for the development of the current arts centre. Then she quotes the Chairman:

> *"The performance area is the next on the list. It has been called a theatre but it can be used for any other purpose, such as exhibitions, lectures and social events, too. ... It is village size, not something wild and huge, not some costly regional centre. It will be built for the local community. ... It is an ongoing development and only circumstances will determine when it will finally be finished."*

Changes to the team increases momentum

It all comes down to having the right people on board and the right support

It is clear that Jack's health was becoming problematic and he pushes hard from the start of 1992 for a new Chairman to take over, but this doesn't happen for over a year. In March 1993 John Dickerson eventually takes over the role. His wife was a volunteer at the Centre and he had recently retired as Professor of Nutrition at Surrey University, having had a distinguished academic career. He was interested in the adult education possibilities and was a committed Christian and lay preacher. In his two-year tenure he is a safe pair of hands as leader and does what he can to raise the funds, the membership and the profile of the Arts Centre.

In June 1993 another significant figure appears – Dr Catherine Pike. She is appointed the Waverley Council arts member to the Council of Management. She has been described as a force of nature, who knew everyone and had a 'why not?' attitude. Together with Carol Sacha, they made sure that Waverley were fully aware of Cranleigh Arts and what it was doing. It needed arts provision on the east side of the Borough, to counteract the pull of Farnham. There was pressure too from Charmian Stowell of South East Arts for Waverley to do more to support the arts. What they achieved was a domino effect that once one funder took the project seriously then more could come on board. Match funding was usually part of the deal and as the subsequent applications were written it sharpened the presentation of the case. With that came a confidence, not only in the inherent need for Jack's vision to finally succeed, but that at long last it might actually be possible. In 1994 things really took off.

The Parish Council were also lobbied on a regular basis. A presentation was given to them on 16 June 1994, following some changes in their membership after elections, seeking support for the application to Waverley's capital funds. Since some sat on Waverley Council as well, this was useful lobbying. They awarded money for lighting equipment and one presumes took the message forward. The Waverley Leisure Committee members were also treated to a tour of the Centre in September to guide them on the project.

Part of the fundraising energy came from the fact that the Centre was busy and working to capacity. The Chairman noted at the end of 1994 in *Vision*, *"we have had our busiest year yet"*. There were about 250 subscribing members and there had been a push to get the message out about what the Arts Centre could do for people. Chris Dubois wrote an article for *Cranfold Life* in August listing the many activities going on, *"Each week over 300 people attend ... as registered students and many more simply visit the exhibitions and have a coffee"*. The emphasis was that it is 'village size', informal and everyone is invited. *The West Sussex County Times* Supplement for July

1994 featured Cranleigh. The centre spread of its 20 pages celebrating the **'Village's proud identity'** proclaimed **'A new era dawns for the arts'**. This was essentially another version of Chris's article with emphasis on the 'fully booked' use of the building, the social and community benefits, and the need for expansion, but only if the money from Waverley came through. It places the Arts Centre at the heart of the village community and explains how it complements other village leisure provisions.

Achieving a critical mass of funding

Which comes first the project plan or the money?

In 1994 the re-application to the Foundation for Sport and the Arts was better received, with the confirmation now of support from Waverley. A visiting consultant, Roy Billington, reviewed it favourably and £45,000 was likely. When asked for more precise details of the project the Chairman had to reply that there were none apart from the outline sent. Concurrently a local government review led to capital projects coming under scrutiny and Waverley was looking to spend some capital reserves, as neighbours Elmbridge and Dorking for their part were doing. The multi-purpose hall was a contender. Cranleigh's application was for £450,000, but Waverley indicated that £250,000 might be available. This period was tantalising in that until a critical mass of money was sourced then the fine detail of what could be done when was out of reach. However in March 1994 a detailed proposal was drawn up to present the case and suggest costings for three options ranging in scope from £450,000 to £800,000. It concluded,

> *"Cranleigh village and surrounding residents (some 30,000) have been presented with a new Leisure Centre, a Day Centre and refurbished village hall, Cranleigh Arts Centre will complete the leisure provision. The whole community whatever its interests, ability or age will be truly served."*

By December 1994 a working group was meeting regularly to push it forward.

The possibility of a grant went back and forth, including a front page *Surrey Advertiser* story in November which suggested that Cranleigh Arts was competing for funding with an all-weather sports training pitch in Cranleigh, which a questionnaire suggested more local people favoured. John Dickerson writing to the management council says:

> *"We had not been told anything about this. One could question the way in which this conclusion was obtained."*

Can one sense the former scientist coming out there?

> *"I was, however pleased to note that the Arts Centre funding has been returned*

to the priority list thanks to the alertness and firm support of the members of the Borough Council who serve on our council of management. Due in large measure to this our hopes of receiving a grant have been restored."

He is referring of course to Catherine Pike and Carol Sacha. The final decision was put off until the following year. With less money forthcoming from the FSA, although a lesser sum confirmed, and the money from Waverley approved with provisos, helped perhaps by the Chief Executive, Geoff Nuttall, being a Cranleigh man, the quest went on for the other major sums needed to complete the building's transformation.

Enter The National Lottery – the game changer

Good luck could make dreams come true

In 1994 the Government introduced the National Lottery. Described as the most significant change in the funding of Britain's arts and cultural sector since the establishment of the Arts Council it was expected to raise £1.8 billion per year for good causes. Money for the arts would be distributed by the Arts Council, changing its role dramatically. The money was for capital projects initially, but in 1996 the Arts for Everyone (A4E) scheme included revenue funding as well, to support new audiences, participation in the arts and the engagement of young people. Two unintended consequences followed. One was that at first by subsidising buildings and not content, it was awash with more money than it could grant, hence the A4E development, and secondly it virtually killed off the Pools, which funded The Foundation for Sport and the Arts, thus their bounty withered on the vine. It was suggested by Dr Pike as early as January 1994 that it was obvious to apply to the Lottery, as was the view of South East Arts. They required not less than 35% of the project costs to be covered by the applicant which could now be fulfilled by the money from the FSA and Waverley, making a bid of c.£550,000 and a total project fund of roughly £843,000! What wonderful things might be achieved with that? Cranleigh Arts could graduate from the basic to the better in its project options.

In January 1995 John Dickerson asked to stand down due to 'pressure of other involvements', but perhaps it was also that being religious he did not approve of gambling nor the profits thereof. Catherine Pike agreed to become Chairman in March and the bid commenced with a new sense of purpose. An Executive committee and a Building Committee were set up and a Development Coordinator, Roger White, appointed. Structural Engineers, Quantity Surveyor, Building Services Engineers, and Consulting Engineers were all engaged, as well as contacts established

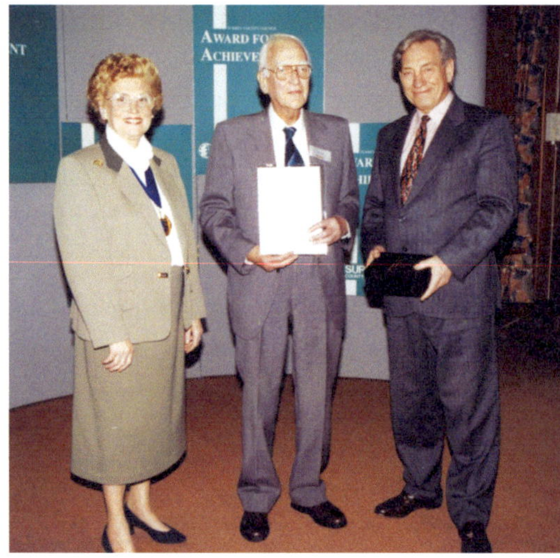

for disability advice, fire regulations and a Safety Supervisor. It is confirmed that Arthur Gomez, who had been with the project since Jack asked him to do it as a 'side project' in 1982, will be chief architect, except for specific artistic commissions. In June Waverley released a sum of money to pay for surveys and initial work and the project really got under way. As if to close a chapter Jack Wagg was given The Surrey Award for Achievement, an engraved glass goblet, by Surrey County Council in recognition for his work in the community. *Vision* records:

"The Council of Management welcomes this recognition of Jack's leadership and example as a 'hands on' working chairman. He has succeeded in establishing a truly community-orientated centre for the arts in Cranleigh and outlying villages. His vision has provided the opportunity for many to practise and enjoy the arts. Jack would like this award to be attributed to the team effort made by all the volunteers at the Cranleigh Arts Centre."

At about this time an article, found in Catherine's papers, appeared in *The Independent* Magazine, part of a growing media debate about the Lottery. As the first Good Causes grants were awarded in March by the different panels – Arts (through the Arts Council), Sports (through the Sports Council), Heritage, Charities (from October) and the Millennium Commission – criticism was voiced about the fairness of the distribution and the criteria being used. The mechanisms were late being appointed and, in the case of the Arts, sniped at for being too privileged. A huge grant to the Royal Opera House unleashed a storm of protest suggesting 'the lottery is milking the poor to fund the hobbies of the rich.' Other critics such as the Rowntree Foundation attacked lottery distribution bodies for giving more money to rich communities than poor ones. The South-east had been quick off the mark at getting bids in, but this was levelled up in later years. *The Independent* article was more supportive of the Lottery saying in its headline that it **'is not the only source of arts funding, just the biggest and the best.'** The opening paragraph went on:

"The pub theatre has a leaking roof. The brass band's old van keeps breaking down. The art gallery has run out of space. Before the Lottery, none of these

organisations would have stood much of a chance of getting public funds to help them. Today their dreams can come true. But to get your share of the arts bonanza you have to go to the right place with the right proposal. ... It is possible to ask for too much, but equally possible to ask for too little."

The article goes on to outline the application procedure and some examples of grants given and compares it to the Foundation for Sports and the Arts process. There are some sly digs at the trustees and the celebrities and not-so-celebrities on the selection panel. Then it looks at case studies such as the Cambridge Arts Theatre who reported, *"The possibility of getting lottery money encouraged us to dream a bit, to look at things in a positive, bright way".* The theme of 'to dream a bit' is developed with other examples, including Hayling Island Amateur Dramatic Society, wanting to convert a railway shed into a theatre. *"The assessor came down and grilled us for four hours. Then he said, 'I don't think you've asked for enough. You need a lighting system and an induction loop. So please put in for an extra £30,000.' We did."*

This climate informed the choices and ambitions that Catherine, Carol, and Rosemary as 'the client' proposed to the project team and the architect. The scheme had already been costed at various stages and in various scenarios. In March an Advance notice form had been sent in where the grant application was estimated to be for £530,000. By the final submission it was for £1,050,00. Needless to say that increase was due to some more realistic costings of elements of the project, but also some 'dreaming' too as suggested by *The Independent* article. Cranleigh could now build not better, but best!

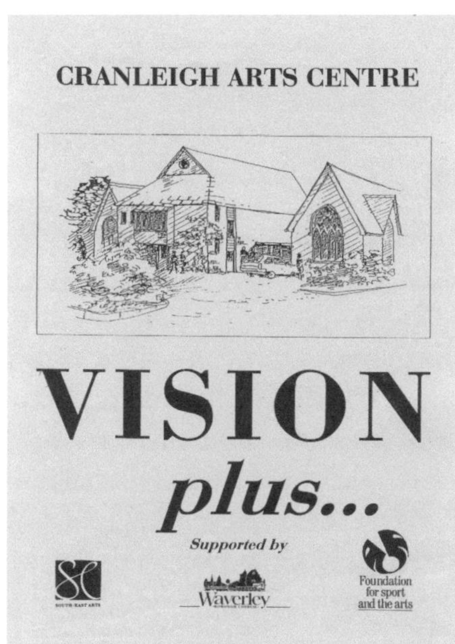

Vision Plus of May introduced Dr Catherine Pike as Chairman and announced the Lottery bid on the back of other funding. The team were featured with pictures, the architect's drawings shown and previous stalwarts gave valedictory comments, including patron Harry Secombe, Jon Hewitt, Reg Lawrence, Jon Horrocks and of course, Jack. Under a heading **'The Time Has Come!'** he sums up the journey and concludes with a description of himself, *"clinging to the wreckage"* hoping to be around for the completion celebrations.

"I venture to ask everyone .. to contribute something tangible – money,

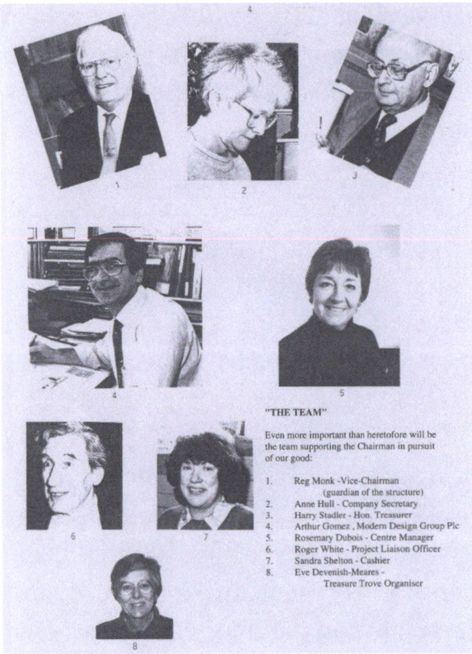
"THE TEAM"

Even more important than heretofore will be the team supporting the Chairman in pursuit of our good:

1. Reg Monk -Vice-Chairman (guardian of the structure)
2. Anne Hull - Company Secretary
3. Harry Stadler - Hon. Treasurer
4. Arthur Gomez , Modern Design Group Plc
5. Rosemary Dubois - Centre Manager
6. Roger White - Project Liaison Officer
7. Sandra Shelton - Cashier
8. Eve Devenish-Meares - Treasure Trove Organiser

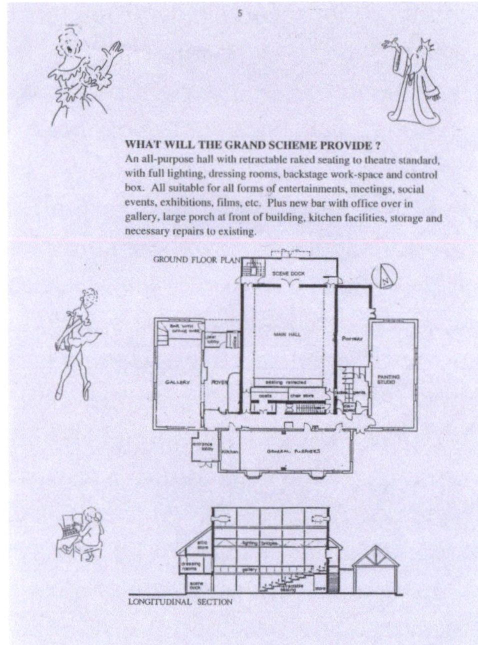
WHAT WILL THE GRAND SCHEME PROVIDE ?
An all-purpose hall with retractable raked seating to theatre standard, with full lighting, dressing rooms, backstage work-space and control box. All suitable for all forms of entertainments, meetings, social events, exhibitions, films, etc. Plus new bar with office over in gallery, large porch at front of building, kitchen facilities, storage and necessary repairs to existing.

effort or kind – so as to guarantee that our Cranleigh Community Arts Centre will be second to none, truly benefitting the needs of all who wish to enjoy the arts in all its forms."

His message was constant to the end.

At the AGM in July 1995 architect Arthur Gomez gave a presentation of the project and showed a model, and letters were sent to all users alerting them of possible closure for rebuilding in Spring 1996 for ten months. Optimistic, as it would prove, but the ball was rolling.

The Bid

It was now time to get serious as there was considerable work to be done which would lead to further professionalism

The preparation of the bid was to take the Centre and its team into uncharted territory. It would involve a review of all working practices and outside scrutiny of the organisation. Outcomes would be projected and measurable and the details of exactly what was required drilled into. The 'family' and slightly closed nature of the operation that had evolved up to now was to be radically remodelled. As well as the need for a business plan and upgraded accounting procedures there was a dawning realisation that after the closure a larger and professional staff team would be needed to manage the reborn Arts Centre. Running costs would therefore need to be subsidised to a greater extent, beyond the expanded programme revenues. But first the bid had to be written.

Carol Sacha had been Waverley's Arts Officer for ten years and had managed successful events in Farnham, as well as negotiations with the Arts Council for money for The Redgrave Theatre, which was starting to struggle. Her boss, Peter Maudsley, was largely sympathetic, but the general attitude of the elected representatives seemed to her to be one of some lack of understanding of the contribution of the arts and *"if it was working with local support then don't rock the boat"*, so that was the policy they had to carry out. As has been established, there were competing interests between the west and east of the borough, with strong characters like Pam Woodroffe, the chairman of the Farnham Maltings, lobbying energetically. The officers tried to balance this out, as best they could, with regard to the Leisure Strategy that the Council had. Seeing a large sum of money coming to Cranleigh would need some political management. This is where Catherine Pike was so effective. As a Tory member she could engage with the long standing Conservative Leader Ann Mugford, who ruled the roost, and she could mobilise other elected members, particularly Cranleigh Councillors John and Celia Savage, for support. John was a sometime tutor at the Arts Centre.

It was clear that more arts knowledge and expertise was needed so Carol approached Brian Harris, an Independent Arts Consultant, for help, although she was honest that there was no money to pay him. He replied, *"I was so intrigued by your cheeky letter that I had to respond to it"*. He visited on 28th September 1995 and got on well with the team. His specialist knowledge of the operation and development of arts centres and past applications ensured that the bid was a strong one and he did get paid after all.

Much of the justification and methodology for the Lottery bid echoed the influential report produced in 1988 by John Myerscough for the Policy Studies Institute 'The Economic Importance of the Arts in Britain'. This had looked at three areas, Merseyside, Glasgow and Ipswich. The introduction suggests,

> *"...we live in an era of industrial restructuring characterised by the growing importance of the service industries (especially in the areas of finance, knowledge, travel and entertainment), and of industries based on new technologies exploiting information and the media. ... The issue now is not so much whether the arts have an economic dimension. Rather, what is the specific and distinctive economic contribution the arts can make? How can this be most appropriately encouraged and exploited?"*

The conclusion, after much data, was that the arts sector contributes significantly to the economic health of the country through employment, exports, ancillary growth, tourism, and urban renewal. More relevant for Cranleigh was that the arts improve the image of a region and make it a better place to live and through a strong cultural infrastructure can be a business asset. Also,

> *"The public placed a positive value on this and on other perceived community benefits arising from the arts, which add to the vitality and attractiveness of a region. Over 90 per cent of the resident population in the three regions studied thought the arts should be available, irrespective of whether they personally made use of local facilities. The arts are a source of local pride, which establishes specific regional and civic identity and inspires new-found confidence."*

This must surely have fed into Waverley's thinking when writing its Leisure Strategy 1996-2001 **'Improving the Quality of Life through Leisure'** and indeed its earlier Arts Strategy, which had placed Farnham Maltings and Cranleigh Arts as the twin pillars of its arts centre provision This suggested to the team that Waverley would be on board with the planned expansion.

By October 1995 the consultants and subcommittees had been working for some months and as the Lottery wanted bids to be for complete projects, the total 'wish list' rebuild was costed out. This came now to £1.4 million. To submit a bid for £1.1 million to the Lottery a further £45,000 of partnership funding was required so Catherine writes to Waverley to request this. She suggests that since Waverley own the building they would be getting a good return from the enhanced real estate. That the bid could fail without this commitment is also a factor. She raises the need for a commitment to greater revenue support in the future but that the new profile should ensure better delivery of the arts to target audiences, *"serving the community needs of the eastern portion of Waverley Borough, some 22,000 people"*.

A formidable team assembles

On 30th November there was a meeting at which the key players reported to the Council of Management. Arthur Gomez and colleagues said that the drawings were complete and ready to go out to tender. The project would comprise the building of a new multi-purpose hall, the construction of a new glass porch at the High Street entrance and the refurbishment of existing accommodation. The whole Centre was to be given a high level of security. Brian Harris gave a presentation reporting:

> *"The detailed feasibility study, together with the Business plan, met the requirements of the National Lottery, the Local Authority, South East Arts and the objectives of the existing organisation. One of the strengths of the...*

> *...existing operation was the well-established track record of users (e.g. Adult Education) which gave the Centre a firm base from which to develop its potential in the community. The Business Plan outlined future needs, including the necessity of employing more paid staff in addition to volunteers. The local authority supported this need. The more complex activity would necessarily mean changes in the management structure and the skills and time offered by the Council of Management. In his opinion the Arts Centre was a very strong applicant for Lottery money."*

Finally Carol Sacha gave a brief report from the Working Group of the planning for the next 12-18 months, *"which included programming, current and future utilisation of space, staffing and funding. She highlighted the benefits of the project to current and potential users and stressed the future need for sponsorship".*

There was great optimism that this was finally about to happen. New people joined the Board and brought extra energy and expertise. Anita Morris, who had recently retired from managing projects at University College, London, came from education. She joined the Board in May 1995 and quickly took on the preparation of the education policy, volunteer role specification and management and staffing structure. She donated her services and this was counted in the budget as an in-kind contribution. Her husband Nick Morris, a lecturer in Photography at Farnham Art College, expanded the ideas for exhibitions and a fine art programme. The heightened security for the Gallery was to enable touring Arts Council exhibitions to visit. Arthur Wren, a local artist, joined and was set to design a new logo.

This was the first Lottery application from the Waverley area and people were a bit in the dark. Says Carol:

> *" It was enormous fun because you were dreaming. Everything was possible; you know, we can have all of this, and somehow everyone believed it was possible. ... The Business Plan was aspirational. It was 'this is what the Arts Council want to read, expect it to be like, and we can make it look like that' with your fingers crossed that it would work."*

Charmian Stowell of South East Arts advised, as she had wider experience across the region and became the 'adult in the room' at meetings. Also at the heart of the team was the Centre Manager, Rosemary Dubois. It was a steep learning curve for her. She knew intimately how the Centre operated and the local politics of the village and the volunteers. She knew the public and what worked. The practicalities of the Centre going forward day to day and of keeping true to the vision of Jack Wagg was essential to her. The Treasurer Harry Stadler knew the financial fine detail and had dealt with Waverley over VAT and fought back when an inflated rent review was proposed. He was concerned by the increased overheads after the rebuild and the loss of revenue during closure. The continuation of Adult Education was starting to be in doubt, meaning the loss of substantial regular letting income. This was due to a shift in government policy, initially by Margaret Thatcher and later Education Secretary David Blunkett for Labour, to reduce funding for non-vocational courses for adults. Although fortuitously, just as closure happened, the local Guildford U3A classes wanted to expand which subsequently filled the gap.

During the summer a host of outside experts were involved. Accountant Michael Pike prepared the Business Plan and budget spreadsheets. A kitchen consultant designed a catering standard kitchen. An acoustic consultant suggested ways of making the hall perform well. Holes were drilled in the car park to ascertain the nature of the foundations and subsoil. Sound Associates Ltd were consulted on projection equipment. A theatre consultant advised on the seating arrangements and sightlines. Chris Dubois, as resident technical expert, was the main person bringing together all the requirements and tempering that with his own practical experience. He was keen also to see that an effective computer system, somewhat in its infancy then compared to today, was included for both ticket sales and administration. D.J. Haley, an IT consultant, was brought in and reported on what hardware and software might be appropriate and how to commission it. The Disabled Citizen's Advice and Support Service was referred to in order to endorse the plans and satisfy the requirements of the application. The form ran to 18 pages and required twelve separate additional studies, plans or documents. The Business Plan alone ran to 22 pages plus appendices. The Feasibility study was much the same.

Ticking the boxes

What was the Arts Council looking for in an Arts Centre?

A first draft was ready by July, but Carol writes to Catherine,

> *"I had a very interesting discussion with the Vice-Chairman of the Arts Council who is familiar with lottery applications and he indicated the key to success was the need to answer every question with reference back to the criteria i.e. once we have done a first draft we need to then go back to the criteria and make sure that we have information against each of their headings. He indicated that to be successful you need to get a score of 60 and the only way of doing that was to have followed their guidelines carefully."*

So more fine tuning went on.

There were eight criteria:

- The benefit to the public.
- The long term effect on the organisation's financial stability.
- The amount of partnership funding.
- The quality of design and construction.
- The contribution of artists, craftspeople and film and video makers.
- The quality of artistic activities planned.
- The relevance of the project to local, regional and national plans for developing the arts.
- The quality of the organisation's plans for education and marketing.

Question C asked, *"Who is the 'project champion' (the person who will see it through to the end)?"* Answer: Dr Catherine Pike. She fulfilled this role admirably and drove through the task with enthusiasm and motivation. Flamboyant tea parties and, on one occasion, a trip to Glyndebourne were her rewards to the team. Helen Cundy says of her, *"She didn't care what people thought. She was so visionary and encouraging. I don't know what would have happened without her".*

With hindsight some of the proposals were ambitious. To open 12 hours a day for six days a week; to have a professional theatre company; to have literary lunches; to have a youth coffee bar 4-7pm; to commission a community opera. But much is based sensibly on expanding what was already being done well and enhancing the quality, availability and breadth of artistic activity on offer. The programming will *"offer excitement and opportunities ... be a home for professionals and give a voice to amateurs".*

The bid was finally submitted in November, but the result would not be known until next September. However at the start of 1996 two problems emerged.

Problems and delays

External and internal pushback over money and representation

In January two issues were reported which put the project in difficulty. The first was with Waverley. After the outcome of the Local Government Review was resolved, the shadow of which had initiated their enthusiasm to spend capital, and things were progressing towards budget and financial planning for 1996/97, the Government cut their revenue support grant by 39%. So the Council needed to draw its horns in. They decided they needed to defer the multi-purpose hall grant of £210,000 to 1997/98. They would instead only provide £85,000 in 1995/96. A new Chief Executive, Christine Pointer, had replaced Geoff Nuttall, and seemed less sympathetic. As a funding partner they would send a letter to the Lottery to confirm this, but it was feared that the whole house of cards might start tumbling down. A Lottery assessor was due to visit to review the bid. Tenders were due to go out later in the year. A crisis meeting was held to review the options and eventualities. This tried to steady the nerves and be positive that the approvals would be given and that a financial pathway would be found, but the resulting uncertainty about when the Centre might close and the financial implications of this made programming difficult moving forward. Additionally there were the public relations to manage and ensure that information was clear to all those involved.

Work began to shore up Waverley's support. Peter Maudsley (Waverley Borough Leisure Manager) and the Leisure Committee members were lobbied. In May 1996 Catherine responded warmly to Peter Maudsley, saying Cranleigh Arts was ideally placed to deliver, with the right support, the cultural objectives of Waverley. He writes back in June saying the Leisure Committee Members had selected arts development as a service objective in the Development of Corporate Strategy 1996-2000 planning and had considered submissions from Cranleigh Arts Centre and Farnham Maltings. Papers had shown how the two could be grown with increased staffing, marketing and core grants and project funding. A service level agreement had been in place for some years. Keeping Waverley on board was key, so a presentation to the Leisure Committee was made in October 1996 following the earlier communications about the four year plan. Apart from the continued commitment to partnership capital funding with the National Lottery, it was becoming obvious that revenue funding would be vital too. South East Arts had been helping with this, but they had made it clear that their funding in the future would be for programming only. They were facing their own reorganisational problems. So negotiations began on an increased Annual Service Agreement with Waverley. On the shopping list were funds for a Centre Manager, two part time assistants, a computerised box office system, outreach workshops and projects, and for marketing.

A second issue was with the Memorandum of Association and Articles (MAA). The Charities Act 1992/3 had changed some of the provisions of the 1960 Act and had implications for charitable governance. It adjusted Charities' obligations with regards to the Companies Acts and also laid down obligations to file accounts and annual reports in a prescribed way. The Commission was given teeth to regulate and sanction those that didn't. It also required charities to have up to date Memorandum and Articles of Association which accurately defined company members for the purposes of passing resolutions and the divisions of responsibility within the Company. The existing MAA had been tinkered with over the years but would not pass the scrutiny that the Lottery Bid required. Representation on the Council still notionally reflected the founder and affiliated societies but Cranleigh Arts needed to expand individual membership to reflect the whole community. Of the original societies only the Bridge Club, which met elsewhere, and the Music Listening Society still existed. An EGM was called for 12th February to make amendments which would bring the MAA in line with the Companies Acts, incorporate the various changes made since inception, regularise the attendance of officials from Waverley Borough Council and South East Arts and abolish the affiliated societies as a category of membership. They passed Resolution 1 which tidied up the Memorandum in minor details, but Resolution 2, which removed reference to founder and affiliated societies *"failed to be passed by a show of hands and subsequent poll as the majority did not reach the necessary 75% of members present and voting as required by the Companies Acts"*. Dr Pike had a revolt on her hands. As with the previous changes that Jack had instituted, the protestors felt that a connection to the origins of the Centre was being lost and that the users of the Centre would not be sufficiently heard by the management. This is a thread that runs through this narrative and as an organisation grows it becomes a bigger conundrum, especially for a community based one.

First off the blocks to protest was Betty Steele, followed by a group letter from six signatories including Ann Horrocks and Peter and Liz Hoad. They make the case that removal of affiliated societies removes the legal requirement for representation on the management committee of local people engaged in the arts. They proposed a compromise of three council members to be elected from members *"who are actively engaged in the arts at the Centre each to be associated with and represent an area of interest among those who use the Centre"*. They hoped that *"under democratic procedure our views should be heard and that they be represented alongside others"*. Brian Hemingway, of the defunct Film Society and longstanding Council member, also writes to Catherine endorsing their view and hoping that it may be accommodated as after expansion *"we will need all the local goodwill and support we can get"*. Catherine replies that another EGM will be held and will include two alternatives, one without and one with the reference to affiliated societies. The Council of Management took the view that change was inevitable and that no interest group should have privileged access to management, instead individual membership widened the scope of representation by all who used the broadening programme of the Centre. Retaining affiliated membership could lead to an unwieldy number on the Council of Management. It is also suggested that a 'Friends of Cranleigh Arts' scheme be developed after reopening to increase membership.

For the AGM on 8th July a letter was sent out outlining the changes proposed as well as a proxy form to get maximum participation. The case is made in a measured way and explains the rationale. The interests of existing council members are given to show that the various arts are well represented and their photos will be displayed at the Centre. *Vision*, the direct link to members, will reflect policy making as well as programme in future. This time the meeting passed the Resolution and that was dealt with for now. Although the inadequacy of the Articles and the definition of membership re-emerged under the Chairmanship of Bob Wild in the 2010s, once the 'Friends' scheme had become the main way of belonging to the Cranleigh Arts community.

The long wait

The bid is assessed and investigated

After the bid had been submitted there were two visits from an external assessor. This was Graham Walne, a respected theatre consultant with a considerable record of lighting and sound design, books and lecturing. He subsequently took his career to Western Australia two years later. He visited the Centre twice, first on 27th June, to understand the project fully. He interviewed ten of the main people involved, including the architect, the South East Arts officer, the project engineers, consultants, representatives of the administration and the executive and met eight others at an informal lunch, who included local councillors, trustees, the Centre manager and users of the Centre. He had some concerns from the case officer at the Lottery to investigate and some questions of his own. He met the architect and the South East Arts officer in closed sessions. Arthur remembers his contributions as being very positive and it was his suggestion to move the rear entrance over to enable the office/store/box office to connect with the store behind the Gallery.

Less happy was a telephone call from John Kennet, an architect at the Arts Council, unaware that Graham had been, raising the same concerns. Catherine records his comments in a letter to Becca Mitchell, the Lottery Officer at South East Arts, *"But more to the point (he) queried our stage area as being unusable – too small, no stage, etc. and was distinctly unhelpful"*. Despite Arthur speaking to him and also Catherine trying to explain the type of room and programme this was to be used for, saying that many small companies were happy to perform *"in our very restricted space"*, the team were obviously spooked. John Kennet had spoken to Fiona Ellis, the Lottery Officer at the Arts Council and despite Catherine speaking to her she had received no assurances. She signs off, *"Yours in some anxiety,"*. This was followed up swiftly by Arthur submitting his revised plans, and an endorsement letter from The Orange Tree Theatre in Richmond for *"an environment and a space which are entirely suitable for a wide range of drama and musical performances, live music and small dance companies as envisaged. I am glad you have maintained the flexible nature of the main theatre space"*. Carol maintains that it was important to involve as many professionals as possible, like Brian Harris and South East Arts and its clients, as they might be taken notice of by the Lottery, rather than just being some amateurs in a leafy Surrey village.

The Verdict

Approval, but with caveats about lack of experience and the need for support

Walne's report came in August 1996. He was very positive about the application saying, *"the overall feeling is very welcoming and the ambiance in many rooms is excellent." "Many contributors have been involved with the project for many years ... thus the plan has grown and developed out of experience and has not been created purely out of the Lottery's existence".* He had an area of concern that the Business Plan was overoptimistic about revenue projections. This had been reviewed, he noted, to be more realistic and he felt it was more a question of presentation than content. *"The applicant's team appear eager to learn from their experiences and to lack an arrogance which blinds people so mistakes are repeated."* He notes, *"It is clear the applicant has little experience of running a performing arts venue on this scale and thus could make expensive mistakes, but the local authority in particular (but not to the exclusion of South East Arts) are very closely involved in day-to-day decisions and have committed themselves to be supportive in real terms".* He comments that *"the relatively high area cost of the new building (£97 per sq. ft.) points to the calibre of the services and finishes involved".* However the architectural panel (John Kennet presumably) had raised some doubts as to whether the design was fit for purpose, criticising the security of the gallery, awkward storage, sightline problems and inadequate changing facilities. He says that the architect has addressed these problems now and come up with solutions which *"considerably improve the Centre's operation and satisfactorily address my concerns as much as it is reasonable to expect".*

In the light of the costed IT proposals he agreed that this was essential to the running of the expanded Centre so supported a slight increase in the sum awarded to cover this. He recommends the applicant receives funding:

> *"Cranleigh Arts Centre is highly regarded by its local population and by the local and regional authorities ... The applicant's team are both conscious of their relative inexperience ... but also appear to be open to advice and guidance as evidenced from their close relationship with their local authority officers. Given such access to expertise there is no reason why the Arts Centre should not achieve its objectives. In terms of the building there is clearly great potential...*

> *...for development without injuring the atmosphere which is part of the Centre's attraction and the proposed performing space fills a gap in the area."*

He places two conditions: that the funding authorities have a hand in appointing the Centre manager and that they monitor the operation and development of the Centre for at least two years from the award. This would be by Waverley, the FSA and the Arts Council.

The close relationship with Carol Sacha, which was such an integral part of the bid, was not to last, however. Feeling unappreciated by Waverley, she moved to Surrey County Council shortly after this. Her boss, Peter Maudsley, thought Cranleigh's success would cause problems in the Borough as it upset the balance. Carol saw the problems for Cranleigh too.

> *"To make the change of an organisation from a voluntary 'we are happy doing it this way, we know what we're doing' to 'now you need to be professional' is a big change, a big ask. But finding a professional who could run it would be difficult. I left you with a problem. But it had to be sorted out in the way Cranleigh could operate it."*

Success and Closure

It would be a long journey to actually make it happen

In September Rosemary Dubois took the telephone call from the National Lottery to say that the application had been approved and that a letter would follow to confirm the money. She remembers the woman saying, *"Now your problems really begin!"*. There were celebrations and a press call. The tenders had been returned but could not be commissioned until the money came through. The work would take about 40 weeks. In fact closure came in March 1997 and the reopening in April 1998. The organisation was run in the interim from a tiny office at Broadoak House, just opposite.

The Technical Meetings of the contractors continued as work commenced. Once started there were the various problems that are thrown up when you deconstruct a building. It was discovered that another £50,000 of work was needed. The roof to the front hall had to be retimbered and re-slated; the front gables had to be replaced and the bellcote taken down and rebuilt. There was dry rot in the Gallery so a concrete floor was laid; the timber floor in the Studio also had to be replaced. The YTS walls proved defective in parts and had to be rebuilt and all re-rendered. A number of subcontractors were summoned to help. Arthur Gomez was on hand too, who knew the building inside out.

Additionally from December 1996 the organisation went into 'brainstorming' mode to draw up the Closure Work Plan. Twenty topics, later reduced to seventeen, had working groups with a Co-ordinator and fitted into a rolling timetable with decision points marked. These topics included Vacating the Building, Computers, Friends and Membership, Programme and Exhibitions, Volunteers, Young people, Publicity, Fixtures and fittings, Staffing, The Opening, Bar and Catering, Lettings, Commissions. The groups took minutes, held by Anne Hull, and reported back to the Management Committee, who would sign off decisions and direct progress, but allowed a degree of delegated responsibility. The membership was spread widely to lighten the load and drew on volunteers and outside people who had experience in each area, but inevitably the bulk fell on the core management team: Catherine, Harry, Rosemary and Anne and other keen members. Every aspect of the operation was put under the microscope and deconstructed, then put together again with tenders out for new equipment, models drawn for new procedures, and endless meetings and lists, lists and more lists. This was a giant exercise carried out by volunteers who loved the Arts Centre and knew that this was the gestation period; that hopefully from the chrysalis they were forming, a wonderful butterfly would emerge.

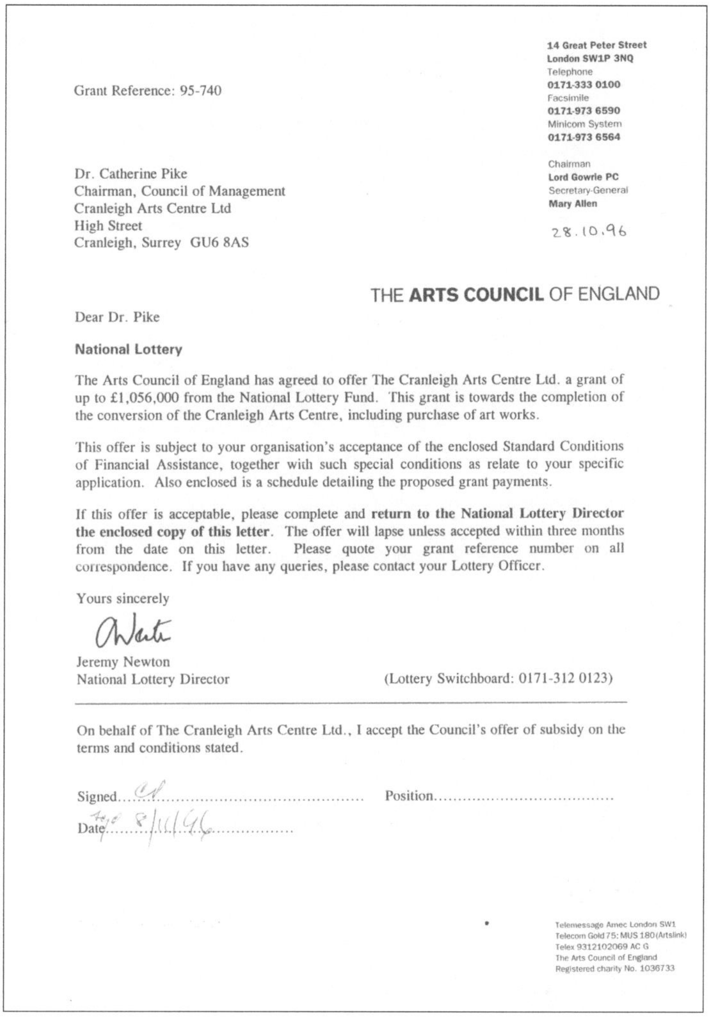

14 Great Peter Street
London SW1P 3NQ
Telephone
0171-333 0100
Facsimile
0171-973 6590
Minicom System
0171-973 6564

Chairman
Lord Gowrie PC
Secretary-General
Mary Allen

Grant Reference: 95-740

Dr. Catherine Pike
Chairman, Council of Management
Cranleigh Arts Centre Ltd
High Street
Cranleigh, Surrey GU6 8AS

28.10.96

THE **ARTS COUNCIL** OF ENGLAND

Dear Dr. Pike

National Lottery

The Arts Council of England has agreed to offer The Cranleigh Arts Centre Ltd. a grant of up to £1,056,000 from the National Lottery Fund. This grant is towards the completion of the conversion of the Cranleigh Arts Centre, including purchase of art works.

This offer is subject to your organisation's acceptance of the enclosed Standard Conditions of Financial Assistance, together with such special conditions as relate to your specific application. Also enclosed is a schedule detailing the proposed grant payments.

If this offer is acceptable, please complete and **return to the National Lottery Director the enclosed copy of this letter**. The offer will lapse unless accepted within three months from the date on this letter. Please quote your grant reference number on all correspondence. If you have any queries, please contact your Lottery Officer.

Yours sincerely

Jeremy Newton
National Lottery Director (Lottery Switchboard: 0171-312 0123)

On behalf of The Cranleigh Arts Centre Ltd., I accept the Council's offer of subsidy on the terms and conditions stated.

Signed.......... Position..........

Date 8/11/96

Telemessage Amec London SW1
Telecom Gold 75: MUS 180 (Artslink)
Telex 9312102069 AC G
The Arts Council of England
Registered charity No. 1036733

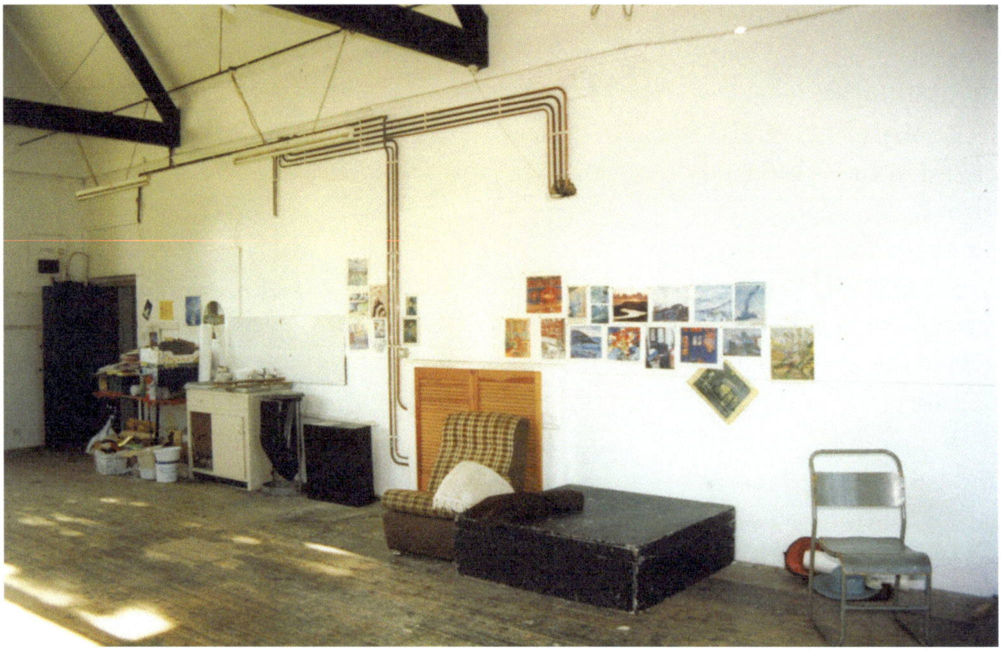

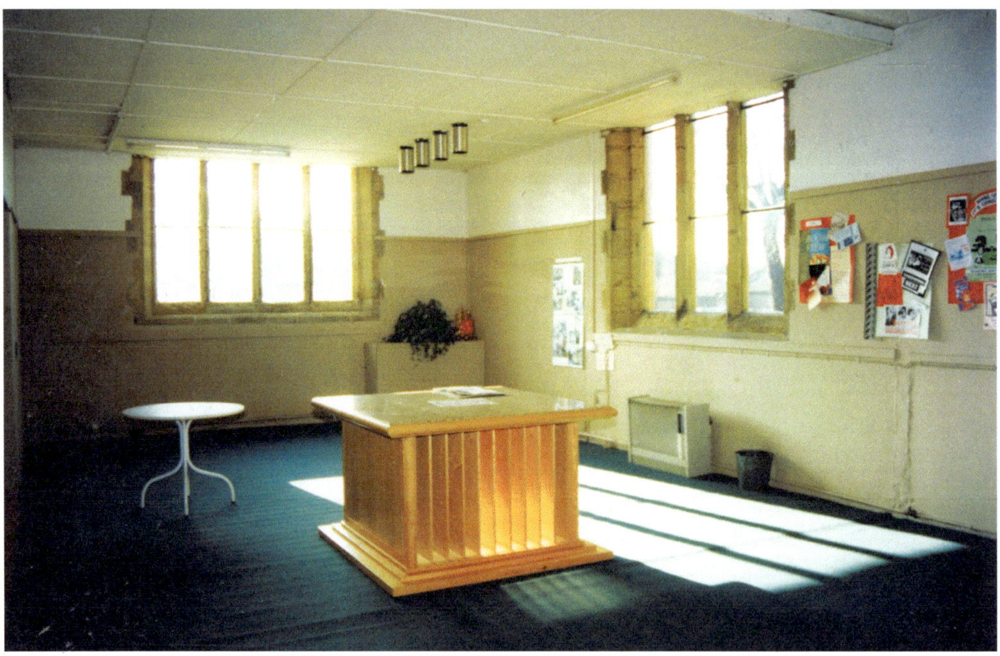

Closing down the rooms before rebuilding, top Studio, bottom Gallery.

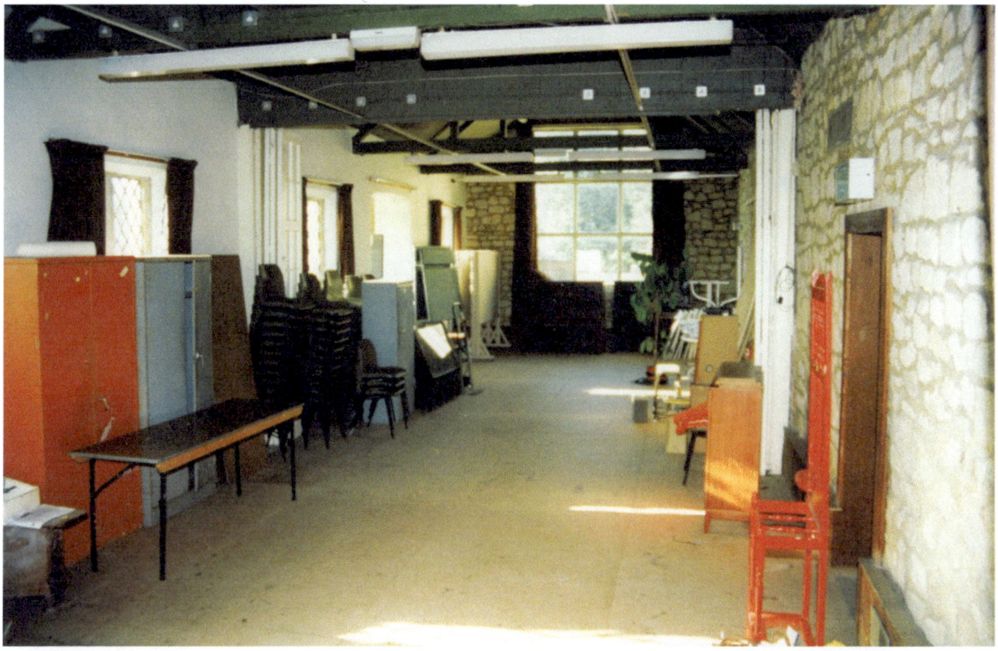

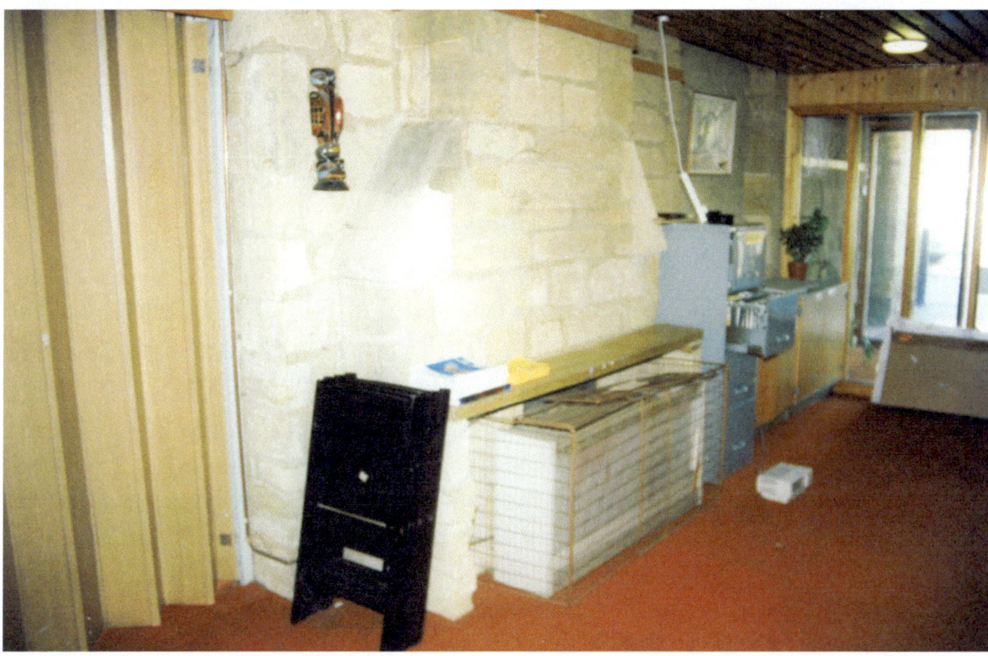

Closing down the rooms before rebuilding, top Crane Room, bottom Foyer and rear entrance.

Chapter Six

A Brave New World in 1998

Reopening and running the new building

Adding to the sadness of closing the building came the news in April 1997 of Jack Wagg's death. He had been unwell for some time but had maintained a keen interest in how things were going and helped persuade the team that closure was necessary for the building to go up economically and quickly, despite Harry Stadler's anxieties about loss of income. He told Arthur Gomez, who was concerned about safety issues if the building remained open, *"Leave it to me"*. A tribute in *The Surrey Advertiser* described Jack as *"the driving force behind the Centre's current major development scheme." ... "Under his leadership the building became a thriving Centre." ... "Rosemary Dubois, Manager, said, 'Jack gave a huge amount of time and effort to the Centre and inspired many volunteers to do the same. His vision is now a becoming a reality.' " Catherine Pike said, "Jack was the real 'architect' of the dream for his beloved Arts Centre which we are now seeing come to fruition."*

Getting Ready

Finding support for the organisation's needs after the rebuilding

Another reality was that there were plenty of things to work on from the little room at Broadoak House. Some events had to be put on to keep the organisation going. Publicity and PR had to be prepared. Every single item to go into the building – doors, doorknobs, furniture, lanterns, worktops – big or small, it all had to be sourced and purchased. Rosemary Dubois admits that it was a steep learning curve when it came to turning the ambitious programme outlined in the Arts Council proposal into a reality. Help was needed beyond the volunteers who had headed up the genres of the Centre's activities so far.

Charmian Stowell of South East Arts, who had been so vital in preparing the bid, knew that the Arts Council were to reallocate some Lottery money away from capital projects towards revenue funding and suggested applying. Also she was retiring, so in March 1997, on her advice, Jem Barnes, the recently retired manager of the West End Centre, Aldershot, was brought in initially on a six month contract as Arts

Development Consultant, with his fees to be covered as part of the closure costs submitted as part of the bid. In the absence of experienced staff at the Centre his brief was to go through each area of administration and lay out a blueprint for how it should be geared up to meet the needs of the expanded operation. He also helped prepare an Arts for Everyone (A4E) bid for £347,500 to the Arts Council for programming support for 1997-2000. He had a proven track record of community engagement, for there had been some criticism that the Arts Centre didn't engage the community sufficiently. He was a large character, abrasive and domineering, but brought some great ideas and was an extra person on the team at this time. His role continued for a year, which was as long as funds allowed. From November Helen Cundy, the newly appointed Waverley Arts Development Officer, provided management support for two days a week.

The bid for A4E was assessed by Alastair Snow who visited the Centre on 26th June. He wanted to measure the application against the five Objectives and four Criteria, plus 'additionality', of the Arts for Everyone scheme. His role was advisory not decision making and he sought to investigate *"the internal and external factors which are critical to the success of the proposed project".* His report, a month later, agrees that the programme as proposed *"represents a dynamic expansion and change to the Arts Centre's original role". "The programme range is progressive and building intensive."* If it goes to plan it will *"create a self-financing and grant subsidy/support structure to enable continuation after A4E year 3. This response will endear the Centre to its people and establish a solid foundation for the Millenium".* He approves of the initiatives to encourage new audiences and broaden participation in arts activity. He praises the work with young people and the activities outlined. He is sceptical of finding a resident theatre company to fulfil the 'supporting new work' objective. He is equivocal about the section on 'building people's creative potential through training or professional development' which included providing NVQ courses, a Jobseekers Theatre Company and a pro/am drama group exploring disability issues and offering businesses theatre events. These he felt would need more professional leadership than seemed available or could be funded. The killer blow comes when he addresses the management and timing of this. He says:

> *"The realisation of this programme is dependent on the appointment of an experienced arts professional as Arts Development Officer, a Marketing Assistant, a technician, and a part time Artist/Curator. ... This staffing and support structure represents a new, critical and testing development to Cranleigh Arts Centre. In this proposed structure there is no overall Director of the Arts Centre but a Centre Manager with responsibility for the building and an Arts Development Officer to appoint and oversee the Arts Team. The A4E application does not detail the responsibilities of the Centre Manager and understates the associative links*

between these two posts. ... This represents the weak point – and timing – of the A4E application. To open and run a substantially larger and extended arts centre building, research and promote a huge increased arts programme both within and outside the Centre, in the same year, is an enormous task for any organisation, especially for a small arts centre run to date by volunteers."

He feels the management viability is dependent on the successful recruitment of professionals – the salary for the Arts Development Officer is regarded as about right; that for the Marketing Assistant and Technician posts as too low. He notes that there is no Marketing Plan and that audience attendance targets seemed high. He praises the Market research undertaken, which suggested strong support for the Arts Centre and indicates *"a settled, wealthy population (22,360) with a plethora of charities, special interest societies and social groups."... "The breadth, vitality and challenge ... takes account of the age distribution of the population."*, which showed equal numbers *"under 15"* as *"over 65"*.

The Arts Council turned down the application. In fact only 11 of 120 applications in the South East region were granted as the Arts Council first attempted 'levelling up'. He was right in his assessment of the overambitious nature of the proposals and its demands on staff. The dreams had to confront reality. When such grandiose programme expansion was trialled some years later it proved disastrous and an affordable staffing model is still work in progress.

The wider context

Locally and nationally the goalposts start to move

Some local support was to be available from the newly formed Waverley Arts Forum. This was instituted at a meeting on 14th January 1997 by the Chairman of Waverley's Leisure Committee Rosemary Thomas, a longstanding Farnham Councillor. The brief was as follows:

"Purpose: primarily a communications forum. Fundamental need to create good networking between the arts organisations to coordinate programmes providing a wide variety of events thus attracting more customers and making the most of the facilities on offer. Waverley seeks a more active role in cooperation and partnership. Cooperation is particularly vital now that Lottery bids are being prepared. Bids to both the Lottery and other funding bodies need to be clearly and coherently reinforced. To achieve this needs a coherent, cooperative and overall view."

Cranleigh's success had evidently caused a bit of a stir so that Waverley, or its councillors, had felt the need to level the playing field. The participants would be Farnham Maltings, Cranleigh Arts Centre, Redgrave Theatre, Farnham College, New Ashgate Gallery, Surrey Institute of Arts and Design, and Council representatives. Looking at the minutes for this first meeting the emphasis is on sharing not competing. With regard to Waverley's position it records:

"Planned Waverley arts officers. Carol Sacha's departure has created an opportunity to move away from giving arts venues financial help alone by developing two Waverley posts. One would be Carol's replacement, with a different emphasis on arts development and the other a team arts officer who would operate within the different arts venues to help develop projects, starting at Cranleigh Arts Centre. Aim to have both posts filled as soon as possible. Waverley investigating A4E to help fund."

This was also explained to the Cranleigh Trustees by Peter Maudsley at their meeting in February. The local context and arts policy was changing.

Nationally meanwhile regular press releases announced that for the Arts Council organisational change was under way and would soon be coming over the horizon. This was in reaction to the impact of the Lottery on arts funding and distribution and a sea change in central arts policy. To understand what was in the wind Harry Stadler attended a meeting at the Arts Council of England (ACE) addressed by Peter Hewitt the Chief Executive in November 1998. His summary notes record the following.

"ACE stood for access, education and excellence. The last five years had seen severe financial restraint and it had become bogged down in small detail of administering funding and not made much difference to the arts. The Labour government under the recently successful Tony Blair was increasing arts funding and with Lottery money as well, forward planning could be more secure. A new contract with government was envisaged. It also acknowledged that Lottery money had been funnelled into buildings and not into programme to fill those buildings. A different structure was coming in with A4E (Arts for Everyone), the Craft Council, ABSA (Association of Business Sponsorship of the Arts) and a separate UK Film Council. The Regional Arts Boards would have delegated flexible funding and its evaluation, leaving ACE to give the national lead, the national portfolio and strategic planning. Money is for artists and art, not institutions, it is a means to creativity. But a rule would be run over the Regional Arts Boards to ensure they could manage this."

The Regional Arts Boards, which had replaced the Regional Arts Associations in a 1990 reorganisation, meant that South East Arts had become Arts Council South

East and it was eventually dissolved in 2002, although some support continued after that. In this narrative it is referred to as South East Arts for simplicity. Their demise, with the need to deal instead with the centralised Arts Council England in London, ended a very fruitful and close relationship.

An article in *The Sunday Times* of 15th November was more critical of policy.

> *"Dozens of arts centres and museums built with millions of pounds in Lottery aid are 'white elephants' which will face closure, reduced opening hours and cancelled exhibitions after running out of money. A national Audit Office report on the Arts Council ... blames the lottery distributors for 'naïve optimism' ... "many 'ill-conceived schemes were approved in the early stages. During 1994-97 the five lottery distribution boards were gripped by a kind of 'gold fever' said an insider ... 'Well the chickens are coming home to roost'. ... It is a looming crisis that Labour warned about in opposition but has been unable to prevent in office. The lottery funded hundreds of new arts centres but, until the effect of lottery regulation changes are (sic) felt late next year the distribution boards cannot offer the money needed to run them."*

This was the problem Cranleigh Arts faced.

Programme planning

What activities are planned for the 'new' Centre and how would they engage with the community?

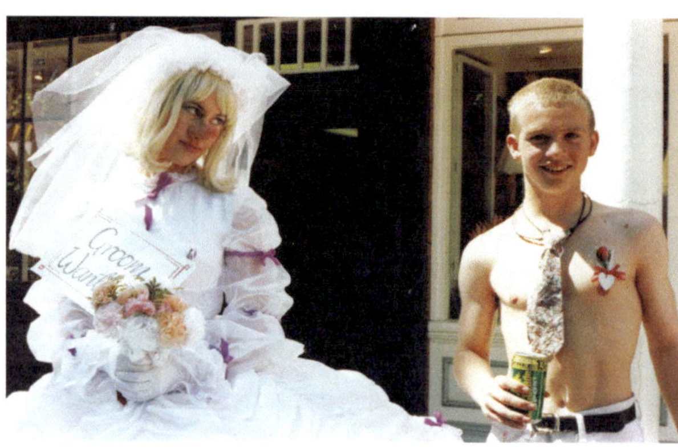

During closure only two street theatre events were presented. Rosemary had got the bug of Street Theatre and, with Catherine, attended the First National Street Arts Meeting organised by South East Arts with Arts Council support, which had grown out of a South East Arts consortium, founded in 1994 when the Tour de France had visited southern England. There were over 120 delegates from up and down the country, foreign representatives and presentations from companies and promoters. The idea was that Cranleigh Arts could now tap into the wider arts picture. In May, Facepack Theatre presented

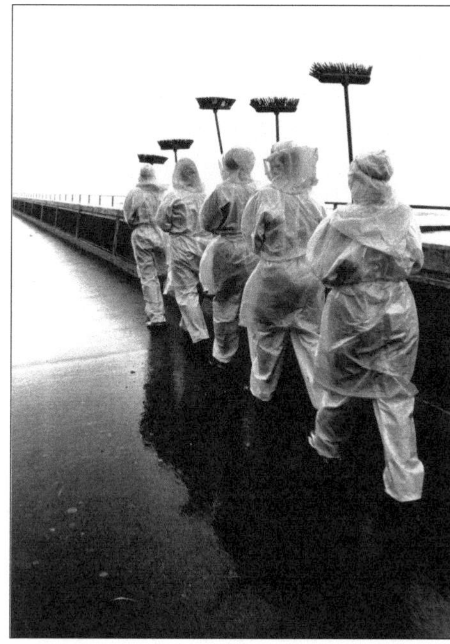

'Wedding Belles' at the Blackheath Festival. Then The Manic Street Cleaners ('a hundred and one things to do with a brush') by Mouth and Trousers Company was booked for the Cranleigh Carnival and Village Fair in June 1997, which also had a manned stand to promote the building development and keep up the profile of the Arts Centre. They would return to spar with Harry Secombe at the titlestone unveiling a year later.

South East Arts had continued to offer support during closure at the level it had previously (£6,565 pa) in order to mount these activities outside the building. However the sword of Damocles had been hovering over South East Arts' head and funding had been at a standstill from the Arts Council for three years and so grants had not increased. For the reopening Rosemary and Catherine applied for a £7,000 grant for 1998/99 under Combined Arts – Presentation of Work – Mixed Programme Venue Scheme. This was granted, however an application for an exhibition and residency to the Visual Arts and Crafts Venue Support Scheme was unsuccessful, but funding for a Ceramics residency did come in 1999 as part of the New Audiences Programme. Application was also made for £3,340 to develop a Dance project, again unsuccessful. There might be many headings to look under and pots within pots if you tweaked the criteria and filled in the right forms.

The 1998/99 South East Arts grant application details the plans after reopening. The ambition was underpinned by new computing and ticketing software, a review of the corporate image and marketing and a generally more professional approach. The artistic aim was defined as follows:

"Cranleigh Arts Centre believes that a broad range of art forms of an appropriately high standard should be available for the people of Cranleigh and the surrounding district to enjoy and practise according to their needs. The artistic programme should be forward looking and varied, seeking to develop and sustain new audiences wherever possible."

There were three key aspects to the delivery of this:

" Building on the Arts Centre's success in the past.

Creating relationships with a range of other community providers including schools, statutory services and voluntary sector organisations

Acting in partnership with both professional and amateur art providers whilst retaining its independence and creating its own unique contribution."

It is accepted that the initial programme will be a 'suck it and see' one, which would seek to gain feedback from the community as to what it wants and then be adjusted for future planning. An educational programme is seen as a key area for development, as it grows audiences and builds on past success, not only with workshops and performances but also through a partnership with Surrey Youth and Adult Education. A Resource Centre for the Arts would be set up as part of this, under the lead of Muriel Longhurst, who had joined the Board in August 1997, having retired from education. She was also one of the organisers of U3A which had been set up in Cranleigh and was to become a key hirer. The opportunities of the new Hall meant that the scope of performances programmed could be expanded, be larger scale and include a mixture of professional and amateur across theatre, dance and music of all kinds. The Visual Arts would include Gallery exhibitions of arts, crafts and photography by local, regional and national artists. A Ceramic residency with education and outreach activities would complete the package. It is accepted that commercial bookings will increase, attracted by the new facilities, *"which although secondary to the community arts activities, will support the arts activities financially"*. Also other special project funding would need to be sought.

Who would deliver this?

Enter Helen Cundy

There had been no resolution to the issue of employing and funding a Centre Manager, although that had been part of the Lottery proposal. Instead there was Rosemary Dubois and other dedicated volunteers who, as had been established by the Arts Council reviewer, Graham Walne, had really no experience of how to manage the much bigger enterprise that the Centre was to become.

Coming to their aid was the newly appointed Waverley Arts Team Development Officer, Helen Cundy, who had been nominated by Paul James, the Manager of the Farnham Maltings. She was to be a key figure in the development and success of the Arts Centre at this time. Her funding came to Waverley through an Arts Council scheme open to local authorities and Waverley seemed to prefer to use her, rather than funding a Centre Manager, wanting to spread her expertise across the Borough. As well as helping three days a week at Cranleigh she had borough-wide projects, including supporting the ailing Redgrave Theatre in Farnham and the expanding Maltings. She assisted Rosemary, Catherine and Harry in their tiny office at

Broadoak House with Programme planning, management strategy and supported the building project as it went on. After reopening she inevitably did much more and Helen says that it quickly became all-consuming for her. She was young, enthusiastic and, she admits, a bit naïve. Christine Barker, the Waverley Visual Arts Officer, helped set up the gallery programme on one day a week.

Pragmatically the programme reflected what had worked before and the passions of individual Board members. Classical Music was Catherine's, Rosemary was keen on children's and street theatre, Brian Hemingway was the film expert, Helen and Christine made up the rest. Quality was the watchword. The extensive education programme planned under Muriel Longhurst made less headway.

The programme was carefully planned for an opening in September 1997 and modelling made of use of space and potential revenue predictions. Some bookings had been pencilled in. But the delayed start and the slow progress, partly due to the extra structural work required, led to painful and frustrating recasting. A publicity handout during the building work confidently proclaimed,

> *"Its transformation into a village arts centre will be complete by January 1998 at which time Cranleigh will be the only village in Surrey to boast its own arts centre run* ***by*** *villagers* ***for*** *villagers."*

Catching here the tone of Jack Wagg, surely. It then listed the new facilities and that in addition to the Main programme there would be an A4E programme to involve:

> Networking: *"We are looking at new ways in which the Arts Centre can work with community groups."*
>
> Volunteers: *"We are recruiting a new band of art lovers to work with us to deliver the highest quality arts experiences to our community."*
>
> And a Schools' Liaison Group *"to provide real arts experiences to local schools both in the Centre and in school".*

Icing the Cake

Commissioning specific items to enhance the artistic impact of the new Centre

It was a condition of the Lottery grant that £37,000 was reserved to commission art for the Centre. This process began in January 1997 with help from Frances Lord, the Visual Arts and Crafts Officer with South East Arts. As well as Catherine and Rosemary the panel for this was complemented by Arthur Gomez, Arthur Wren, local artist and trustee, and Betty Steele, longtime critical friend. The theme 'Amuse and Smile' was chosen and proposals were sought for a clock for the foyer, architectural glass for the entrance lobby, a memorial titlestone on the façade and a coffee bar for the foyer. Added to this later was the design of railings outside together with an ironwork poster display feature. The search began with Frances's suggestions then expanded to the Crafts Council extensive database which had colour slides of work to look at. No internet searches then! A brief was drawn up according to Craft Council guidelines and sent to a short list in each category. Then in the light of their responses the artists were invited to view the site and be interviewed, then a final selection made and contracts issued, again to Craft Council templates. To judge from the files it was an interactive process with various tweaks and amendments made as it went along. David Gregson was so liked that his brief was extended to include the adjoining box office counter and gallery benches.

Four leading award-winning nationally famous artists were chosen in September 1997. The titlestone outside, by Richard Kindersley, carved on York stone modestly announces the Centre. In the Entrance sandblasted and acid-etched glass panels by Martin Donlin depict the Nine Muses in abstract forms based on migratory birds' flight influenced by the Crane, with areas of text relating to each muse. In the Foyer on the old chimney breast is a 'Smile' clock by Marianne Forest in patinated brass with a mottled finish and gold leaf hands with polished studs for numbers. Also here is the Coffee Bar (since redecorated), reception and two benches designed by David Gregson with geometric and flowing lines in ash and Corian. Outside bold stainless steel rails guided people to the entrance and a three sided poster display stand encloses a tree with metal grid beneath, echoing, it was hoped, a Parisian street feature. The tree was a gingko biloba donated by Waverley and was ceremonially planted by popular local TV artist Tony Hart. Due to delays with the building work, because of more extensive renewal of stonework and the 'firm employed working at a snail's pace', the installation of these commissions was put off from January 1998 to February when the building might possibly be handed over. In fact it was signed off in April 1998.

Open at last!

A series of events celebrate the new Centre's opening as chaos gives way to congratulations

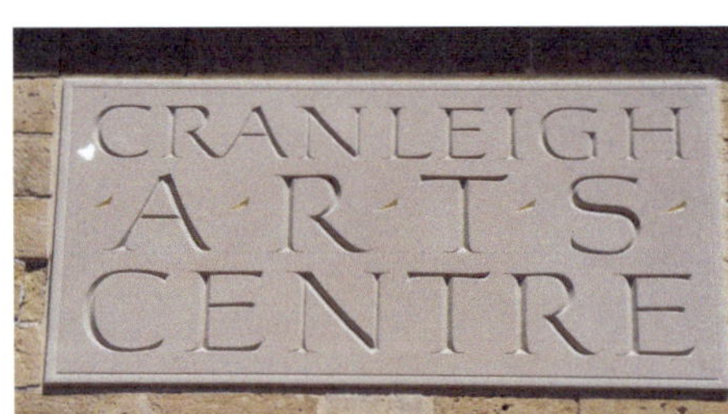

There was pressure to reopen as soon as possible to get some money coming in, so a rolling launch was planned for Spring 1998. Two major hirers, Surrey Adult Education & Youth Service and U3A, had been kept up in the air over the delays and were pressuring to finalise their programmes.

On the ground it was a bit chaotic as the building was only three quarters finished

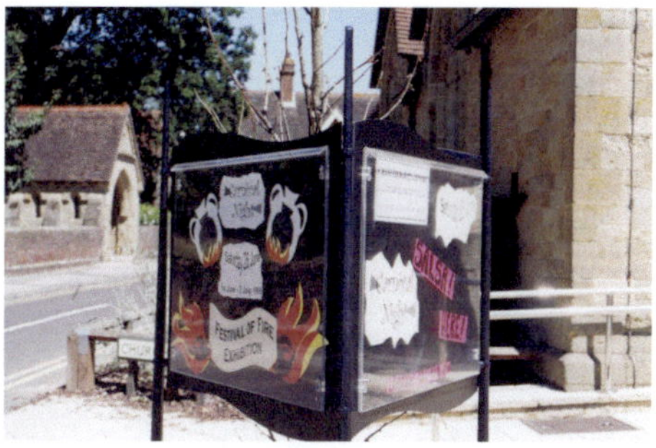

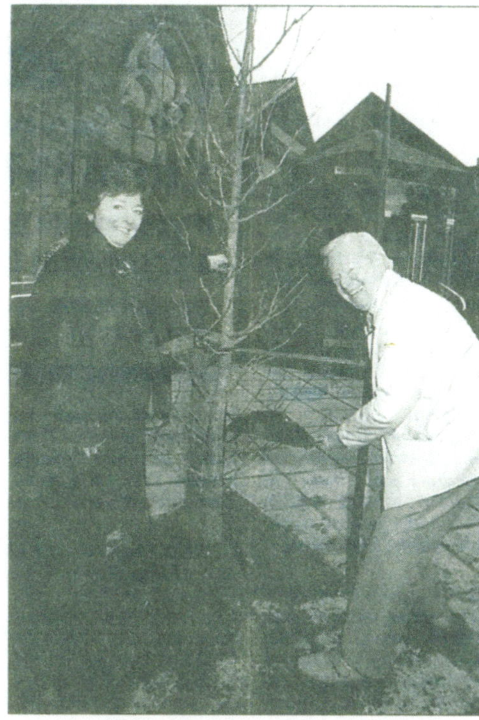

Cranleigh Arts Centre's drama co-ordinator, Rosemary Dubois, watches as Tony Hart plants the tree outside the building.

New tree for arts centre

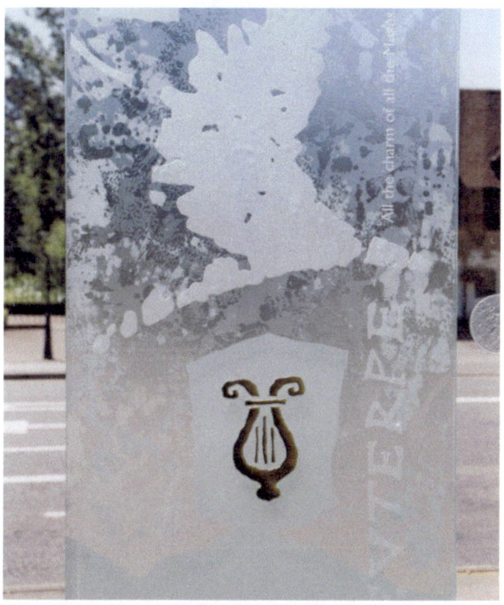

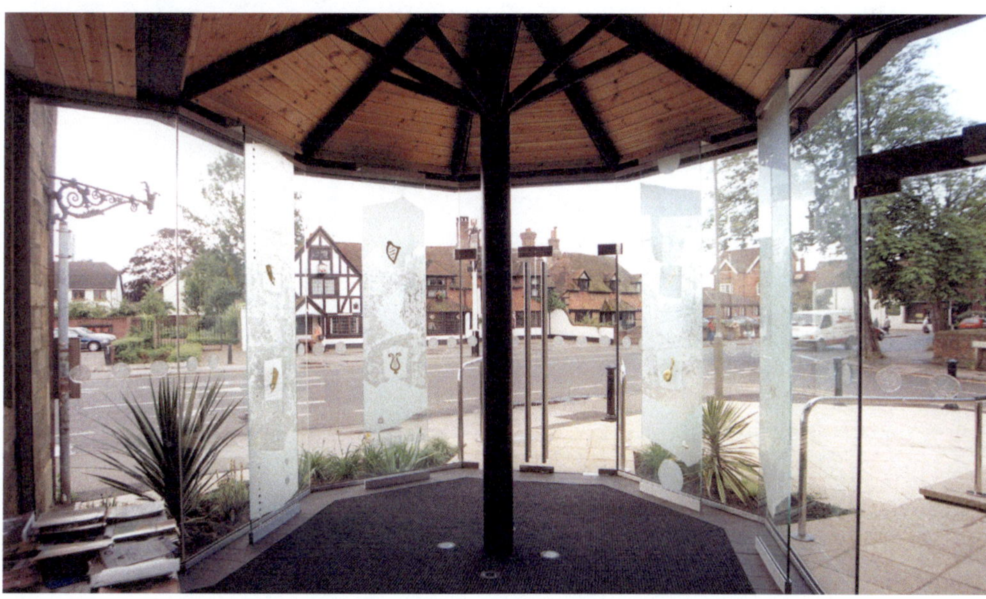

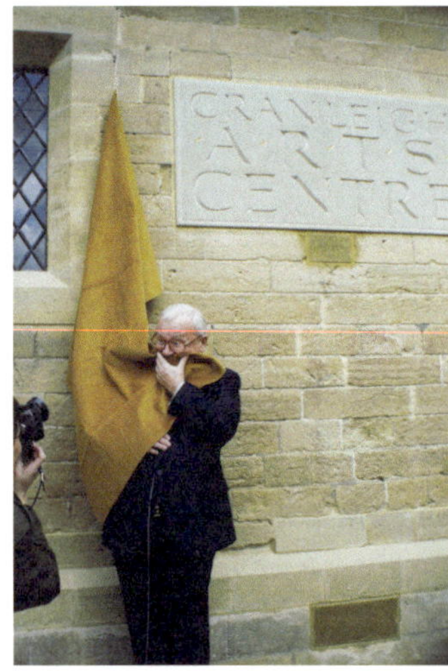

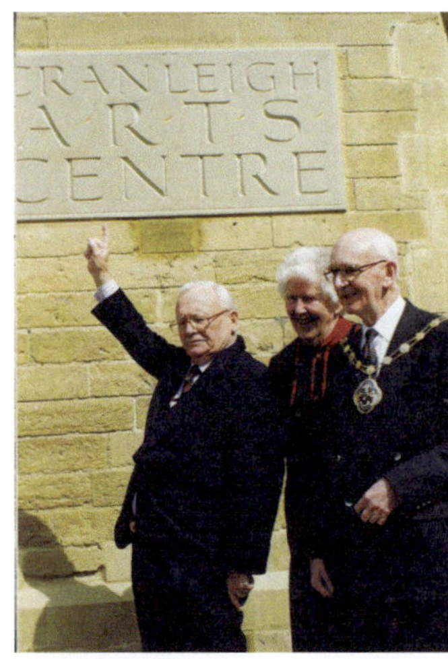

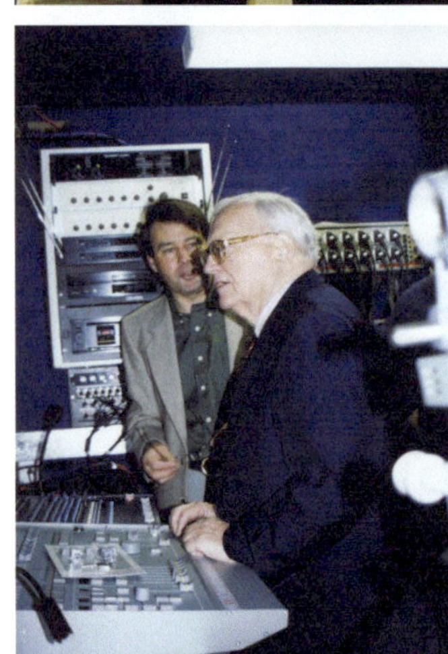

so there were electricians and technical people still working. Through the build the oversight had been loose, despite Roger White's efforts, and hard decisions and conversations not had, with the contractors pretty much having a free hand. Vaughan Mitchell, who joined the Board after re-opening, says he was given the job of snagging the build and found many faults, some emerging only months later. Examples were the programming of the air handling, which for months was coming on through the night unbeknown to anyone; vents were installed upside down, so didn't work; pipes were the wrong material and rusted and then leaked; the cistern in the gents didn't flush as it was filled with builders' rubble. His list went on. As anyone who has had oversight of the Centre will know, the additions and adaptations over the years have meant that clearly appreciating every nuance of its working is a tangled web, with useful information and tips and wrinkles not always being passed on.

The first reopening event was on Saturday 18th April, when there was a tour of the building followed by the unveiling of the commissioned titlestone at the front of the building by Sir Harry Secombe, introduced by the Mayor of Waverley, Michael Biddiscombe. This was billed as a 'preview' as there were understandable concerns that all might not have been complete and was really forced on Catherine Pike by Waverley Borough Council, as the Mayor and Councillors were due to change for 1998/99 in May's elections. The popular street theatre group Mouth and Trousers performed as 'The Manic Street Cleaners' entertaining passersby in the High Street during the morning, providing photo opportunities to catch the eye and lead people to the unveiling. It was also the most suitable date for our very busy Patron, who was celebrating his golden wedding and booked for multiple television commitments. He entertained the crowds in his

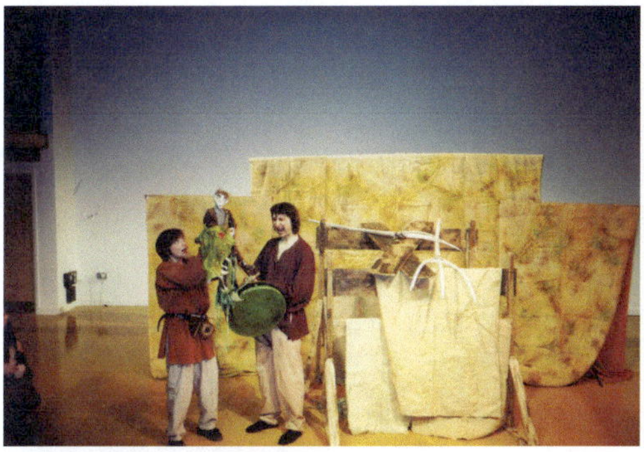

Garlic Theatre Company.

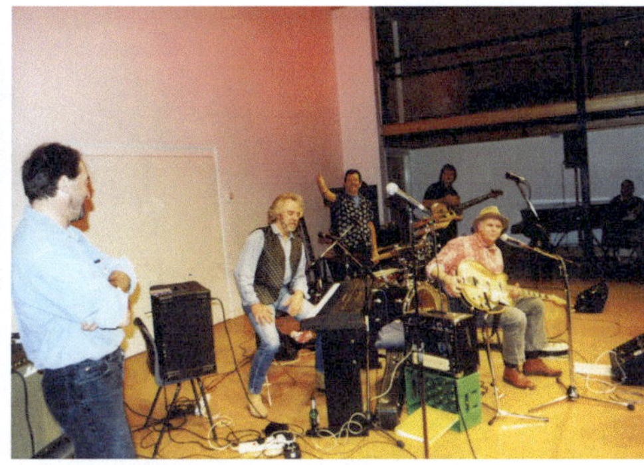

King Earl Boogie Band.

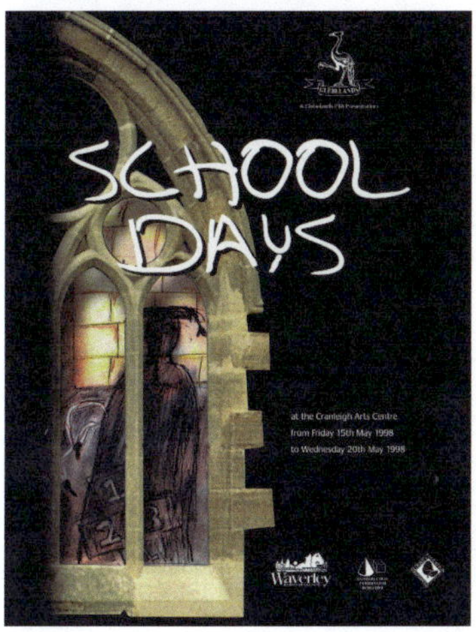

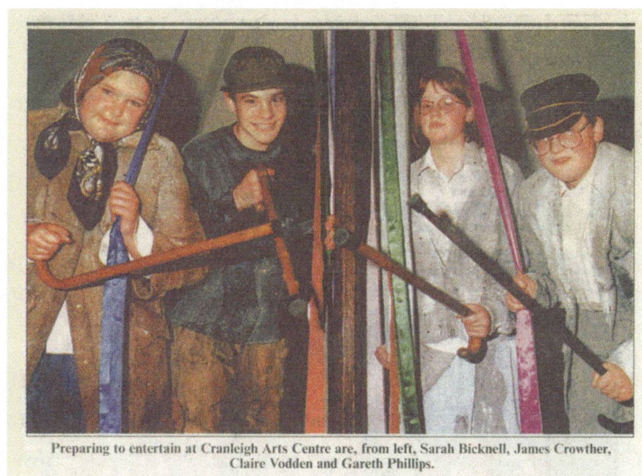

Preparing to entertain at Cranleigh Arts Centre are, from left, Sarah Bicknell, James Crowther, Claire Vodden and Gareth Phillips.

inimitable way. The invitees were largely the Borough council members and officers plus all the supporters of the Centre over the years – the volunteers who had given so much to the project and the societies and clubs that had made it their home.

Drama led the way subsequently with a professional performance of a one man version of 'Under Milk Wood' by Guy Masterson and a children's theatre company, Garlic Theatre, with 'George and the Dragon'. In the Gallery was the first art exhibition by Shazia Mahmood. Film, Rock bands and classical music swiftly followed, along with dance classes and arts and crafts workshops. Gradually the Centre came to life again.

On Wednesday 20th May there was a Gala evening performance of Glebelands production 'School Days' which celebrated the history of the building. This was a big community event with guests from local education, business, politics and the arts. It was billed thus:

"A sixty strong cast and crew perform from Friday 15th an epic drama and musical production based on the life of the Cranleigh Arts Centre building. From 1847 until 1966 the solid sandstone walls of the village school will come alive. The students

have for months, with the help of local people, researched the background to this show. A kaleidoscope of significant and entertaining bygone moments is the outcome."

The gala evening included a pre-show talk and demonstration as well as a buffet supper.

Finally, the planned main event on Thursday 11th June, was an evening reception for all those involved in the Lottery application and build, plus local dignitaries. The following day the new Mayor, John Savage, wrote to Catherine,

"There is much to congratulate you on, and so much to thank you for. The new Centre is well-designed and beautiful and welcoming and visitor-friendly and audience-friendly ... Now the friendly reception one always received is enhanced by the building. ... How fortunate Cranleigh is. ... I don't remember hearing anyone congratulate you last night. I think you were far too modest: you have worked so hard to achieve the new Centre and you must have been exhausted and frustrated and discouraged at times. So, thank you very much for all your efforts; Cranleigh owes you a great debt."

In an attempt to get user feedback a poll was taken in June at the afternoon meeting of the Women's Institute. Of 50 members present half were canvassed on their opinion of the new Centre. 17 out of 25 had been in and generally the building was liked, although there were reservations about the modern porch. Other criticisms were of the coffee bar as lacking in character, *"not conducive to a cosy morning's coffee with friends"* and *"why no plants?"*. Failings which have only recently been addressed by the current artistic director. In the theatre the lack of a hearing loop and the noisy air handling were faulted and were later to be fixed by Vaughan Mitchell and Mark Matthews on the long list of post-build snagging tasks. As far as the programme went the ladies wanted more plays, lunchtime concerts with sandwiches, fewer run of the

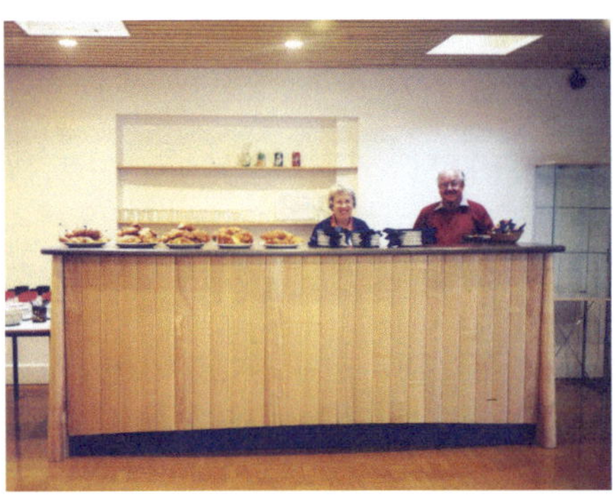

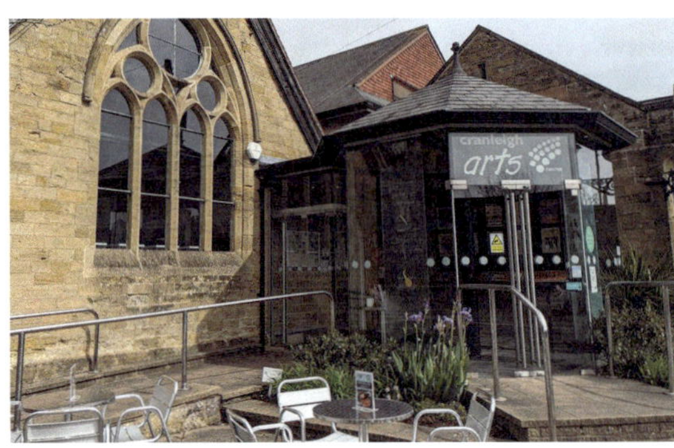

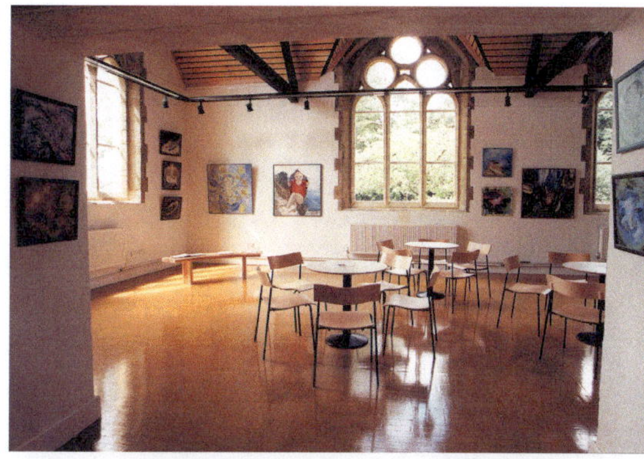

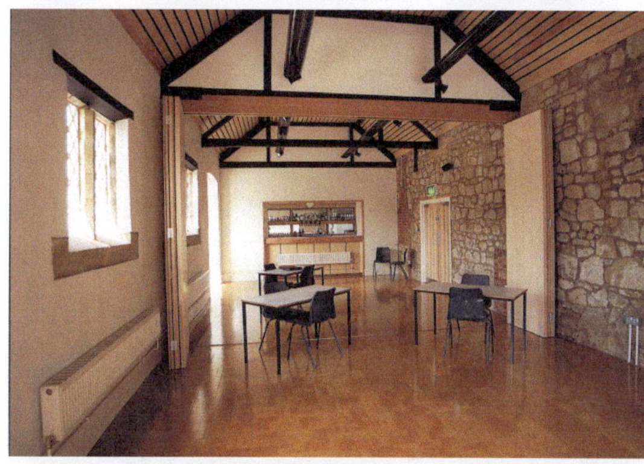

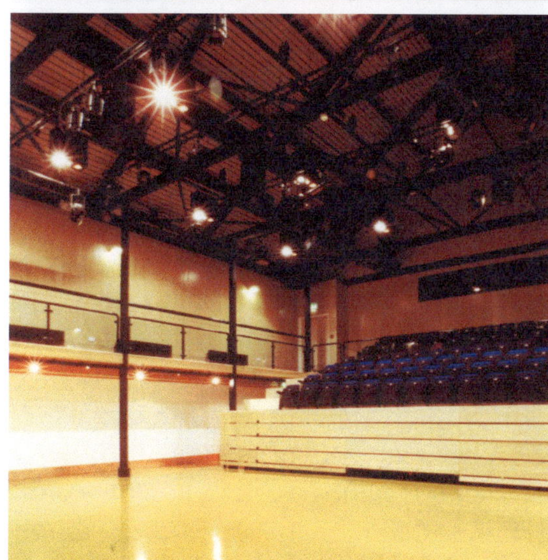

mill films and possibly tea dances. All these would be tried with varying success. Perhaps not fully representative this poll was at least one way of starting a conversation with the Cranleigh community.

But the consensus was that the money had been well spent. The building was transformed. The addition of the multi-purpose hall to accommodate small scale theatre, music and musical theatre constructed within the central space between the two old wings of the school, fully equipped with sprung floor, technical equipment, retractable seating and backstage facilities, was the main element and saw the completion of Jack Wagg's vision, nurtured for almost twenty years. As a tribute to 'his unstinting work and devotion' it bears his name. The gallery was refitted for professional touring exhibitions with security glass and shutter; the first being illustrations by Ralph Steadman for 'Animal Farm'. A new entrance foyer was built on the front with disabled access, providing a welcoming face to the High Street. Insulation and new ceilings were installed. The rear entrance was remodelled and the box office, admin office area and coffee bar refitted and re-equipped with computers and software. The old performance space was equipped with a new bar, kitchen and dividing screen and named the Crane Room, ready for hirings and hospitality, classes and literary lunches. Externally the crumbling stonework was repaired and landscaping carried out to the side and rear.

More Problems – no money, no staff
How will the Centre be managed now it is open?

Problems were developing at Waverley however to rain on the parade. In January 1998 they had written to confirm that

> *"Waverley has had to cut back on the annual revenue contribution the council makes towards the Centre's running costs. We had hoped to keep the contribution at £3,500, but despite strenuous efforts during the difficult financial debates in committee and at Council meetings we have been forced to reduce it to £2,700 owing to the severe cut backs in the Government's grant settlements to local authorities."*

This was a shock, just as more money was needed not less to run the Centre. To recap: back in 1996 the picture had seemed rosy and envisioned The Maltings and Cranleigh Arts being developed side by side to deliver the Waverley Leisure Strategy. Catherine had lobbied for that with Peter Maudsley and the Council had agreed a total of £250,000 in its 1995/6 Capital programme to support the Lottery bid. Although there had been a wobble when they asked to defer part of it, it was understood that they were still on side. Once the Lottery bid had been approved then a presentation was made to the Leisure Committee on 28th October 1996 by Arthur Gomez, Brian Harris, Catherine Pike and Harry Stadler selling the project and reinforcing the step change this represented. The need for a Centre Manager was essential if the organisation was to evolve. The Committee published its recommendations on 7th January 1997 approving the release of the capital, suggesting a service agreement and endorsing the appointment of an arts development officer to work at Cranleigh and the wider borough for three years (Helen Cundy). Previously it had recommended increasing staffing and marketing grants for the Maltings and Cranleigh in a paper called 'Safeguarding the Future of Waverley's Arts Centres'. This had been heralded by an article in *The Surrey Advertiser:* **'Arts Centre cash go-ahead'**.

In January 1998 three candidates for Centre Manager had applied after advertisements had been posted. They were interviewed, but two were not sufficiently qualified and the one who was offered it withdrew, perhaps realising the precariousness of their salary. In the interim a management team was instituted comprising of Catherine Pike, Muriel Longhurst and Anne Hull until the Manager situation was resolved. Rosemary Dubois continued in her role as daily factotum. Muriel Longhurst, who had already made lots of suggestions for programme ideas, threw herself into problem solving and produced papers and schedules, routines and checklists, as befitted an ex-Headmistress. In August she was appointed Vice-Chair, perhaps with a view to taking over from Catherine. In October and November she led a review of the Management Structure together with Catherine, Helen Cundy, and Treasurer Harry Stadler. This grapples with responsibilities but looks on paper like a power grab by Muriel and a down grade of Catherine's role. The minutes of the November council meeting are missing so it is conjectural as to what happened. Rosemary Dubois remembers an occasion when they had to meet to decide between Muriel and Catherine. Perhaps this was it. However by the next meeting in March 1999 Muriel has resigned. Helen remembers there was a difference of opinion (code perhaps for a blazing row?) with Catherine. This was not surprising as they were very different people with very different approaches, but despite the difficult situation it seems the trustees lined up behind their chairman. *"The Management Team was working well but it was agreed that a Centre Manager with arts professional management skills was still needed."* Minutes March 1999. However Christine Barker had finished her secondment as Exhibitions Organiser, so that was being advertised, as well as the post of Caretaker and there was still an urgent need for someone with Marketing expertise. It was proving hard to get the organisation operating as it should do to maximise the potential of the new building and it was only just solvent. The organisation was under stress.

In June 1998 Catherine and Harry had written to Peter Maudsley at Waverley alerting him that the refurbishment had overspent due to extra costs of the unforeseen defects found.

> *"The state of the building not least the stonework, roofs and floors, were found to be in a far worse state than could have been expected", as no survey was made when the building was taken on, "which was clearly culpable. However, the building belongs to Waverley and it may be thought that they had some responsibility in the matter."*

They also say that the annual grant goes back almost totally in rent and that insurance, provided by Waverley for a much enhanced building will likely be £4,000. Since the programme is still building up there will be shortfalls in both the capital and revenue account and that the Centre will be insolvent in three to four months. The bank may not extend credit. They request either an interest free loan or suspension of rental and insurance payments. They continue,

> *"As a quite separate but very important issue we must revert to the question of a Centre Manager. While since the Centre re-opened all the voluntary staff have coped as best they could and while we appreciate the help given by Waverley Arts staff without which we could not have managed, these arrangements are temporary and cannot therefore be regarded as a long-term solution. We have been asked by our Lottery Officer to advise them formally that we are unable to*

comply with their condition under this heading since we clearly cannot afford to fund such an appointment. We feel we must ask you to have a second look at this problem."

In July Catherine escalates the matter and writes to Christine Pointer, Chief Executive at Waverley, explaining that unless the Artistic Director was appointed Cranleigh Arts would not fulfil the terms of the Lottery grant and might not receive final payment from them. She had pushback in this immediate reply from Christine Pointer.

"In the letter from Fiona Wright (Arts Council), which you appended, she clearly states that 'I understand from the application that this post was to be funded by Waverley Borough Council.' I have to say that as Chief Executive this has never been my understanding of the situation, nor is any revenue funding provided within our budgets for this post.

I am at a loss to understand how this situation has arisen. Over the last twelve months we have been giving you support in kind from our Arts Officer, but this was always designed to be temporary support to enable you to programme and open the Centre. Waverley cannot and indeed has not the resources to pick up the salary for your manager and no matter how many people sit round a table to discuss this issue, the funds are simply not available.

I passed your letter to Peter Maudsley and to our Partnership Funding officer, Wendy Varcoe, in the hope they may be able to offer you assistance in generating funding elsewhere, but given our budget situation this year, and the further cuts we are expecting to make in 1999/2000, there is nothing at this present time which could provide the measure of support you are seeking."

After what must have been a much needed holiday Catherine replies to Christine Pointer in two pages of closely worded defence. She evidences the Waverley Leisure Strategy 1996-2001. She makes telling comparisons to Godalming Museum and the Farnham Maltings. She quotes Christine Pointer's own warm words on the reopening of the Centre printed in the WBC magazine: *"I am delighted that Waverley has been able to help by providing capital and revenue funding for this very exciting project. ... it will be a great benefit to the community and an asset to Waverley and the region as a whole."* She notes in fact that the grant has been cut and is anyway offset by the rent. She measures what Cranleigh Arts can deliver against the 'corporate purposes' of the Borough Council and ticks the boxes. She argues for Cranleigh to be the centre for arts provision in the east of the borough. She acknowledges the contribution of the Arts Development Officer (Helen Cundy), partly funded by South East Arts, to the first few months of start-up but says there must be a full time Centre Manager to make a commercial success of the new facilities. She asks for a meeting with the Arts Council, South East Arts and Waverley. Her son, David, recalls that *"she rarely brought problems home with her, but just got on with it. However, Waverley not paying for a Manager broke through that and made her very angry. She was principled and saw it as bad faith to renege on that. You just don't do that."*

This 'all interested parties' meeting, an effort to add pressure, was turned down. Harry Stadler was gloomy that, as Waverley's building project reviewer Steve Tilbury had already flagged up, there was no more money available, so they seemed to be unlikely to budge. However there is a meeting on 7th September with Maudsley and Linda Salway, the new Arts Officer replacing Carol Sacha, which Peter Maudsley summarised in a letter to Catherine afterwards:

> *"They had discussed and reviewed the paper trail and established that although the Officer report had advocated a funded manager and a subsequent study had taken place in the Arts Development Service Plan, the members' consideration of this decided that Waverley was not in a position to fund this and this was acknowledged by both sides. Going forward there were options to be explored:*
> *The Arts Task Group was of the view that a team-based approach to managing the arts in Waverley was preferred to a venue-based one, to spread expertise. This would be resolved by Christmas.* (It is true that this had been flagged up in February 1996 when the Capital Grant had been awarded initially.)
> *The longstanding friendship and support of South East Arts was productive and should be developed as opportunities arise.*
> *The external Funding Officer could be helpful in generating funding for the Centre. Perhaps taking on the freehold would have financial benefits and that could be considered."*

Additionally Waverley raised the issue of succession planning for Catherine and Harry and the need for a twenty-five year plan, to include widening the Board of Management away from local representation and towards an imperative *"in having those who can contribute significantly to your survival and success"*. He concludes *"I remain committed to seeing the Centre survive and be successful and to use the best endeavours of me and my department to ensure that this happens"*.

In the end they agree to continue to offer Helen Cundy's expertise on a part-time basis of three days a week. This was great for the Centre as she got on well with the team and was in sympathy with their aims. Her involvement gradually snowballed until it became all-consuming for her, lured in like many others before her. Trying to bring together borough resources she developed a two year summer project with the Leisure Centre of sport and crafts for young people, but it didn't really work as the two were not really compatible. She was also trying to represent the Council at the Redgrave Theatre in Farnham, which was in deep trouble, and report back on the situation there. It was clear that she was overstretched and her boss became nervous at her executive engagement. A local authority in London had been blamed when something went wrong in a similar situation. She resigned to move to Newcastle. This was a big blow and brought matters to a head.

Breakthrough

A bit of moral blackmail or facing reality?

However in June 1999 South East Arts was able to make an offer of £15,000 towards the development of activities and events at the Arts Centre. *"Special conditions attached to this grant are that second payment will be on confirmation of funding from Waverley Borough Council for a Centre Manager."* The Arts Council equally had been stalling the final payments of the project until there were signs that this condition was met. Harry Stadler had written to Fiona Wright, the Lottery Projects Officer after the gala opening in June 1998,

> *"I am glad you are speaking to South East Arts on the question of a Centre Manager. We are doing the same and Waverley have been in touch. We urgently need someone to fill this post and as you probably know it was originally hoped that Waverley would fund this position as they do for at least one other Arts organisation in the Borough."*

In November in the aftermath of the above debate he writes again,

> *"Although as you know Waverley has steadfastly refused any financial assistance towards a Centre Manager, we are currently exploring with the help of their staff possible sponsorship funding for such a post as well as for artistic activities. With overheads coming in at above even my own pessimistic estimates there is no chance of finding the money from our own resources."*

Meanwhile he has to send in details of itemised equipment and fittings costs to explain increases and decreases in expenditure as well as invoices for ex-gratia work. There is haggling going on with the builders over extra construction work and fees to be explained as well as snagging issues. There is a query too over Chris Newman and Sector's fees as consultant quantity surveyor and services consultants. The juggling of payment is tricky, as to settle an account 75% comes from the Arts Council, with the Centre funding the other 25%. This can cause a cash flow problem, so Harry has to arrange an overdraft facility. But light comes at the end of the tunnel as Harry writes to Fiona again in October.

> *" You will be interested to learn that we are about to acquire a Centre Manager,*

Mark Wright, who will be starting on 1st December. The post will initially be funded largely, but not entirely, by Waverley, the amount of the funding decreasing after 2000/01, so that Mark will need to earn his keep by increasing the volume of money coming into the Centre, which we are confident he will be able to do. It is of course only due to pressure from yourselves that Waverley have come up with any money at all, having previously told us emphatically on a number of occasions that none would be forthcoming. Even so it has been like getting blood out of a stone, for having originally promised to let us have the first instalment of the grant as soon as the ad for the post went into the papers in the second week of September, we are still waiting for the money, which we do not consider professional behaviour. This is particularly embarrassing as it has for the first time forced us into a small overdraft position at the bank."

Fiona is delighted but needs to check that the composition of the interview panel is as per their conditions. Harry reassures her that funders were well represented by Steve Tilbury and Linda Salway from Waverley.

So by giving way to the inevitable, Waverley has established its control over the future of the Arts Centre and its direction of travel. Despite its own financial troubles and its potentially divided nature with the members and the officers sometimes having competing agendas, they perhaps realise that it is too important to fail. They do consistently a number of times eventually bail it out, but in line with their bigger picture of what function they need Cranleigh Arts to fulfil and how it should operate. Would this then be the start of a new dawn for the Arts Centre at the start of the new Millenium?

Chapter Seven

The 2000s – going up a gear

A new beginning and initial success

A bright tomorrow

Mark Wright arrives, the first professional Centre Manager, who quickly gets to grips with how things need to be changed

At the first Management Council Meeting of the new Millenium there was cause for celebration. Mark Wright, the first professionally qualified Centre Manager and Artistic Director, was welcomed, having been appointed in November. His CV is not recorded but he was evidently experienced enough to see what was required. He presented a Preliminary Action Plan. The tone of his introduction suggests his style.

> *"This document represents my initial impression of the Centre's activities and the issues that can be usefully addressed in the coming months that will set the foundation for future development. It is important to emphasise again that some of these comments and ideas are not necessarily new and many are the result of conversations with people already involved with the Centre. I recognise that there may be many good reasons why some developments have not taken place before and there is absolutely no implied criticism of those who have worked for the benefit of the Centre previously."*

The four page document lists Policies and Priorities as: Education, Quality, Community. The Principles of Programming are to be: Sustainable building blocks and Integration and Consistency. He addresses the Role of the Governors, seeking to define the relationship between the Board and management drawing on Arts Council guidelines. He tackles Accounts and Budgeting, Marketing, Facility Hiring and finally Housekeeping. It is an astute strategic summary of the key areas that must run effectively and identifies areas of growth. It is evident that he has already 'got' what Cranleigh Arts is trying to do, its role in the community and where it could go.

Other changes of personnel were recorded at the start of this year. Harry Stadler, who had been Treasurer for ten years, including keeping track of the labyrinthine accounts of the Arts Council bid and grant spend, stood down in November. In his place had come John Pearce, formerly Manager of Cranleigh's NatWest Bank, who presented a financial appraisal at this meeting too. In the eighteen months since opening the Centre has experienced cash flow problems and posted losses of several thousand each accounting year. He is evidently a forensic accountant and has drilled down into Income and Expenditure looking at the last nine months and analysing what percentage each element represents and what targets should be set to achieve a balanced budget and potential growth. He posits a possible surplus of £22k with this 'stretched' budget. As ever he concludes that largely fixed operating costs will be tight against variable income.

> *"The Company remains well-endowed with fixed Assets but short in the Income stream. Costs offer little opportunity for improvement beyond prudent control and in my opinion we should concentrate our energies firmly on the expansion of our Letting and Production income."*

However he resigns as Treasurer, for reasons not given at this meeting, to be replaced by Richard Paton in May. He was a seasoned local chartered accountant, with experience of being Treasurer of other local organisations including the Village Hospital Trust, CAB and the Day Centre.

Another longstanding member was Anne Hull. She had been the first paid Administrative Secretary in 1988 and Company Secretary from 1992. Together with Rosemary Dubois and Jack Wagg, then with Catherine Pike, she had been an anchor for the daily running of the Centre through the many ups and downs of the nineties. She felt, wrongly perhaps, that the new Centre would be very different and not have a place for her. She stood down after the reopening, being replaced initially by Manisha Thaker and then by Sarah Underhill who began in September 1999 and quickly got in step with Mark and at the end of 2000 added the role of Accounts Manager, taking over from a volunteer, with an increase in her hours and salary.

Mark quickly moved on three fronts. Get the money right. Get the support right. Get the marketing right. In February he takes the process of the monthly operational accounting into his own hands and institutes tight control over expenditure. There are forms on which spending must be approved and by which payment can be tracked through comprehensive coding. He allocates a budget to Marketing. The chain of command, via Mark and Sarah to the Bookkeeper Miss Skelton and the accounts supervisor Mrs Parry, was clear. Richard Paton, as the new Treasurer, would have oversight.

Marketing, Programme and Volunteers

Mark makes progress in all areas

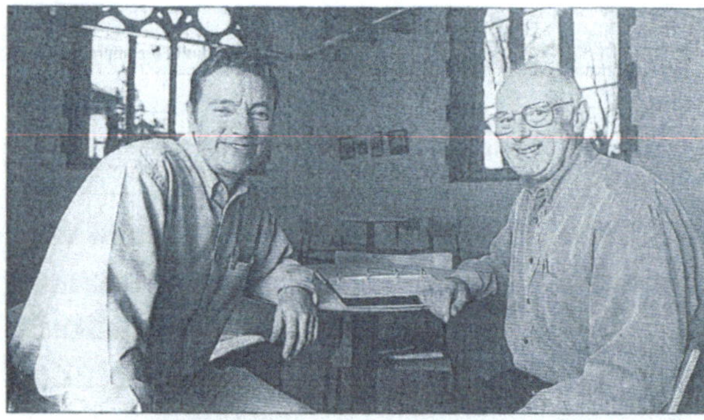

Skill share: Mark Wright (left) and Arthur Nicholls

Another new face was Arthur Nicholls. He was seconded on a six month mentoring project financed by Arts and Business to devise a Marketing Strategy for Cranleigh Arts. This results in a comprehensive document which has the intention *"to provide more creative challenges and experiences that engage more people more often"*. It offers clear analysis of the landscape, a SWOT breakdown, discusses ambitions for the Centre and finalises eleven objectives translated into a three year schedule of actions with measurable targets. It is another exemplary document, clear-headed, practical and reflecting professional expertise. Too often Marketing is the Cinderella of the organisation, understaffed and underfunded. Inevitably lots of people have great suggestions but without a sense of strategy or evaluation these are stabs in the dark. The cost in time and money of such marketing is often a waste. Mark was sure of his priorities and necessary actions in the Strategy presented to the Board and it was unanimously approved.

Reports on Marketing had been done before. In January 1998, on the verge of reopening Catherine received a Marketing Plan commissioned from Sally Anne Lowe, a local marketing expert. She focusses on Revenue, largely from business and commercial use and sponsorship, and Audience, having a strong corporate identity and contacting people directly by better use of Databox. It makes some encouraging suggestions but as it comes from an outsider it lacks the identification with the primary aims and objectives that Mark's has. Perhaps the vision had become clearer in the interim now that the Centre was open. Coming over the horizon too we know there is a radical change in digital communication on the way, that is only hinted at in references to the website and emails, that make it sound so dated. These are areas that Mark is also engaged in. He takes on overview of the website and also has a redesign of the logo, moving to the 'circles' one that is still in use today, showing what a good choice that was.

As a result of the Arts Council bid, with its projected outcomes, and the continued support of regional South East Arts, the activities of the Centre are reasonably well

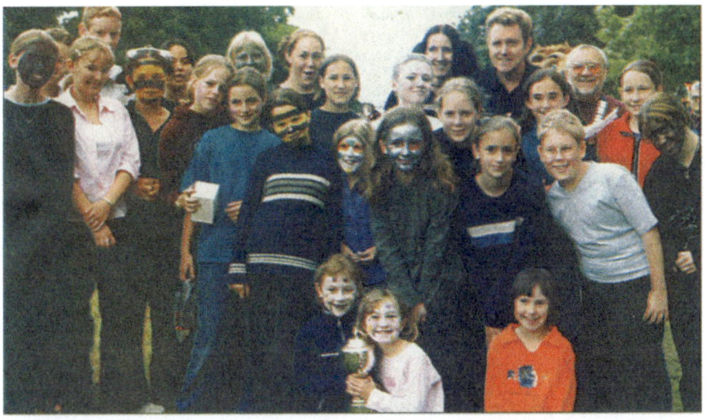

Youth Theatre Carnival Float winners.

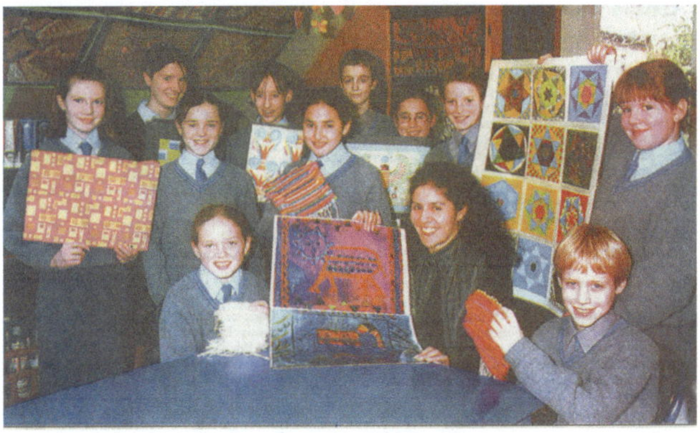

Floral Females Exhibition Duke of Kent School.

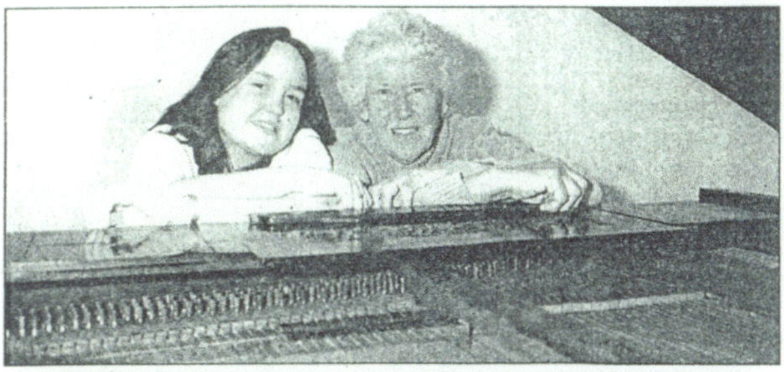

Teamwork: Cranleigh Arts Centre administrator Sarah Underhill and chairman, Catherine Pike, are urging people to sponsor a piano string.

planned and monitored. What went well was repeated, new strands and projects were devised in order to apply for funding, feedback came from ticket sales and take-up.

Community engagement came from being part of the Cranleigh Pageant and linking a project to the annual Carnival. A youth drama group and a youth orchestra had been started. New initiatives like Arts at the Arboretum at Winkworth became a regular fixture. A link with Tony Smith and Eclectic Music brought regular Rhythm and Blues nights for the first time. In the course of 2000 such was the success of the drama that three youth groups had to be run, with the addition of an adult group. Films were being run as matinees as well as in the evening. The donation in 1999 of an 1885 Broadwood Grand Piano strengthened the classical music offering, although an appeal had to be made to 'sponsor a key' to replace the 225 strings. This saved the £360 hire fee previously incurred each time. Lunchtime concerts gathered support aided by Catherine's advocacy.

With a busy programme the volunteers, without whom the Centre couldn't operate, had been building in numbers. There was an opportunity to meet monthly to socialise, be updated and contribute ideas. In January in line with his aim to strengthen support Mark arranges a meeting headed **'Your opinion counts!'** where, over a glass of wine, he says, *"I am keen to ensure that you feel your time is well spent and to hear directly how you think we could move things forward".* There was a write in option too for those unable to attend. There are no minutes from this but one must assume that as a 'tell and sell' exercise it did the trick. His Marketing Strategy stresses that unless 'staff' feel positive about and understand what an organisation stands for then the result is poor customer service. Support also comes from the members of Cranleigh Arts and the newly formed Friends. He identifies this as another key area. *"Wherever possible we should try to give value back to those who support us most strongly. ... Rewarding loyalty is, in essence, a question of recognition and appreciation."* To do this he suggests the confusion over the legal status of some subscribers be sorted out. Subscriptions from members and friends were bringing in almost £7k a year, after its introduction and development at relaunch. 'Members' were legally part of the limited company and voted at the AGM, appointed Trustees and were liable, if the company went bust, to contribute £1. 'Friends' were supporters of Cranleigh Arts and received some benefits for an annual fee. Mark wanted the two to be amalgamated and for it to be put to the AGM in July that all should be designated 'friends'. The Council agreed but a vote was deferred and the matter was to be reconsidered when memberships came up for renewal in February. It was thought that there would not be a need to change the Memorandum and Articles of Association. The issue was complicated by the fact that the two groups were administered separately but could all be assimilated into Databox should this happen. In the New Year all were written to, the two categories explained and they could tick a box if they wanted to be a Member as well as a Friend. 10% opted to become members as well as friends, but some confusion remained and this issue would keep coming up and has still not fully been resolved today as the register of voting members declines.

Mark gets involved helping Harry Stadler in signing off the final payment from the Arts Council. The final sign off required no less than eight forms, reports and summaries to be completed and sent to the Arts Council Capital Services Officer and an external assessor. In February 2001 Mark provides reports on the programme, the marketing strategy and the Business Plan. Eventually after concerns over access and disability provision are sorted out, the last payment is made in April and the file is passed to the Post Completion team in November 2001.

Mark also has a bead on grant applications, bidding to South East Arts to be a Recurrently Funded Organisation (RFO) and to Waverley to be a Sponsored Organisation.

He even had a strategy for the car park, which since the days of Jack Wagg had proved impossible to police. He intended to introduce clamping after a warning. In talks with the churchwarden it had been accepted that they had no rights to park at the Centre but might join in on a common clamping policy.

By the December Council Meeting Mark Wright receives a vote of confidence from the meeting proposed by Catherine Pike after his first year as Centre Manager. The trustees must have been heaving a sigh of relief that at last the Centre was forging ahead on all fronts with a dynamic leader. He had certainly made his mark. The place was buzzing.

Or back to square one?

A resignation and a return means changing leadership just as progress is being made

However at the next meeting in March change is in the air. Mark has put in his resignation from April 2001. This was a bit of a body blow but necessitated by his wife being relocated to Yorkshire. As some recompense his new job was only four days a week and he offered to work for the Centre one day a week from Yorkshire, to be available by phone and email to deal with any queries and complete administration such as payroll. Harry Stadler wrote once more to update the Arts Council.

> *"As to his successor the post is being readvertised and it is hoped that interviews will be conducted next month (April); as before representatives of Waverley and South East Arts will be in attendance. I mentioned to you that among the applicants is likely to be Helen Cundy who was Arts Development Officer at Waverley until towards the end of 1999 and in that capacity was seconded to Cranleigh Arts Centre for much of her time and performed there an invaluable role in the administration of many of the activities that needed to be started or restarted upon the reopening of the Centre. If she succeeded in being chosen as Mark's successor this would very nearly eliminate any difficulties which are otherwise bound to arise from the lack of a proper handover."*

His next letter on 27th April confirms this.

> *"You will be interested to hear that Helen Cundy whom I mentioned in my last letter rang us yesterday to accept the job as Mark's successor and is expected to take up her duties sometime in June. Everyone at the Centre is very happy at this outcome and breathing a sigh of relief."*

Catherine Pike had been very keen to get Helen back and had approached her to apply. She was working for Gateshead Council's Arts team and had completed a postgrad diploma in Arts Management and was wanting to move back south from Gateshead. On her appointment she was able to arrange a handover with Mark in

Yorkshire over an extended coffee morning! She knew the core team so slotted back in easily. In her absence Mark had set up administrative structures, but cash flow was still a big problem. Adult Education which had been a solid income stream had virtually folded. Waverley's funding was tapering down and they had put up the rent after a revaluation and were demanding arrears. The new Rhythm and Blues nights were a lifesaver and films were also on the up which helped. But things were far from secure. She says, *"The only strategy I had really was, I just have to get people into the building. Before the Lottery it felt like all these little clubs".* She had a good group of people to help. Chris and Rosemary Dubois were dedicated long serving contributors. Helen would cry, *"at last the cavalry has arrived!"* when they rallied round, often at unsocial hours, to help set up or clear up for events or undertake key activities. She could rely on Catherine's support too. *"She wasn't a people pleaser, she did what she believed was best for the Centre. She was so visionary and encouraging. I don't know what would have happened without her."* Another new arrival was Emma Rafferty, who took over as Administrative Secretary from Sarah Underhill who moved on in July. She would be Helen's loyal lieutenant as they grew what Mark and Sarah had established.

Two significant additions to the Board happened at this time which strengthened the team further. Arthur Nicholls, who had mentored the Marketing Strategy, maintained his links and expert contribution to the Centre by accepting an invitation to join. The other was Chrissy Matthews, who was to be a key player over the next ten years, working tirelessly for Cranleigh Arts. She had retired from various management roles at BA and was getting involved in local things. The first project had been the Cranleigh Pageant the previous year, where the Centre had provided ticketing and Front of House support. She had met Mark Wright, helped set up the relevant Databox programme, had worked with volunteers before at the Royal Horticultural Society and had been drawn in to Cranleigh Arts, as would her husband, Mark, subsequently. She was a co-founder of the Cranleigh Initiative, a spinoff project panel of the Chamber of Commerce, and so was well connected with the local business chiefs. The possibility of sponsorship to augment grant funding of elements of the programme could perhaps now be developed. From her very first meeting in June she makes lots of practical, useful suggestions such as finding a new Patron or indeed several, after the sad death of Sir Harry Secombe in April, and arranging a Draws licence. She went full steam ahead on business sponsorship.

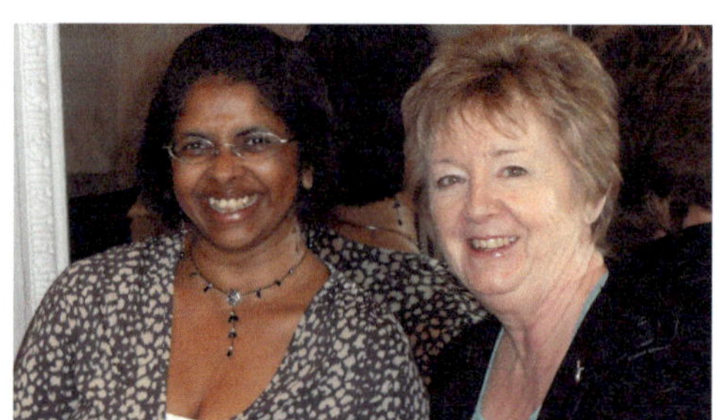

Chrissy Matthews and Rosemary Dubois.

The money starts to run out

How to avoid insolvency and the dilemmas involved

In March 2001 Mark tabled his budget report and usage figures. His approaches for funding had been successful. Looking at the new Budget for 2001/2002 £18,000 had been awarded by South East Arts under a new annual Recurrently Funded Organisation (RFO) scheme, subject to a service level agreement being concluded. Waverley had awarded £17,700 under their sponsored organisation scheme but proposed to claw back some of that to pay the rent. £5,000 was still to come from the Arts Council. The new accounting procedures made it more possible to accurately reflect what might happen. Richard Paton tabled his figures for the current year and showed an operating loss of £3,612 to which had to be added £3,000 still to be spent on the rebuilding to match the Arts Council share. Subsequently Richard Paton addressed the Council in June.

> *"We had no reserves at the start of the year and the loss puts the Company in quite a delicate financial position. ... Thus it could be said that the Company is insolvent. [He assumes the positive paper value of assets would have little actual value in the event of a break up.] In fact I do not believe it is insolvent because (i) we are budgeting for a surplus this year (ii) the picture as regards the value of the company's assets in a break-up situations may not be as bleak as I have painted it and (iii) we have negotiated an unsecured loan facility of £7,000 with our bank, which should enable us to pay our debts as they fall due, provided that we earn a surplus this year.*
>
> *"It is imperative that we do earn a surplus this year and I believe we need to take positive action to ensure that we do. I am nervous of the budget which Mark Wright warned us prior to his departure "had no fat in it". I fear that it is over-optimistic – for example it includes grants receivable which appear to have no real basis for inclusion and it is not clear how the estimates of cost and income for the arts activities have been arrived at. I hope that it may be one of our new manager's first jobs to review the budget in respect of arts activities.*
>
> *"I am sure that it will also be one of her priorities to consider ways of increasing income, but I think we need to take some action sooner rather than later, if we can. Ideally I would like to see £10,000 put back into the Company by way of increased income this year."*

This was the situation that Helen was taking on.

It is a truth universally acknowledged that no one gets rich from the arts. It is expensive to produce due to the people and facilities that it often needs. Even workshops and classes come with overheads that may not be covered by what people are willing to pay. Over the years the value of the arts to health and wellbeing has been reinforced and the need for support to make it available to all is accepted. Nonetheless grants are not always forthcoming often restricted by political imperatives and, unlike in some other countries, government support for the arts, sponsorship and charitable donation is less developed here. Often the subsidy comes from the time and energy of the people delivering the art that they love and care for, be they professional, amateur or volunteer, sometimes at the expense of their own wellbeing. This is as true of Cranleigh Arts as in the wider national picture. From the start it had been a hand to mouth existence. Now however the stakes were higher. Richard Paton's analysis above would be repeated by future Treasurers. The existential threat would come more often, here in 2001/2, again in 2006 and in 2017. How to square the circle between commercial survival and delivering the portfolio of potential loss making activities that the charity was set up to provide for the community of Cranleigh would be debated over and over again. But the trustees had a duty to safeguard the survival of the Company and that meant adjusting the budget and finding money. It is evident from the records that over the years individuals had helped cash flow with short term unsecured personal loans. At the following meetings many ideas were suggested, adding to a list started by the Treasurer. But like turning a tanker there are considerable delays until change happens. The programme is booked months in advance; grant bids and sponsorship may take many months to achieve also. New initiatives need time and promoters, neither of which the sole two full-time members of staff had, and money was running out fast.

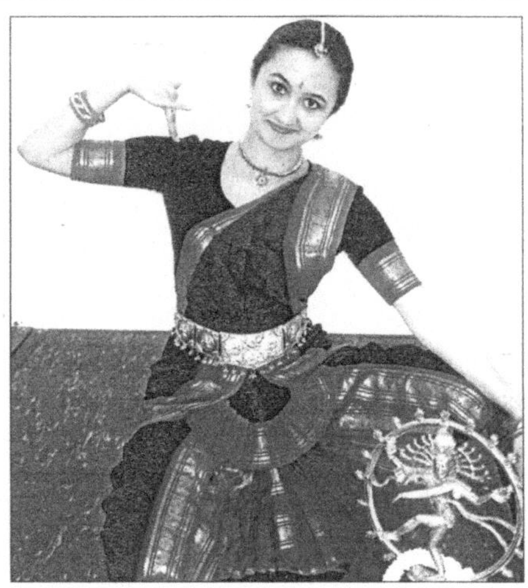

Shalini Bhalla, who will be helping children taste a touch of Bollywood next week. (c)

Discovering the joy of Bollywood

In her first few months Helen was able to report some success. In the midst of this deepening financial crisis the Centre put on a 'phenomenally' successful David Hockney exhibition, with an associated storytelling workshop and Summer Madness had run again with great success. By September Hire rates were increased for new hirers and conversations held with regular hirers explaining the situation, with a Council member in attendance to support Helen. There was some pushback from U3A. Businesses were being targeted for hires or sponsorship. The Friends

Scheme was (re)launched. Operational and project funding bids were in with South East Arts and with Waverley for small grants as well as ongoing conversations about support. Good personal relations were built up with Paul Ackerley at South East Arts and Linda Salway continued to do what she could at Waverley. At the time there was quite a large arts team and they could offer a lot of support through advice and secondment. Press coverage had increased. The new brochure was bringing in bookings including new classes for parents and toddlers and dance.

In September Richard Paton was on holiday but the next crucial financial low point was identified as coming in November. Two Special Financial meetings were held in October where he stated that although technically insolvent for a period the finances would be cushioned by ticket advances and by South East Arts agreeing to release grant monies early so bills could be paid. Managing the message was crucial too. Helen writes to council members on 2nd October,

> *"I am very concerned that gossip appears to be going around the village about our situation. As we agreed at the meeting, this is not public information, it would be very damaging if it were to hit the press at this stage. I am very grateful for all your support in dealing with this situation, but I would appreciate if you could let me know any ideas so that we can make sure that things happen through the correct channels. There are a number of sensitive issues involved and I do not want to upset any of our relationships with customers or funders."*

At the second meeting two, perhaps conflicting, approaches emerge from the Minutes. First in programming that the aim should be to raise the profile by linking to national events and activities and Gala fundraising. The other was to look to Waverley to provide extra 'bail-out' support, but their agenda would have to be satisfied too. *"Following a public meeting in Cranleigh the feedback had been that the Councillors were looking for the Centre to be viewed in a more community context."* It was suggested that every Councillor be written to asking for their support. Linda Salway, Arts Development Officer, advised writing to Peter Maudsley to ask for assistance. *"She expressed her view that it had become obvious that the Arts Centre was not going to be self-financing and was in need of core funding."*

In December a presentation was made to Peter Maudsley that showed on Richard Paton's figures an overdraft of £16,000 by the end of the financial year. This was agreed and application made to Waverley for £20,000 to clear it. The Executive Committee was inclined to give £15,000 with the expectation that the Parish Council provide the rest. Mrs Staats, the Parish Council representative, thought this was unlikely as they only allocated money to capital projects, it had all been allocated and only up to a maximum of £1,500! As this was now in the public domain the local paper ran the story under the headlines **'Fate of arts centre lies in parish**

council hands' and **'Arts Centre waits on cash vote'**. The articles explained that at their December meeting Waverley Council

> *"... has agreed to provide £15,000 but only if Cranleigh Parish Council 'seriously considers' coming up with the other £5,000. The art centre is under the new management of Helen Cundy and since her arrival she had addressed the reality of the financial situation facing the Centre as well as taking a strenuous commercial line with its activities and uses. There is great hope for its future and success under the new management regime. The council has warned the art centre that it is unlikely to consider giving any further rescue payments in the future."*

In January the Parish Council met. Here the arts centre had some strong supporters who rallied round and were able to see a way round the difficulties. Brian Ellis suggested that as some of the deficit was the portion of building costs not met by the Arts Council, that would count as a capital grant and so could be acceptable. *"We have a rather unique Centre in this village – it is not something that can be boasted of by Haslemere or Godalming."* John Savage said he would like to see it given *"as much money as possible"*. He went on to highlight the *"ambitious quality of the programme"* the arts centre has, with concerts, plays, exhibitions and workshops. *"It's a place that needs to be supported because it is so vital to the emotional life of the community"*, he added. And Jean Dodd said the manager, Helen Cundy, was also trying to open *"some kind of drop-in centre for young people"*. It was referred to the finance committee and ratified by the full council for £3,000. Heading into 2002, and the new financial year, disaster had been averted.

Having dodged the sword of Damocles a postscript was offered by Richard Paton on the liabilities of Directors. He presented reading material for guidance and highlighted that, while relatively safe from financial culpability and prosecution unless deliberate fraud was undertaken, council members should be aware of their obligations under Health and Safety Laws. More strictures to worry about. It was agreed that this would be put under regular review going forward.

Growing the organisation to get out of trouble

Programme, projects and profile are expanded

In March the Centre was back in the black but still needed to keep very tight control of the numbers. The net cost of running the Centre was about £96,000. While hirings were up and the programme expanding this led to a need for more staff and greater wear and tear. Grant income was not guaranteed. New lines included a Comedy Club, local bands and DJ evenings to get young people in. By the summer the bands had attendance of 120, the DJ 180. Another potential boost could come from film. With the demise of the Regal Cinema the developers had offered a sum to support the showing of films elsewhere. Helen and a working group did a detailed appraisal of this including market research and concluded that for a donation of £15,000 there was a viable market for the expansion of the Centre's film offering. Crownhall Estates had originally offered £10,000. In the course of the year the Council agreed and the money was paid after a legal service agreement was signed. The R&B nights were restructured as hires thus reducing risk. A regional project entitled 'Family Friendly' set up a family advisory group to guide on projects which would provide for that market. Summer Live – a series of drop-in music and 'takeaway' evenings and an extended Summer Madness programme for children were also planned. Arts at the Arboretum at Winkworth, now in its third year, had a £2,000 grant from WBC and would include street theatre, raku firing and a storyteller. 600+ people attended. One council member expressed frustration that this hadn't generated any income, but it was explained that the grant had covered costs and that the arrangement with the National Trust precluded charging. It had to be free. Richard Paton continued to drive the numbers hard, such that Arthur Nicholls remarked at one meeting that *"financial success should not be the main objective of an event"*. Helen recalls having similar discussions with trustees to maintain that the arts were the core of what they did.

Chrissy Matthews had been working hard on sponsorship and patrons. In September 2002 she updates the Council. Kenney Jones (Rock musician/Hurtwood Polo Club) and Colin Young (Cranleigh Freight Services) were interested in sponsorship. Richard Womack (David Mann & Sons) and Colin Young wanted to be Patrons. Paul Getty had been approached too, but turned it down. Other letters inviting them to become a patron had been sent to Hannah Gordon, Annabelle Levington, Ringo Starr, Judi Dench, Anna Carteret, David Shepherd, Tony Hart (who had planted the tree at the entrance) and Julie Walters (who many years later accepted).

Another Management Review

Mark Courtice, consultant, investigates the management to find a model that might work

By mid-year the pressures on the organisation were beginning to tell. An application to the Regional Arts Lottery Programme for organisational development was successful and paid for an arts management consultant to review the organisation, assist with business and financial planning and to review the Council of Management. This had been at the instigation of Paul Ackerley of South East Arts, with the support of Waverley, who, after several possible people had been suggested, endorsed Mark Courtice, who had a range of experience of venues, companies and agencies, including at the Nuffield Theatre Southampton and St Mary at the Castle in Hastings. He would observe from November and reported in June 2003. The intention was to find a sustainable model for the way forward. He is very active. He shadowed Helen for a week to see what she did and at the end had to admit *"I'm exhausted"*. This was the main problem – the toll on the staff.

In their first year Emma and Helen had thrown themselves into the running of the Centre, working long hours and even delaying paying themselves when cash flow had been crucial. Turning events round often came down to just them, as cleaning staff and caretaking were not always available. Emma went above and beyond her responsibilities, producing lunches for conferences, canapés for parties, cleaning and resetting rooms on top of her administrative role and working all hours. By September 2002 room usage analysis shows a significant increase over the last six to twelve months, up to 100% in some months. The Centre is also operating seven days a week, opening on Sunday for the Kings Church. The loss of some Duty Managers had led to the pair regularly working up to 50% more than their paid hours, it was reported to Council in July 2002. In January 2003 Emma Rafferty was off sick with chronic fatigue, having had periods off through the summer and autumn of 2002 and hospitalised with appendicitis. Mark Courtice reported that the staffing position had become unacceptable. The Directors had a legal duty as employers to act responsibly and care for their staff. He strongly recommended increasing staff despite the poor financial position. When this came up for approval at Council in January 2003 *"Miss Cundy pointed out that the organisation had lost a couple of bookings due to poor customer service because of pressure on staff. Also a Marketing Assistant would only need to sell an additional 20 tickets a week to cover the cost of employing them."* As a result Shalini Bhalla came in as Marketing Assistant, initially for three months, and Louise Grundy increased her role as Administrative Assistant, which she had been doing ad hoc for the last year. Sue Palmer-Jones takes on bookkeeping with help and Chris Strawson backs up admin. Office space was now at a premium, so proposals were made to fix that. The back office behind the Box Office would be partitioned to allow for a two-person private space. There was a need too for more and better computers, so application was made to the Parish Council to fund them which was granted. Emma eventually returned as accounts manager after her illness and in June 2003 Kate Pearson was appointed Administrator. More Duty Managers were recruited, including Chris Dubois. Nonetheless Mark notes that Helen has so

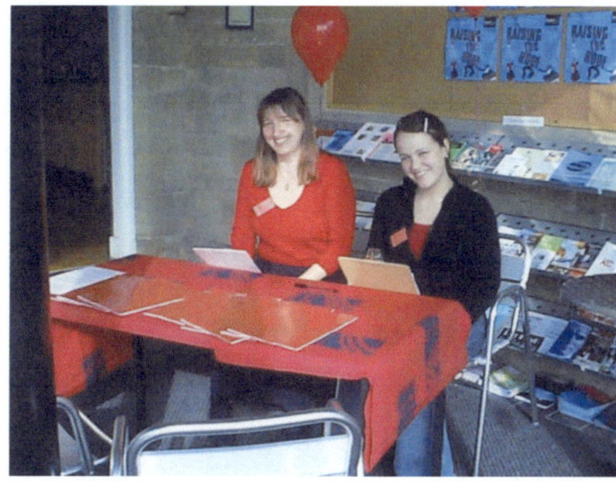
Kate Pearson and Louise Grundy at a Volunteer drive.

much daily stuff to deal with there is little time or headspace for strategic policy development. It was at this time that formal contracts of employment were introduced. Previously it had been by letter of appointment and Job Descriptions. This provided more protection for both the staff and their employer.

The stress factor and Mark Courtice's interventions led to some waves. Such that Helen had to write to all the Friends on 21st February 2003.

> *"You may have heard rumours about the arts centre closing. I am writing to assure you that this is not true. Over the past year we have built up the programme at the arts centre and our room hiring, so that we are now being used much more, and obviously bringing in more income. However we are currently undergoing an organisational review."*

She goes on to further explain:

> *" .. this is to establish a clear identity for Cranleigh Arts Centre, which is reflected in the programme and managed and staffed appropriately in order to make this happen. ... In terms of staffing, the Centre has grown to a state where we cannot cope with the level of activity with the current staffing."*

She goes on to reinforce that Cranleigh Arts is an independent company and not run or fully funded by Waverley or the Arts Council. It has to generate its own income. *"I think it is important that everyone knows!"* However in terms of local messaging it was important to be upbeat about things and not to suggest that the Centre was struggling unduly, as a major fundraising push was going on for the Village Hospital Trust at the same time. A fifth birthday party in June 2003 gave the opportunity to shout about the Centre's successes since reopening.

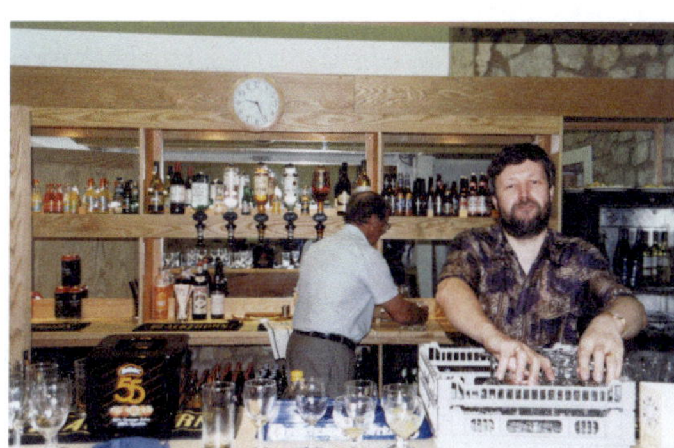
David Shelton, Licensee, behind the Bar.

Mark Courtice next turned his focus on The Council of Management (CoM) and presented a paper for discussion.

> *"He commented that it was not unusual for such organisations that had originally come together to save a building, to lose sight of the fact they are now running an organisation that is responsible for providing art for the people of Cranleigh."*

He identifies that the CoM has grown in a rather ad hoc way and, while effective up to now, lacks definition of the roles of members and any system to ensure it is doing the right thing. Could there be a conflict between members volunteering and also being the monitors of that work? The Council members lack training. They should perhaps serve for a defined time and contribute specific skills with regard to running an Arts Centre and delivering its mission. He proposes a skills audit of members, the identification of gaps and the recruitment of new members to fill them. He also circulates **'Care, Diligence and Skill'** a handbook for board members of arts organisations just produced by the Scottish Arts Council. This useful guide was produced 'to encourage well-informed discussion and good 'corporate governance': the establishment of effective systems of management and control'. If members read the fifty pages carefully then a first step in their training was achieved. It is interesting to note the composition of the Council of Management at this time. Listed in April 2003 we have Catherine Pike (Chair), Richard Paton (Treasurer), Rosemary Dubois (programme), Chrissy Matthews (community), Vaughan Mitchell (building), Chris Dubois (admin/tech), Brian Hemingway (film), Geoff Tresman (financial). These are the voting members. In attendance are Helen Cundy (Centre Director), Jean Dodd and P Betlem (Waverley Councillors), Linda Salway (Waverley Arts Officer), Rebecca Ball (South East Arts), Mrs D Staats (Cranleigh Parish Council), and Mark Courtice (Consultant). The eight elected long serving company members certainly had plenty of advice and scrutiny from the other seven invitees to guide their decision making.

Mark Courtice's third strand was to look at programme revitalisation, assuming that the under-resourced and understaffed current programme was stabilised. Currently the components were film, theatre, exhibitions, music: folk, classical, R&B and jazz, and children's theatre. Regular hirers included U3A, NDFAS, Bridge Club, Camera Club and some Adult Education. He suggested adding to this three projects a year working with regular partners, which could be focussed on creativity, community, inter-generational, youth based, multi art form and even residential. Partners and funding would need to be sought and a time line was suggested to set this up. Some running costs could be off set against these projects.

This was already happening to a degree as with the very successful 'Yatra – a journey', part of a national project promoting culturally diverse arts. It linked to Manisha Thaker who had worked as Administrator previously at Cranleigh Arts, and was the story of two families, the Thakers and Figueiredos, who had travelled from India via East Africa to Surrey. A journey shared by Shalini Bhalla too. It included several concerts, films, children's theatre, storytelling to school groups, an exhibition and a performance which intermingled storytelling, dance, visual arts and music. Another project in the pipeline was FLY - For Local Youth – aimed at teenagers. This came out of Cranleigh's Healthcheck initiative and brought together the youth service, police and local business sponsorship to provide regular events at the Centre. A sixth month pilot started in January 2004.

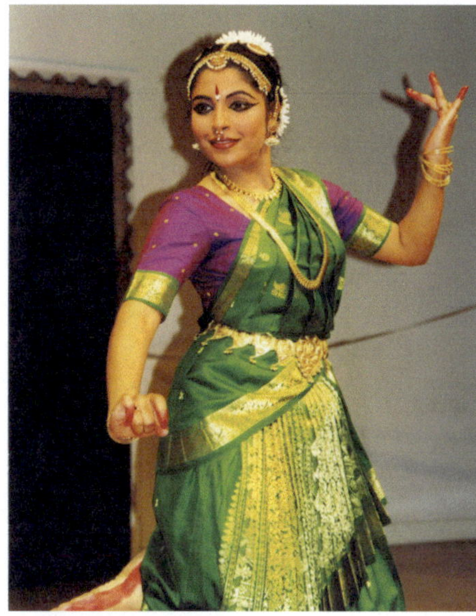

Manisha Thaker in 'Yatra'.

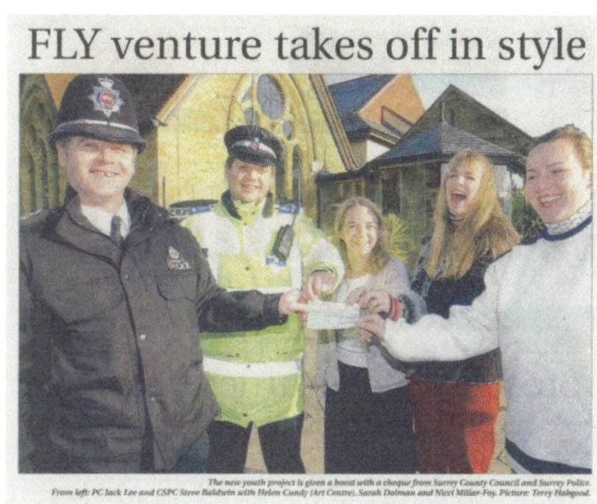

FLY venture takes off in style

The new youth project is given a boost with a cheque from Surrey County Council and Surrey Police. From left: PC Jack Lee and CSPC Steve Baldwin with Helen Cundy (Art Centre), Sarah Dolman and Nicci Millar-Foy. Picture: Terry Habgood.

He presented his final report to the Council in June 2003 where the meeting also heard of upcoming developments from Rebecca Ball of South East Arts. His recommendations would need to be reviewed in their light. Quite a debate ensued. The Arts Council was shifting its ground regarding its funding policy. She explained that RFOs would no longer be able to apply for project funding unless it was of exceptional national or regional importance. National policy was to spread funding to other organisations and post 2006 it would go to exciting, innovative, collaborative projects rather than allocated on an historical basis. 'Yatra' was an excellent example. She suggested that the aim of the arts centre long term, supported by marketing, should be to develop a reputation for innovative work. She also said that funding could be sought from other bodies than the Arts Council, such as the Countryside Agency. Linda Salway on behalf of Waverley said that organisations in receipt of organisational development funding would naturally expect money to be available to enable further development and it was understandable that the director and management of Cranleigh Arts should feel frustrated, more so in view of the fact that it was not possible to apply for project funding. The Treasurer adds that with building overheads then the financial picture for 2004/5 may be problematic. We will see that this dilemma and the shift in central policy would lead indeed to future

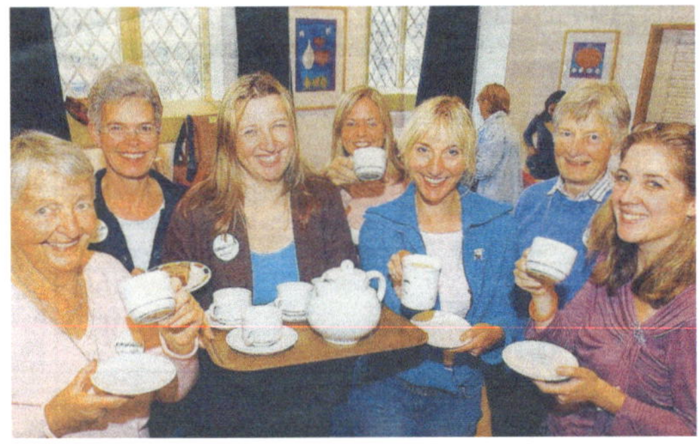

Fundraising coffee morning.

problems and near disaster in 2006. The Chairman thanked Mr Courtice for carrying out his work *"in such a pleasant, non-confrontational and stimulating atmosphere. It was very satisfactory that we were seen to be a well-managed organisation".* His report is thorough and lengthy. The minutes record that *"23 of the recommendations have been completed, recommendations 37, 40, 41, 43, which were urgent, are being dealt with."* Later reviews of progress go up to number 49 and seem largely to have been acted upon. They are across all areas of the operation and range from big to small – from risk analysis and health and safety to offering sandwiches at lunchtime concerts. He concedes *"The organisation has performed miracles with tiny resources. ... There are now real challenges to face".* He would like to see a more aspirational programme, including an artist in residence, better volunteer management and better marketing.

The autumn programme starts to introduce a shift in artistic policy to try out new elements such as puppetry for adults and introduce one off community projects with less artistic content with outside funding. However Rosemary Dubois complains that it was becoming increasingly difficult to programme arts activities and events due to the occupancy of the building by outside hirers from the expansion of commercial lettings.

Children's parties were a popular booking. On one occasion it was all set up in the Jack Wagg Hall with a mini trampoline, tables for refreshments and a showing of 'The Lion King'. Mark Matthews, the projectionist, had just set it going when reception phoned up to say that there were some suspicious people in the car park. He went to investigate and saw two women dripping in gold jewellery and four burly East European men in sunglasses in three large Range Rovers. He didn't approach them but got the manager to check the booking. The address was a large house in Hambledon and it turned out to be Roman Abramovich's brother who had made the booking, which explained the bodyguards. But really, in Cranleigh?

The winds of change and some gathering clouds

New people take charge as the financial prospect looks bleak

As 2003 changed to 2004 it was clear that the dial had not moved much on recurrent difficulties. A Risk and Health and Safety subcommittee had been instituted and had reviewed insurance and staff stress at its first meeting but hadn't managed to meet again. The accounts were looking better, but probably as a result of not paying the massive staff overtime bill that had accrued. Staff appraisals confirmed that despite the appointments made previously there was still a shortfall of 24 hrs per week and that they felt stressed and overstretched. Office space, with more people working was becoming a pressing issue and it was agreed to approach Arthur Gomez, the architect, to look at the feasibility of a rear extension, but where could the £30,000 come from for it? The building was five years old and already beginning to show some deficiencies. Vaughan Mitchell had a list including, boilers, air handling, blinds, tables and chairs and a dodgy computer system that had recently been hacked.

In May a third staff member was appointed – a Box Office Supervisor. Funds were in surplus and some reserves were in place thanks to the increased hires and the programme, which had averaged 76% capacity, so Richard Paton conceded that *"our top priority should now be to sort out our staff and salary structure before we contemplate more risky/less profitable programming or any diminution of commercial activity".* So additional staff costs were put in the 2004/05 budget. Emma Rafferty left to be replaced by Sue Palmer-Jones and Katy Gower was appointed Box Office Supervisor. This was a blow to Louise Grundy who had applied, but she was promoted to be Helen's PA and would deputise for her when she dropped to four days a week in September having been signed off sick in the summer with stress and anxiety.

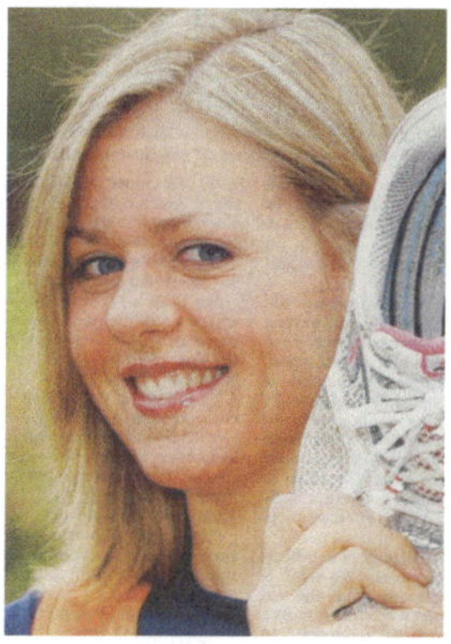

Katy Gower.

Catherine Pike felt that it was time to find her successor and wanted to take further Mark Courtice's review of the function and makeup of the Board. His skills audit had thrown up only a few gaps but he had said he favoured a larger number of members than at present, maybe ten. The crux was whether it needed now to evolve from what had been originally set up before the expansion. The search for new Board members resulted in five potential candidates. They were interviewed and three invited to join. They were: Joanne Barber, Director of the New Ashgate Gallery in Farnham, who only attends a few meetings in an eighteen month period; Nick Morris, retired Dean of the Arts and Media Surrey Institute, who had been involved before, with his wife Anita, when the Arts Council bid had been prepared. He resigns in 2006 after some frustration with delays and machinations. The last one was Rosemary French, Chief Executive of Surrey Business Link. She had been rung up by Ian Lynch of Waverley and asked to apply as *"there were financial issues at Cranleigh Arts and can you look at it? They have deep problems and can you help?"* She admits that she had lived in Cranleigh for a number of years and was a supporter of the arts but didn't know it existed as her work had taken her abroad a lot. She thought it would just be a couple of years, but like many before she was drawn in and became a key player when she had to tackle another of the episodic crises that the Centre faced in 2006.

This was foreshadowed at the November 2004 Board meeting when Catherine, Richard and Helen reported back on a meeting with South East Arts. While the meeting was positive and the programme received with approval it was made clear that the Centre would lose its Recurrently Funded Organisation (RFO) support from 2006 and only be eligible for Project funding. This was in line with other small centres such as Windsor and Havant as Rebecca Ball had flagged up over a year ago. By April 2005 two applications, for capital and project expenditure had to be submitted. Thereafter it was likely to be a three year application process. This appears not to have caused any immediate worry, perhaps as Rosemary French identified later, there was an attitude that *"oh well, the Arts Council won't let us down"*. But soundings by Helen and Linda Salway were that this was a settled policy and that all effort should be directed to project funding and the business plan redrawn.

2005 was set to be a crucial year of change. Just before Christmas Helen had put in her resignation to leave in February. Even on four days a week she realised that for her health and sanity she couldn't continue. She had given her heart and soul to the place and seen it through expansion, building the team, finding the right programme and embedding it in Cranleigh life. She felt she couldn't go through the cycle of financial instability and reinvention again. It was time. The front page of *The Surrey Advertiser* highlighted the funding struggle saying she *"left with a blast at the bureaucrats who determine the funding"*, quoting her: *"The frustration of having to constantly find funding rather than putting energy and expertise into extending the programme and opportunities for more people is something I did not personally want to undertake"*. At her leaving party Catherine Pike declared *"We all love Helen. She has built this place up into what it is"*. Helen admitted to having mixed feelings about leaving adding *"it's that community feeling in Cranleigh that I shall miss because I have never come across it so strongly anywhere else. ... I believe the arts can transform lives and a community and the arts centre can make a huge difference"*.

The Board agree a plan of action. Adverts went out for applications by the start of February and the interview panel of Catherine, Rosemary French, Rebecca Ball (South East Arts) and Linda Salway (Waverley) suggested. To cover the gap between Artistic Directors Shalini and Louise Grundy would be paid to take on extra responsibilities with Kate Pearson, the Administrator. Helen would have the arts programme in place up to August before she left. Together she was working with Nick Morris on a redraft of the Artistic Policy which was predicated on three strands: Children and young people, Nurturing emerging artists, and New audience development. Before she left Helen would ensure that Job Descriptions were updated to reflect current responsibilities.

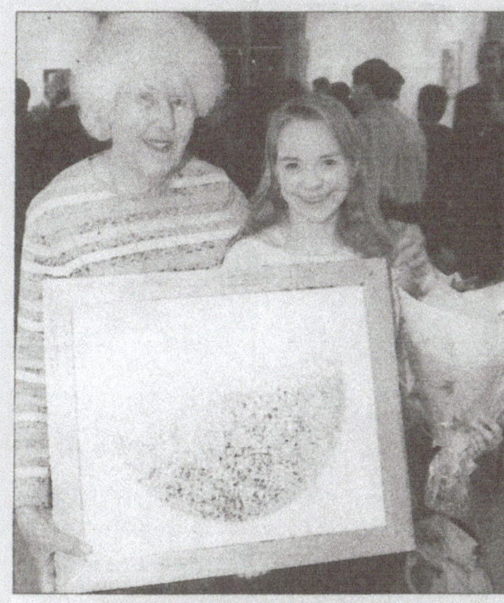

Dr Catherine Pike presents Helen Cundy with her leaving gift.

Fond farewell as arts centre director leaves

Richard Paton, Helen, Chrissy and Rosemary French were tasked to redraw the Business Plan. The successful stretched arts programme under Helen had contributed £30,000 profit to the nine month budget but going forward, with the loss of South East Arts RFO funding, that profitability needed to continue and perhaps increase. In total a further £65,000 subsidy would be needed from somewhere. Operational costs were up and some income streams down. Investigation into these was needed. There were plenty of numbers but the story behind them wasn't always clear. Richard Paton did a model budget on a Project Funding basis and found *"Somewhat to my surprise the model shows that Project Funding could work, if certain assumptions are true and/or acceptable"*. By this he refers to the loading of substantial 'overhead' costs as management fees to the projects and assumes the carry forward of many existing activities as 'projects'. This would be optimistic and a potential fatal flaw.

A new Centre Director, a new Chairman, a new direction

The two new people have high hopes but does either have a full grasp of the situation as the implications of policy changes become very real

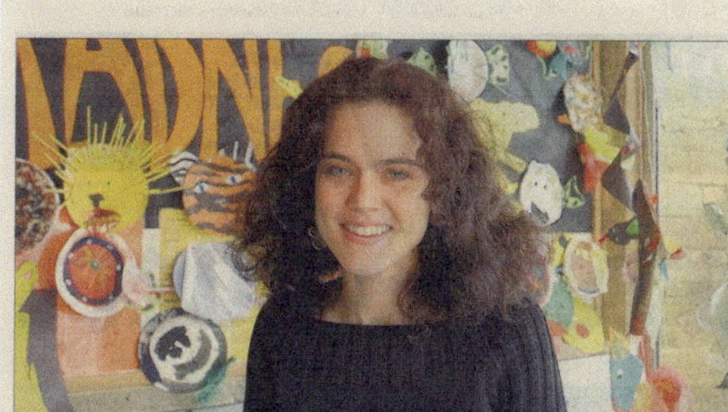

Debbie Stubbs is the new manager at Cranleigh Arts Centre.

Creativity is the game for new manager

In April 2005 Debbie Stubbs was appointed Centre Director. Whether she was to prove to be the Arts Centre's saviour or its nemesis depends on who you talk to. She had previously been Director of Windsor Arts Centre and been a community arts development officer for Kensington and Chelsea and South Buckinghamshire councils. Her brief, which she seemingly had a track record of, was to formulate the project bids to ensure the continued funding of the Centre. A newspaper profile of her in May is headed **'Creativity is the game for new manager'**. It reports:

> *"She is keen to build on the arts centre's successes, including the FLY project and sees great opportunities for 'creative visioning'. Debbie said: 'It's a chance now for real creative thinking in terms of where it is going and in terms of artistic output and input. It depends on the community and what they aspire to – the building has the potential for so much.' She is attracted by the potential for working outside the actual building, pointing to next month's repeat of last year's successful open air theatre production at Snoxhall and to involvement in the Cranleigh festival. 'I'm just planning to see where we can take it really,' she added."*

One of her colleagues described her: *"She was beautiful, had lovely hair, the most beautiful piercing blue eyes, she wore wacky clothes. Couldn't navigate her way out of a paper bag. Came from Windsor a different way every day."* Her expansionist plans resulted in various trips out to buy things for the Centre, making light of queries as to where the money would come from. She often referenced the successful Battersea Arts Centre as a model. She drew up budgets and spreadsheets, but when the numbers were checked with colleagues they often had to be revised, one wondering whether she might have had dyscalculia. She did report to the Board that they were overspending, which had become increasingly clear to the Bookkeeper and Treasurer, but she reassured them that all would be well and they believed her.

In May Kate Pearson, the Administrator, resigns to continue her MA and move north back to her family. In June Catherine Pike hands over the Chairmanship to Rosemary French, who asks for Nick Morris to be her Vice-Chairman. She writes to the volunteers to introduce herself.

> *"It is a great honour to be elected to take over from Catherine Pike as Chair. ... I will not be an exact replacement for Catherine because inevitably we are all individuals and will do things differently. However I will bring a new pair of eyes to the Cranleigh Arts Centre at a pivotal moment in its funding history. ... As Chair I bring 24 years of business experience and 4 years leading a government funded business support agency. I am still fully employed by Business Link Surrey as its Chief Executive. The added value that I hope to bring to the Board is that of business nous and working relationships at a very senior level with key organisations such as SEEDA, Surrey Economic Partnership, Waverley Borough...*

> *...Council, Surrey Community Action and Surrey Learning and Skills Council. You will not see as much of me as you did of Catherine on a day to day basis .. therefore the Board has agreed to appoint a Vice Chairman to support me. [she gives details about Nick Morris] Between us we believe we have the bases covered!"*

Nick will have the artistic overview, Rosemary the business.

She is true to her word and presents a plan to recover from the loss of RFO funding at the June Board meeting for approval. This has three strands: increasing income from existing activities, sponsorship, and bids for funding arts projects, which would include a 20% overhead recovery element. *"Debbie will be the key driver of this programme and she must be given adequate time out to prepare funding bids, chase sponsorship and raise charges. Her background provides her with considerable experience in this area."* A risk analysis concludes, *"If this is planned properly and is managed by the Board properly and regularly we should be able to see our way through the first year. Other centres have successfully won this battle"*. Debbie is tasked to bring in £100k per year in quarterly successful bids. This was a big ask. Rosemary writes in the annual AGM report,

> *"Although the Arts Centre retains its charity status it is becoming increasingly clear that its activities, which are so important to the community of Cranleigh, will only be sustained through a commercially focussed view of the way ahead."*

Another change came in July when Derek Sanders is appointed Operational Manager to replace Kate Pearson, after a redefinition of the admin role which aims to ease the burden on the Centre Director. He was an interesting man who had been a litigation lawyer and drawn into the Centre through his passion for jazz, which he had promoted at the Centre. He becomes a key person moving forward, although one suspects he is having to 'learn on the job'. He is joined in September by Emma Terry as Part-time Marketing Executive, replacing Shalini. Despite warnings that Debbie would not be seen much as she would be heavily engaged in bid writing, she deputises in both these roles as part of her induction before their eventual appointments. Once they are in place she is able to rewrite the Business Plan: 'Footsteps for the Future 2005-2008' by November, but she is given a day out a week by Rosemary to work at home to draft bids, as she was concerned to find Debbie hadn't yet started on the current quarter's target of £25,000 of project funding. Debbie reports to the October Board a list of what she and Derek have been doing. This tends more towards recording activity rather than outcomes. Her Business plan in draft, which is on file, contains much narrative and summative material and policy appendices. It has aspirations couched in general terms and makes much of previous or already set up initiatives. The aims and objectives are broad:

"to celebrate our environmental heritage, diverse audiences and multicultural community.

"to empower and provide active involvement in quality creative experiences.

"to provide a significant cultural resource for all ages and abilities.

"to develop our business into new realms.

"to be a value for money social enterprise."

The specifics and measurable outcomes are sparce and the page 'Resourcing our new Strategy' blank. Maybe this was what the potential funders might have wanted to see but Chris Dubois, no slouch intellectually, recalls his frustration at a meeting on this with Debbie. He had to stop her and say *"I'm sorry I don't have a clue what you are talking about. Can you please put it in plain words".*

More change comes in August when Linda Salway announces she is leaving Waverley to be replaced by Emma Waters. She had given great support over the last few years, had contacts at the Arts Council and was well in with members. However the arrival of the very experienced, well-connected and dynamic Gavin Stride at the helm of Farnham Maltings had tilted the balance westwards. Emma was advised *"don't get embroiled in Cranleigh"*. Relations between the two cultural hubs in the borough became less easy as Cranleigh struggled. Some councillors were quite openly hostile. However Rosemary knew Gavin and felt that his support could be helpful, things could be learnt from him and that he did care about Cranleigh. In September she visits the Farnham Maltings with Debbie to meet the key people there and see what initiatives were working for them. It had held on to its RFO funding so was more secure. The Maltings could boast up to 700 members who paid subscriptions, a cash cow car park, as well as limitless rooms that could be made profitable. But still lessons could be learnt from our big brother, thought Rosemary.

What Debbie comes up with is a project called FUEL. There is some evidence that this is a Windsor Arts proposal that is being repurposed. A PowerPoint slide presentation on file is headed **'Plans for an international based Art and New Technology Platform Event'**. This envisioned a unique flagship event, breaking down barriers, to include flash mobbing, street art, local and national media engagement, concert, dance and theatre performances, innovative films, to bring new art practices to new audiences and to invigorate imaginations. While this might eventually have been refined for submission, Nick Morris, who had the artistic oversight, recalls going with Debbie to pitch this to the Arts Council, where *"she couldn't explain what this grand project was!".*

The fate of the Arts Centre rested largely in her hands now.

Chapter Eight

2006 The fight for survival

The big crash and the fight back

2006 Annus horribilis

Hard choices have to be made to stave off disaster

Over the course of 2006 the house of cards would gradually collapse and tough decisions had to be made to avoid extinction. However with the commitment of some key players and the support, yet again, of Waverley Borough Council, who were not going to allow failure, disaster was averted. But not without a lot of pain and heart searching. This was the closest Cranleigh Arts came to folding; some similar organisations were not so lucky. By examining the events in detail as they unfolded we can see how it is a combination of factors. The Board don't always know clearly what is going on at ground level. The staff either lack the skills or the resources to honestly deal with the problems this crisis brings. The community and funders lose confidence in the team to deliver. Poor communication and a 'head in the sand' tendency of some also doesn't help. Despite being triggered by a shift in national circumstances and policy it was the complexity of the problems and the character of the participants that nearly brought about the demise of the Centre.

The bleak financial prospects were spelled out by Richard Paton at January's Board. Here there was frustration that margins were not sufficiently monitored and that *"we need to know where CAC makes money and where it loses money"*. Rosemary French summed it up, *"We are always looking back at cash flow, but cannot budget forward as we do not know in advance what profit contribution each activity will make"*. Procedures for expenditure approval were also required urgently. The bookkeeper, Sue Palmer-Jones, had raised her concerns about all the unrestricted spending that was going through the accounts with Richard, but feels she has no authority to intervene. She resigns shortly after. What had happened to all Mark Wright's systems one wonders? Rosemary was frustrated and wanted more than historical interim accounts. She was astonished to find Databox (events and sales) and Sage (the accounts) were not integrated. However, an IT upgrade might improve that. Richard Paton argued that he was not a Finance Director, with the time to pore over every number, but rather a traditional Treasurer who has oversight, but not direct involvement. He is clear that Reserves were being depleted. Unless the Arts Council and other funding bids, which had just been submitted, bore fruit quickly insolvency loomed in March. Trust applications could take up to a year and Emma Waters, Arts Officer, said that budgets at Waverley had been frozen so no more money was likely from them. Future programming and ticket sales of the summer season must be reviewed in March 'to see if we can continue to trade'. A request from Debbie for increased staff hours was deemed 'absolutely impossible'. Debbie had some good news however that staff were working well, the Light up Cranleigh project with grant support had been successful and a Friends relaunch event had had a 20% uptake, taking Friends to 185. Increased audience limits from a new licence had helped expand capacity for popular events and prices had also been raised across the board. Oil on troubled waters?

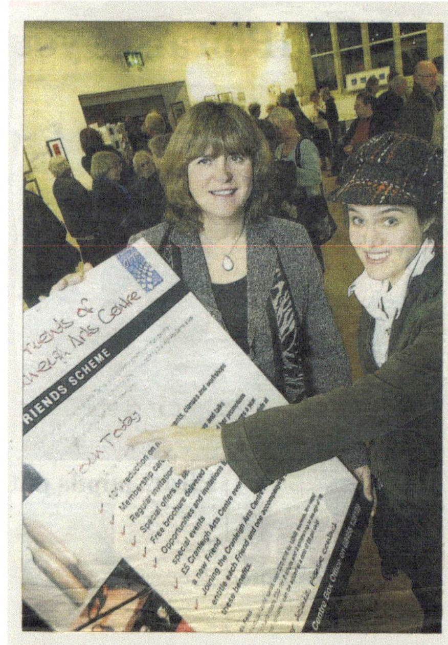

Rosemary and Debbie

However things had come into much sharper focus by March. Rosemary could see that staff levels could not be sustained and takes firm action. She writes to all staff *"informing you of the unfortunate need to reduce our headcount to make savings as a result of the loss of the Arts Council RFO grant"* and put all on notice of redundancy, a legal requirement if staff cuts were eventually to be made. The first to go was Louise Grundy, Director's PA, although she continued to serve as an art tutor and, as we will see, waits in the wings for future developments. Her letter to the Board expresses mixed feelings.

"I have enjoyed working at CAC over the past six years, starting with the Arts and Crafts Club, being asked to do "a bit of admin just up to Easter" and here I am 5 years later being made redundant! I worked my socks off supporting the Arts Centre, when people were ill and money tight, I was there. The challenge gave me confidence to have a go at anything ... from organising the Lantern parade with its 19 workshops 150 lanterns 300 participants and 30 stewards within a £5,000 budget to manning the box office and balancing the takings...

...I will miss working with the volunteers ... They are most important to the running of the Arts Centre, look after them, you can't do without them. I will miss the children and their parents, who not only come to the art classes to learn something but also come to gain confidence in a loving and sharing environment. I believe this important aspect is slipping away from the Arts Centre. ... I will have good memories, putting away the raised seating whilst irate Bridge players wait outside the door, driving a 25ft paper mâché Hare to Winkworth Arboretum on the top of my car ... the Madness premier with everyone dressed up ... I am sad to go and I still don't understand why. You knew nearly a year ago we had this deficit and, it seems, little has been done about it in time."

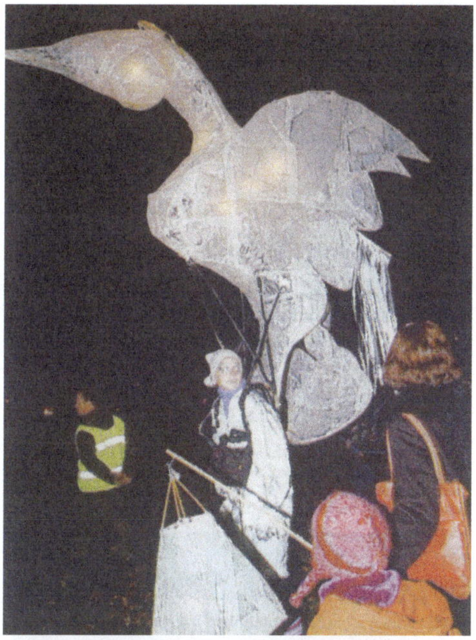

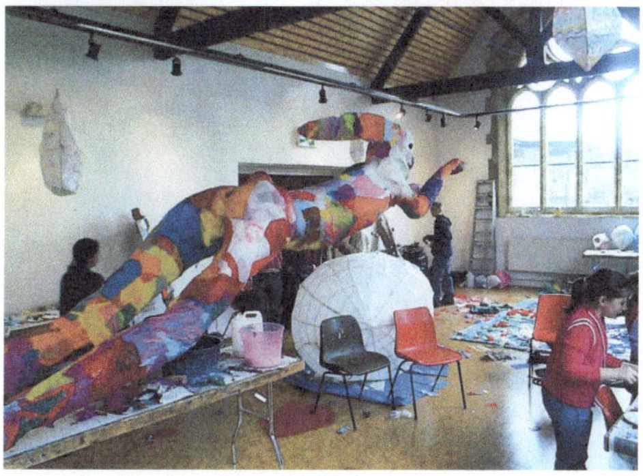

The Board meeting on 29th March signals how bad things were becoming. Richard Paton presented his budget for the new financial year and a concluding summary for 2005/06. Despite a 10% increase in revenue, staff costs had wiped that out by increasing too. Richard Paton is clear in his report. The deficit of £15,000 for the current year would wipe out the reserves. Going forward the FUEL project grant of £34,500 would be crucial income in July, losses in the first quarter would not be covered without it. But insolvency was a strong possibility despite the positive cash flow being sustained by advance sales and grant payments. A working party of Nick Morris, Richard, Rosemary and Chris Dubois had come up with a financial model to recommend to the Board.

Rosemary French reported on a consultation meeting with Waverley at the end of February, and her own thoughts about the finances and strategy. The meeting with Waverley was to get assurances that CAC was in full control of its resources and was taking appropriate action. Brian Long (Waverley Finance Director), Julie Maskery (Waverley Head of Leisure Services) and Emma Waters (Waverley Arts Link Officer) attended with Rosemary, Richard and Debbie. Julie led that they really wanted to support CAC but there was no more from her funding. She felt that CAC had been let down by the Arts Council, who perhaps had an aim for small centres to disappear, but that she was not going to let that happen. A vicious circle developed that project funding potentially drove out regular activity, and that innovative new work would come at the expense of community arts. Julie said that it was necessary to weigh up where money could be found and follow that route. The community role is worthwhile but not key to survival. She would try to engineer some pressure on the Arts Council and wanted CAC to push for more than moral support from the Parish Council. Rosemary suggested some joint bidding with Farnham Maltings.

> *"Julie said that Gavin Stride was already keen to do so but had been concerned that he might be 'railroading' CAC. Rosemary said that she felt that we could cope with that in return for the joint benefits both organisations could reap."*

The minutes conclude: *"Julie wanted to know if we were prepared to take hard decisions to improve profitability and we said we are and that it was good to have Waverley's backing"*. To a great extent this set the direction of travel for the next few years.

Rosemary also presents them with her thoughts on Richard's *"valiant attempts to make the Budget balance for next year"* and begins in reflective mood.

> *"I look back and wonder what I had missed to get into this situation. Certainly being new to the job does not help. But it is more than that. I came into it believing that the Arts Centre was in a breakeven/small profit position and that we were losing £25,000 of Arts Council funding in 2006/7. What I had not reckoned on was that the performance this year has resulted in such a huge loss and will be compounded to a total £45,000 loss next year without a brave strategy to combat this. And yet this year has been one of the busiest, most active, most events, most diverse activity etc in the history of the Centre. I wonder if we have tried to be a city, or at least a town-based arts centre instead of a rural village centre of arts related activities. You can take a horse to water but you cannot make it drink and Cranleigh is that horse. We have seen fantastic events that have been well marketed and well-priced half empty or worse. We have seen little enthusiasm for becoming a Friend of the Centre and we have seen little will by retailers and business people to support the Centre. ...*

> *... We have been busy fools. It is probably time to stop battling for audiences and face facts. We need to cut back and cut back hard to survive. And we need to make that decision very, very soon."*

She goes through the numbers and finds some overoptimistic. More staff cuts save money but reduce activity. Higher prices lead to a drop in numbers,

> *"but that could lead to a rationalisation of offering, concentrating on attendees who are willing to pay for classes that they really want. If we do not have an arts centre anymore then the classes go down the pan anyway. So our strategy could be that children's and adult workshops and theatre can only occur if full price is paid or if a subsidy is provided through a grant. A brave move but one we have to face."*

She concludes that a worst case scenario would be no FUEL grant and a loss of £26k on operations would then be untenable and *"I would not proceed, but hand in the towel"*. A better outcome would be the grant coming through and retrenchment to reduce costs and maximise profitable activity *"but still hugely difficult"*.

The Board approves the following actions. That Debbie should work three days a week on bids. Derek will run the Centre when she is not there. The Trustees back their staff despite a lack of confidence in them from the rest of the users of the Centre. A subgroup is set up to work out a 'core' programme for May-August. A subgroup is instituted to work on a fundraising survival campaign. Communication of the situation to staff and the wider stakeholders is to be carefully managed by Rosemary and Debbie. A press release is issued which having outlined the situation includes this.

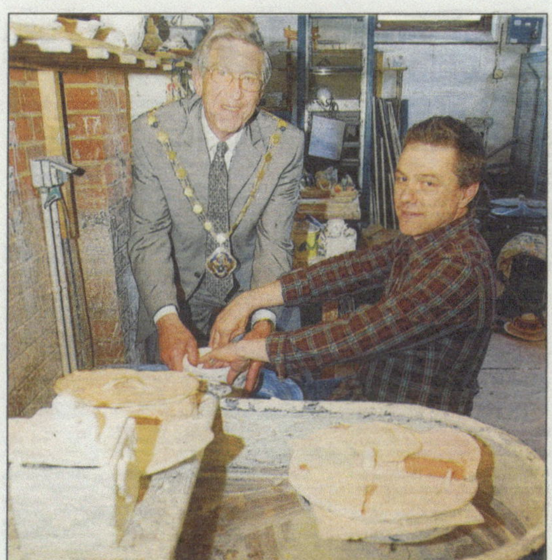

The Mayor of Waverley, David Inman, tries his hand at pottery with operations manager, Derek Sanders on a visit to Cranleigh Arts Centre.

Being arty at open day

> *"Staff are being made redundant and activities curtailed in order to balance the books. Over the next few months it will become clear what level of project grant*

funding the Arts Centre can expect. To be prudent the Board of Directors has agreed as of now a programme which reduces our current expenditure and those activities which are no longer financially viable. The future level of project grant funding will determine our programme – indeed the existence of the Centre – over the next year."

Rosemary writes to all staff and volunteers in more detail on 7th April. She outlines the situation and the measures that have been put in place. Again stress is put on the outcome of the FUEL bid in June. She concludes:

"Our situation is not unusual in the voluntary Arts Centre world. There are another 100 similar organisations in England at the moment that have had their annual Arts Council funding removed. They, like us now, are having to apply for individual projects instead – these projects need to be of very high artistic standard and preferably should attract new audiences from disadvantaged groups, which makes it even harder for Cranleigh. ... The Board knows that there will be huge disappointment at losing so many of our popular activities but we are in a position where 'needs must' to survive."

Cutbacks and resignations

Rosemary circles the wagons to defend against insolvency

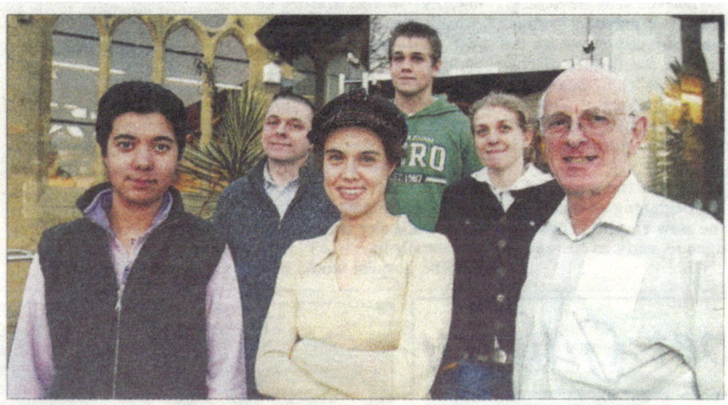

Arts Centre staff. Director Debbie Stubbs (centre) with, from left, Anita Lala, Derek Sanders, Ryan Pannell, Ruth Eastelow, and Vaughan Mitchell. C5470813

Finally at March's critical meeting Vaughan Mitchell had reported on the state of the building. His report lists difficulties with electrical supply, the boilers and IT. He remembers some disagreements with Debbie at the time, where she seems to have been slow picking up on the requirements of the building and the expertise of the volunteers who dealt with the technical side. His final items show his frustrations.

"The Ladies loo remains unfit for its purpose, despite promises that it would be finished by now and is a major turnoff among many of our customers. The decision to start a major refurbishment of the loos, while admirable in itself, was a bad

decision, being a text book example of the consequences of starting a project without having the necessary resources to see it through. Hopefully those responsible will have learned from this experience. In the last few days I have learned of the FUEL project, and its likely consequences – major building structural and usage changes. The level of my involvement in this project makes it impossible for me to continue to report on the state of the building to the Board."

Richard Paton has also had enough and puts in his resignation at the March meeting. He writes:

"This is not a sudden or spur-of-the-moment decision and the reasons are largely personal. ... I am probably doing three or four times as much voluntary work as I ever intended in retirement. It is time to cut back and the only way is to be firm and resolute about it. ... I think it is best to go at the Company's year end and before it enters the next stage of its financial life. There is a secondary reason for resigning, which is the scope of the Treasure's responsibilities. ... It has become clear in recent months that a much more pro-active financial control role is required at Board level and this represents a commitment that I am neither willing nor able to make."

Four days later Nick Morris writes a confirmation of his resignation to Rosemary:

"When I joined the Board I believed that my particular experience in Art, Design and Media would be a useful addition to the range of skills that Board members bring to the oversight of the Centre. At that time the revised Arts Policy provided an opportunity for activities at CAC to develop into new areas which I felt would be exciting and beneficial to its future. I fully appreciate that present financial constraints must put any such developments low on the list of priorities. I fully support the strategy that the Board agreed at its last meeting but believe that for at least the medium term future CAC does not require the particular skills that I can offer."

The Board meets next in mid-May. Rosemary's report is blunt. While acknowledging the progress made with establishing the core programme (Chris Dubois and subgroup) and the Fund Raising Public Appeal Campaign (Chrissy Matthews and Emma Terry) she was blunt that if the FUEL bid is not granted in July then there would be no alternative but to wind down the staff and activities and become a hiring and cinema venue. Meetings with Waverley had taken place in April and May at which they seemed reassured and said they would do all they could to help. But they had concern that there was now no director with financial oversight. Suggestions were canvassed. However they had appreciated being informed of the situation as early as this, unlike the Redgrave Theatre in Farnham which had not, and subsequently closed.

Debbie's report to the Board covered the bids made. There was a long list of possibles but little progress, if the file copy of the spreadsheet is anything to go by. Apart from the pending FUEL bid there was only one received from the Parish Council. Debbie explained the FUEL project as submitted in April. It involved three artists in residence to create new work and workshops, as well as support for existing artists. There were three strands or subprojects – FIRE – digital arts and presentations. SALT – dance and performance. EXPO – visual arts and exhibition. Also FRONT ROW – for seat sponsorship and fundraising and TASTE – for a healthy eating café and creative arts workshops. *"In delivering FUEL we will generate a heightened concentration of new innovative artistic energy."* Collaborators had been identified. A transformation of the spaces in the Centre for exhibition and creativity was proposed. In year one it would be indoor commissions, in year two outdoor commissions and in year three street works using mobile phones and a flash mob. All the bids were interwoven except FRONT ROW. There were a lot of eggs in this particular basket.

After these heady dynamic aspirations the Board moved to consider more mundane suggestions such as a banner outside saying **'Support us or lose us!'** and Chris's practical suggestions to stagger hours, when to close and how to manage cost and revenue. He also alerted the meeting to the fact that Derek, now largely in control, was a bit disorganised and needed clear direction. Other colleagues testify that he gave his time generously, had good engagement with the public and was enthusiastic for the arts, if a bit of a dreamer. Finally, Rosemary paid tribute to Chris and Chrissy *"who have worked beyond their remit as volunteer Directors to help us pull through this. All three of us have full time jobs and the CAC work over the past two months has been considerable. We cannot go on behaving as CEOs for ever, but we think we need to last out until September before handing the Centre back to the Management Team".* The Trustees had been working hard to prop things up, but did she know what would happen next?

A sudden departure

The lynchpin is removed

On the 15th June Rosemary writes to the Board.

"I regret to inform you that Debbie Stubbs has decided to leave Cranleigh Arts Centre and to move to the North. This is a lifestyle decision for her and her partner so they can actually afford a house of their own. Her decision has absolutely not

been influenced by the campaign of harassment by a certain tutor in the Centre. I have been unable to persuade her to remain and she will leave next week. Chris Dubois and myself have been aware of Debbie's decision for two weeks but unable to share it with you due to the both of us taking holidays."

She and Chris would meet when he gets back to formulate a plan for July's meeting but otherwise 'keep calm and carry on' is the message. The timing of this could not have been more catastrophic and one must question Debbie's motivation. Was she crumbling under the pressures of the job or did she have a premonition that the FUEL bid, on which so much depended, would not be successful? She had not always got on with the team, despite her positive messaging back to the Board. *"You could never get hold of her,"* one colleague said. *"I would find her crying in the toilet,"* said another. Whatever the truth of the matter, she was gone with immediate effect. She had been in post for just over a year. Both within the Centre and outside there had been reservations about her leadership. Complaints had been circulating about her which had reached Waverley. Both John Savage (Waverley Councillor) and Emma Waters (Waverley Arts Officer) had privately expressed concerns. An outside observer must wonder, did she jump or was she pushed? When contacted for this book she replied,

"I had the privilege of serving as Director of the Arts Centre for a brief period, during which I formed many cherished memories from around 2005. [She continues by listing and praising Catherine Pike, Rosemary French, Rosemary Dubois and many of the staff team at the time.] *It was truly a privilege to work with such a dedicated and talented team. Feel free to ask any questions that would be helpful for your publication."*

When asked some follow up questions about the bid, her management and her sudden exit she did not respond. The Board members of that time have been similarly reluctant to comment.

Rallying round to keep the Centre open

Efforts from all quarters enable a change of direction and survival

Two weeks later Rosemary French calls an emergency meeting. She has had meetings with the Arts Council and with Julie Maskery (Waverley Leisure Officer) and Gavin Stride (Farnham Maltings). The FUEL bid is unlikely to succeed without a project director and would probably not bring in enough, so should be withdrawn as it is now dead in the water. Cashflow is exhausted so insolvency threatens. Calls for sponsorship and local support has resulted in little interest. Waverley is supportive but very clear about what should happen. Julie writes:

> *"Further to our discussions on Monday I would like to reiterate Waverley's position. It is acknowledged that the current model for delivery is unsustainable and that the Centre has been facing both operational and financial problems for some time. We also appreciate that the current Board must take immediate action to deal with the cash flow deficit. However the Council as a key funder must be assured that any future model of management is established on a sound basis and I am of the opinion that the consideration of a partnership with the Maltings is a commendable proposal and may lead to a longer-term sustainable and more strategic way forward."*

She goes on to say that the council has offered core funding in order for the Centre to provide cultural activities and develop arts initiatives.

> *"If no long term sustainable and financially viable model of operation can be established, which would enable such activities to be delivered by the Centre, then there would be question over whether the Council would continue to provide the same level of funding as currently offered. The Council would also want to ensure that the Users, Friends, Members and Volunteers of the Centre are fully engaged in the process, and we welcome your commitment to this involvement."*

So the die is cast. Waverley will only offer a bailout if radical change is instituted to go back to first principles of arts management and provision.

First the cash flow had to be stabilised. The Board agreed that the Centre would be run as a low-level operation for the next three months with a no-risk programme and reduced opening hours. During this period only the Operations Manager and a cleaner would be retained, the rest of the staff would be made redundant. The aim would be to relaunch in the autumn and subgroups with set terms of reference were immediately constituted to move forward quickly.

Group One – to manage the Funding Stakeholders
Group Two – Cashflow and analysis of Creditors
Group Three – Programme Management during suspension and for relaunch
Group Four – The Farnham Maltings Collaboration Group
Group Five – Public Relations

The membership consisted of the remaining Board members, key volunteers and Emma and Katy, the two staff, for their four weeks' notice period.

The Arts Council offered £5,000 grant for operational development and Waverley seconded Brian Long, their Finance Director.

This flurry of activity steadied the ship and brought a sense of purpose, but it did not go down well. Rosemary French says that she received abusive letters pushed through her door. Rosemary Dubois reported back on a meeting with volunteers that there was 'much anger' at how things had been managed, sympathy for staff, and questions asking justifiably why this hadn't been foreseen by the Board, as well as critical of the effects of overexpansion. Since volunteers were a major stakeholder they wanted access to the Board. Sharon Duggan, who ran regular singing courses, workshops and the Cranleigh Community Choir at the Centre as well as previously helping as a volunteer, was typical of the many people who had loyally supported the Centre for years and felt let down by the bad management by the Board and by the recently departed Centre Manager. She had also set up The Cranfold Collective which represented a group of about 25 local artists, many of whom were connected to the Arts Centre. The volunteers and hirers had been dissatisfied with how things were being run for the last year and had made complaints to the Board and anyone else who would listen, including the Charity Commission. This disconnect between the Trustees and the users of the Centre became a big problem, with the staff being caught in the middle.

Inevitably this hit the press on 14th July: **'Arts Centre in cash crisis'** *Surrey Advertiser*. **'Arts Centre staff axed'** *County Times*. Front page articles explained the situation and quoted from a press release from Rosemary. In this the stress is put on rallying round to keep the Centre going, and the prospect of public consultation going forward. Part of this was also in a statement which was read out to the audience before ticketed events.

There were also personal issues putting additional stress on staff, especially Derek, at this crucial time. Over the last six months he had been having a clandestine relationship with Emma Terry, despite both being already married. She was signed off with stress for a week at the beginning of June, writing to explain to Debbie, *"I have realised that I am no longer able to effectively keep my personal stress out of the building and away from my colleagues and I feel being afforded the opportunity to focus on this particularly difficult period during my divorce proceedings for a short time will help towards me getting back on top of things"*. She will work from home in the interim and be back on the 14th. She was a very good marketing person and had been commended for her good work. The following Monday she and Derek, who is working with little back-up trying to manage staff hours, have a blazing row over her work and hours, with her accusing him of discrimination, which is overheard by a volunteer and she storms out saying she is leaving. This is presumably smoothed over and within a month she has been made redundant, but works her notice productively, although he is kept on. The volatility of the relationship is shown by her coming back repeatedly later to see him at the Centre. On one occasion Derek and Chrissy Matthews were meeting in the office and saw her drive into the carpark, take a hammer from her car and smash his windscreen. Chrissy calls the police and has her escorted from the premises. It is understood they did subsequently settle happily together and had a child in due course.

The Board next meet at the end of July to take stock, at a crowded meeting with 18 round the table, comprised of eight trustees and ten stakeholders and consultants. While being reassured that each subgroup was delivering on their immediate tasks, discussion centred on how to move forward. The Arts Council and Waverley were offering short term funding to allow breathing space for organisational development and strategizing to *"get the future 'vision' for CAC right"*. In summary they heard the Operations Manager had an impossible brief at present and needed much support in the running of things. Events and programme could be delivered, but not the wider range of managerial tasks. Currently trustees, notably Chrissy, Rosemary Dubois, Chris Dubois, Vaughan and Catherine, were covering much of this. Gavin Stride offered to help achieve the essential separation of governance, management and leadership by seconding one of his team from the Maltings for one day a week. So it transpired.

Another key person new to the meeting was Stephen Dennison. He knew the Centre through the involvement of his wife, Gina, as a regular box office volunteer and Friend. Rosemary had used his company Strategic Planning Solutions (SPS) at Business Link Surrey. SPS consulted on financial restructuring. Initially she had asked his accounting partner Dick Haynes to run the rule over the finances, now that Richard Paton was no longer available, and to report back to Brian Long, Finance Director at Waverley. Some of the money from the Arts Council for organisational development would enable Stephen to facilitate two strategic group discussions in the autumn. He would be a key player in the years to come, joining the Board in March and taking over from Rosemary as Chair, when her time was up.

By the September Board meeting the dust is settling, although things are completely being run by trustees Catherine Pike, Rosemary Dubois and Chrissy Matthews and three part time duty managers, as Derek has been off sick with depression, which continues through the autumn and he eventually resigns in December. Dick Haynes and Chrissy have done wonders for the accounts and procedures, which had gone to pot previously. Despite the 'core' programme restriction having to meet the 20% margin threshold, the Centre was busy and money coming in. A bid had gone to Waverley for a £20,000 'lifeline' to pay off creditors now and stay solvent until March 2007, which was likely to be given now that they knew things were stable and transparent. Small Project funding had been granted by the Arts Council to pay for Jane Friend, Deputy Director of Farnham Maltings, to spend one day a week at Cranleigh for twelve weeks. Each week she was focussing on one aspect of the Centre's operation. This would result in a summary report. She gathered evidence from everyone including the key stakeholders. She found a lack of systems, poor communication between Board members, staff and volunteers, uneven pricing and delivery, but excitement at the potential of the Arts Centre. She concluded that *"she felt optimistic that the Centre could emerge more robust from the present situation"*.

On 26th September the Charity Commission wrote to the Trustees with good and bad news. A complaint had been made about the trustees making changes to the activities of the charity and about unresolved difficulties in obtaining tickets. With regard to the first the Commissioners said, *"the trustees of a charity have considerable powers to act in the best interests of the charity and we will not normally intervene simply because there is a disagreement with a decision that the charity's trustees have lawfully taken, even if it is an unpopular one"*. They are satisfied that Cranleigh Arts has taken professional advice regarding the strategic planning of the charity's activities and financial planning in the current circumstances. Regarding the second they are concerned that beneficiaries are complaining and recommend that the trustees have a policy to involve themselves where concerns cannot be dealt with at an administrative level. Criticism is made in that they also pick up that the accounts for 2004 and 2005 have not been audited as required, and for 2006 have not yet been submitted.

The November Board meeting can be optimistic. Waverley had granted the money so good headlines can be posted: **'Funding reprieve allows art centre to plan for future'**. Councillor Byron Grainger-Jones had spoken up in support and having outlined all the reviews that had taken place concluded, *"The Arts Centre is such an important resource to this part of the borough and we are now optimistic about its future"*. A new bookkeeper is now in place so Chrissy can turn to marketing, posting stories about exhibitions, upcoming events and fundraising, which include a celebrity concert by Paul Jones, which raises £6,000 and the sale of a Cranleigh Calendar at Cranleigh

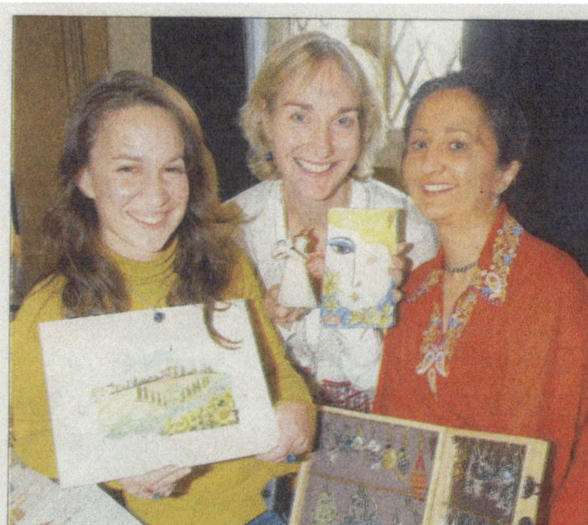

Mariana D'Ambrosio, Katharine Gordon and Shalini Bhalla.

It's a beauty of a bazaar

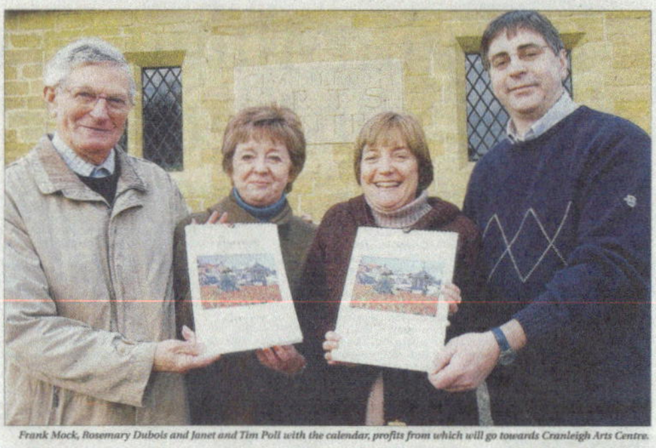

Frank Mock, Rosemary Dubois and Janet and Tim Poll with the calendar, profits from which will go towards Cranleigh Arts Centre.

Villagers make a date for charity

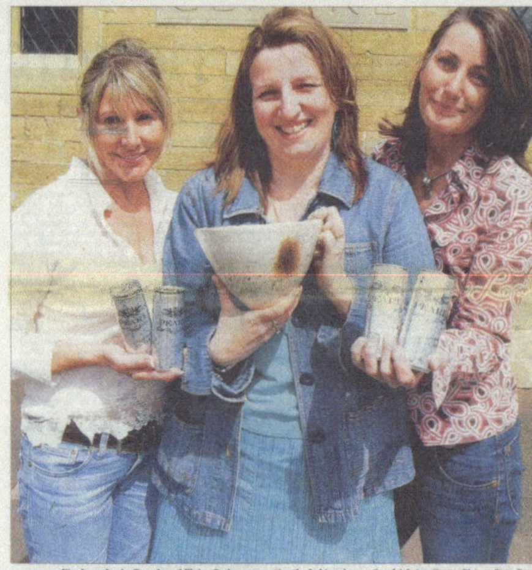

Kim Lowe, Louise Grundy and Elaine Graham promoting the fashion show at Cranleigh Arts Centre. Picture: Steve Porter.

Models go potty in style

News, which makes £1,000. This will build towards a Spring season relaunch. It had been a close call, but the vision had survived, just.

Partnership and restructuring 2007 – 2009

Management support from Farnham Maltings allows a new professionalism to stabilise the running of the Centre with not one but two managers

In the New Year Rosemary writes a letter to volunteers, staff, tutors, users and the community. She pays tribute to the support of local councillors and other people for helping CAC get back on its feet. She confirms the vision '**to enrich, entertain and inspire our community**' and says how that will be achieved going forward in eight bullet points. A core part of this will be *"by forming a strong strategic alliance with Farnham Maltings"*. This will *"increase the profile of cultural activity in Waverley, improve our ability to deliver creative activities, enrich existing strands of work and benefit from shared resources"*. This is as a result of Jane Friend's Report and Recommendations. There she took a dispassionate look at the running of the Centre, having talked, listened and delved into what had gone on. She finds the systems lacking, volunteers disenchanted, staff demoralised and the Board so busy firefighting that it can't see the wood for the trees. Her solution is to offer a service contract that the Maltings will provide management support for the next one to three years. This is strongly endorsed by Waverley who agree to fund it. There is a meeting to negotiate the detail and ensure that Cranleigh Arts does not lose its independence and that lines of authority and reporting are clear. Rosemary adds,

> *"We have learnt a salutary lesson through the Debbie Stubbs experience of the difficulties of applying for revenue funding for projects and activities. However*

with the help of Farnham Maltings we believe that we can rectify this."

A done deal is reported to the January meeting of the Board, subject to £12,000 funding approval in February. This is received and a three-year contract is drawn up.

Despite the previous loss of trust and goodwill over redundancy, Louise Grundy comes back as part-time temporary General Manager until the post can be advertised later in the year. *"I didn't want to see it going down the tube."* Emma Rafferty also returns as bookkeeper. However the Board is down to six as Vaughan has resigned along with Geoff Tresman and Joanne Barber steps down on maternity leave. Only Stephen Dennison has joined. The need for a Treasurer is urgent and soundings are made in all directions.

By May things were further stabilised. Paul Jones has taken on the role of Patron amidst much glowing publicity. Mike Kiernan has been suggested for Treasurer by Gavin Stride and he prepares the end of year accounts with a view to taking this on. Not one but two Operations Managers were appointed after advertising and interviews. They are Louise Grundy and Jenny Squire who will each do three days a week and were seen to have complementary skills, knowledge and experience. This gets good coverage. On the distaff side there had been criticism in the local paper of the cancellation of one of Tony Smith's Eclectic R&B concerts due to low bookings, which led to a flurry of letters to the editor, mostly in support and praising the Centre as a venue. At this time his concerts are seen as critical to the Centre's income. The money from Paul Jones goes into capital reserves and it pays for 40 extra seats to be installed upstairs in the Jack Wagg Hall to increase capacity, with further funds needed for more staging and new boilers, the old temperamental ones having been nursed through the winter by Vaughan, who has continued to volunteer in the building. All this makes good stories for the newspapers and show that things are improving.

By September things have bedded down. Mike Kiernan is on top of the numbers, although bookkeeper Emma Rafferty has now gone. He has simplified the system so that the Operations Managers can handle some of the finance and have a weekly check on things. The support of Chris Maddocks, Operations Manager at the Farnham Maltings, has been invaluable in all areas. The staff even have a small pay rise and the proposal is made to increase Louise and Jenny's hours. The autumn brochure, produced by Rosemary Dubois, is front page news in *The Advertiser* and there is a sense that the old confidence is returning. The differing approaches in the pairing of Louise and Jenny is typified by an anecdote. On one occasion an old man had an accident outside and came in with blood pouring from his head. The two leapt into action with the First Aid kit. Jenny was reading the instructions and procedures while it was Louise who actually mopped up the blood.

In November the bread-and-butter issues are to the fore; now the crisis has been averted the quotidian takes over again: the boilers, an attempted break in damaging the roof, the website's accuracy, the telephone system, Performing Rights liability, First Aid courses and CRB checks. The role of volunteers is being developed to provide 'back office' support and hospitality management for big hires is given to Janet Baverstock, Duty Manager. She is joined by newly recruited son Tom. Rosemary French can conclude the year in her quarterly letter with a celebration of a six months' period of success. She also announces that the joint managers roles are to be divided into: Louise: Operations, and Jenny: Administration, and new Board member applications are invited.

Confidence returns

An upward trend from working smarter shows that success breeds success

As 2008 gets under way contracts are reviewed, savings made on utilities, the Waverley grant renewed, and the Arts Council confirm funding to Waverley for three years of the 'Creative Alliance' with Farnham Maltings. There is evidence of a lot of learning from the Maltings which saves effort. Regarding the website there is access to their two days a week IT expert. There is a tightening up of volunteers' responsibilities and training, drawing on the Maltings' routines and paperwork. Chris Maddocks has become a trusted mentor to both Jenny and Louise. By March the Treasurer can report that *"the forecast for the full year continues to indicate a healthy surplus"*. Indeed it comes in at £18k which brings the reserves back up to 2003 level. The Friends are going to be relaunched (again!) with Diane Girling and Ken Tyrrell at the helm and help from Stephen Dennison. One perk is advance booking. With the Paul Jones Christmas Concert being so popular a trend develops that some people join as Friends just for that. Fundraising goes well generally with an Art Auction and a total of £6,000 for the boiler appeal raised from grants and donations. This is still only hallway to what is required but the Board decide to go ahead for June, eventually in fact September, and to push hard to get the extra needed. Three new initiatives emerge – an Awayday to help focus staff and Board on planning for the medium term in October; the

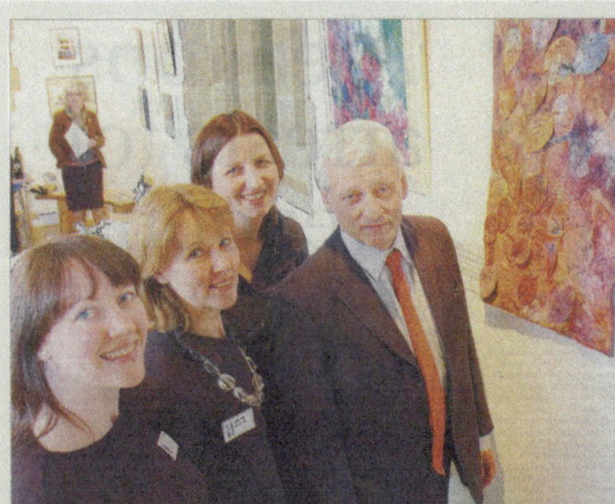

Centre managers Jenny Squire and Louise Grundy, with Lesley Jones, exhibition co-ordinator, and auctioneer Walter Benzie.

Auction of artworks helps centre

refurbishment of the Studio to make its use more efficient and attractive; and a complete overhaul of the IT systems. Closure in the summer in order to do maintenance, cleaning and painting is well supported. Another old friend returns – Shalini Bhalla as Dancer in Residence.

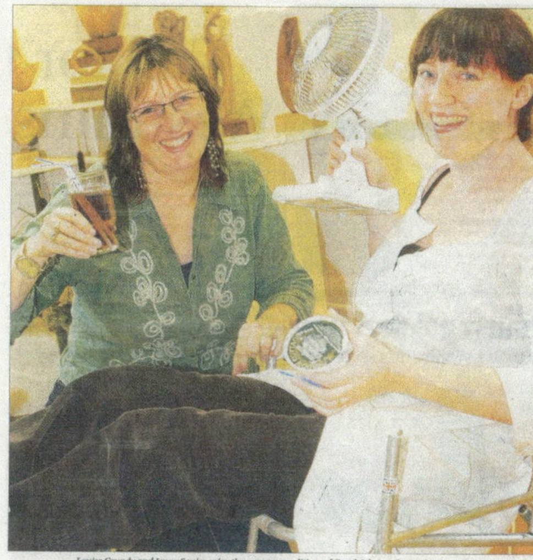

Louise Grundy and Jenny Squire enjoy the warmer conditions of Cranleigh Arts Centre thanks to the two new boilers.

Warm front ahead as boilers kick in

The Awayday has a packed agenda for its five hours with five submitted papers to lead discussion. Joining in was new Board member Hannah Kester, formerly a technician at CAC, now Manager at Chequer Mead Arts Centre, East Grinstead. The topics included: Involving Youth, which looked at policies and projects currently running and which could be enhanced; the area of Room Hire, and Volunteer Management, asking whether a dedicated administrator was needed. Obviously this couldn't be afforded at present but might be an option in the future. The oddities of the Board were discussed and the use of trustees as volunteers. A skills audit was taken but it had already been identified that the gaps of legal and fundraising expertise needed to be filled. To ensure membership of the Board continued to change it was proposed that time limits should be introduced. Changing the Memorandum and Articles of Association was complicated but should be looked at next year. The Alliance was reviewed from the Annual Report and seemed to be working well. Another Awayday was pencilled for next October.

By the end of 2008 the Centre is fizzing. Paul Jones presents his concert. Chris Dubois has retired and now has even more time to help in the running of the Centre. He focuses on policies and projects, particularly the Studio refurbishment and a rolling programme of capital expenditure for renewal as money becomes available, in the spirit of Jack Wagg. A big project combining a concert with an exhibition by Patti Boulaye is in the pipeline, which happens in 2009. International photojournalist Terry Fincher has a knockout exhibition, Cards for Good Causes set up their stall for Christmas, and even the Cranleigh Locality Office are considering moving in. Volunteers now number over 60 and Friends membership has doubled.

The confidence the organisation has had from its renewal has radiated out into the community. Rosemary is able to report to the AGM,

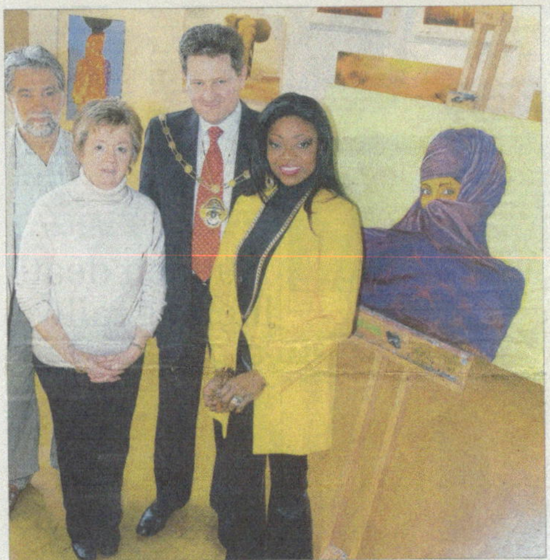

Patti Boulaye welcomes Tony Smith, Rosemary Dubois and the Mayor of Waverley, Cllr Len Bate, to her exhibition at Cranleigh Arts Centre. Picture: Chris Whiteoak.

Patti puts Africa in the picture

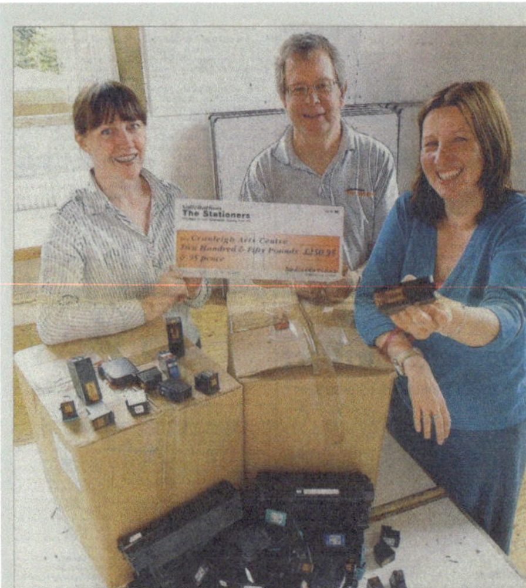

Bob Melvin of Solicitations presents a cheque to Jenny Quire and Louise Grundy of Cranleigh Arts Centre. The money was raised through a cartridge recycling project. Picture: Grahame Larter.

Making cartridges count

> *"CAC enters 2008/9 on a stronger position than for many years. The Board of Management will continue to oversee and drive CAC towards a future of financial sustainability which is the stated desire of our sole funder, Waverley Borough Council. However ... CAC will also work ever harder to deliver a service to the local community, which is of the highest quality, is well regarded, which attracts new audiences from all parts of the local population and which, most importantly, is used and appreciated by all."*

The confidence continues into 2009 as Waverley finds some money for the refurbishment of the Studio.

However staff overload is being reported by Louise and Jenny, backed by Chris Maddocks. Since the 'overstaffing' crisis of 2006 Rosemary had been of the view that the Centre should not pay staff to do work that volunteers could undertake. Indeed some had voiced opinions that the skills they had from their former careers were not always being recognised. Chris Dubois is tasked to undertake an organisational review to see who does what and who might do what, moving forward. Another cloud was that between Paul Jones's two Concerts, at which the surprise guest had been Eric Clapton, a break in had taken place and the safe was burgled. Over four thousand pounds had been in there, representing bar, ticket and raffle takings and floats. Although insurance covered it to an extent, it was still a financial hit. There were suspicions that it might have been an 'inside job' as some knowledge of what was where was needed and the mess made was superficial and cosmetic. The police did not find enough evidence to proceed with an investigation. Later receipts and other paperwork were discovered abandoned in a car park bin at Winterfold Heath. This crime followed the theft of lead from the Pottery roof a few months earlier. The episode cast a shadow, so security and procedures were tightened up as a result.

Some fine tuning

Stability at last as the organisation becomes streamlined and old issues resolved

In March 2009 Chris Dubois presents the results of his Organisational and Resources Study with his proposals. It is thorough and detailed as expected. He finds that there are not enough staff for the activities that are carried out. Of 52 'man-days' per week of work needed there is a shortfall of about 6 which would equal a person. The work done is made up of 20 days' worth by paid staff (which includes Duty Managers and Cleaning), 20 by volunteers and 6 by 'super-volunteers', experienced trusted people who know the Centre inside out, such as Rosemary Dubois, who is still backing up many areas, including Exhibitions and Programme. He finds that the dual Managers situation is unsatisfactory as they are often distracted away from their central tasks, too often firefighting; there is uncertainty over who does what, leading to poor delegation and supervision; there is little cover for absence and leave and there has been little time available to train and enhance their skills. There is not the headroom to develop procedures, external links, fundraising, marketing and the necessary growth of the organisation to match its recent success. He suggests appointing a third member of staff to oversee Box Office, Volunteers and Duty Managers. The Board discuss this and agree to start by moving to one Centre Manager, who, once appointed, can review and recommend other subsequent staff requirements. With a careful eye on employment legislation both current post holders are invited to apply for the job.

This again causes some concern amongst the supporters, so Rosemary French writes to volunteers, staff, tutors, users and the community in April to explain. She confirms that additional expenditure has been approved for an additional member of staff. She explains that there will be,

> *"a single Centre Manager, that has leadership responsibility for the whole Centre strategically, operationally, financially and artistically. Yesterday I spoke to Jenny and Louise and informed them of this restructure. Both of them welcomed the direction we were taking even though it effectively means that both their present roles are redundant. I have invited both Jenny and Louise to apply … Let me finally make clear that although the dreaded word redundancy had been mentioned in my letter, that this refers to the roles only and not to people. There is no reason*

why anybody who is presently employed by the Centre will no longer be employed by the Centre in the future, in particular Jenny and Louise. We have two excellent employees in Jenny and Louise and we hope to continue with both of them, albeit in different roles. Let me also dispel any myths that we are making these changes because of financial problems. This is absolutely not the case. We are making these changes because we have 'growing' pains!"

The village rumour mill had been working overtime once again it seems.

In May she writes again.

"Jenny Squire was the sole applicant for the new role of Arts Centre Manager. She will start in her new role on 11th May. … She is now planning three sets of actions to prepare the Arts Centre for future growth: review current activity; arrive at an appropriate staffing structure; review all income and expenditure."

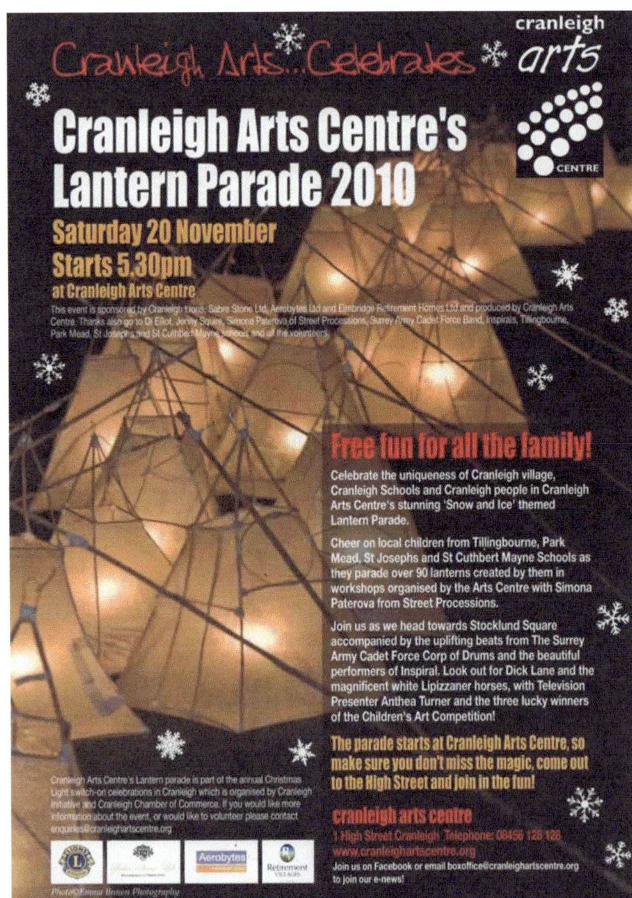

Louise had reduced her hours and taken some time off as sick leave. Once again the Centre was taking a toll on one of its staff. Apart from being an art tutor, Louise had been employed by the Arts Centre in three guises: working with Helen Cundy, saving the day after Debbie Stubbs's departure and latterly in partnership with Jenny Squire. Like many who have served the Arts Centre she gave it her all and worked over and above the call of duty. The projects she managed were headline events, like the Lantern Parade and FLY. She says,

"It was fun. We wanted it to survive. But after five staff had mental break-

> *downs you had to question. People worked their socks off, became ill. Worked their socks off, became ill. Reinvented the wheel, again! I became ill because I stopped making art. So I had to step back."*

Jenny Squire in sole charge proposes a new staff structure which the Board accepts. This is to have three staff reporting to the Centre Manager: Marketing and Box Office f/t (Tom Baverstock), Programme and Planning f/t (Ruth Eastelow), and Functions and Services p/t (Janet Baverstock). They settle into their posts as the autumn approaches and there is optimism that a stable staff team has been achieved, but volunteer support is still heavily engaged in the back office administration. Jenny outlined her vision for the future of a thriving, busy venue as *"Imagine having the best films, best concerts, best theatre, best exhibitions right on your doorstep".*

By July there is progress on some long 'ongoing' issues. TWM, local solicitors, have accepted a request from the Board for help with disentangling 'Members' and 'Friends', which could be submitted to the AGM. They want to be more supportive of Cranleigh Arts and suggest pro bono work in return for some advertising. There has been a better understanding of Waverley's position on the erection of a notice board outside, with one recently having arrived outside Mann's in the High Street. Made by Cranleigh School, they quote £2,500 for another one to be made! So it is put back onto the 'ongoing' list. A Risk Register has been instituted for Board review each meeting. This has thrown up issues of Health and Safety with regard to the equipment in the Jack Wagg Hall, so Chris Wilson, a freelance local theatre technician, is brought in to advise, an association which continues for many years. Storage, a perennial problem, has led the Youth Orchestra to move to the Band Room, as CAC cannot offer storage space for their instruments. However a big success is the refurbishment of the Studio with funds from Waverley and other fundraising. This was designed by Louise Grundy's father, John Malyon, and completed with volunteer

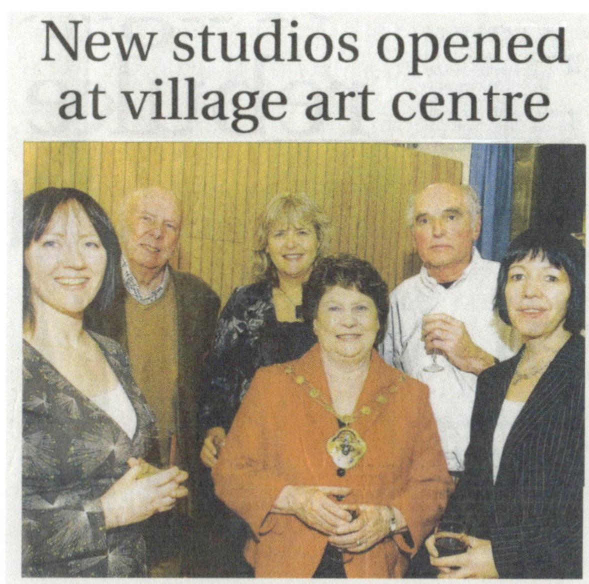

Jenny Squire, John Malyon, Rosemary French, Mayor Pat Frost, Andrew Maunder and Mary Orton.

labour, tightly managed by Chris Dubois. Such is his skill that they come in under budget and are able to pay for the mirrors down one wall which enables the room to double as both dance and art studio. The partitioned cupboards and mezzanine at one end solved some of the perennial storage problems and allowed for a swifter turnaround between hires. The accumulated archive was boxed up and partially listed to be stored on the mezzanine. At the opening by the Mayor of Waverley, Pat Frost, she said,

> *"This is a fantastic Centre – Waverley doesn't have much money and the fact that you had this grant means that in Waverley's eyes you are very important to their vision of the arts. You are the jewel in the crown."*

At the September Awayday Charles Fuente of TWM leads a review and discussion of the Memorandum and Articles of Association. The changes and review came as a result of the implementation of the 2006 Companies Act which simplified what was required. However, as subsequent Chairmen have found, the different amendments that had happened in the past had created quite a tangle. There were procedures not followed and records and renewals not kept, with some clauses seemingly contradicting each other. Also the process to change them is quite a high bar as 75% of members have to approve. The Board at this time decided to keep Friends and Members separate from each other and even consider a charge for Membership. This followed the thinking when the Friends was first set up after reopening. The confusing and unsatisfactory situation however continues to the present day. The Meeting concluded with consideration, led by Rosemary and Ed Baker of Surrey Community Action, to try to reestablish and define the role and parameters for the Board membership. The introduction of limited terms, a succession policy, training and induction, allocated responsibilities and diversity in recruitment were all considered and approved. Subsequently subgroups were set up to work on Governance, Policies and Board Nominations.

Setting a new path in 2010

The Centre moves forward as a mature organisation with improved management structures and a growing confidence in its mission

This work was made concrete in 2010 as the initiatives started by Rosemary French came to fruition. An EGM was called in June to pass the new Articles of Association. The 61 registered members were circulated with the details. It had been decided not to have a joining fee or subscription. Two resolutions were passed by a quorum of members including 14 proxy votes.

The new Centre Manager, Jenny Squire, had her annual appraisal and presented her Vision of the Future to the Board. This involved developing the Centre as a community venue, developing the creativity happening within it, developing local artists, developing participation and developing village culture and heritage. She had an associated marketing plan and a series of creative initiatives to go with each strand, budgeting for £16,000 project grant income. However a cloud on the horizon is that Waverley warn that grant funding was likely to be cut by10%, a familiar story. Thankfully there is some good legwork being done by Chris Dubois on possible grant applications, work which he continues to pick up for a number of years, becoming very adept at writing the bids. At the Awayday in September how to budget for a reduction of Local Authority grant support and how to tap into philanthropic giving are key issues for discussion. The financial crisis of 2009 had led to a national debate on funding. Under consideration are papers from many corners including the Arts Council on what David Cameron's 'Big Society' meant and how the funding model for the arts and other sectors of social enterprise that had been previously centrally financed might operate.

There is only one staff change in this year, Tom Baverstock being replaced by Katie Morris. In November Jenny reports to the Board:

> *"With a full complement of staff for the first time since January 2009, more than 18 months ago, our small team is finally getting into its stride. 4 FTE staff working to one vision, one business plan and reporting to one person is producing results. With 2.2 FTE less staff and a reduced salary budget, our hard working and dedicated team are achieving roughly the same income, and with considerably less resources, as our expenditure budget is maintained in a climate of rising prices. In a buoyant and strong economy we would be making considerable gains and investing those gains back into increasing staffing levels, however this challenging economy, which is seeing the end of many arts organisations, is for Cranleigh Arts ensuring a standstill."*

She notes too that *"all staff have considerable leave outstanding"*, so the problem of overstretched staff, despite more having been appointed, continued.

Five new Board members were recruited and appointed to replace those who would be unable to be re-elected due to the new two term rule instituted in the new Articles. They were Frances Haywood, Antonia Wilson, Clive Wouters, Callum Paterson and Stephen Fowler. With more people available Rosemary is keen to get them to be responsible for specific areas. IT, Volunteer management, the oversight of the Building and the Technical resources are all suggested and eventually apportioned. It takes a while for the relationship between these new trustees and the paid staff to evolve, but the support is eventually appreciated. At the AGM in

November two stalwarts left the Board, Catherine Pike and Chris Dubois, taking between them 36 years of wisdom and achievement with them. Both continued as volunteers and were on hand to help out when required. However change has to be balanced by continuity or there is a danger of constantly reinventing the wheel if corporate memory is lost. As has been shown, the issues, problems and mistakes tend to come round again and again.

The three-year Creative Alliance with The Maltings came to an end. A report was written by Jane Friend, bookending the one she started the project with. Her conclusions are that both organisations have benefitted from this and that it could be a model for other partnership arts arrangements. The Alliance had sprung from a crisis at Cranleigh Arts which had *"brought about change and enabled CAC to overcome the inertia and inbuilt resistance that exists in most organisations." "The role of the funding local authority was, and remains, key. ... It took a neutral and professional stance whilst maintaining an active interest".* She suggests that the relationship could continue with the local authority arts officer retaining *"an ability to influence new areas of cooperation".* She suggests that rather than being crisis led, the collaboration could involve shared resources moving forward and that this should be explored at Board and senior level.

As the new decade got under way it was clear that Cranleigh Arts had survived existential threat, was turning a corner and had evolved once again under the leadership of Rosemary French and the support of loyal staff and Board members. The tendency to boom and bust, the vagaries of funding and the personalities of the key players would continue to shape the story through the 2010s, up to the next major shock of Covid.

Chapter Nine

Trying to Progress in the 2010s

Can a stable financial model be found?

The social and economic background

The great recession leads to grants and income falling

The financial crisis of 2008/9, the great recession, was to cast a long shadow across the next decade. The arts were not immune to this as the UK and the world faced the deepest recession since the Second World War. Sources of income from central and local government, from business sponsorship and from philanthropy were all reduced. An Arts Index Report states that from 2008 to 2018 there was a per capita drop in public funding for the arts of 35%, while local government funding for the arts fell by 43% and business sponsorship by 39% in the same period. The arts had to become more self-sufficient and be more commercial. So a gradual rethink of budgets was undertaken but the change could not be immediate. For consumers the squeeze on household budgets meant that discretionary spending on arts activities, hospitality and nights out was often the first to go.

A microcosm of this can be seen in 2011 where the January Board Minutes report that income would be reduced due to a 12% cut in the Waverley grant (it had been cut by 17% the previous year) and that since room rates had been increased some hirers were moving elsewhere, including much of U3A and the Film Club, reducing income further. Apart from the room rate review, Jenny Squire had tackled the difficult issue of the spread and times of regular bookings. She proposed closing on Mondays and tried to get regular bookings grouped together so they did not get in the way of other commercial hires or arts bookings that might come up. It made clear sense to try and optimise the space, but this met with some resistance from those who had always met at the same times each week. Long established hirers such as U3A were vocal in their disapproval. Rather than change their routine some groups chose to move elsewhere, others understood the logic and were more flexible.

New income had to be sought. A deliberate expansion of the hospitality offering was developed by marketing the Centre as ideal for weddings, wakes and celebrations, with a part time Hospitality Coordinator, Janet Baverstock, a former Duty Manager to run this. These could bring in substantial sums. One wedding was a two day booking of the whole Centre. The bride, her family and the caterers took over all the rooms. However at the end the family and caterers just left everything for the Centre staff to clear up, who were there until 2.00am! However if external staffing costs were factored in, instead of using volunteers, then a professional service could be provided for a premium price and gave a welcome boost to the coffers. Adverts were offered in the new Brochure to subsidise its cost for the first time. Later in the year there are ambitions to develop the Friends further to include local business discounts as a perk, and to expand the hospitality provision to increase income. The alliance of the Centre with local businesses was a good move, encouraging people to shop locally and for the Cranleigh community to support each other. Even two parking spaces would be rented out. Research begins on upgrading the ticketing programme and to improve the website in order to facilitate the growing trend for online sales.

At this time there is also some limited discussion of a change to the business model in order to manage more clearly the aspects of the charity. Should the building be bought and hived off into a separate charitable entity with its own fundraising to keep it maintained? Should the hospitality and lettings be a commercial business that fed profits into the core charity of arts endeavours? There were other arts centres with such arrangements. This didn't get very far however as no one had the headspace to think about it in any detail. It must also be supposed that since there were barely the resources and energy to manage the charity as it was, to expand into three contiguous parts was likely to be beyond current means and merely bring a load more problems.

In line with the national tightening of belts, 2012 brings another fall in the Waverley grant. Other income is similarly depressed, despite everyone's best efforts, so that there would be a small loss for the first time in five years. Historically Waverley's grants had been:
2009/10: £31,325;
2010/11: £29,000;
2011/12: £24,000;
2012/13: £22,300.
Some hope was held out for the possibility of a three-year Service Level Agreement (SLA) which would allow for more certain for-

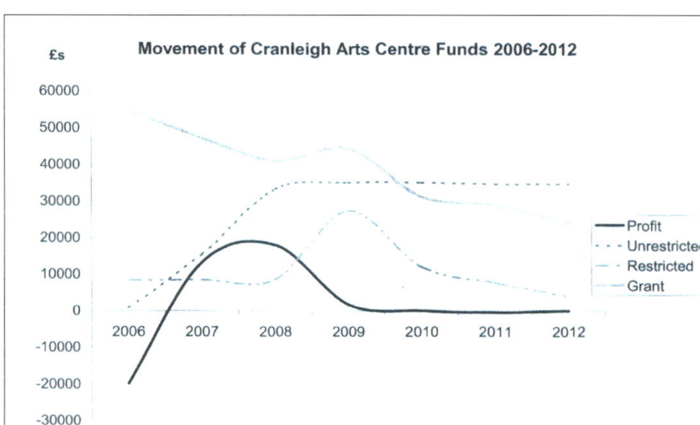

ward budgeting and guarantee the money to be received. It would however come with the requirement for clear deliverable outcomes which would be reviewed and measured annually. This model was initially trialled by Farnham Maltings and is eventually signed off for Cranleigh Arts in 2015.

Less positive were the negotiations with Waverley over street signage. Too many people still drove past the Centre thinking it was part of the church and many supporters wanted a more vibrant kerbside image. The local councillor Brian Ellis thought he could get a brown tourist sign put up on the approaches to Cranleigh. The difficulties were that the lease prohibited anything being affixed to the Victorian building, but Rosemary craftily got an illuminated sign put up inside over the modern porch entrance door instead. This was a battle that would continue for years up to the present day with incremental development of exterior lighting, signs, lettered boards and poster cabinets as the council's planning officers softened.

Finding the right people

Changes to staff and Board members mean that continuity and consistency are hard to achieve

Staffing continues to be an issue. There are large amounts of overtime accruing but increased activity requires more management. The Board set up seven sub-committees to promote, support and consult on key areas of the operation. Jenny Squire proposes a restructure to save money. She would step down to two days a week from four and move to an Artistic Director role on projects, while Ruth Eastelow would add Venue Manager to her Programmer role. To fill the shortfall she proposed unpaid 'super' volunteers be tasked with taking on Duty Managing and other responsibilities and there would be self-governing volunteer teams under the current coordinators. To a degree this would be an extension of the subcommittees, but already they were running into some difficulties regarding who they reported to and what authority they had. This proposal does not get Board approval, who concluded that at the moment a well-run venue was more important than artistic projects to overcome the income deficit. They feel there is a need for more leadership not less. It is identified that there is a risk that Jenny might leave, but in a recession that might be an opportunity to attract a candidate with new skills. She resigns in May.

Of 22 candidates for the Manager five are interviewed and Jenny-Anne Dexter appointed. She was 29 and although she had a background in arts promotion and administration, she had been marketing 'We Will Rock You' in the West End and had a spell at the Yvonne Arnaud, she hadn't run a building before. Rosemary said to her, *"you don't have all the aspects we need, but we think you have the potential to gain them"*. She supported Jenny-Anne to the hilt; *"perhaps she saw me as someone she could mould"* comments Jenny-Anne. Both Rosemary and her successor, Stephen Dennison, had fortnightly meetings with her and were able to have frank discussions of problems. There was continuing support too from Chris Maddocks of the Farnham Maltings with whom she had a week of induction, in lieu of handover notes from Jenny Squire. Hannah Kester, a Board member who ran Chequer Mead in East Grinstead, was another resource. Jenny-Anne also sat down straight away with the staff team and consulted them *"before they hated me"*, to see what their concerns were and how the operation worked. This was a measure of her energy and enthusiasm.

Ambitious plans for arts centre

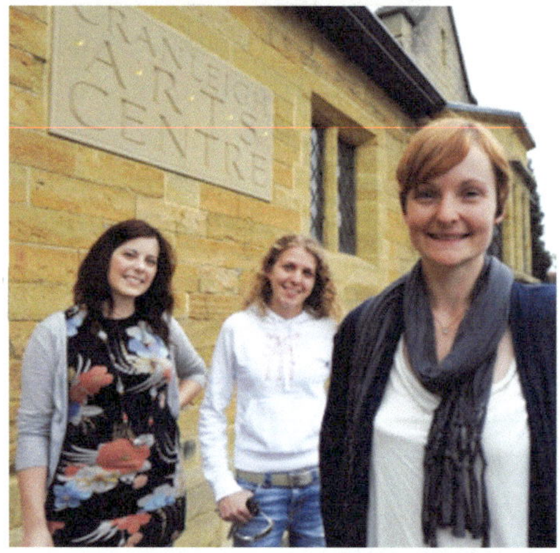

New manager Jenny-Anne Dexter with assistants Katie Morris and Ruth East.
Picture: Terry Habgood. (Ref: SA114031_4)

2011 sees other changes of personnel. Mike Kiernan hands over to John Gill as Treasurer. The cashier of 20 years, Sandra Shelton steps down. Chrissy Matthews, who had been so instrumental and inspirational in running the Centre for the last decade, moves on to other local charitable projects. Stephen Dennison is appointed Deputy Chairman, as Rosemary French is due to stand down in 2012. Ruth Farmer, Board Secretary for eight years, wants to go too. Janet Baverstock resigns as Hospitality coordinator, so there are gaps to fill in key staff areas.

Changes to the Board

Broadening the expertise available and getting them more involved

In September 2012 three new Trustees join: Kary Backhouse, Phil Rickett and Chris Wilson. Phil, who was due to help manage the building, resigns after six months finding it difficult to work with some of the team, but the other two will make quite an impact. Kary, a longtime friend of Rosemary French, is put to work on the new Business Plan with Jenny-Anne. Stephen Fowler has already taken on the technical side and has oversight of that. Clive Wouters moves from Building oversight to Resources and helps bridge the gap between volunteers and staff.

In 2011 Jane Sharpe and David Goff had become Volunteer Co-ordinators. This was largely because Jane had offered to volunteer and it had taken such a long time to sign her on that she felt that it should be better organised. They wanted to make volunteering a more sociable experience and moved to set up teams to work together and arrange cover more effectively. They also introduced a 'Thank you' reward scheme of free cinema tickets, later coffees, that built up each time someone volunteered. They held regular sessions with volunteers to 'meet and greet' and share ideas. A new Volunteer handbook came out of this in 2013.

Callum Paterson, a high-level computer specialist, had oversight of IT and specified an upgrade to the system. He had improved the website which had been very static by writing a back-end database, which allowed it to be more easily updated, He struck problems initially as the Centre had lost the password and the man who had originally set it up was not altogether co-operative. Callum became the go-to person at all hours for solving computer problems. The subgroups are restructured by Stephen Dennison when he becomes Chairman and this seems to strengthen the management of the operations. No one has time for fundraising however and this pillar of the budget, which covers some capital expenditure and should build reserves is missing at this time but will be addressed in future years.

In September 2013 four more new trustees join: Rob Kerby, Ken Rushton, Stephen White and Gaynor Wilson, replacing Phil Rickett, Frances Heywood and Stephen Fowler, who sadly had a serious car accident. Gaynor is a potter who revitalises the Pottery and also brings for the board the expertise of her husband Mike, an architect, who eventually takes on the long-term vision of the development of the building. Rob, and his wife, a Duty Manager, will also do vital practical service before emigrating to Australia in 2016. Ken takes on fundraising, but sadly ill health forces him to step down after only ten months. Stephen White has experience of charitable trusts through his work with the Clothworkers Guild and takes the role of 'critical friend'. Thus the board has transitioned, as Rosemary French had envisioned, from being *"rather parochial and inward looking"* to one that reflected wider expertise and is actively contributing support, whilst not losing touch with the local community or deskilling the staff.

Another new broom

The crossover with the Board becomes greater when a Trustee takes on the Manager role

However in July 2013 Jenny-Anne Dexter resigns after only two years. She had found it a steep learning curve but had enjoyed the challenge. *"You don't just manage the*

Arts Centre you manage the village and its expectations", she said. *"They were good fun times. We used to laugh a lot. There was so much going on. It far outstrips any other job I've done. It had so many aspects. You have to shapeshift all the time."* Jenny-Anne also developed catering offers and better organisation of the volunteers. Although she got on well with the staff she felt that they were not a happy team with poor working conditions and low morale and that they had reached an impasse. *"I didn't want to drive it into a ditch so I went."* She left to work in donor giving and fundraising for three major charities. Her spare time activity has changed from mixed martial arts to park runs, which perhaps is a comment on her style then and now.

With the Marketing Coordinator, Katie Morris, taking maternity leave and Jenny-Anne going, the Board had a problem. However Kary Backhouse, who had a background in business and marketing, stepped forward to offer to take on the Centre Manager role. After an interview and discussion this was agreed from 1st August as an interim measure to provide continuity and reassurance. She would be paid for three days and volunteer for two days. Having had a year on the Board she knew what she was taking on and had definite ideas about what was needed. She believed in firm leadership and started by moving the administration up to the dressing room space and funding is eventually found to remodel it as an Office. Here, in contrast to the Gallery mezzanine or behind the Box Office, staff could work in private and uninterrupted. Her paper to the Board in September is a clear analysis of the key areas she wants to focus on. This is a root and branch review to reinvent the Arts Centre and tackle what she sees are its operational problems. It is a critical time as the new Business plan for 2014-17 needs to be crystallised. She wants to strengthen community projects, lift the profile of the Gallery, mobilise and motivate the volunteers and become more customer focussed. This receives approval.

However in November 2013 the Hospitality Co-ordinator and the Marketing Maternity Cover both resign. One is replaced fairly quickly but Marketing has to be covered by a volunteer, Jane Bowden, and the fallout, despite her best efforts, means that some momentum is lost with a consequent drop in sales. There is added pressure on Ruth Eastelow, the Programmer, and on Kary. Some staff restructuring is proposed with part-time posts introduced, which will bring in additional paid evening Duty Managers and financial administrative support, as well as a volunteer group to help Ruth with programming. Kary's performance is reviewed favourably by the Board and her achievements noted, along with *"being uncompromising on quality, standards and policies"*. She is reappointed until the end of March 2015, having expressed a willingness and says she is *"enjoying the job; so much still to do"*. She is clear about what should be her managerial responsibility and what is delegated to Trustees, taking some areas back under her control. In the next year the Fundraising Committee and Volunteer Forums are dissolved. She steadies the ship while riding stormy waters. The Broadband is upgraded and the Centre e-news reaches almost two thousand on the mailing list. The volunteers undergo regular training and are led by separate staff members according to what task team they are in. Customer service gets special emphasis. However in May 2014 Ruth resigns, followed by the Venue Manager and the news that Katie Morris would not return as Marketing Co-ordinator. So three posts are advertised with three new appointments in the summer.

For Ruth, who had programmed fourteen seasons, she felt she had achieved what she wanted to do. *"I'd honed it. Building was better, programme was solid, making money. ... But a number of little things made me feel compromised.... I felt I was not getting the credit."* She had brought back the open exhibition, developed pop-up films and children's theatre, all with a keen sense of balancing the artistic with the commercial; she also had improved the building by better internal signage and music in the foyer. But she was managing hired-in staff, bookings, contracts and deals and many volunteers. *"In the end it was time to go."*

Success with the Programme

New initiatives and creative ideas take the seasonal programme to a new level

During Jenny-Anne's tenure she established the link with Mick Perrin, the agency who managed top comedians, persuading him that Cranleigh would be a perfect try-out venue, beginning with Ross Noble. This would be an enduring and popular strand of the programme. Ruth was keen to make Films a good seller too, with pre-show supper deals with local restaurant Rania and later with the Richard Onslow. 'Mamma Mia' was packaged with a bottle of fizz and the largely female audience got into it so much that the projectionist had to shut himself in the box to avoid their advances.

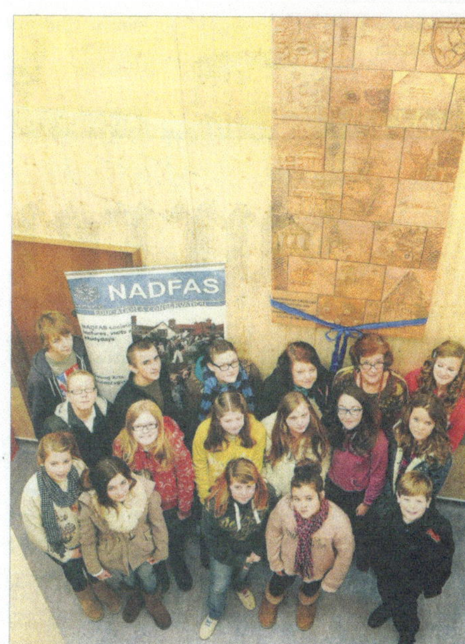

The unveiling of a ceramic mural created by teenagers for Cranleigh Medical Practice.
Picture: Jake Darling. (Ref: SA127447_3)

By the AGM in November 2013 there is some celebration that there is a profit after some years of losses. Eclectic R&B nights, the Eat and Drink Festival, which saw attendance of 700, and a successful fundraiser concert with Joe Stilgoe, arranged by Antonia Wilson, all suggest that the Centre is back on track in business terms, even if the delivery of it has had some wobbles.

A donation for equipment in memory of Chrissy Matthews, who had passed away in March 2014, enabled the Centre to start Live Streaming, which had begun in 2009 to cinemas but was now filtering down to smaller venues. This was an audience pleaser and boosted programme income. A Classical Music strand is brought back into the programme too, although this would take longer to become established.

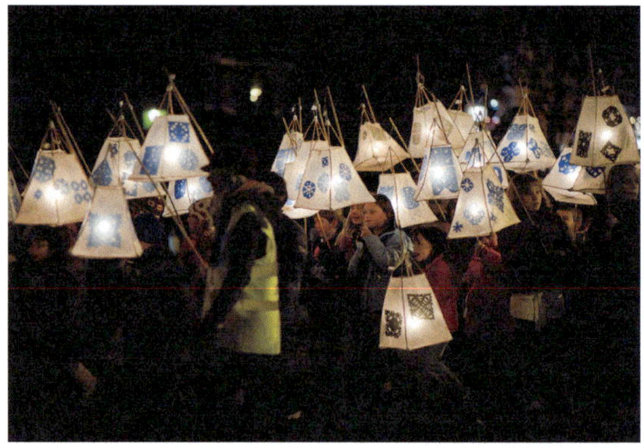

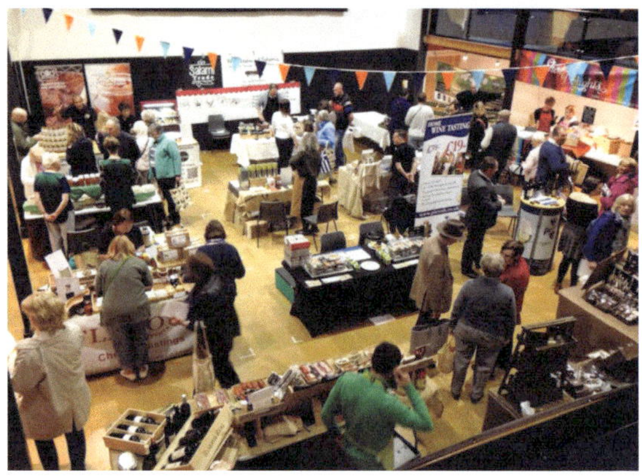

The Lantern Parade.
Food and Drink Festival.

Connecting to the community has to be evidenced for grants and is also part of Kary's strategy. This bore fruit in the successful second Food and Drink Festival with footfall of 1200, which also involved live music in the High Street. A Literary Festival was mooted for 2016. There was funding for a community project, 'Times of Our Lives', where 45 local people who had been at school in the Centre created an oral history and accompanying booklet, led by Gill Collins. Men in Sheds took up weekly residence to do their woodworking projects in a social setting. Thus the Arts Centre was fulfilling its brief to serve the community as required by its Service Level Agreement with Waverley, but the increased activity put stress on the staff and volunteers. Income was increased, but margins were reduced due to the need to employ more staff on occasions for technical support or Duty Managing.

In 2016 Stephen launches a new fundraising event – the celebrity interview. He knew the theatre producer Robert Fox who arranges for actor Bill Nighy to be interviewed by Paul Jones. This proves to be very successful and is followed in subsequent years by interviews with Virginia McKenna, Julie Walters, Imelda Staunton and Jim Carter. Stephen also now has time to develop the Classical Music programme, which leads to a high profile recital by Richard Saxel, and a joint concert which helps to reestablish links with Cranleigh School, as well as an English National Opera evening.

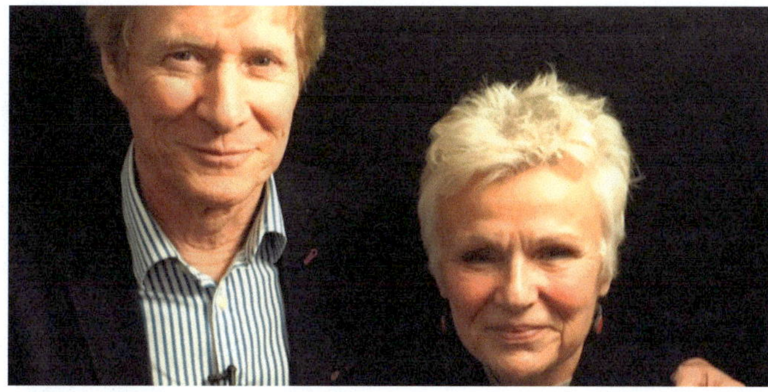

2015 Fundraising for the Building

Concerted efforts are made to get outside funding for both the building and the operation

Despite edging into a small profit, it was realised that budgetary dependence on a volatile programme needed fixing and the route proposed by the Centre Manager was to drive towards more sponsorship and fundraising, for both capital expenditure but also operations. This had a number of elements over the year. Led by Stephen Dennison applications were made to Biffa and to the Foyles Foundation for £80,000 repairs to the outside of the building and roof and some other enhancements, like outside illumination and the long-awaited signage, which might be supplemented by S106 developers' money from Waverley. Following a donation, a Fundraising consultant, Helen Shone, was engaged to report on possible strategies and sources. Seeking to raise the profile of the Arts Centre additional Patrons would be sought for each of the art forms, initially getting a positive response from local television mogul, Paul Smith. A project called Target 25 was launched, based on a rather arbitrary anniversary, to celebrate 25 years of the Centre and to raise £25,000 to secure the Centre for the next 25 years. There would be an Open Day to get the CA message out to the community on 25th April and it would culminate in a Fundraising Dinner and auction in November, organised by Antonia Wilson, which did successfully raise in excess

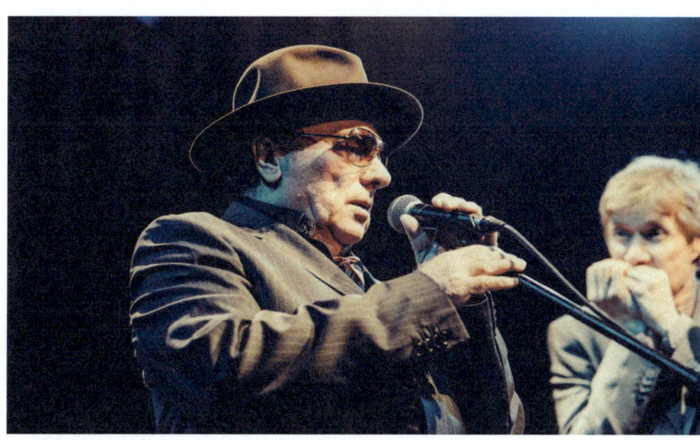

Van Morrison and Paul Jones

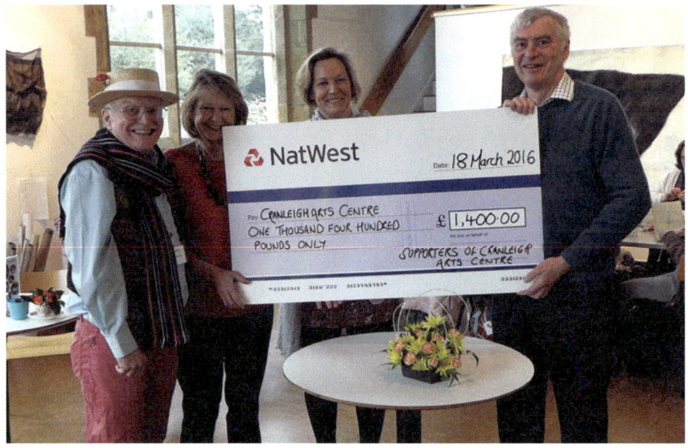

of £14,000. A group of supporters had set up a 100 Club, separate from Cranleigh Arts and over the year raised £3,400 with a further £2,800 in 2016. This is invested in various small projects within the building. It should not be forgotten that the annual two sell-out 'Paul Jones and Friends' Concerts also made a significant contribution to the funds, both by way of his donation of some of the proceeds, but also from raffle and bar profits.

Underpinning these strategies were an Arts Council workshop on Fundraising which Kary attended and Helen Shone's report. These were brought together in a paper she put to the Board which underlined the intention of the Arts Council to encourage organisations to raise more money from private giving by offering match funding through 'Catalyst: Evolve Funding'. This could unlock up to £150,000 over three years. The Arts Council found that grant-making trusts and statutory sources of income had flatlined and may decline. So any strategy must be a mixed portfolio to reduce financial risk. Helen Shone is clear that fundraising must be an organisation-wide activity which needs a commitment for the long haul. She rightly states that this is time heavy and that staff alone cannot deliver it. Trustees and other volunteers must be proactive and develop skills and relationships that will bring in the money to sustain the organisation. The Arts Council will need to see evidence of this if it is to contribute funds. The point is also made that the Arts Council does not fund 'arts for art's sake' but sees it as having instrumental value, with a measurable impact on our economy, health and wellbeing, society and education. The Board find Helen Shone's roadmap a coherent and convincing document, dealing as it does with all aspects of the task, but it leaves the big question of who would do all the extensive things she suggests. Kary is very firm in requesting the Board's commitment. In the end the Arts Council's Catalyst scheme is agreed to, with a hope that sufficient progress can be made with an ongoing strategy building on Target 25 to achieve the match funds required.

Continuity at this time was seen to be important so an EGM was held mid-year to extend Stephen Dennison's tenure as Chairman by a year. After a positive appraisal in February, *"Kary has made excellent progress but there are many challenges ahead. I am delighted overall with her achievements"*, her tenure as Centre Manager is renewed in April. Two new trustees join in 2015 both of whom would be critical to the future success of Cranleigh Arts: Peter Adams and Bob Wild.

Struggling again to keep afloat

It becomes increasingly clear that the strategies pursued are not having the desired effect

Despite the successes in fundraising, with margins squeezed, attendance falling and less taken on profitable areas such as hospitality, there is still a hole of £25,000 in the breakeven budget to be made up from donations. As a result Reserves have fallen to £17,000 against a target of £80,000. In January 2016 it is agreed to introduce a ticket levy in line with many other arts organisations that pays towards the development of the building and/or the costs of processing the ticket. In the meantime a pay rise is granted to staff; the first in three years. Unfortunately, the staff churn continues with Naomi Elliott, Ruth's replacement, leaving and an ongoing vacancy for the Venue Manager post. The problem is that the salary that can be afforded by the Centre is too low for anyone to afford accommodation, unless they are established here already, either a young person living at home, who would

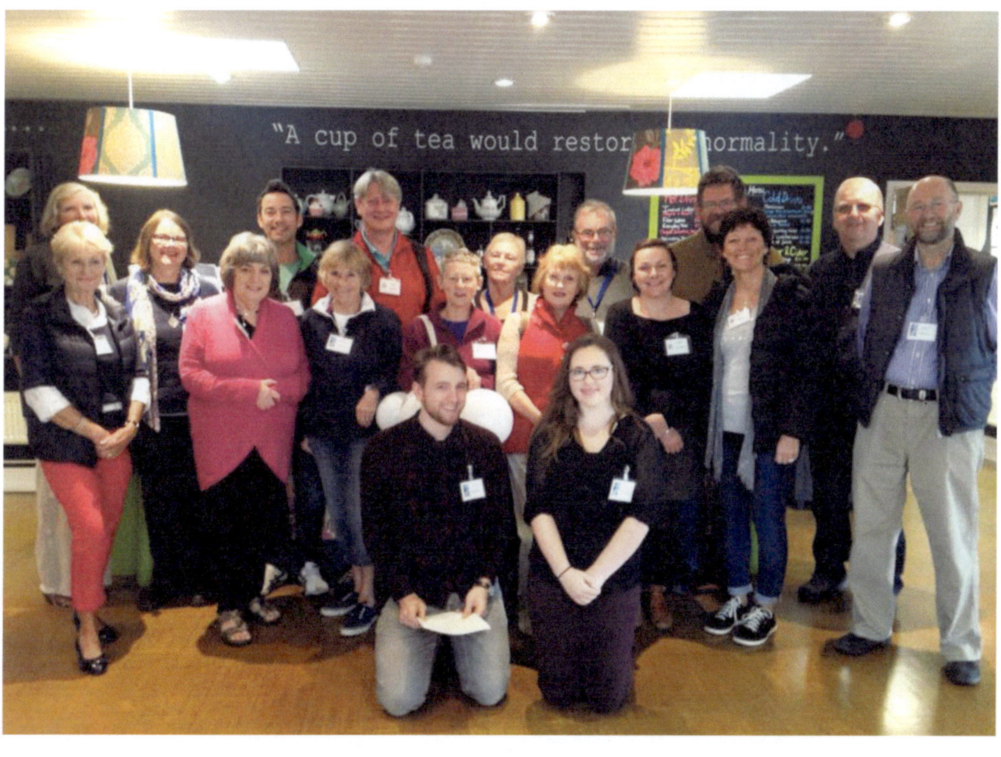

move on fairly quickly, or an older person, who may be experienced, perhaps with a family and mortgage, but who would expect considerably more remuneration in return. The staff churn continued through 2016/17 with Beth Mathieson, recruited as Programmer, lasting only a year and Rob Kerby, trustee, who steps in to take on the Venue Manager post, but only for six months while waiting for his emigration visa to Australia to come through. Rob is a very experienced manager who brings a welcome efficiency and stability to his role. Jane Howard, Marketing Manager, leaves in May, to be replaced by Rosie Townsend, who only stays a year. In a small team the interplay of personalities and the managerial style can have an undue impact. All this is detrimental to the running of the organisation and unsettling for the volunteers who see their managers come and go. There is some evidence that nationally volunteers are becoming harder to find and are more discriminating as to how they want to participate. Between 2013 and 2016 a total of 112 people participated as volunteers. As of October 2016: 40 of them have retired, died, moved or left; 42 remain weekly volunteers; 20 have monthly engagement and 10 are more occasional, such as trustees.

Kary has to work hard to keep positive momentum, maintain routines and standards and to plug the gaps. This eventually has a detrimental effect on her health in 2017 when she has to take sick leave.

A forward budget for 2016-17 has a loss of £11,400 written in, to be made up by donations, which increases the pressure on everyone. To help develop strands of the arts programme a part-time Arts Development Co-ordinator, Gill Collins, is appointed to help, but this adds more to the staff budget. John Gill steps down as Treasurer in March, having done four years, and Bob Wild, a former banker, takes this on. Bob makes a forensic examination of the accounts and sees that unless things change the Centre will go bust in six months. He is adamant that ongoing costs, such as staff salaries, must be covered by operating revenue. The Board cannot rely on unpredictable and serendipitous gifts and grants to keep solvent. A change of policy is needed. With his extended tenure up Stephen Dennison has to step down in November 2016 and as the year goes on it is clear that Bob will be the best person to succeed him in November. Robert Watkins, a local accountant, is recruited to replace him as Treasurer.

As the year closes there is further discouraging news. The ambitious Arts Council bid is unsuccessful, as in 2006, which puts the future financial security and business plan for 2017-20 in doubt. A major hirer, Eclectic Live Music which programmes R&B, withdraws after disagreements over terms, meaning a potential reduction in income of up to £6,000. Small sums do come in: from Surrey CC for the boilers, from Waverley BC for redesigning the office space, and from Foyles for roof repairs. The best news however is that funding has been secured from the Wates Trust for a part-time Volunteer Coordinator. This meant that for the first time a designated person would manage the volunteers, not as an adjunct to another role and ease the staff budget.

2017 – difficult decisions again

The Board and Manager have differing views on what the future course should be but ultimately financial imperatives dictate the solution

At the February Board Kary presents some research from the Arts Council into the proportion of earned income, private donation and public subsidy that went into arts organisations of different sizes. Its conclusion was that private investment was increasing and that the sector was becoming less reliant on public funding. Small arts companies tended to earn only 40% of their income. In comparison Cranleigh Arts generated over 80% of its income from earnings and a relatively small amount from private or public funds. She argued that to run the operation as it should be then much more income must be sought from these two sources to allow for full running and the desired expansion. This was opposed by the Chairman who argued that the operation should be self-funding, apart from specific project and SLA funding, or, better still, profitable, with any extra funds from donations and fundraising going into reserves against a rainy day and to fund capital improvements. In hindsight it was the latter of these models which allowed companies to successfully survive Covid, when it came along, and many small companies who followed the former went to the wall.

To some extent this was an ideological debate between left and right models of how the arts should be provided. Is it a fundamental social provision that should be funded by society and the community through taxation, like other social services? Or be self-funding from the desirability and quality of its offering in the marketplace? The pendulum swung back and forth depending on the government of the day, its arts policy and the economic climate. To some extent the administrators, like Bob, leaning to the right, and the artists and creatives, like Kary, to the left. Fundamentally however, as Rosemary French had argued in the previous crisis, if you aren't there, you can't do any good work for people anyway, so survival by any means must be the bottom line.

The Business Plan details a total of eleven paid staff, full and part-time, going forward, although filling and funding them is problematic at the start of the year as two potential appointees turn the jobs down. The Marketing Co-ordinator resigns in February and the programmer Beth is likely to go too. Bob reviews the situation with Kary who wants to put up salaries to make it more attractive and secure experienced staff. Bob presents a paper to the Board asking some questions.

> The posts are being readvertised but why is there such staff turnover: fourteen in three and a half years?
> Is it money, lack of talent in the area or a dislike of the Arts Centre?
> If appointments cannot be made then there are stark choices. If salaries are increased then the budget would be blown and there are very limited reserves.
> If we have fewer staff then activity and income would reduce and so does turnover.
> If we recruit apprentice level staff we could pay less, but may have a reduction in effectiveness.
> Do we revert to just a Centre Manager with volunteers in other roles?

The Board throw back some suggestions: that trustees are involved in the interview process and could become mentors to new staff; that exit interviews should take place; that salaries seem to be in line with other local organisations. There is expressed frustration that the activities and atmosphere in the Centre are at last generally very positive and that staff issues shouldn't disrupt or sour this momentum. There is scepticism at the use of interns or apprentices, who would need more induction and supervision and so would not be cost effective in the long run.

By May the past financial year's data is available and there is some reassurance with staffing. A Volunteer Co-ordinator has been recruited. Katie Wilson joins in April, having worked for the National Trust at the recently fire-damaged Clandon Park House. She is extremely able and is to be a mainstay of the organisation for the next five years. Also in the pipeline are a new Programmer, Peter Hunt, and a new Marketing Coordinator, Phoebe Farr, who join in June and July, with salaries at current rates. The numbers are pored over to try to predict what the future course should be. The small loss in the year 2016-17 can be met from reserves, but the direction of travel must be right for the budget for 2017-18, already under way, and for the ongoing business plan. Analysis suggests that income continues to fall, margins have reduced and costs, particularly on staff, are rising. The budget goes through four drafts as predictions are adjusted to make it balance. Some on the Board feel that the income targets are unlikely. Alongside this is the possibility of bidding for S106 money, a levy received by Waverley from developers to invest in the community, to expand and improve the Arts Centre for the future. Greater capacity and better facilities could improve the financial prospects in the years to come but is only likely to be given if good financial governance is shown now.

In July discussion continued as to how to stabilise the finances. For the year 2012-

13 staff costs had made up 49% of operating costs. For 2016-17 this had risen to 64% and was budgeted ahead to be 66%. To get this down a radical plan was conceived looking at redundancies, as Rosemary French had done ten years previously. Could the role of Centre Manager be removed? This would create a flattened structure, empower the newly engaged staff team, involve the Trustees in active oversight and use the skills of key experienced volunteers in a positive way. A model was drawn up to reallocate the responsibilities of the Centre Manager. Discussions began with Kary in August about this proposal in line with employment practice. Unsurprisingly she was not convinced and was forthright about the risks that it entailed. Lots of questions were thrown up and discussions continued amongst the Trustees. At the beginning of September the decision is made by the Board to proceed with this restructuring, so meetings commence towards agreeing with Kary a redundancy or severance settlement. Due to legal consultation delays this takes most of the month to resolve. However in mid-October the new structure is implemented, Kary retires and briefing meetings are held with the main stakeholders, the Volunteers and Waverley almost immediately, and subsequently more widely at the AGM. There is scepticism from some, but the Chairman and the Board Members most closely involved explain the reasons and solutions and assure them that they will make it work. After the dust settles this proves to be the case. The four staff team have clear authorities and are each mentored by a Trustee, who make up an Executive group reporting back to the full Board. Others, such as the Chairman, Treasurer, and Clive Wouters as Operations Coordinator, take on areas not covered by the staff. The Q1 and Q2 results show losses of £7k and £13k respectively, showing how necessary the strategy had been. There is a united and committed Board and an energised staff team to take the Arts Centre forward after some difficult years.

2018-19 Stability and growth

With a lot to prove the new team build a successful operation and S106 money allows for improvements to the building and confidence returns

In the course of these two years the staff grow into their roles. Paul Grover, who initially was just Buildings Manager, had worked closely with Kary on improving the quality of service for commercial hires, such as wakes and presentations. He gradually had increased his hours and now took on a full facilities role delivering on all non-arts hires as well. Phoebe Farr, who came from assistant marketing at the Lighthouse, Woking, takes clear hold of the brochure and publicity, including social media and branding. With Clive, she pushes forward the stalled ideas for a new website and ticketing provider, which is in place by the end of 2018, together with contactless payment. They also crunch some data on audiences, refine the e-newsletter and expand the brochure's distribution. Peter Hunt is very quick to pick up on the nuances of programming and creative in seeing new opportunities. He discovers, as others before had done, the perils of 'running too hot' but finds the balance. Katie Wilson brings a new professionalism to the management of the volunteers, with her friendly and open manner, which ensures a successful tightening of training and procedures. Community outreach is added to her portfolio, her hours extended by additional funding. For what is possibly the first time the operational budgets are shared with the staff team who know clearly what their parameters and outcomes are and gives them ownership. Regular staff appraisal, shared writing of policies and mentoring from trustees helps bind the team together and aids communication, whether paid or volunteer. By September sales are up 32% and the staff get a rise of 3%, in appreciation of their efforts. At the AGM a longstanding member gives credit to *"the best group of paid staff that CAC has ever had"*.

Other good news comes in the award of £125k S106 money from Waverley which is put into phase one of improving the building – the redesign of the toilets, which allows for the addition of a corridor to join the Pottery to the main building and a reorganisation of storage. Mike Wilson is the architect and Peter Adams the trustee in charge of this. It is planned through 2018 and carried out in summer 2019. Following her Celebrity Interview Fundraiser with Paul Jones, Dame Julie Walters agrees to become another Patron.

Other changes involve the creation of a garden at the rear of the car park by David and Rene Seume and Jane Heathcott, the garden gurus of Cranleigh Arts, in association with Cranleigh in Bloom; the installation of CCTV to deter youngsters getting on the roof and to improve security; the implications of GDPR are tackled and a substantial anonymous donation allows for the purchase of a new grand piano, which raises the profile of the classical music programme.

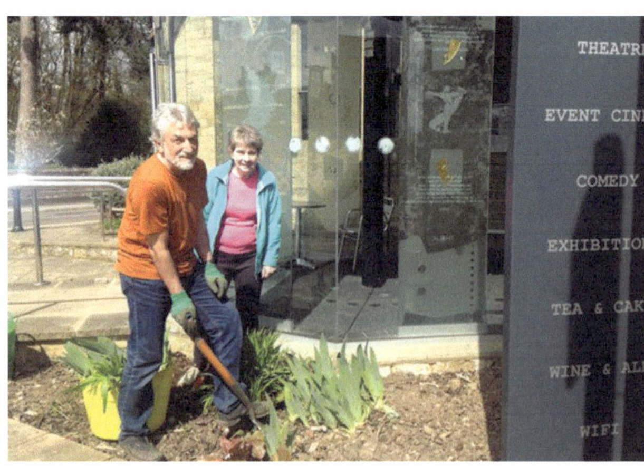

David and Rene Seume.

Personnel changes happen at Board level inevitably. Robert Watkins stands down as Treasurer, covered temporarily for three months by Bob until David Whitaker joins in July 2019. Antonia

Wilson and Clive Wouters have to come off the Board at the end of 2018 as their eight year tenure is up, but Clive stays on as Operations Coordinator, a senior volunteer reporting to and seconded to the Board as an observer. Two industry recruits, Danyah Miller, a local actor/storyteller, and Lil Lambley, a theatre producer, lend their expertise for a year each. James Mainwaring, an IT specialist, joins too. Simon Rabinowitz, coming from a hospitality background, joins in 2018 and is helpful in formulating longer term plans for development. Lynn Murray, a local solicitor, had joined in 2017 and brought legal and local knowledge and contacts. Sadly Peter Adams dies after a short illness in November 2019, having successfully completed the rebuilding project. The diversity of the makeup and recruitment to the Board reflected Bob's aim to make it fulfil the range of expertise and knowledge needed for the effective oversight and planning of such an operation as the Arts Centre.

Subsidy for free tickets for young disadvantaged people is obtained from St James's Place Charitable Foundation, which helps fulfil the Centre's commitment to make the arts accessible to all in the community.

The stability and success of the Centre is reflected in the metrics so beloved of Bob at the AGMs and other presentations. The small loss of £4k in 2018-19 becomes a profit of £21k in 2019-20. Outstanding progress had been made. Ticket sales increase in those two years from 9,263 to 13,150. Annual footfall is roughly 40,000. Reserves increase from March 2018: £55k, to March 2019: £72k, to March 2020: £104k, exceeding the target. The priorities of the 2018-21 Strategic and Business Plan were: Sound sustainable financial footing to 'Future Proof' CA; Enhance image and marketing delivery; Invest in staff and volunteer training; Grow audience and ticket sales; Fundraising; Invest in Building maintenance and refurbishment. As the Chairman reported at the AGM in November 2019 it was clear that there had been significant progress in all these. But just as the ledgers were closing on that most successful financial year in March 2020, so did the Arts Centre as the next existential threat hit.

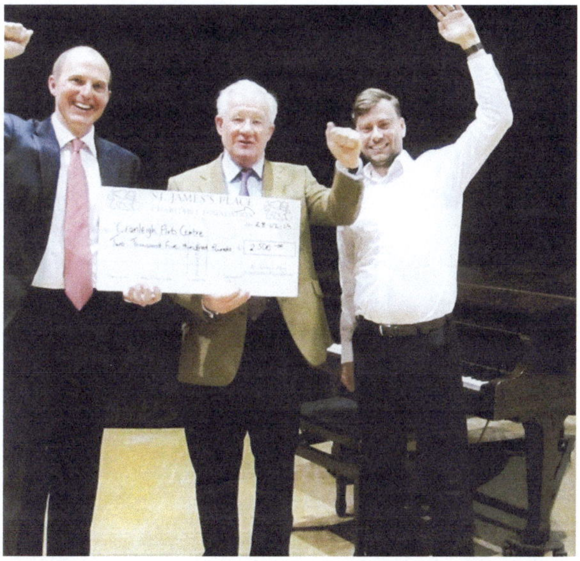

Alan Young, Bob Wild and Peter Hunt.

Chapter Ten

Lockdown and survival in the 2020s

Prudence prevails and the show goes on

2020 The impact of Covid

An emergency stop and into the unknown

At the start of 2020 it was not quite business as usual. There was one staff change as Phoebe Farr had been attracted to a post at G Live. Her replacement was Eloise Hulme who had some marketing experience, was young and seemed keen to learn. The budget assumptions for the year to come were reviewed by the staff who felt the income lines were a bit high, so they were revised down. Bob Wild reporting back to the Board in February was disappointed but said that the team needed to own the budget. *"While he and the Board owned the financial consequences of the Arts Centre's financial performance it would be counterproductive for the Board to impose financial targets that did not have their commitment."* Under the Risk Review the appearance of a coronavirus on the horizon was noted. More urgent was a Fire Inspection Report. In the light of the Grenfell disaster regulations had been tightened up and there was an urgent need to upgrade some provisions. This would be implemented immediately. Approval was also given to upgrade the coffee machine and tea bar as the next stage of improvements. Katie Wilson's funding from Wates Charitable Foundation was to expire in April, but an application to the National Lottery Community Fund had been successful and they would fund her post for five years. Announcing this in the February Newsletter to volunteers she writes:

> *"It's been another great month here at Cranleigh Arts with sold out shows, new volunteers joining us and the lunchtime concert seeing around 75 people. All these factors have helped create a real buzz about the building and continues to show the strength of our programme and what we can offer the Cranleigh community. My role in Cranleigh Arts and a key part of our overall mission is to maintain and grow our involvement and links with the community and ensure the volunteer experience we offer is one where our volunteers feel supported and valued."*

However all this came to a sudden stop after an emergency board meeting on the afternoon of 17th March when immediate closure was confirmed. The staff had already cancelled an evening showing of 'Fidelio', following what other ATG theatres and the Yvonne Arnaud were doing, after a press briefing by Boris Johnson. His advice was, *"you should avoid .. theatres .."* unhelpfully leaving the choice to venues. The industry contacts of Lil Lambley and Danyah Miller would be very helpful as this situation unfolded. On 24th March the Centre was mothballed as the country was locked down and headed into the unknown. The business plan objective of 'survival' now became very pertinent and very real. As this was largely about money and the organisation's operation in the interim the two lead players would be Bob Wild and Clive Wouters, who quickly formulated strategic plans to present to the Board. Initially government responses and information were hard to come by, but the restrictions, penalties and opportunities gradually became clearer.

At May's Board Meeting, via the newly discovered Zoom, the key parameters were emerging. It was agreed unanimously to continue to keep staff on full salary as they were a major asset. Katie was funded separately so could continue to work from home at no cost to the organisation, but the other three were furloughed once the details of that scheme became clear. Optimism that 'it'll all be over by Easter' meant that the programme had been on a rolling cancellation through until then and subsequently to the end of May. But it became clear that this virus wasn't going away any time soon. As content providers were cancelling too, activity was suspended through to August. Ticket refunds were offered and could mostly be quite easily done through Ticketsolve, but a proportion of the audiences took the option of making it a donation instead, which was gratefully received. Regular updates were made to all supporters through newsletters and social media and there was a regular Cranleigh Arts slot on the newly set up fortnightly Destination Cranleigh Radio podcast, which eventually reached between two and three thousand downloads A national survey of audience intentions 'After the Interval' was sent out and so some indicative guide was obtained as to what customers' attitudes might be when lockdown was lifted.

A 'start-up' group was set up to begin strategic planning of what would need to be done to protect customers, volunteers and staff and what the cost benefit would be in different scenarios of re-starting. Katie and Clive tried to keep up with the changing government guidelines as they evolved – some versions running to over 50 pages. Often the arts were not specifically mentioned so what applied was opaque until qualified later. Risk assessments were drafted and re-drafted. Re-opening with probable restrictions at this stage was posited as October or March. Bob's concern was to calculate with no income at what stage would the money run out– the 'survival horizon'. Thankfully the reserves had been built up to a record level in the last few years, which suggested CA could hold out until the end of 2021. There might be Arts Council grants to be had, but they seemed initially to be aimed to prop up less prudent organisations more in danger of extinction. Once reserves were down to 50% then more cost cutting might be needed if the pandemic continued too long. As it was, the only outgoings sanctioned were salaries and the essentials of the building. If any revenue could be generated within the restrictions that would be a bonus.

Where there's a will, there's a way

The introduction of streaming and how to protect the audience

By July there was some relaxation of the rules but the programme had been cancelled until the end of September. One option was to explore the streaming of filmed events, which some other arts organisations had embraced. This was investigated as a business opportunity both for now and the future. The possibility of using S106 money to cover the cost of £13k for buying the equipment was mooted with Waverley. Already a 'virtual gallery' was running on the website for artists to submit work done in lockdown, following Grayson Perry's lead on television. The volunteers were surveyed on their likelihood of returning and the mailing list were sent 'Act 2', the follow up of the national audience survey, which had 682 responses from CA's customers. The community were still supporting the Centre. The start-up group noted that the priority was to ensure the survival of the Centre and the care of the people using it. People said they would return but only if they felt safe. The Chairman's conclusion was,

> *"It would be calamitous for several reasons (image/reputation/good corporate citizenship/duty of care to volunteers, staff and public) if we were to open, incur or cause a Covid19 outbreak through a superspreader and to be forced to shut down again publicly. Comparable places are being cautious and there is no immediate pressure to re-open before we feel it is right in our context. Costs of reopening are significant and we are unlikely to make much gross profit in offset until social distancing is removed, confidence returns and participation levels are as before. This would reduce reserves faster than currently in 'sleep' mode."*

So people 'bubbled', 'ate out, to help out' and, if they could, took a quick trip to the EU, while the Centre remained closed.

In September it was confirmed that Waverley would continue to support the

Centre and had agreed to the use of S106 money to buy the streaming equipment. It was thought that some limited events could be delivered, either broadcast or with a socially distanced audience, so staff time on flexi-furlough was put towards this end. Start-up swung into action. The necessary servicing of the building was carried out, a one-way route round the Centre laid out, and signage, protective masks and visors, sanitisers and thermometers, and even a spray disinfectant machine purchased. Katie and Clive added detailed routines for every volunteer and staff member who would have a role with the public or performers to support the risk assessments already written. Plans were stalled however as on 5th November, reaping the whirlwind of the summer's laissez-faire, England went into its second lockdown. Three live streamed concerts did go ahead and proved the efficacy of the new facility and had the bonus of upgrading the broadband provision. The performers had the strange experience of playing to a completely empty auditorium. At the next Board meeting on Zoom it was noted that Friends' membership was dropping as the closure militated against renewal. The Arts Council grant applications for extra support had also been unsuccessful. The survival horizon had closed in a bit due to the recent expenditure, but as the Chairman reported to the AGM in November, on Zoom of course, *"he had a quiet confidence that the Arts Centre would endure"*.

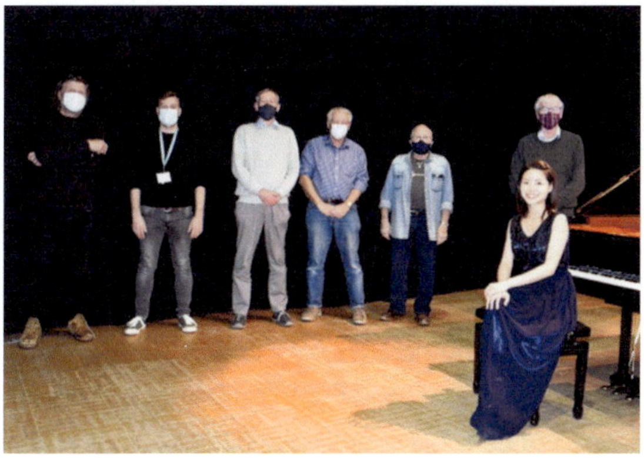

The Streaming team with Mengyang Pan.

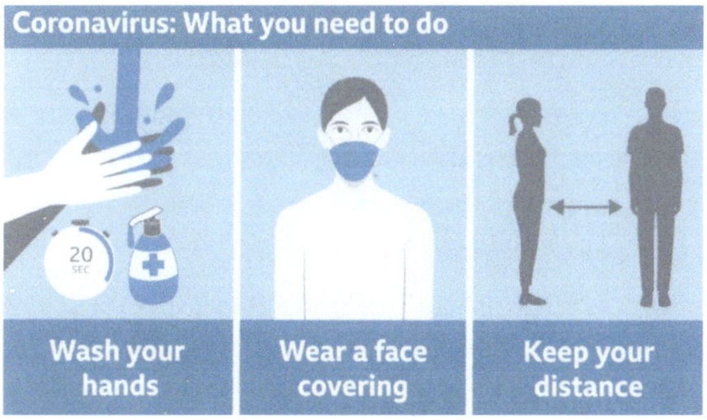

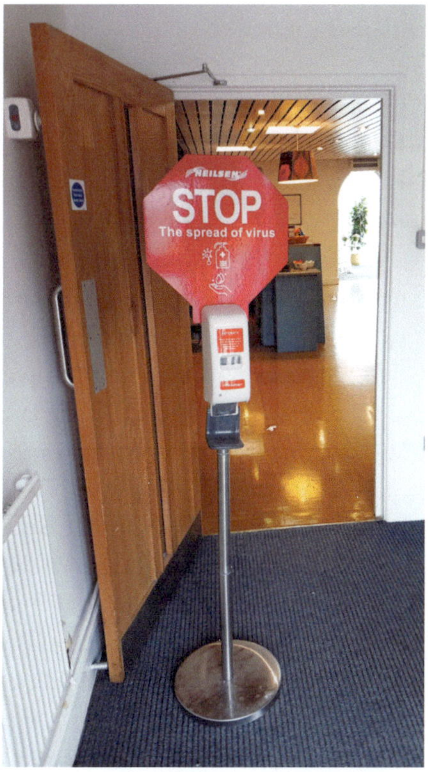

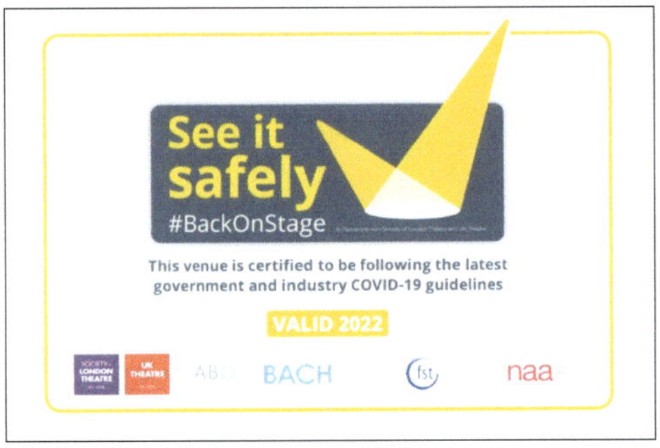

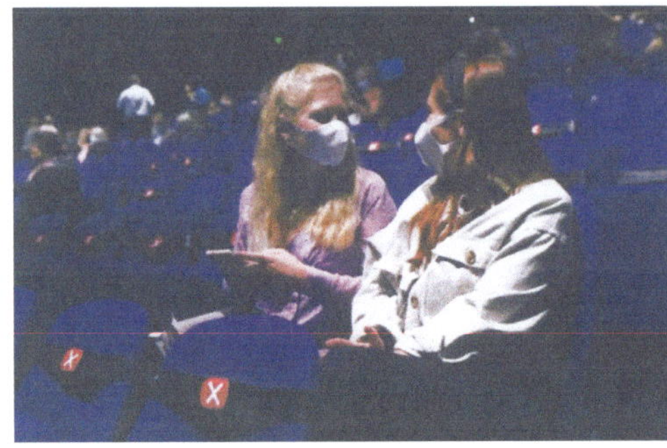

A chink of light came with the news in December of the approval of a vaccine, the start of a vaccination programme and a less draconian three tier system of restrictions. In December that meant that four performances, two classical concerts, a children's show and a folk duo, went ahead for a socially distanced and protected audience (capacity 32). This did not make any money but did wonders for the morale of all involved. The training had been effective and the audience, surveyed afterwards, said they had felt safe and had really appreciated all the efforts made. Things closed down again as Christmas approached and the alpha variant appeared with the next full lockdown on 5th January. The Centre would remain closed from then until May 2021. Sad news too of deaths: Lesley Mason, who had run Bookworms and Friends, and of the partners of two other volunteers.

Looking to the future

Getting back up to speed is not without difficulties as personnel problems arise

The work of the Board continued. In January, looking further forward, the Chairman kicked off discussion of the new 2021-24 Three year Strategic and Business Plan. Chris Wilson had had his tenure extended by a year at the AGM due to his experience in formulating this in the past. A job he relished. The aim of the previous one 'Future Proof and Sustainable Growth' had seen some success, but what would need to be the direction of travel post-Covid? Apart from making operational profits and maintaining financial security, which for him was a given, Bob suggested that aiming for artistic excellence, increasing reputation and reach, and enhancing the community role and impact of Cranleigh Arts might be appropriate starting points. He emphasised that it needed to be a team effort.

> *"We look for agreement in dialogue with other key stakeholders whose operating responsibilities and knowledge are essential factors in providing a reality check, fleshing out our strategies and plans, buy-in and ultimate delivery."*

This plan, built on three pillars, '**Stability, Continuity and Improvement**', was expanded and approved at the March Board.

The March Board also considered the immediate outlook. It was hoped to re-open according to the government's road map around May. In the meantime Live Streams had begun again. Regular hires and classes had indicated they would probably not start again until September. There was interest by some promoters but it was thought it would take until the end of the year before things were up to speed again. In the light of this no annual August closure was envisaged. As a hedge against delays an outdoor season of two concerts and a Shakespeare play were planned for July and August. It would be necessary to juggle income from the government's furlough support scheme, which had been extended to September, against the potential income to be generated from the activities that staff needed to do, Ellie Hulme in Marketing for example. Some trustees wanted to err on the side of financial caution. The Waverley representative gave the view that organisations in receipt of community funding from them had a duty to re-open as soon as possible in order to deliver those outcomes. This was duly noted.

Unfortunately the '**Stability**' pillar was about to take a knock. In May Peter Hunt and Ellie Hulme resigned; Peter to move to RHS Wisley and Ellie to stewardess sailing boats in the Mediterranean and subsequently fly high as cabin crew for Virgin. In June Paul Grover, the Venue Manager, left suddenly due to personal circumstances. He had been a stalwart since 2016, gradually taking on more responsibilities over the years. His knowledge of the building and its quirks was extensive and his customer service to the hirers and public often went over and above what was required. Additionally Clive Wouters had flagged up his wish to step down from Operations in October, after four years. In July Sophie Woods was appointed as Artistic Director and had oversight of Marketing as well as programme, to be joined by a

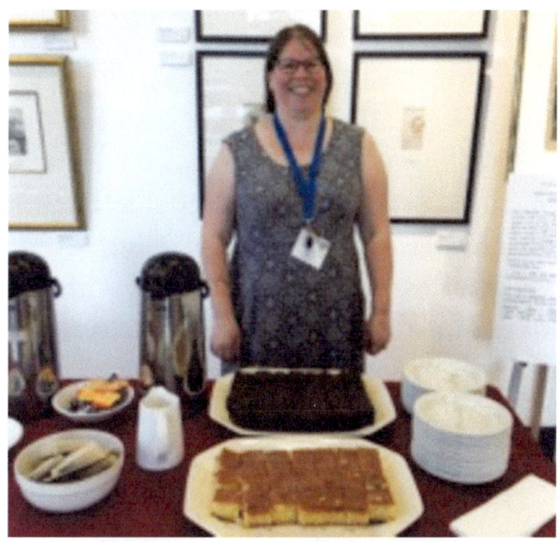

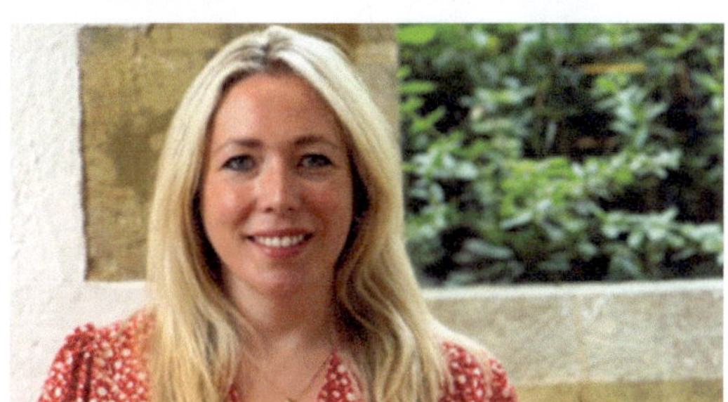

Top Katie Wilson, below Sophie Woods.

Marketing Assistant, Anna Kedge, in September. The Venue Manager role proved harder to replace, but finally it was filled from just two candidates. In the meantime Katie Wilson held it all together and provided some continuity as the last woman standing, but who would herself leave to join Sight for Surrey in February 2022.

A financial buffer of £30k had come from the Garfield Weston Trust and the Arts Council and there was optimism that audiences could return with restrictions in May and unrestricted from June, however this was put back by a month due to the new delta strain. Some hirers had expressed an interest in getting going again before September, such as the youth theatre, pottery and art. The personnel churn meant that there was threat to a speedy re-opening. In this context a review was undertaken to redefine roles and responsibilities. Yet again the need for trustees to assume more oversight and mentoring comes into play and senior volunteers such as Chris Dubois, who had been preparing grant bids in the background, Stephen Dennison, with the Music programme, and Chris Wilson, are given more to do. So successful is Sophie in managing what Peter had left her and adding new ideas that she can report in September that since July there had been in excess of 1,000 customers, the Centre finally having opened fully. There is a shadow cast by the rise of the Omicron variant in December which restricts things again, but by and large normal operations return. Finally on 28th March 2022 Boris Johnson lifts all restrictions. After two years the global pandemic is over and Cranleigh Arts can move forward again.

The long awaited coffee machine is installed and the photocopier upgraded to enable more marketing material to be produced in-house to a better quality. Both were improvements in the pipeline before lockdown but insisted upon by Sophie. She puts her stamp on the building with many inspired touches, softening the Gallery for example and uses her marketing experience to boost the brand with tweaks to the website and an enhanced social media presence. She says she felt she was walking into an unloved space after covid and needed to revitalise it. She took a pragmatic view on the programme and has revelled in the diversity of what she can offer. As she prepared to step down for maternity leave in 2024 she reflected:

> *"It's been one of the best and worst jobs I've had. You have to live and breathe it; you have to turn your hand to anything. When you are in it, you are really in it. It does become an obsession. ... But who else has as cool things as we have? Musicians and comedians love the space. It's unique."*

On her first Duty Manager event she had to deal with the fire alarm going off at the end of a History of Rock concert. Since this was unusual, the staff present were new in post and the stewards a bit rusty, the procedures were not properly followed. One audience member commented *"that was a good way to get us out"* and a steward was still handing out fliers to emerging attendees thinking it was not a real emergency! Sophie rang Clive and Bob who rushed to the scene to be confronted by a fire tender and a crowd of people milling about. It transpired the kiln had not been properly loaded in the Pottery and caused a smoke alarm to go off. All was well and lessons were learnt for the future, but it was literally a baptism of fire for her!

At the November 2021 AGM Bob Wild was pleased to report that the Centre was back on track and paid tribute to the staff, trustees and volunteers who had made that happen. Two new trustees were appointed: Kavita Agarwal, a businesswoman, and David Hitchen, an actor/teacher, to replace Chris Wilson and Lil Lambley. Gaynor Wilson had her tenure extended by a year to provide continuity. He presented a Business Plan for 2021-24 with an aim for reserves to be £150k. There were also plans for further improvements to the building at a cost of £160-180k. There was criticism of the absence of a guiding hand managerially for the volunteers. He acknowledged the vacuum and mentioned the lack of funds for a General Manager position. *"He noted however that there were many knowledgeable and responsible individuals investing their time and expertise into the successful running of the Centre".*

2022 – 2024. The baton is passed on

More people come and go as there is a search for stability, however the programme goes from strength to strength despite the cost of living crisis

As well as Katie needing to be replaced as Volunteer and Community Coordinator, Anna Kedge, the Marketing Assistant, left in November. This begins an uncertain era for staffing as it is difficult to find the right people for the right roles. Some redefinition and re-ordering of responsibilities and recruitment from within the volunteer body fills the gaps. To replace Katy, Clive Jones, Jo Edge and Jane Heathcott share elements of her job each on part-time contracts, each playing to their individual strengths and time available. Jo, who had been the Front of House Manager becomes the Volunteer Coordinator, Jane takes on Front of House, while Clive, a Duty Manager, handles the rotas and communication. The monthly newsletter is replaced with a weekly bulletin and update. By the end of the year they introduce an online volunteer management system, RotaCentral, which had been explored before lockdown. The resident computer expert Alasdair Mackie does the computer integration of it. Bethany Cosgrove, a recent graduate of Guildford School of Acting, starts as an Event Duty Manager in February, and moves up to be full time Production Coordinator from April to November. This helps fill the gap left when Charlie Parkinson, the Technical and Facilities Manager, leaves in April after only eight months. From July she is helped by Harry Brown on the maintenance side. This staff churn led to a lot of pressure on Sophie who admitted the challenge and pressure of feeling ultimately responsible. She says it would have been impossible without Jackie Sanctuary and Bernice Harris, who returns to assist with administration as volunteer Secretary, providing continuity, support and a wealth of knowledge. This indomitable woman had been Bookkeeper for many years, worked closely with Kary Backhouse, served on the bar, been a cashier and had the best practical understanding of how the operations worked of anybody. If the newbies needed to know anything it was a case of 'ask Bernice'. Deepak Laxman, the volunteer bookkeeper who had taken over from Bernice in that role, feels that it has all become too much, despite his best efforts to streamline it with spreadsheets, and the Board finally accepts that this is a role that must be contracted out to a paid person.

Chris Wilson is able to offer some support and coordination for the changing staff and the facilities provision. A recently appointed new trustee, Jackie Sanctuary, who began as a Duty Manager, gradually assumes wider responsibility and eventually takes over formally as Operations Director (unpaid) at the start of 2023. Chris Dubois meanwhile continues as ever quietly behind the scenes assisting with data collection, grant applications, PRS and contracts. Bob Wild decides that he would like to step down after seven years and lines up another new appointee, Brian Belcher, to be his successor from the November 2022 AGM. Brian, like Bob, is a former banker and has been a Duty Manager since retirement. Another new trustee is Brian Freeston, who has a background in film and for two years had been the Parish Council observer on the Board. His work in Cranleigh had included the Memorial Garden and he, together with Simon Rabinowitz and architect consultant Mike Wilson, takes on the next phase of the rebuilding project, now that more CIL (formerly S106) money has become available. Bob had presented these plans at a public meeting in June attended by volunteers and friends. It involved a rearrangement of the Crane Room, Bar and Kitchen, the development of a bar in the Gallery, relocation of the box office and improvement to the inside and outside public spaces. He was surprised perhaps at the resistance to some elements of it. Apart from highlighting some of the practical operational difficulties that the changes might bring if implemented, there was considerable disquiet at making the Gallery another bar. He promised to review the plans but said that the staff team and Board had approved them. Lobbying from the grass roots continued through the rest of the year and changes were made in due course, which modified the project as executed in August 2023.

In November the staff changes continued. Jo, Bethany and Harry all moved on to other things and the Centre was struggling to cope yet again. Clive Jones also indicated that he would prefer to remain just as a Duty Manager going forward, after some ill health. More advertisements and interviews were held and in February 2023 the team welcomed Ian Mortlock as Facilities Manager and Helen Steward as Volunteer and Community Manager, but both on part-time contracts. At last things began to settle down.

Despite the cost of living crisis, the business was looking up as the ticket sales through the year increased month on month. The total for the year reached almost 14,000 which was in excess of 2019's record level. Helen re-instated the monthly newsletter and the Christmas volunteer party with great success. A core team of fundraising volunteers, Caroline Todman, Shelagh Mitchell and Iris Evans restarted their activities from before covid, with a successful Quiz Night and Bridge Tea afternoon. Also this year the Centre moved towards being cashless and iPads replaced the cash registers on the Tea Bar, Bar and

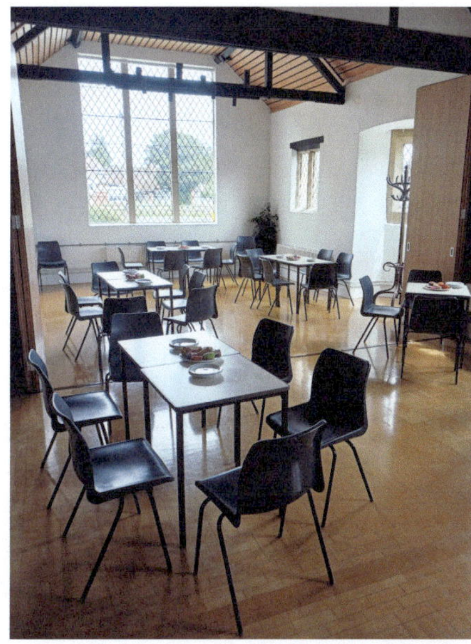

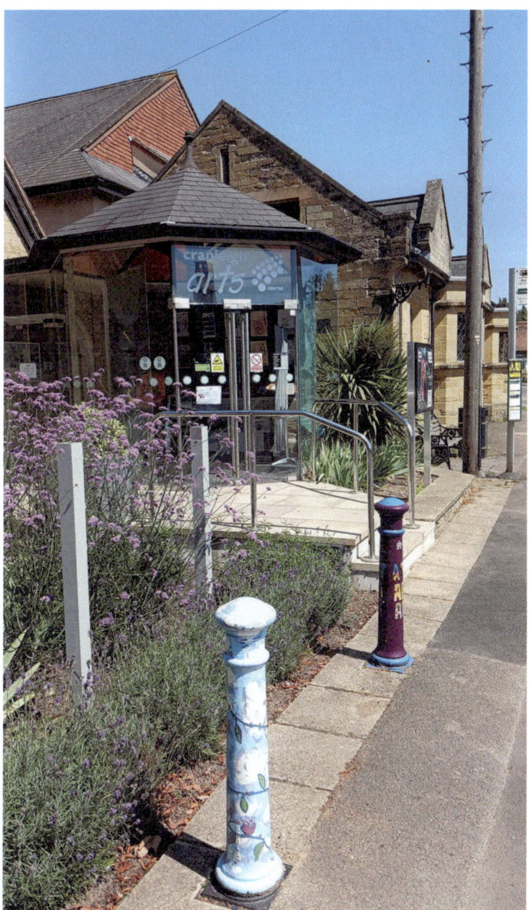

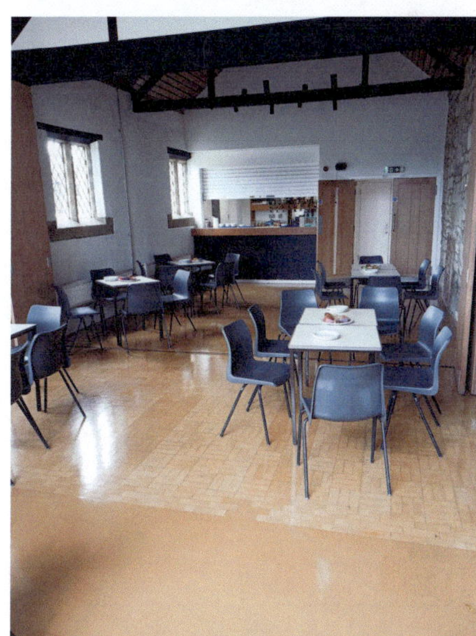

eventually the Box Office. Friends' membership gets back up to 300 due to the dedicated hard work of Elizabeth Campbell. The highlight of 2023 was the redesign of the Crane Room and Kitchen area in the summer, which gave the opportunity to open up the large East window and create a more attractive hospitality space. The foyer was also opened up to help the flow of people. Outside landscaping added to the kerb appeal, and extra noticeboards boosted publicity and made the Centre more visible.

More changes happened at Board level in 2023. Extra trustees were sought in the year and Caroline Heslop, Stephanie Gallo, John Burford and Alan Froggatt joined the Board, with John Haile taking over as a non-trustee Treasurer. Caroline and Stephanie had both been loyal volunteers, Stephanie as queen of the interval tea bar for many years. These replaced recent resignations. The surprise at the end of 2023 was that Brian Belcher stood down after a year as Chairman and handed over to Brian Freeston to take the Centre forward. He outlined his approach in a letter to all:

> *"The Board has decided to increase the involvement of trustees,"* and went on to show how each trustee now had an area of oversight. *"In these challenging times with the help of our skilled and experienced volunteers at all levels as well as our small band of committed, professional staff, we are weathering them. ... The new arrangements at Board level should allow for a closer connection between Board, staff and volunteers. This will in turn make us more of a community with a stronger common purpose."*

Although income had been positive costs had soared. Reserves had been reduced by an overspend on the improvements, understandable with inflation so high. Money was again tight and it would be a case of all hands to the pumps. In the course of 2024 there are more personnel change as Helen Steward leaves, Sophie Woods takes maternity leave to be covered by Paul Scott and Jackie Sanctuary steps down. Their roles are filled, but not without a bit of difficulty and some luck. The struggle to get the right people in the right jobs for the right time continues. But somehow Cranleigh Arts survives, as the wheel turns yet again.

Chapter Eleven

'All things to all people'

How the arts programme has fared over the years

The Strategy

The background to the changing activities of the Arts Centre and the constraints

It has been a frustration to those tasked with programming the Centre that its brief is so wide. In its aims it is clear that all the art forms, as so decoratively engraved on the glass panels of the entrance, should be provided for the community, either to participate in or to experience. From the beginning these were to be art and crafts, drama and dance, music and comedy, film and photography, and later included local history and adult education. This reflected the core societies that brought Cranleigh Arts into being. The strength of the offering at any time over the years has depended partly on the enthusiasms and knowledge of the people involved in organising or booking them, but also on the economic environment. South East Arts early on were able to give grants to support the programme, and audiences or workshop class participants voted with their feet or their wallets for what they wanted. After the rebuild a more professional approach was needed to live up to the business plan and the budget. To the regular fare was added rhythm and blues, comedy and Live Streaming which moved the dial by giving access to top class entertainment. A range of community arts projects brought creative diversity, either funded by the Arts Council or Waverley.

It is a romantic fallacy that 'if you build it they will come'. It takes hard work and a lot of luck to make running an arts operation profitable, or just to break even. There are several factors at play. Firstly, there is no logic to what people will be drawn to; a popular booking one time may see empty seats when they return. The weather, competing attractions, too many events in a week or a financial squeeze can lead an audience to stay away. Diversification may help, but risks diluting the brand. Secondly, margins vary from event to event. In the successful 2018-19 Programme the profit margin was 34%. The Bar and Coffee bar adding half as much again. The split with the artist or producer may only result in keeping 20% of the box office.

This is true of the Popular Music bookings which netted only 11%, despite usually high volumes of sales. However when showing a film there is only the purchase and distribution fee to cover but it requires a lower ticket price. Exhibitions are similarly low cost but can provide commission income if sales are made. Theatre, particularly Children's, can be loss makers as the number of performers usually increases the cost and the short length of the show limits the seat price, thus reducing the take. Ideally the sell-out NT Live and Royal Opera House showings cross subsidise the loss makers and so a balanced budget can be achieved. Thirdly, the costs of running the building in which these events take place is ever increasing. Not only are there staff costs, sales and marketing but the infrastructure, both permanent and expendable, is a constant source of unpredictable expense, be it boilers, IT, changing fire regulations or a leaking roof. Sponsorship of particular events or projects can help boost the programme and grants can help keep the building going, but the biggest dilemma is the cost of staffing, which is a necessary high priority. There never seems to be enough money generated to employ the people that are needed to sustain the operation.

From time to time at the behest of the Board or from the initiative of the Centre Manager or the Programmer there has been analysis of the profitability of different strands and of the utilisation and income from different spaces against capacity. Is it better to have a regular hiring of a small class for a lesser fee, or one-offs that may bring in more but leave a room empty? Too intensive use of the spaces makes demands on staff to clean and repurpose them, often having to shift tables and chairs or other equipment. Leaving aside hires, just with a full programme of presentations and screenings there are considerable demands for volunteers as bar staff, box office and stewards, which may not be easily met at key times of the year. Running 'too hot' has been a problem in some seasons when the organisation has been stretched to breaking point.

In 2006 the Centre Manager in her introduction to the brochure claimed that Cranleigh Arts had 80,000 visitors a year. The programme lists 64 events in October to December 2005 and 61 in January to April 2006. In 2016 one of her successor Centre Managers is claiming *"the busiest season ever"* making the Centre *"a creative, progressive and vibrant place"*. In Autumn 2017 she writes, *"On average each year we offer 50 films, 27 popular music concerts, 15 live theatre performances, 10 comedy shows, 6 talks and 15 live streamed performances. We also have 55 types of arts events ranging from craft workshops for adults and children to our book club"*.

Looking through the events brochures from the past fifty years some trends and ebbs and flows can be identified. But what is clear is that those responsible were driven by wanting to deliver the best quality that could be provided and ensuring that the Centre punched above its weight. This has become one of its distinguishing features and is perhaps why it has been so valued by its community. Here is an outline of how the different arts activities have fared over the years.

Art and Crafts

From the beginning the Arts and Crafts Society provided a core of activities and exhibitions for the Centre. The diversity of its tutors and the loyalty of its many members were very valuable. Saturday exhibitions were a money spinner through sales and by increasing footfall to the coffee bar. These mini exhibitions were curated by Ann Horrocks, Liz Hoad and Corrie Ahearn and included ceramics, calligraphy, soft toys, watercolours, photography, jewellery, batik, enamelling and wood turning, quite often related to current classes or their tutors, sometimes linked to Adult Education. Glass blowing and raku firings also provided spectacular demonstrations. There were regular fundraising craft markets and flea markets and for years a 'Treasure Trove' sold donated articles run by Eve Devenish-Meares.

As facilities were expanded then regular pottery and art classes became a mainstay, with a Life Class started in 1984 and a Monday painting group from1994. Collaborative themed projects, linking visual arts to film and song, were tried with success, as with the 'Celebration of Birds' in October 1987 which brought together an

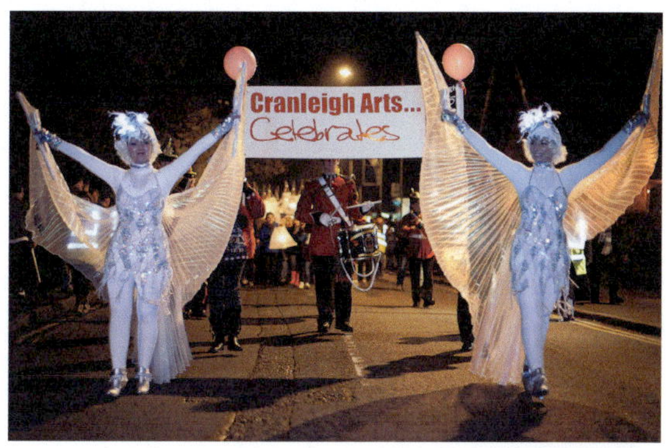

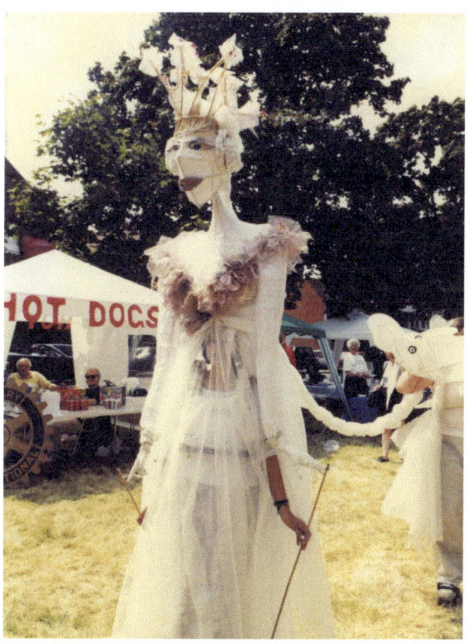

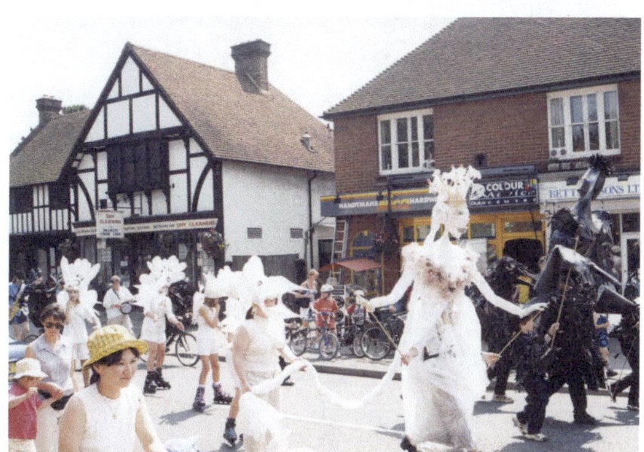

exhibition, an RSPB film and a concert. Similar ventures were run after the reopening, such as 'Art at the Arboretum' at Winkworth which was a day of arts activities to participate in and watch. Subsequent creative projects like the Lantern Parade, the design of Carnival floats and costumes and the Festival of Light were public examples of group creativity on display, celebrating what Cranleigh Arts could offer.

The re-opening of the Centre in 1998 led with a mix of exhibitions: paintings by a local artist, a school exhibition, Kiln Magic from the Wey Ceramics Society, followed by a fund raiser for Task Force Romania, glove puppets, the Camera Club's annual exhibition and the first Open Exhibition competition. This surely covered all the interest groups in the first year. The new building was equipped with enhanced security to be able to show national touring exhibitions. This paid off by attracting the work of Ralph Steadman, David Hockney, L.S. Lowry, Peter Blake and the Brooking Collection in the first five years. More recently there has been the **'Laws of England'** Arts Council tour and, in partnership with the Belgravia Gallery, works by the Royal Family and Nelson Mandela.

The regular annual Open Competition has been a window for local artists to be seen, complementing the Arts and Crafts Society Exhibitions in the Village Hall. A key strand has been regular showing of the work of local schools and charitable arts organisations. These have included The Meath, Art Venture Trust and The Women's Support Centre. Artists-in-residence have often been a stimulus for the school work exhibited and have in particular projects had the support of The Arts Society (CDFAS), who also nominate a selected work for display in the foyer.

In 1999 funding up to £15,000 was obtained from South East Arts and others for a project called Mix and Match. This was a set of twenty workshops and events led by artist in residence Andy Glass, joined by Jutka Fisher, who engaged the Skate Club, the Youth Club, clients from Cheshire Homes, people with disabilities and the general public in building kilns and making pottery and sculpture, both at the Centre and at the Youth Club, culminating in an event at Winkworth Arboretum and an exhibition at the Centre.

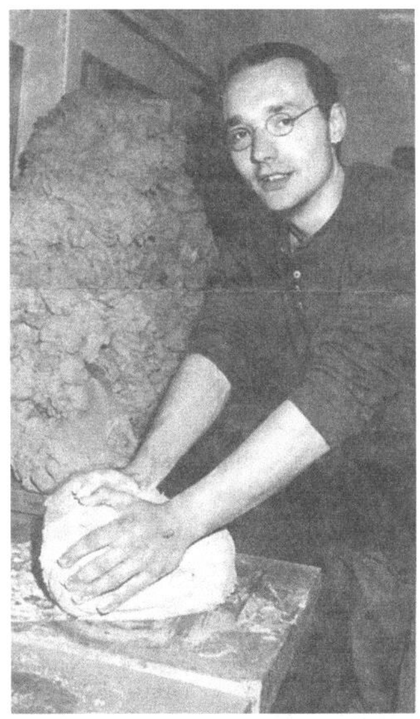

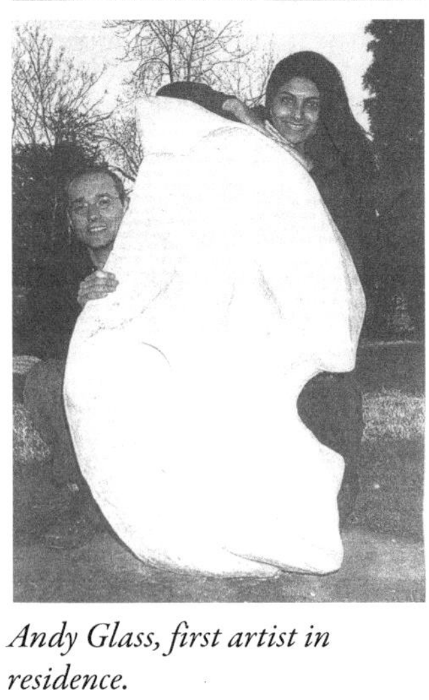

Andy Glass, first artist in residence.

Classes have continued to be run on either a term basis or as one-offs. Having a Potter in Residence, such as Rich Miller in 2004, gives a boost to such activity and has been done when funds permitted. Other regular art tutors have included Betty Steele, Garth Allen, Sam Maynard, Nick Galpin, Louise Grundy and Miriana D'Ambrosio. Some classes are run by Cranleigh Arts, some as hires by an artist or franchise that wants the space. The craft offering has experimented with felting, beadwork, stained glass and bookbinding. Two regular and committed groups have been Knit and Natter and Stitching for Pleasure. An informal Friday art group started to meet regularly from 2010 added to by a tutored Monday group more recently. Popular also has been Brush Party, which combines an art class with an open bar, allowing for convivial socialising whilst copying the tutor's demonstration and is always a sellout. The national initiative The Big Draw in 2014 and 2016 was another way of encouraging wider participation to just pick up a pencil and have a go.

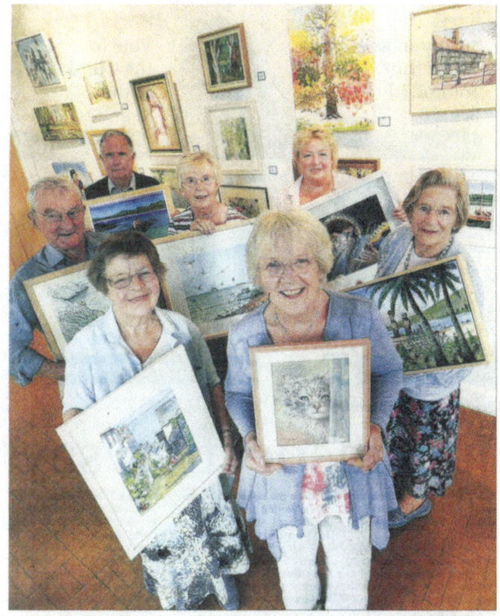

Members of the Friday Art Group Painters' at their exhibition at Cranleigh Arts Centre.
Picture: Alistair Wilson (Ref: SA135421)

'Come join us' says art group

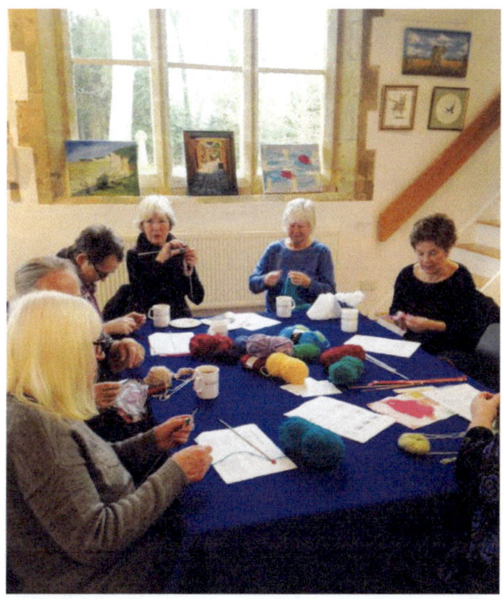

A boost to the visual arts has come with the 'Exhibition on Screen' series from film maker Phil Grabsky. These films focus on an artist and a particular theme or recent exhibition to bring together a close viewing of their work alongside informed commentary from experts and curators. Begun in 2014 at first these showings included a Q&A with Phil himself, who lived locally, but as his company has grown that is no longer an option, and they have now even become available on Sky Arts at home; but seeing masterpieces on the big screen, as with many other films and plays, can't be beaten just yet. A close-up view of Munch, Vermeer, Matisse, Van Gogh, Monet and many others has been a regular treat for art lovers at the Centre.

Drama and Dance

The influence of the Players in the early development of the Centre has been recorded in Chapters 2 and 3. Their major shows continued for a while in the Village Hall, but from the beginning they contributed small entertainments and social events to the programme. In 1981 'Hay Fever' is part of a Twenties Week and they added a Junior drama group. An 'Evening of One Act Plays' follows in 1982, with 'Absurd Person Singular' the next year. However, despite changes of personnel trying to keep it alive, the key people move away or retire and the Players fold in September 1985. Good contacts with South East Arts meant that professional theatre fared better. For fifteen years they financially supported the booking of small-scale touring theatre shows, which included a Polish Mime Company, Snap Peoples' Theatre Company, a professional Panto 'Cinderella', the English Shakespeare Company, the Pickwick Players and engagement with the South East Arts Street Theatre Consortium. Members also had the benefit of joining theatre trips to London, Chichester and other local venues. There were links too with the Guildford School of Acting, whose students came with shows several times, usually Musical Theatre.

After re-opening the possibilities are expanded. Although the stage area and backstage impose limitations, for workshops the seats can be retracted and a large sprung floor area made available. Dance is explored as links with South East Arts are strengthened. In 1999 Salsa is all the rage and in July 2003 a 'Celebration of Dance' is run which develops from a series of workshops into a performance. While not a convenient art form to programme at the Centre there are occasional bookings of Contemporary dance and in 2018 Quicksilver Dance Company, which consisted of older dancers, again linking performance to workshops or classes. Street Dance and Bollywood classes also come and go according to tutors and demand.

As shown in Chapter 7 the Arts agenda shifts from investing in buildings or supporting revenue to project funding with specific outcomes. In 2003 there is a national project on cultural diversity in the arts. Cranleigh joined a creative partnership with Riverhouse Barn, Walton-on-Thames, and the Farnham Maltings to develop 'YATRA – a Journey'. This focused on the story of British Asians in Surrey and centred on an Exhibition, together with an education programme, participatory events and performances which included storytelling, oral history, film, dance and music. This focussed on two families, one of whom was the Thakers. Their daughter Manisha had worked at Cranleigh Arts. Her mother Bakula had been a Saturday Duty Manager. She was also a classical Indian dancer and teacher alongside her day job. Four local artists, a painter, a sculptor, a photographer and a jewellery maker, provided material for the exhibition, alongside memorabilia, pictures and artifacts from the Thaker and Figueiredo families relating to their journey from Gujerat and

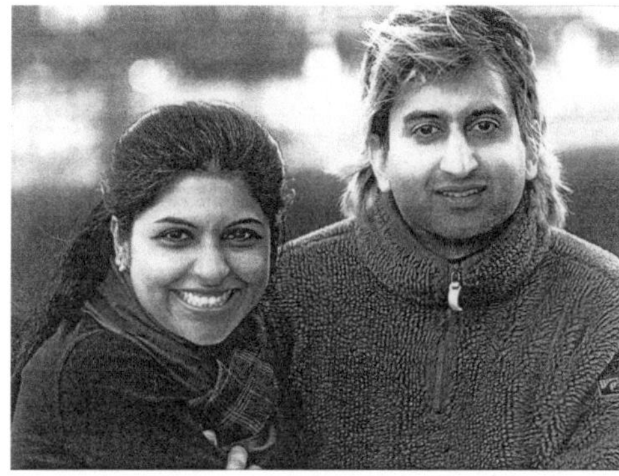

Goa to East Africa and then to Surrey. To go with this there was a performance of 'The Trodden Path', a dance and storytelling piece that told the journey of the families as a folktale. It was performed by Manisha with visual design by Andre Figueiredo, written and narrated by Helen East, who also ran related educational classes with schools. This received a £24,000 grant from The Arts Council and had further subsidies from other funds, including Waverley Small Grants, to cover the £34,400 budget. Nothing on this scale had been attempted before and it gave a great boost to the identity of the Centre.

This strand was continued in 2006 when dancer Shalini Bhalla, who also was part of the staff team, created 'Asmakam' with Payal Akuja, with music by Eleanore Duggan. Such was its success that it was revived in 2008 and went to the Edinburgh Fringe. Shalini became Dancer in Residence and as well as teaching Indian dance presented a Bollywood themed evening with dance, food and a film in 2012.

Presenting off-site outdoor events was a regular feature. Touring theatre included Lighted Fools Theatre Company and the Rude Mechanicals, who took a show to Snoxhall Fields in 2008. This has been maintained more recently since 2016 with seven annual summer Shakespeare plays next door in the Rector's garden. Currently there is a partnership evolving with Knowle Park and their amphitheatre for future projects. A link with Farnham Maltings' House producing arm gave access to their small scale touring projects and saw regular visits to Cranleigh by their companies. In 2006 perhaps the most bizarre production was a one hour circus performance 'FZ', which included an artist *"suspended over the stage shedding clouds of flour and slithering in the pools of water that rained on the stage"*. Otherwise various companies have brought more conventional fare: 'Austentatious' - improvised Jane Austen; 'The Knicker Lady'; as well as plays honouring Joyce Grenfell, Agatha Christie, the Titanic, Shackleton, Dickens's characters, the gardener 'Old Herbaceous' and many more.

In 2015 NT Live brought the experience of the South Bank, West End and Covent Garden to the big screen, giving audiences a front row seat to the most desirable plays, opera and dance. The first season was 'The Beaux Stratagem', Tom Hiddleston as Coriolanus, Benedict Cumberbatch as Hamlet, 'The Nutcracker' and 'Le Nozze di Figaro'. It has continued to excel and is now a key part of the Centre's cultural offering.

While there had been peripheral involvement in the Cranleigh Pageant in 2000, it was not until 2004 that amateur adult theatre began again since the demise of the Players. The Company of Waggs grew up alongside the youth theatre (CRYPT), that was being run by Pete Allen and Sue Palmer-Jones. So named because it echoed the name Jack Wagg and because Sue was known as Sue Moo and its acronym was COWS! Like the junior group this had an 'open to all' policy and put on 'My Fair Lady' in 2009 followed by 'Cold Comfort Farm' and 'Habeus Corpus'. But changes of Centre Manager and differences over policy led to their operations coming to an end. The Ewhurst Players have brought two evenings to Cranleigh but tend to remain in their Village Hall, as do other local amateur drama groups.

Children's activities

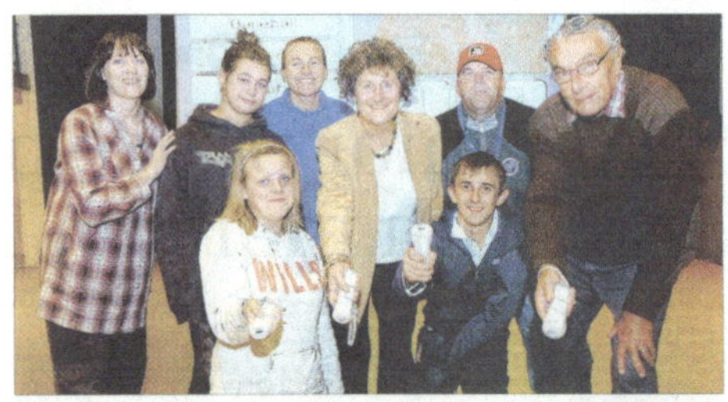
Jane Charlton (centre), with Jenny Squire, Nicci Millar-Foy, Nick Jolly, Alan Goldsmith and youngsters, get to grips with Wii handsets.

Wii event unites young and old

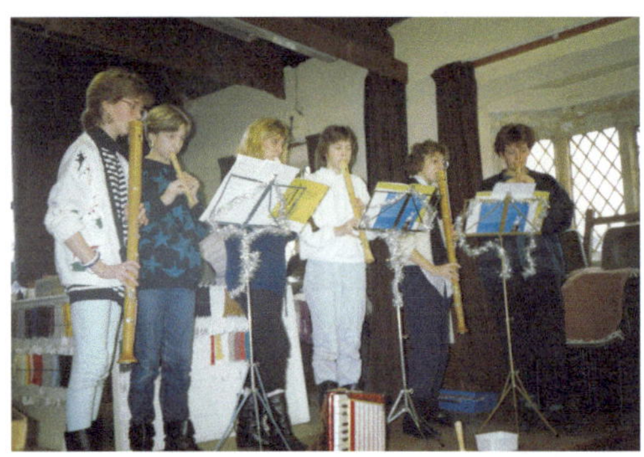

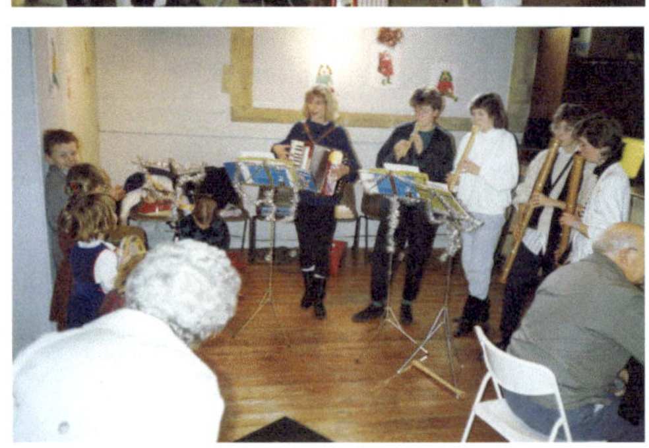

Providing arts opportunities for children has been a core part of the mission from the start, not only for imaginative, creative and social development but because they will be the arts consumers of the future. So in all the genres 'junior' access was a necessary part. A number of key people and projects stand out that show the philosophy and attempts by programmers to engage this demographic at the other end of the scale from the core supporters. Even bringing them together on occasions.

In the 1980s there were regular art, pottery and drama classes for children, with special offerings on some Saturday mornings such as a theatre group, music and mime or cartoon films. These were put together in various combinations for the holidays, first in the summer and then additionally at Christmas and Easter. Lucy Buchanan was the tutor for many of these working with Rosemary Dubois and other tutors. She was inspirational at combining music and drama for all ages. She had first arrived

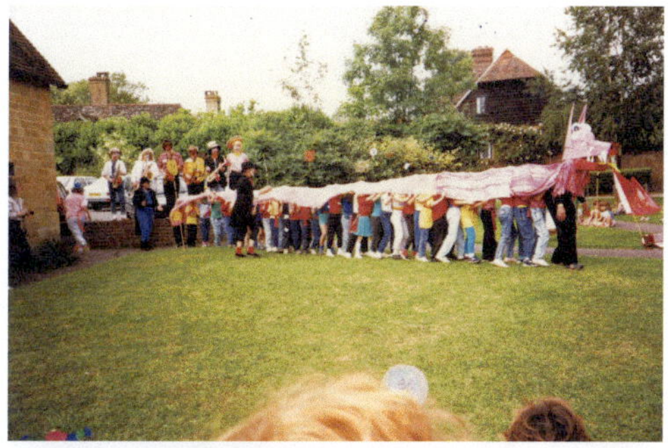

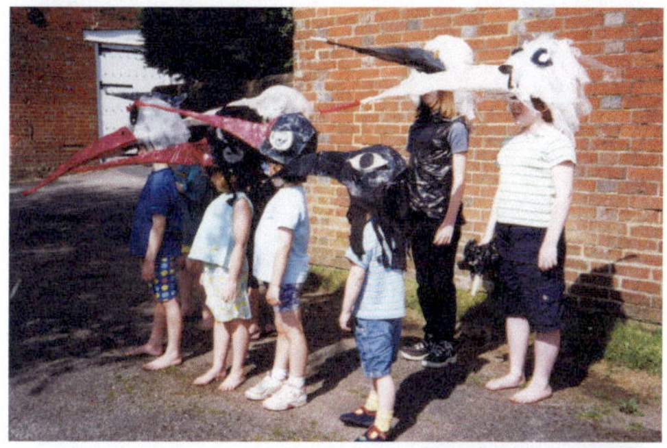

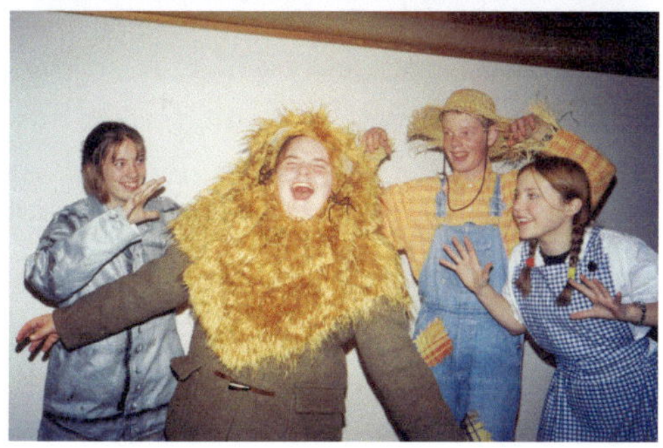

at the Centre on a motorbike looking for work and Jack thought, *"she's got something!"*. He was right and she became a fixture for a number of years.

Pied Piper Theatre Company were regulars in 1986/7 coming three times with shows, later to be joined by Masque Dance Company, the Man in the Moon Theatre Company and Garlic Theatre Company. These bookings were all masterminded by Rosemary Dubois. From her passion and desire to provide ever more interesting things there came shadow puppet workshops, storytelling for Halloween, fun French and a Young Writers Group, who saw their poems published in the monthly edition of *Vision*. The culmination was 'Summer Madness' in 1996, a three week festival of creative activities for children based on Lewis Carroll. This was such a success that it would be repeated in following years.

After reopening there was more space for activities. A Mother and toddler dance group was established as well as regular pottery and art and crafts classes. A Youth Theatre Group was started in 2000 by Amanda Farrell. So popular did drama become that it quickly grew to three groups of two age ranges. They performed 'The Wizard of Oz' in 1999, 'Oliver' in 2001 and 'Our Day Out' in 2002. A Youth Orchestra followed in 2001. In 2000 the summer menu included clown and drumming workshops as well as a 'play in a day'. The involvement of Louise Grundy at this time, who ran a range of textiles and arts and crafts classes for toddlers and young people, expanded the offering in the next few years. She was also behind successful initiatives such as the Carnival procession creations, the Mix and Match Arts at the Arboretum projects in 1999 and the Lantern Parade in 2009, all of which had young people to the fore and gave a prominent profile to what Cranleigh Arts was doing, not least a giant papier mâché Easter Hare. Competitions, such as to design an anti-litter poster in 2004, or to decorate a bollard, and summer 'Big Art

Weeks' have continued to try to engage young people.

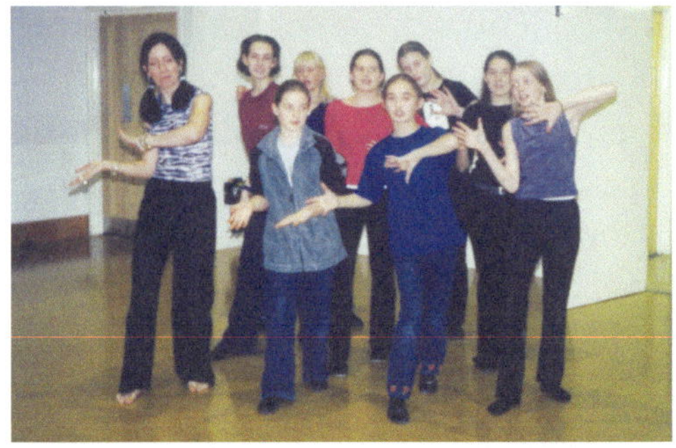

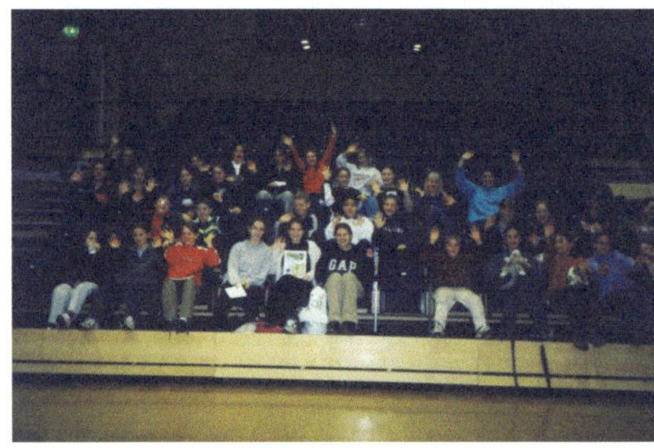

In 2004 two major initiatives were launched. First, the indomitable Pete Allen joined Sue Palmer-Jones to run the youth group started by Amanda. It was renamed CRYPT (CRanleigh Young People's Theatre) as he hated the youth theatre tag. They had an open access policy and were highly creative and individual leaders; inspirational and energetic they won a large following and great devotion. They empowered the young people and if good theatre happened as well, then all well and good. Sue tells of one young boy, very nervous and not a natural, having his moment in the spotlight. He dried up from nerves and had to be fed every line. Meeting him afterwards she thought he would be distraught. Instead he beamed up at her saying, *"That was the best thing I've done in my whole life!"*. They put on devised work or mash-ups of established plays with the emphasis on fun and engagement. Adults in Cranleigh today still look back fondly on their involvement. Their work eventually went under the banner of Whirligig Arts and added a filmmaking course in 2007/8. In 2012 they were part of Mayday celebrations putting on a Mummers play. They continued until 2015 when their own circumstances and changes at the Arts Centre led first to a move to the Village Hall and then closure. Since 2017 Surrey Youth Theatre Cranleigh, under Mitch Jenkins, has run classes and showcase productions, with fluctuating numbers, continuing this tradition. An increasing number of franchised performing arts groups have also used the Centre for shows, including Cranleigh Dance and Theatre Arts, Showdown Theatre and In2Drama who have run summer courses. Schools too: Glebelands and Cranleigh Prep School for special events. Hurtwood House, the local independent specialist sixth form school for the arts, has also presented an evening of its finest actors each June for over twelve years and taken the Gallery for art exam work exhibitions.

A major contribution for the young people of Cranleigh in 2004 was FLY (For Local Youth) which came out of a Cranleigh Healthcheck exercise This was a project set up in partnership with Cranleigh Youth Club, run by Sarah Dolman and Nicci Millar-Foy, to respond to the cry *"There's nothing for us to do in Cranleigh!"*.

Applications for funding were sent far and wide and got a positive response from Community Action, Cranleigh Initiative, the Surrey County Councillor Andrew Povey and local businesses. The Police were involved and backed it, also providing funds and a regular presence. The aim was to present 'sociable, affordable events for young people in Cranleigh' through a range of events twice a month at the Centre. These included local bands nights, DJ Club nights, a Valentine's Dance, LAN nights and films. The rules were that it was drug, alcohol and smoke free and a Hoppa bus, paid for by the Cranleigh Lions, enabled the youngsters, aged 13-19, to get home to the outlying villages. There was an element of self-rule in that the youngsters helped choose the events and got involved in the planning, marketing and running of each one. After an initial six month pilot it ran successfully for a number of years. In 2006 Nicci Millar-Foy was given a Respect Award for Taking a Stand from Home Office minister, Hazel Blears. This recognised the FLY work and its success in reducing anti-social behaviour by 74%.

However in 2007 meetings were held to review and tighten up the operation. It appeared that Debbie Stubbs had said CA would pay for a number of events in 2006 without any record, so the finances were disputed. CRB checks were becoming an issue. There were problems with the security firm used to supplement the Community Police Officers who attended and the young people's behaviour was getting rowdier. Although the bouncers would confiscate alcohol if anyone was found with it, they drank outside, bringing angry complaints from the Rector who found revellers with a bottle of vodka in the churchyard. Mums would ring Louise Grundy, the Centre Manager, complaining that *"my daughter came home drunk!"* to get the reply *"We can only supervise them when they're here".* The changes of personnel with the Centre Manager meant that relations became more difficult. There were some clashes over dates, the setting up of the Centre and the clause in the agreement that FLY had sole use of

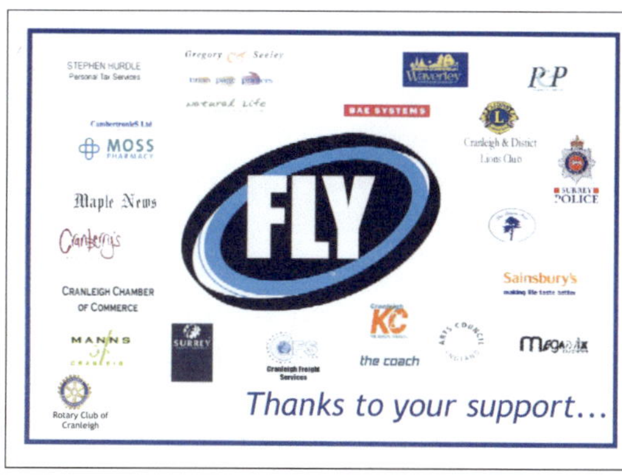

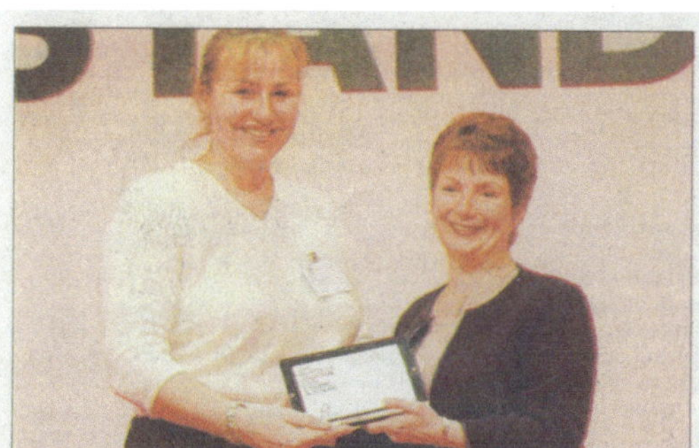

Nicci Millar-Foy (left) receives her award from Home Office minister Hazel Blears.

the Centre. The context in 2008 was very different to when it was originally set up and Nicci Millar-Foy went to Waverley's Community Arts Officer Charlotte Hall (nee Gardiner) who was a Board observer to mediate. However it seems to have come to an end in 2008.

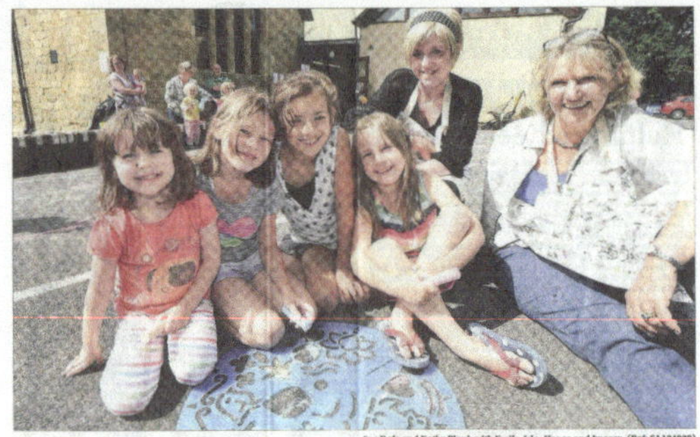

Sue Dale and Kathy Plank with Emily, Isla, Honor and Imogen. (Ref: SA134932)

Chance for children to get arty at new sessions

Different arts engagement groups have come and gone. Cranleigh Arts Monkeys was run by Kathy Plank and Maureen Dormoney as an afterschool drop off art club from 2014 and later continued by Sue Dale. Little Sparks was an under 5s Saturday morning group of music, games, songs and stories. Art Hub, an afterschool art class franchise, have recently taken over some provision. In 2015 and 2016 summer courses were run in theatre skills, dance and flag making. Popular for a while were Street Dance and Pop 'n' Lock Classes. Over the years the Arts Society (formerly CDFAS) have sponsored exhibitions and concerts involving young people and local schools. A major project was the design and making of a tile sculpture for the new Health Centre.

Film and Photography

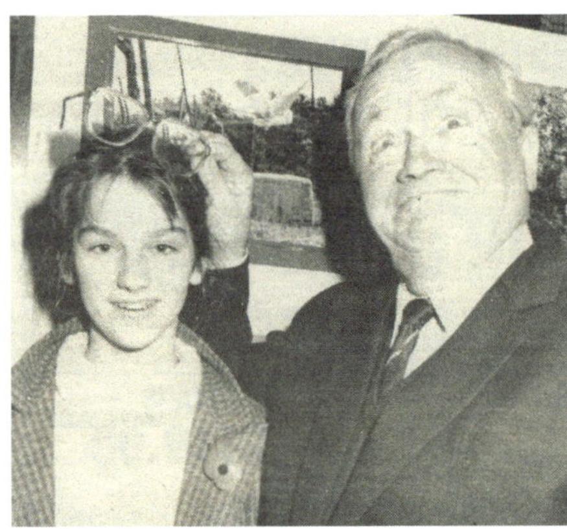

The Cranleigh Camera Club was one of the founding societies and despite the poor facilities in the old school building managed to have a damp dark room, host workshops and hold exhibitions and competitions. They also supported the social events and pitched in with fundraising. Eventually it proved less than ideal and they moved out to meet instead at the Baptist Church and to exhibit in the Village Hall. However they still retained links and held occasional photographic presentations in the Gallery, their in-house profile given a boost by the Secombe Photographic Competitions in 1988-92. The Gallery has regularly hosted photographic exhibitions, including one by

Picture tells a story

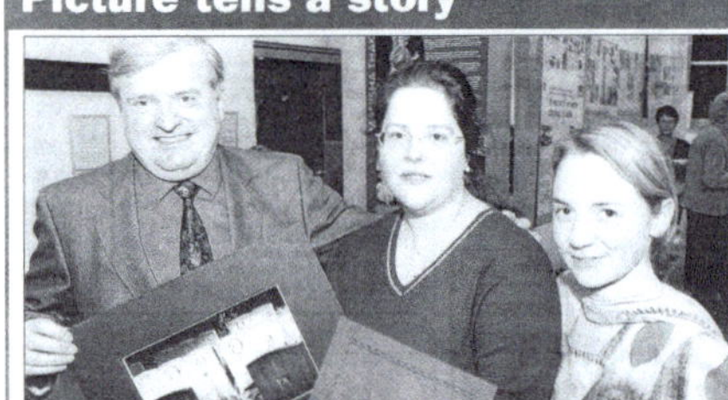

Catherine Humes of Bishops Square, runner-up in Cranleigh Arts Centre photographic competition, receives her prize from Richard Womac, chairman of Cranleigh Initiative and Helen Cundy, director of Cranleigh Arts Centre, right.

celebrated leading photojournalist Terry Fincher.

In 1976 the Cranleigh Film Society joined the core members of the Trust. Led by cineastes Brian Hemingway and Edie Goodfellow they organised regular monthly showings of available recent films with a smattering of foreign films for the buffs and silent movies for the kids. However by 1991 the Film Society is wound up due to no one wanting to be on the committee, as had happened to the Players, but Brian continued to show films for the Centre and donated the balance of funds, £250, to the general coffers. There is a gap then until winter 1993 when South East Arts provide some money to support one film being shown per season.

After re-opening the offering is boosted to a regular Wednesday each month and the Centre shows popular films on second run. In 2001 'vintage' matinees are tried and research is undertaken as to what the public want. In 2002 The Regal Cinema closes when Bernard Tonks retires. He has struggled to keep the 400-seater cinema going. This is the era of Blockbuster video hire when the seeds of the nascent home cinema experience are sown. In a deal with Crownhall Estates, who will develop the site for housing, Cranleigh Arts gets money to support the showing of films and to upgrade its equipment. This gives the programme a boost, as the 170-seater Jack Wagg Hall is easier to fill. A Judi Dench season is a success. Foreign films are mixed in and supported. Saturday morning family cinema is established. Very popular is a showing of a Buster Keaton silent epic 'The General', with commentary and piano accompaniment from expert Neil Brand. This is followed up by 'Sherlock Jr' in similar fashion.

In 2005 Brian Hemingway died and a few years later, in his memory, the Hemingway Film Club is launched in June 2008 to show award-winning international films each month on a Thursday. Subscription-based, with a nominal entry fee, it is separate from but subsidised by the Arts Centre. For the first three years it struggles to gain traction with a membership of about a hundred. Eventually there is a parting of the ways and they move to the Band Room where they have continued successfully since. Financially this worked better for both parties in the end. It also allowed Ruth Eastelow to move regular films to Thursday and thus avoid a clash with the Orange 'Two for One Wednesday' promotion.

Other groups who hired the facility include Circle Eight Film Group, to show double bills of local history and railway shorts. SERIAC (South East Region of the Institute of Amateur Cinematographers) had an annual Film and Video Festival for a number of years. In 2007/8 a Young Filmmakers group meet regularly to create films in term time workshops.

Subsequent programmers have followed their instincts to make the films on offer be something beyond the reach of the couch potato. Festivals are one way: in 2012 for the Diamond Jubilee – royal films. In 2014 the hook is a 'Handpicked' strand in the season – one international, one documentary and one British film. In 2019 it is Music on Film – 'Amazing Grace', 'Wild Rose', 'Grease' singalong and 'Singing in the Rain'. Add-ons are another way. In 2002 'Bridget Jones's Diary' is shown with a pre-show pampering package for a girls' night out, which includes a drink, cake and a makeup or manicure session. In 2009 'Mamma Mia' is shown with a side of mezes and fizz, while in 2022 you can order a pizza to go with the family film. You can even bring your baby to special matinee showings for young mums. With the technology having been upgraded for the NT Live showings and all that is needed is a blue ray disc and projector, the possibility of pop-up films, as soon as they become available, gives a flexibility now that was not so before. Recently sponsorship has come from Box Broadband who seem to want to encourage big screen cinema at the same time as their ever faster fibre is bringing on-demand content into every home. Surely some irony there?

Music

Like a microcosm of the bigger arts programme Music is a broad church and has many denominations with their distinct devotees. Weighted towards audiences more than participation, unless dancing in the aisles counts, there have been opportunities to engage through classes and regular groups over the years, alongside watching some top rate performers of their genre. Sometimes subsidy has enabled events, sometimes the events have been fundraisers for the Centre. But the music never dies.

Initially in the 1980s the focus was on local music with occasional concerts. There was a regular Folk Club, and performances by the Cranleigh Youth Musicians. Peter Trevelyan, the St Nicholas organist, gave a recital, the Bramley Music Competition prize winners performed. There were links established with Goldsmiths and the Royal College of Music for young musicians to come and perform, including a Cellist from the BBC Young Musician of the Year Competition in 1985. That year South East Arts gave an ongoing grant to support live music. Jazz appeared in 1986. In 1987 there was a social 1940s Party, with music, dancing and some drama. More exotic perhaps was the visit of a Danish choir who gave a fundraising concert in the Church and a Balkan Folk group in 1990. Show tunes made an appearance with a Gershwin presentation in 1996.

Appearing odd perhaps to us now, but well supported at the time, was the Music Listening Group established in 1985. This had spun off from the Guildford Recorded Music Society and ran for over ten years. The group would sit and listen to a member introducing and playing their favourite recordings. Perhaps the culmination of this came in a whole Lecture series 'Aspects of Rigoletto' in 1996.

After re-opening initially it was 'suck it and see'. An approach by a promoter, Geronimo, to Rosemary Dubois led her to try Rhythm and Blues. It seemed popular. Classical music went well at lunchtime. The Dominic Alldis Trio, whose crossover jazz and cabaret was starting to make waves, were well received and have recently returned to become regulars. The pattern for the next few years had a mix of classical, folk, R&B and jazz every season. In 2005 a 'Boozy Blues' weekend was put on in association with Hogs Back Brewery who brought out a limited edition 'Arts Centre' Ale.

After two years the promoter of R&B changed from Geronimo to Tony Smith and Eclectic Live Music. This would prove to be a profitable relationship over the years. He brought some top names to Cranleigh including Osibisa, Mike Sanchez, Dr Feelgood, Geno Washington, Georgie Fame, Alan Price and, of course, Paul Jones. There were some occasional disputes at times, but when someone wrote to *The Surrey Advertiser* claiming that the offering had gone stale which was why ticket sales had fallen off, his supporters rallied to his side, as did the Centre. His audience now might prefer to sit rather than stand in the mosh pit, reflecting the passing of the years, but R&B still burns bright.

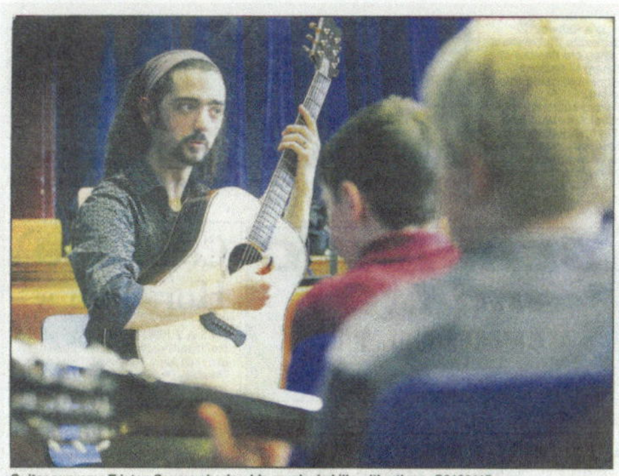

Guitar supremo Tristan Seume sharing his musical skills with others. C6180115.

'Rock' masterclass given to pupils

Local participation was another key strand. Since 2000 Sharon Duggan had been the Centre's singing tutor, running numerous courses and workshops and was encouraged in 2006 to start a Community Choir alongside her singing classes. This became very popular and her annual 'Big Night Out ... with Bells On!' show (the culmination of a sixteen-week performance course) was a firm favourite with audiences running for over ten years. Sharon also ran (and continues to do so) a summer show and a Christmas show 'The Cranleigh Community Choir and Friends', a mix of professionals and talented amateurs as well as the choir. The longest standing hirer, Sharon has been at times a mainstay and ongoing critical friend to the team, while engaging

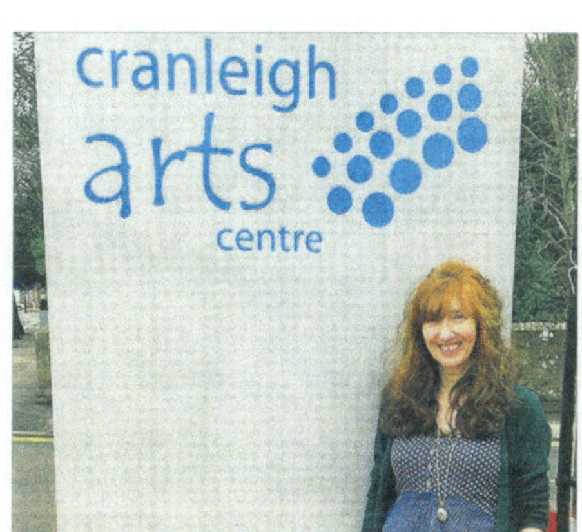

Sharon Duggan celebrates the choir's 10-year anniversary.

many residents in the joy of singing and performing. Similarly, local guitar player and performer Tristan Seume, whose parents are long serving volunteers, gave classes and concerts as he established his music career. In 2003, with Waverley funding, a 'Battle of the Bands' competition was introduced and well attended. Other Open Mic events have peppered the programme as demand has arisen. In 2010 another local performer Richard Poll took the lead on this, sponsored on one occasion by Home Brew.

Various diverse local groups have showcased their work in concerts at the Centre including The Crawley Accordion Orchestra, the Methodist Youth Band, The Guildford Opera Company, the Surrey International Harp Ensemble and the Surrey County Youth Orchestra. Another regular and popular one has been the Ron Green Big Band who, despite several changes of personnel, still pull in their loyal fans. In 2018 Community Drum Circle was programmed. Such was its success it has returned again and again when young and old regularly gather to delight in beating the hell out of all kinds of percussion.

Through the 2000s/2010s various changes of promoter happen in different genres as the programmers realise that this is a cost effective way of booking acts. Julian Lewry takes over Folk, Modular take over jazz, Electric Voices provide contemporary acts and DK Music Academy start 'Live at the Crane Room' to showcase local acts. In 2017 acoustic acts become appealing again. Most recently Nigel Sanctuary has revived Open Mic evenings and local market stall holder Paul Rich has brought Frank Sinatra to life in a full concert.

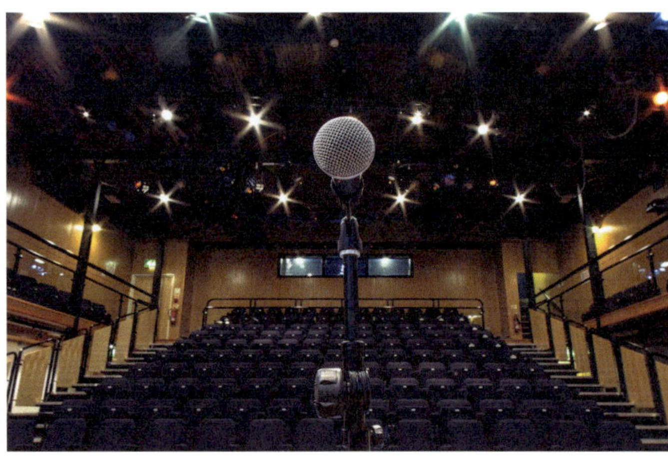

Another development has been the growing popularity of Tribute acts. They begin to be programmed in 2007 with one a year building up to the present day with at least one a season. There is a strong appetite from the audience to relive their musical memories through acts such as Purple Zepplin, the Counterfeit Stones, the Alter Eagles and the Jackie Generation.

Classical music was sometimes a hard sell having a usually small but appreciative audience and was the Cinderella until Stephen Dennison took it over, when he stood down as Chairman. It had been a passion of earlier Chairman, Catherine Pike, who made sure that there was a decent piano at the Centre and on one occasion took the staff to Glyndebourne as a thank you for their hard work. In 2014 sponsorship from the Martin Music Scholarship Fund gave the opportunity to present up-and-coming young musicians. Stephen's drive to increase the audience by extensive marketing and his development of other funding, both local and national, saw this part of the programme expand and excel. Some concerts were fundraisers and the quality grew exponentially. Members of the ENO, Richard Saxel, Head of Music at Cranleigh School, the Queen's Six, Dame Imogen Cooper and Leslie Howard all took to the stage and entranced the audience. Over lockdown a classical recital was the ideal thing to stream, with a performer interview, in lieu of an actual event. This kept the audience in touch with Cranleigh Arts and gave the performers work, whilst obeying government guidelines. In a locally crowded field Stephen established Canleigh Arts as a market leader for classical music. So much so that an anonymous donor bought a new Shigeru Kawai grand piano on the strength of it.

Comedy

Before the re-opening Comedy, as in stand up, was largely unexplored. Comedy meant skits or entertainments put on by the Players as part of a fundraiser or social event, or a performer such as David Kossoff, where comedy was part of a talk. It has since 1998 had two strands: a comedy club and headline acts, one more successful than the other. As with Music, the performers are booked through a promoter, the allegiances and relationships varying over the years.

In 2002 Good Sense of Humour started a comedy club on the first Tuesday in July, August and September with young comedians including Natalie Haynes. Then in 2004 Creased Up Comedy took over and in the next eighteen months brought Tim Vine, Zoe Lyons, Chris McCausland, Mitch Benn, Jeremy Hardy (a Farnham lad), Jo Caulfield and Rich Hall. In 2006 Blast Comedy Cabaret Club was tried for a while, with Creased Up and GSOH also providing performers, who now included Mark Steel, Andy Parsons, Russell Howard, Jon Richardson and Greg Davies. It has become a Cranleigh boast that *"we saw them here first"* as acts have gone on since to become ubiquitous and established TV performers. After some complaints at the content of some of the acts a rating system was introduced in the publicity, grading them from 'family' to 'blue'" in 2009. In 2011 the Comedy Club idea was relaunched by Just Fair Laughs and included a meal deal while watching largely new TV comics. Another promoter Lakin McCarthy brought Arthur Smith and Fred MacAulay to keep the higher profile up.

A step change was made in 2014 with the association with Off the Kerb, a leading agent who saw Cranleigh as a good pre-tour try-out venue for his top names. So Shappi Khorsandi, Kevin Bridges, Jo Brand, Rob Beckett, Dom Joly and Romesh Ranganathan, together with the return of Andy Parsons, Mark Steel and Jeremy Hardy, made this a great success for the next ten years with sellouts almost immediately tickets were put on sale. The performers appreciated the intimate venue and warm welcome. One noted that, *"In South London they throw bottles at you if they don't like you. In Cranleigh they just go quiet".*

In 2015 and 2016 a pre-Edinburgh comics' warm-up was tried but as this was in July and the names not well-known it had less success. Better was a booking of The Noise Next Door, a comedy impro group, who did separate shows for adults and for children. They were very popular and returned in 2023.

Education

Apart from classes in the art forms, many being provided as part of the Adult Education programme in the early days, a broader educational strand can be found in the users of the Centre. The History and Archaeological Society became affiliated in 1980, the Bridge Club joined in 1987 and a writers' group and poetry group were running on and off through this period. The Adult Education branch in Cranleigh was a mainstay from 1976, not only financially, but also because its chief officer, Dilys Savedra, was de facto Centre Manager for a long while. Eventually after re-organisation, loss of funding and changes of personnel they stopped running classes at the Centre, concentrating on Glebelands instead. But U3A expanded to Cranleigh in 1995 and took their place with a wide range of classes as they became established. These regular bookings became an important, if somewhat limiting, underpinning of the finances. Another is Cranleigh Decorative and Fine Arts Society (CDFAS) which has met monthly at the Centre from 2007, taking an afternoon and/or evening booking for a speaker and runs occasional special interest days. There is an illustrated lecture on a wide range of topics to a membership of over a hundred. Prestigious and well supported this is part of a national organisation, NADFAS, *"which brings people together through a shared curiosity for the arts".* It changed its name to The Arts Society in 2017.

In 2004 a book group Wine and Words meet regularly for a time, a part of the Tabasco Book Club franchise. From 2007 onwards the Cranleigh Writers' Group start to meet at the Centre. They publish an anthology 'Gallery' to showcase their work and take part in various open mic nights. The first Literary Festival happens in 2016. This involves poetry, star speakers, a linked film, a new writing showcase, workshops and a presentation from the Guildford Shakespeare Company 'The Bard's not that hard!'. There is a presentation by work from Hurtwood House School of student work. The Festival is successful and was repeated each year up to Covid. Local writers and poets participate alongside guest performers such as Ian McMillan and Danyah Miller. Workshops provide skills and advice to aspiring authors. It has been revived in 2024. Other projects have included 'The Best Days of our Lives', a reminiscence project curated by the Arts Development officer, Gill Collins. This brought together those who had been at school in the Centre in the time of Claude Bloggs and their memories of its use then. A booklet was produced and launched at a tea with the Mayor.

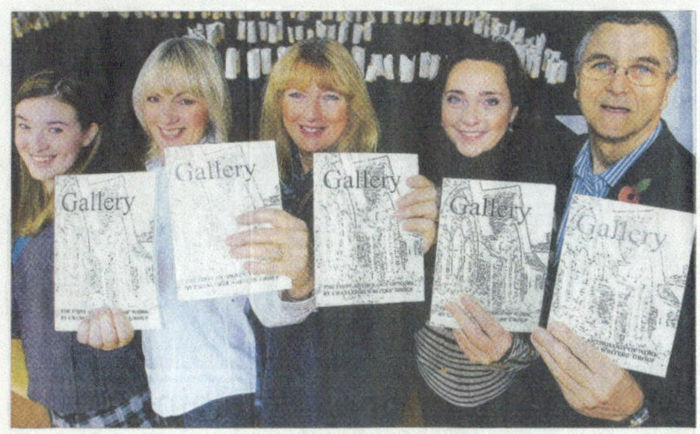

Writers Hannah Perrin, Tricia Broomfield, Bridged Fayers, Jane Terris and Colin Ward with copies of their book. (Ref: SA105752a)

Talks have been a regular booking from the start and usually in those days had an arts bias. So initially they were actors, artists or musicians informing the audience about their craft. There was Antony Hopkins on music and John Labanowski on 'Shakespeare's Fools'. Later this extended to hearing John Challis on playing Boycie in 'Only Fools and Horses', Sunny Ormonde from 'The Archers', Cranleigh actress Melanie Parr in 'The Sound of Music with Gretl', and 'The Making of War Horse'. Eventually this widened to include science: The story of Apollo 11; history: 'Surrey on Film 1914-1953', Bletchley Codebreakers and 'Violette Szabo by Tania her daughter'; politics: Alan Johnson and (separately) Ann Widdecombe; and even sport: David Gower, Henry Blofeld and Peter Baxter. Wildlife featured from Ben Law 'The craft of the woodsman' and Virginia McKenna on 'Born Free'.

Events are sometimes programmed to catch the wave. National Storytelling Week was celebrated in February 2001. In 2002 there is a National Science week, which has two talks and a linked exhibition. Later in 2002 Local History Week was similarly celebrated. In more recent times there have been visits from the Supersonic Science Show, the Bubble Theatre Show and the Lego Show by the Brick People, all repeat bookings and entertaining, inspiring and educating full houses of young people.

Wellbeing

Within the aims of the charity 'to promote leisure time activities (apart from sport)' wellbeing activities are a relatively recent arrival. Apart from a Girls Night Out in

October 2001 and February 2002, which promised *"gossip, a bar, manicures and makeovers"* the first identifiable class in the programme is in 2008 when Yoga starts. which increases to three classes a week in the following year. It may be that U3A were offering some classes in this area which are not identifiable as Cranleigh Arts promotions. Yoga is followed by Tai Chi and a regular Health and Hygiene class, as well as First Aid.

In 2014 there is a Baby Massage class and in 2015 Mindfulness. 2016 sees more growth, reflecting a broader trend, as two drop-in groups start: Colour at Cranleigh, a mindful colouring-in session and Knit and Natter, a knitting group. Pilates and Fit Steps groups begin regular classes. In 2017 Mummas and Beans, a support group for new mothers and their babies, also proves popular. All this culminated in 2019 in a Health and Wellbeing Fayre which was an open day offering taster experiences and information on all the courses and classes offered. A more recent addition has been a regular Sound Bath session to promote relaxation.

At the older end of the community in 2016 Singing for the Brain starts meetings in April which in Autumn becomes Melody Memories. This is a dementia support group which moved out to Rowleys after funding problems. Their place was taken by Memory Lane Café, a similar support group under the Alzheimer's Society umbrella, which is self-funding and has grown successfully in what it offers to those living with dementia and their carers. Operating on a Monday when the Centre is closed it is a safe and exclusive space for those involved.

Two other initiatives to improve the access of the community to the arts have been a scheme to offer young carers free cinema tickets, sponsored by St James's Place, and the introduction of neurodiverse screenings in 2019/20. Sensory Friendly Films are a special opportunity for individuals living with autism and others, perhaps dementia, to enjoy films in a safe and accepting environment. Lights in the theatre are turned slightly up, dim lights remain on and the sound is turned slightly down.

Festivals, fads and fundraising

Getting people through the door and raising money are the two drivers of activity. Both are methods of involving the community in what happens at the Centre. In the early decades, when the societies and Adult Education dominated, the letting of spare space was not exploited very much. Early hirers of the facilities were the Vallendar Friendship Club, the Hitherwood Residents Group and the RSPB. Cranleigh Arts was represented at 'Welcome to Cranleigh', a biennial evening in the Village Hall organised by Michael Wild and the Parish Church, which introduced newcomers to Cranleigh to the many social groups and activities on offer. Similar community fairs have been run in recent years to enable sharing of resources and knowledge of support groups within Cranleigh. Churches Together in Cranleigh also ran a series of interfaith talks at the Centre in 2004.

After re-opening the non-arts hires were expanded to include at different times: wrestling, mediums, antique valuations, retro gaming evenings, quizzes and magicians. It may be breaching the Magic Circle code but on one occasion the performer relied on electronic cues from a device activated by a technician in the control box. He was blindfolded and had to arrange various people from the audience into an order. When he said *"I'm sensing a man in a blue shirt"* or *"a woman in a red dress"* the technician would buzz once for yes and twice for no. However on this occasion there were two people in blue and so an argument broke out in the control box between the two techies as to whether it was 'yes' or 'no'. The magician was ill advised and got muddled by the cues and ground to a halt. Red faces all round.

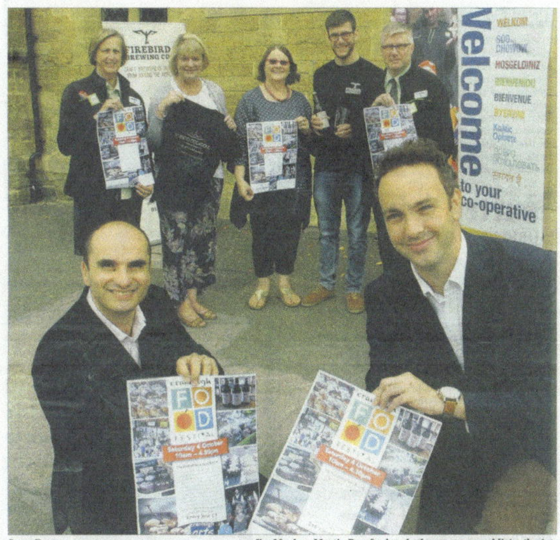

Steve Porter SA145565

Jim Markos, Martin Bamford and other sponsors publicise the Arts Centre Food Festival, in Cranleigh.

Putting the art in artisanal food

For a while Festivals were the thing, a trend encouraged by Gavin Stride at the Farnham Maltings. So Eat and Drink Cranleigh in 2013 morphed into the Cranleigh Food Festival and then the Cranleigh Food and Music Festival in later years. Support for Spring into Cranleigh and Cranleigh in Bloom also engaged the Centre with the community. In 2017 The Great Get-Together started and was another way annually of reaching the wider public in the spirit of community, honouring the murdered MP Jo Cox. Providing 'rooms for hire' have also brought groups together for weddings, funerals and celebratory birthdays in a welcoming atmosphere. Fundraising needs led to special events too. When things were dire in 2007 a fundraising fashion show was put on by Elaine Graham and Julie Stardust. In 2015 a series of events were held for the slightly miscalculated 25th Anniversary, including a dinner and an auction. The high-profile Celebrity Interviews and the nomination of prestigious concerts also counted as fundraisers and were hot tickets. But there were humbler ways to turn a profit such as the sell-out Bridge Teas or smaller auctions and quizzes which meant that all could make a contribution in some way.

Mission accomplished?

Reviewing the last fifty years the diversity of the activities at Cranleigh Arts is striking. Those putting together the programme, be it individuals or a committee, have always tried to offer the widest range of opportunities possible, both mainstream and the more unusual, within the limits of available resources. Ambition to deliver the best has been built into the DNA right from the start and continues today, fuelled by the passion of those involved. It does deliver its mission. The outcome is many faceted, which is perhaps why it shines so brightly and attracts the numbers of participants it does from across the community.

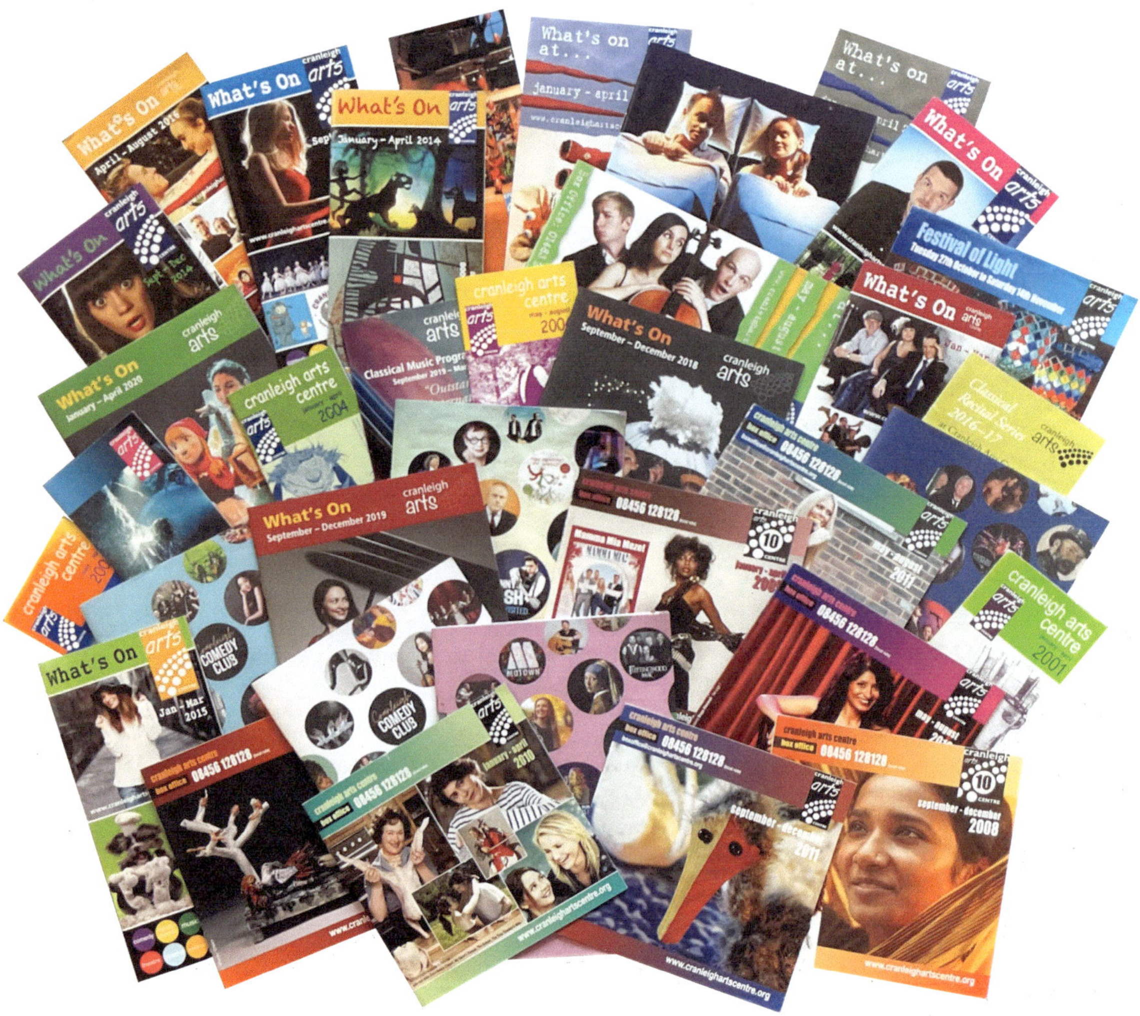

Chapter Twelve

The Patrons, Trustees and Volunteers

The people who make a difference

The success and survival of the Arts Centre has been due to the input of many remarkable people. In the narrative of this history there have been some significant contributions, either at a particular moment in time, or over a period, which have bolstered the enterprise and enabled its growth. But there are many pieces that make up the whole picture. It is understandable that often the most obvious have been those who gave it its public profile or led the organisation.

The Patrons

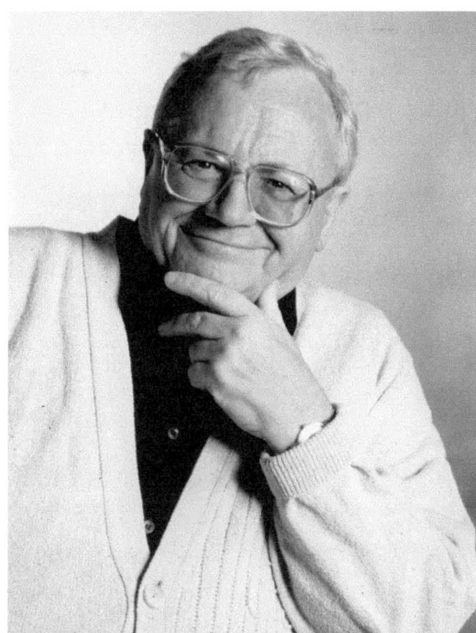

Sir Harry Secombe

Harry Secombe, his wife and family had been living in the area since 1984 and were often seen round the village. He had a record of aiding good causes, including the Cranleigh Youth Band, having opened the Band Room in 1985. Jack Wagg wrote to him in April 1987 asking for his support *"for our diverse activities including the bolstering of our Building Fund. ...your Vice-Presidency of South East Arts and our backs-to-the-wall struggle tempts me to hope you will at least be able to consider this letter with understanding."* His secretary replies that Sir Harry is very committed to the TV filming of 'Highway' (ITV's version of BBC's 'Songs of Praise', which he also went on to present) and Concert tours and has little time to be engaged other than to lend his name. Jack replies that a short private visit could be arranged to meet a few leading members and *"hopefully one or two ideas would emerge"*. This is agreed in July but it is not until February 1988 that he and his assistant make a visit. On finding out that there was a need for some basic equipment like a desk, typewriter and a telephone he immediately sent a cheque for £500 and agreed that becoming a Patron would be a good idea. This happened formally in May 1988. The local paper had a front page picture of Harry getting a welcoming lick by Jack's dog and the headline **'Sir Harry to be Arts Centre patron'**. It went on:

> *"He agreed to become patron as he said he was so impressed by the variety of programmes offered at the Centre and the opportunities for handicapped centre-goers. ... Sir Harry's active interest and involvement with the Centre will provide a much valued focus to the future fundraising efforts."*

The County Times had a different picture showing Centre Manager Rosemary Dubois with Sir Harry and Mayor Alan Lazarus holding carved wood mallets from an exhibition as earrings.

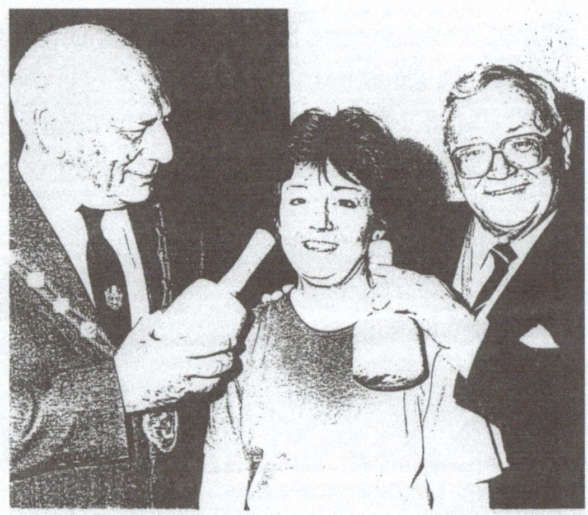

Photo by courtesy of the West Sussex County Times.

Originally the photographer had suggested they could be hitting Rosemary over the head with them, but Sir Harry said he couldn't do that as his 'Highway' viewers wouldn't like it. He became part of a fundraising group set up in September 1989 to get the ball rolling, which had its inaugural meeting at Willinghurst, Sir Harry's home. He opened his contacts book and drafted an appeal letter describing the work of the Centre and its ambitions. He continued,

> *"Last year I became so impressed with what was being achieved on a voluntary basis both for the community and in the specific interest of the visual and performing arts, that I willingly became Patron of the Arts Centre as a charity well-deserving of my support. I have promised to help with a substantial fund-raising project in 1990. I am impressed that this is community arts at its best which you would wish to support generously – I invite you to do so. Our immediate target is £10,000."*

Rosemary Dubois remembers going for tea with him and how his sitting room had a grand piano and his own paintings on the wall. He had studied art, written poems and two novels, as well as being a singer and actor. So he was very much aligned to all the activities of the Arts Centre. His involvement came at a crucial time which gave a boost both to the people working at the Arts Centre and for the customers too, in that it raised the status and profile of the organisation. The ambition of raising the money to complete the development of the building became more feasible and its potential for growth more concrete.

One of the first projects was a photographic competition and exhibition held in December 1989 which was to be judged by David Secombe, his son, a professional photographer, Bill Ward the ITV producer of 'Highway' and himself. There were Junior and Adult categories with substantial prizes donated by Sir Harry. This was a great success and repeated in 1990 and 1992 with 120 entries. In 1990 an extra category was added to link to the Celebrity Cricket Match which was held on Sunday 23rd September.

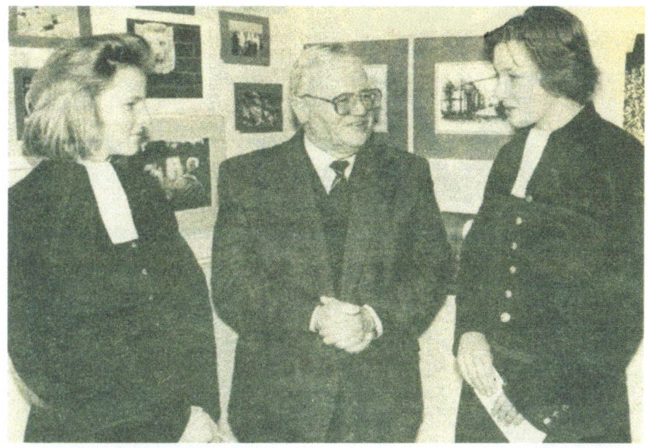

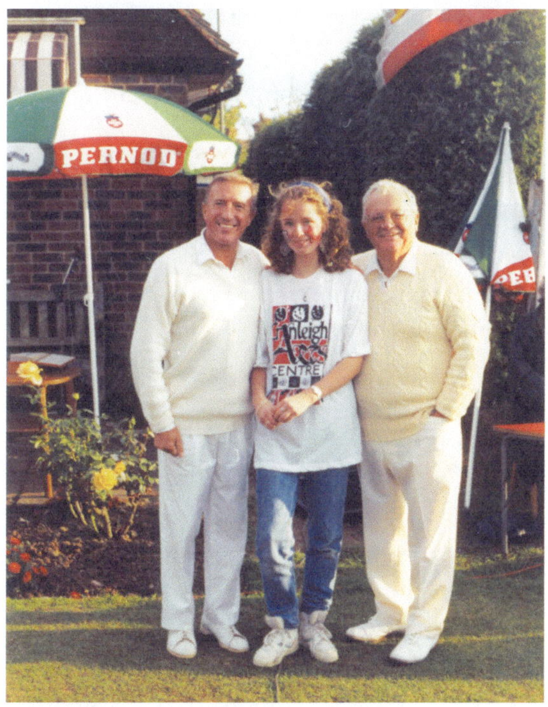

Roy Castle and Harry Secombe.

In contrast to any previous fundraisers the Cricket Match was an organisational test for everyone in terms of scale and profile. After the planned Gala Concert had been rejected as being too ambitious for the scarce resources of the Arts Centre, this event had to show Harry that they were serious. The committee met regularly to get every detail planned. The neighbours and police had to be informed. Catering had to be arranged, including a buffet lunch in the Cricket Pavilion. At the start of September the to-do list still ran to 30 items from organising the crafts stall, the funfair and the ice-creams, to PR, photography and autograph booths, a marquee, bunting and a band. Even a steam engine! A PA for the commentator, Christopher

Martin-Jenkins, and appropriate changing space for the players completed the list.

On the day there were showers on and off and Charles Collingwood's wife joked to Rosemary that she must have her *"own personal rain cloud"* following her. Chris Dubois was in charge of meet and greet, but as he rarely had time to watch TV he worried that he wasn't going to recognise any of the Star Eleven, so he arranged for someone to be at his ear telling him who they were. They included Richard Stilgoe, Charles Collingwood, Roy Castle, Neil Durden-Smith, Christopher Martin-Jenkins, Mike Denness and Kieran Prendeville.

Sir Harry followed this with a fundraising concert on 2nd November 1991 in the Davenport Hall at Cranleigh School, promising 'indoor fireworks' as it clashed with Bonfire Night but was the only date he could manage in his busy schedule. The first half was provided by the New Entertainers giving songs and readings while Sir Harry, with his pianist Ronnie Cass, took the second half with familiar songs including 'Love is a many Splendored Thing' and 'Nessun Dorma' interspersed with goonery, jokes and anecdotes. The £3,000 raised helped to offset the £40k costs of constructing the new Pottery at the end of the East Wing.

He re-opened the fully rebuilt Centre in April 1998. The entertainment was the Manic Street Sweepers street theatre group, which gave Harry a chance to improvise some repartee with them first. Unveiling the title stone Sir Harry declared *"God bless all who sail in her! ... It's fantastic what they have done, absolutely wonderful. It's so important in the community to have this facility. It's better than a lot of cities."* He also said, *"It's absolutely fantastic in there. It's like an Aladdin's cave, a wonderful place"*. His irrepressible sense of fun ensured a truly memorable occasion. There is a nice contrast on the front page of *The Surrey Advertiser* that carried a teaser photo of Sir Harry covered in a cloth with his glasses over it and the heading **'Who is the mystery man?'** ... *"Goonish behaviour abounded in Cranleigh at the opening of Cranleigh Arts Centre. Find out more on page 13."* Alongside it was an article announcing *"Calls to pull down the Yvonne Arnaud. Board advocates building £21m theatre on new site"*. Thankfully twenty-five years later both buildings are still standing.

Sir Harry died in April 2001, after fighting a string of illnesses including a stroke, diabetes and prostate cancer. There had been talk of maybe arranging an 'Evening with ...' event with stories and clips but sadly that was not to be. On YouTube there is a BBC documentary filmed eighteen months previously showing him recuperating at his home in Shamley Green and making light of his ill health. There was a service in Cranleigh Parish Church attended by the family, local residents and a host of show business celebrities. Villagers lined the route of the cortege. Floral tributes included those from Spike Milligan, Norman Wisdom and the Prince of Wales. The Rector of Cranleigh Nigel Nicholson led the service, with the Vicar of Shamley Green assisting. Sir Harry's brother Prebendary Fred Secombe gave the address. He said,

> *"His love was as large as his circumference once was. He was generous and kind. He was generous to charitable causes, generous to individuals and generous to my churches. He was always finding fun wherever he was, even in dying."*

In October Catherine Pike and Rosemary Dubois represented Cranleigh Arts at a Service of Thanksgiving in Westminster Abbey. This was attended by the Prince of Wales and Representatives of the Royal Family. Bill Cotton read one of Harry's poems and there were addresses by Michael Parkinson and Jimmy Tarbuck. The Dean said in his opening remarks,

> *"Today we remember Sir Harry Secombe, the clown. The clown has an honoured place in human history. He is the one who can make people both laugh and weep, who can puncture pomposity, and from any of life's situations conjure a critical yet funny view."*

Certainly that was the person whom Cranleigh remembered. The Centre could not have had a better patron. He embodied both passion and fun in the arts and championed what Cranleigh Arts could achieve.

Paul Jones

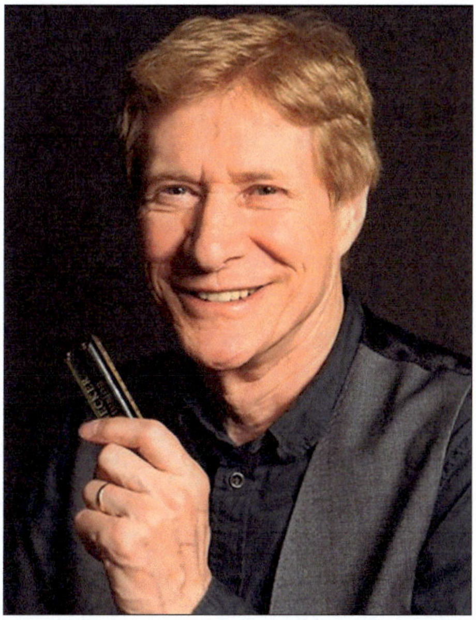

This corner of Surrey has become well known as a haven for rock'n'roll royalty. Ringo Starr lived for a while on the outskirts of the village. Kenney Jones owned Hurtwood Polo Club. Eric Clapton, Bill Bruford and Alvin Stardust were also to be spotted in the High Street on occasions. Indeed Alvin had been in discussions over becoming a patron and he and his wife were supporters. Rosemary Dubois remembers seeing Phil Collins several times shopping in Budgens in the 1980s. Patti Boyd (wife to George Harrison and Eric Clapton) came to one of Dominic Alldis's first concerts at Cranleigh Arts. Down the road at Chiddingfold, the Mulberry Inn, owned by Chris Evans, had pop icons drop in regularly and the Chiddingfold Club held an annual gig led by Gary Brooker with local pop artists and friends. Tony Smith (Eclectic Live Music) stepped in to help organise them in 1997 with a Dr Feelgood concert for Macmillan Nurses.

In 2000 Eclectic Live Music had been presenting acts at the Arts Centre including

Mike Sanchez, Alan Price and Zoot Money. In 2004 Paul Jones was invited to join a concert organised by Gary Brooker at the Guildford Civic, which included Eric, Kenney and Alvin. Recalls Paul,

> *"It was at that great concert that I met Tony Smith, who promoted gigs for Cranleigh Arts Centre. They'd been looking for a patron since Harry Secombe passed away and, after a while, asked whether I'd be interested. It took me some time to consider but eventually I couldn't resist. The first concert we actually organised together was at Chiddingfold. It was a charity fundraiser for Hurricane Katrina. From then, we've done it every year in Cranleigh, to raise money for the centre and various charities."*

His first Cranleigh Arts fundraising concert was in 2006 at Christmas to help get out of the financial crisis and they would continue for ten years. It raised over £6,000 which, together with grants from the Parish Council and Surrey County Council, paid for the installation of forty more seats on the balcony, thus increasing the capacity and earning potential. In April 2007 in the publicity for his appointment Rosemary French was quoted as saying,

> *"We are seriously delighted – it really is fantastic because I think he brings in the right mix of the old and the young. To secure Paul Jones is truly a scoop! Our grateful thanks go to Tony Smith of Eclectic Live Music who orchestrated the 'match' between us."*

Paul helped too by publicising some of the live music gigs on his radio programme and used the venue to film a TV programme. He also brought the Blues Band and Manfreds tours to the Arts Centre to great acclaim.

The following year's concert, 'Paul Jones and Friends', was just as successful, sharing the proceeds this time with a Romanian refugee charity. This became the model going forward increasing to two nights. Each year the Friends who would be sharing the stage with Paul were a secret until the night, but included the great and the good from his little black book. The roll call included Eric Clapton, Paul Weller, Van Morrison, Steve Brookes, Reuben James Richards, Chris Barber, Andy Fairweather-Low and Debbie Giles. Since it could be a different one on each of the two nights tickets were a hot property; people often came to both nights resulting in a sellout within hours of the box office opening. Not only did the Arts Centre benefit from a share of the proceeds, some going to other charities nominated by Paul or his special guests, but additionally Friends' membership went up as they had priority booking. A Friend application even came from someone living in Austria! Huge Bar sales and a raffle helped to further increase the income.

This injection of funds helped over the years to support the revenue account and capital reserves at a time when money was tight. The next Chairman, Stephen Dennison commented, *"I don't think CA would have survived without Paul Jones"*. There were problems only in 2008, when there was a break in and the theft of some of the takings, and in 2010 when it had to be postponed due to heavy snow. At one concert there was a power cut, not unusual in Cranleigh, just after the interval. After a brief discussion about emptying the building Paul decided to carry on with acoustic instruments and the emergency lighting. The show must go on! The event was transferred to G Live in 2017 when Paul wanted to raise more money for his charities in a larger space. The wisdom of this was shown in 2018 when his concerts with Tom Jones and Van Morrison raised £30,000. However he generously continued to give some of it to Cranleigh Arts. Stephen Dennison recalls meeting with Paul and his wife at 140 in the High Street for coffee and saying that Cranleigh Arts would miss his contribution. After a long pause Paul said, *"how much are my gigs worth to you?"*. Stephen told him. Paul reassured him of his continued support. The association with Eric Clapton continued as he has also used the Centre for filming and as a rehearsal venue, as have other performers such as Elio Pace.

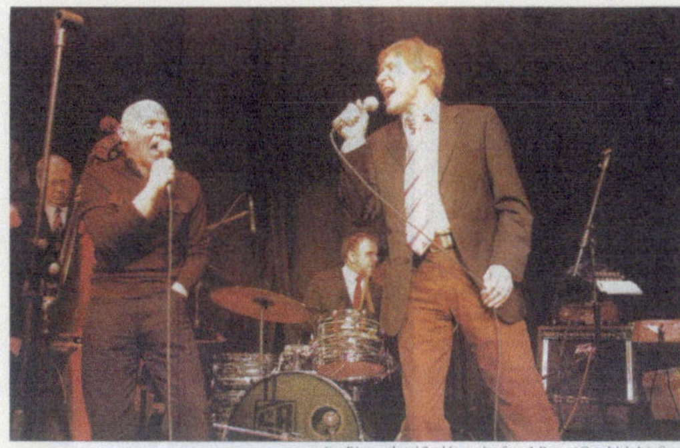

Jim Diamond and Paul Jones sing Sam & Dave at Cranleigh Arts Centre.

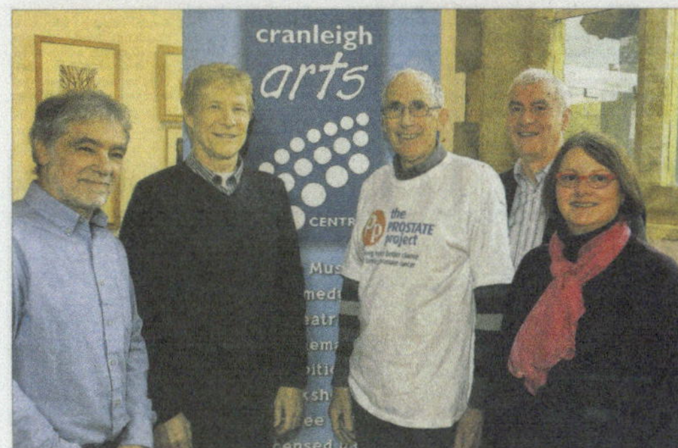

Pete Gardner
SA140686

Tony Smith of Eclectic Live Music, Paul Jones, Cranleigh Arts Centre chairman Stephen Dennison, Prostate Project chairman Colin Stokes and arts centre manager, Kary Backhouse.

When Paul Smith suggested the idea of Celebrity interviews, which other theatres such as the Yvonne Arnaud did, Stephen Dennison took it on and tapped up an old showbiz contact for guests. He had been at school with Robert Fox, the theatrical agent and part of the Fox theatrical dynasty. Stephen still had his cricket bat so with the excuse of returning it he asked him if he could help. *"Who do you want?"* he replied and reeled off a list of top stars. This became 'An Evening with ...'. Paul was very willing to be the host, as he regularly did interviews on his radio programme, thus doubling the star attraction! These began in October 2016 with Bill Nighy, whom it turned out Paul had acted with, following on with Virginia McKenna in June 2017. It was back to actors in December with local resident Julie Walters who

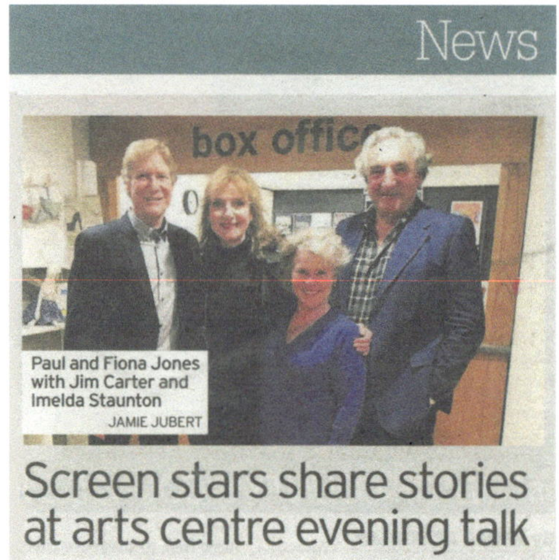

seemed charmed by her visit. In April 2018 Rick Wakeman took the stand, having been persuaded by Bill Bruford, Stephen's neighbour in Ewhurst. He and Rick had both recently been inducted into the Hollywood Rock and Roll Hall of Fame. Although not part of the brief Rick delighted the audience with some impromptu music too. He tweeted afterwards, *"Had a wonderful time last night at Cranleigh Arts Centre. Lovely people and great friends such as Bill Bruford and Peter Egan in attendance. Paul Jones and I had a great fun chat on stage. I scored 9 on the waffling meter!"*. (His son Adam and musical partner Damien Wilson, have also been regulars in the centre's diary performing as Wilson and Wakeman). The climax of this series was the reunion in October 2019 with the husband and wife couple Imelda Staunton and Jim Carter, when Paul was joined by his wife, Fiona Hendley-Jones. They had all first met in 1983 when acting in the National Theatre production of 'Guys and Dolls'. This quartet of stars made for a memorable evening. The one that got away? Dame Judi Dench was very close to being signed up but it didn't quite happen.

Paul Smith CBE

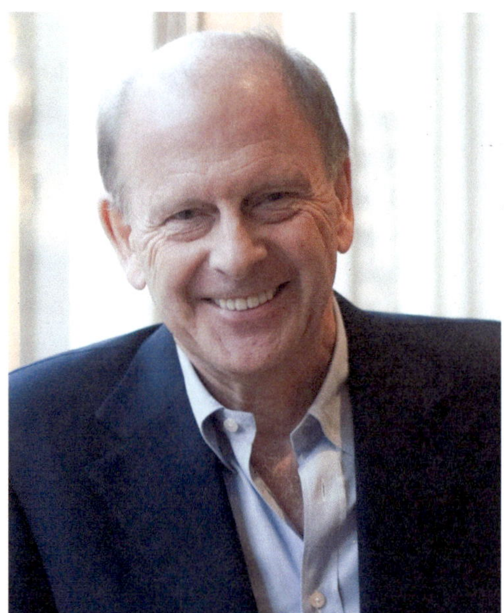

It was the Annual Garden Party of the Shamley Green Garden Club in 2015 that brought Stephen Dennison and Paul Smith together among the roses in his garden. A senior media figure, he has played various roles across broadcasting and film-making. He is the Chairman and founder of Celador. Since 1981 he has led the business from its early days as a pioneering television post-production company through BAFTA and Emmy award winning global TV production to Oscar triumph in the film industry and most recently as a significant owner and operator of UK local radio stations.

Wanting to support the arts locally he agreed after some persuasion from mutual friends to be an Honorary Patron. On being asked for advice on sound equipment for the Live Streaming upgrade he generously made a contribution towards it and has given further support and advice over the years.

Dame Julie Walters

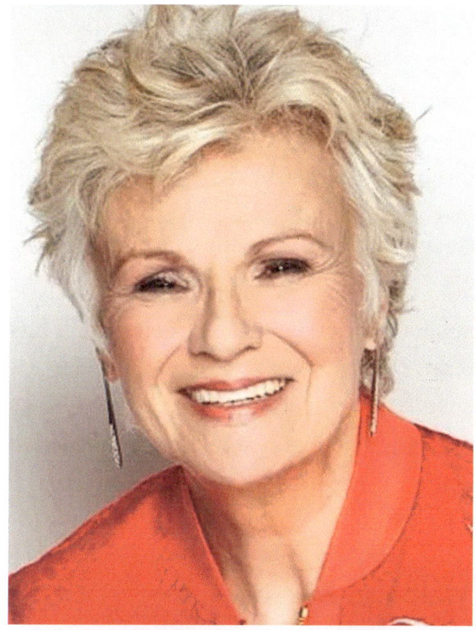

In April 2018, having enjoyed her meeting with Paul Jones, and following some persuasion, she agreed to be added to the Patrons. She has shown an interest in the Centre and was kept up to date by Bob Wild, donating a portrait to the Centre to mark her presence. But due first to work commitments and then to a health scare she has not been able to be involved further, apart from keeping in touch by popping in now and again.

Rich Miller

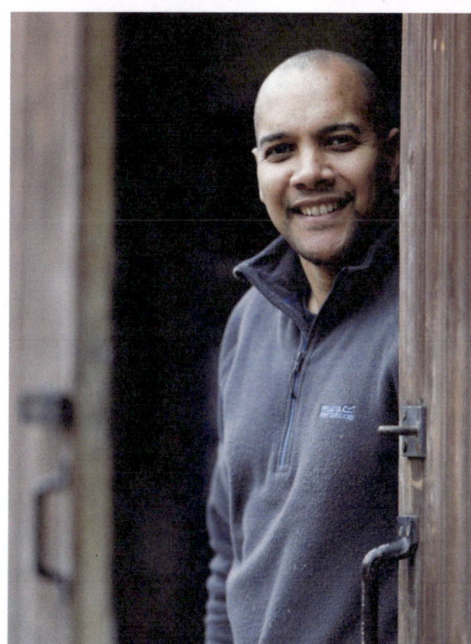

Another old friend making a return as a Patron in 2022 was Rich Miller. He was the Potter in Residence from 2003-04 and very popular with all whom he worked with. *"Lovely Richard, we used to call him. A really nice chap,"* recalls Louise Grundy. *"But occasionally he would forget to come in for classes. I'd have a group of middle-aged ladies waiting on a Wednesday morning and I'd have to ring him up and say, 'Hello Richard, shouldn't you be somewhere?' to remind him."* Since then he has been a Judge on TV's 'The Great Pottery Throwdown' for the last four of the seven series, having been involved from series one, as well as taking on other TV work and running his internationally successful Froyle Tiles business. His involvement so far has been to judge the Open Exhibition.

The Trustees

The Trustees (or Directors) are unpaid volunteers. Their role is to have oversight, decide strategy and take accountability for seeing that the aims of the charity are delivered (trustees) and that the limited company is operating legally (directors). Inevitably they are drawn in to the operations too. At times their leadership or sheer hard graft has ensured that the organisation has survived. In every recent survey of volunteers a common response has been *"Who are the trustees? What do they do? We never see them"*. That would not have been so at the beginning when they were directly representative of the user groups of the Centre. However as the business matured and expanded so the danger of a disconnect became greater. They are elected by the Members at the annual AGM. But once the Friends scheme was introduced then the Members' role became confused and more honoured in the breach than the observance. Attendance at AGMs has dwindled to a precious few. Once limited tenure was introduced the Trustee turnover increased. To date well over 60 trustees have been registered over the years at the Charity Commission and to pick out individuals from them may seem invidious. However some do stand out, without whom Cranleigh Arts might never have survived fifty years, starting with the Chairmen.

Malcolm Beeson

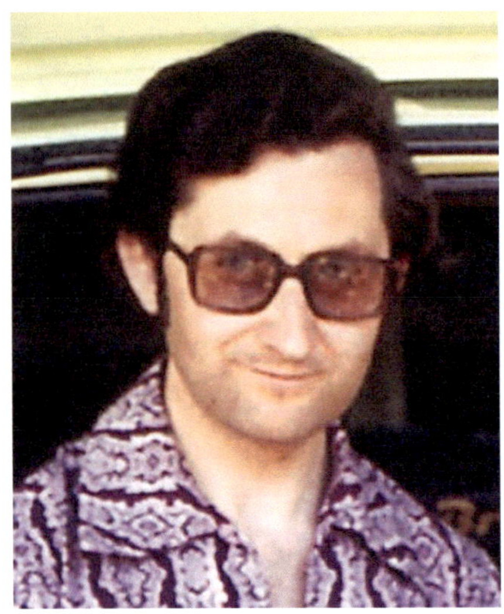

He was the founder Chairman and first Director of the Cranleigh Arts and Leisure Trust and the person who in the early days did much of the administration and organisation, including drafting the Constitution. He kept the Trustees informed and coordinated the relations with the founder societies. He organised the public meetings that instituted the original Trust. It was he who dealt with Hambledon District Council over land, buildings and planning permissions. He was involved in the programming of the Festivals and provided much of the technical support once the building had been brought into use. During shows he would be found in the corridor operating the lighting desk that he had constructed himself.

He had moved to Cranleigh in 1970 when his work with Beecham Pharmaceuticals relocated him to Brockham Park near Dorking. He was part of the new arrivals to the recently completed Summerlands estate, residing in Kilncopse.

He was drawn in to The Cranleigh Players and became their 'chief sparks' building electronic dimmers to supplant older linear resistors, manufacturing his own circuit boards and backstage communication system.

In 1979 his work moved again to Epsom and he left Cranleigh. The new Chairman Jack Wagg wrote to him in July 1980:

"I am asked to tell you that the Management Committee wish you to know of their profound appreciation of all you have done in your leadership of the struggle to put the Art Centre on the map. Having just spent some time reading the early files I am amazed at your tenacity and capacity for hard work. Please accept best thanks from all of us."

Jack Wagg

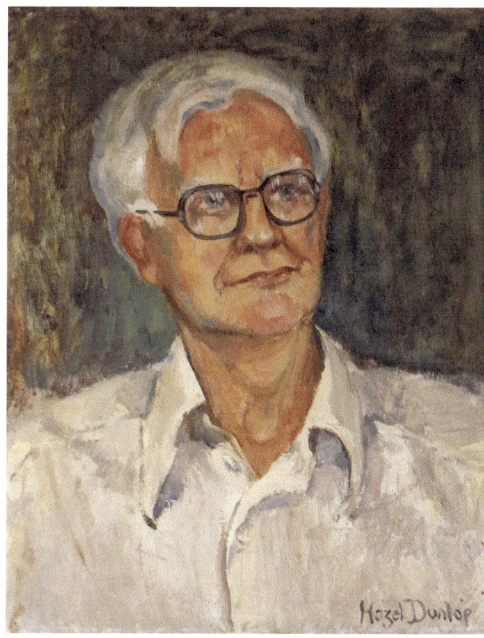

'Captain Jack' steered the ship and his vision developed the initial ideas of the Cranleigh Arts and Leisure Trust's founders into a community arts centre. He had the political nous and management skill to see what needed doing and to engage people to join him on the journey. He wasn't afraid to take on opposition whether it was from individual vested interests or corporate local authorities. He was determined to achieve the best possible community arts centre for all ages and all groups.

Arthur Gomez, whom he had brought in as architect right at the beginning, characterized him as *"a benevolent dictator. Ferociously intelligent. Very entrepreneurial. Not so much a team player but put good people in to do what he wanted to do."*

Chris Dubois described him thus:

"He wasn't in it for power or kudos. He had huge confidence in his vision for the place. He would seek consensus when he needed it and would drive on when he didn't need it. Not after a gong. A strategic and detailed thinker. You could always see his mind working: 'I'm here. I need to be there; this is in the way – so I need to go there and there.' A schemer perhaps, but for the common cause. On balance a warm man socially, but goal driven at work."

His Chairman's pieces in *Vision* are a rallying cry, season by season, to supporters to keep the faith and step by step work towards the goal. His summaries at AGMs are markers of the progress made and the struggles undergone. He never lost his faith that it could be achieved. He received an Award for Achievement from Surrey County Council in 1994, recognising outstanding achievement in working on behalf of the community. In 1995, with Catherine Pike now at the helm and Lottery money on the horizon, he summed up his efforts in his own characteristic way in *Vision*,

> *"In 1978 I returned from a long trip to North America, arriving in Cranleigh in full bloom on a wonderful summer day. Although retired from paid employment, I knew that Cranleigh deserved all I could offer, so readily accepted an invitation to join the Management Committee ... then struggling with the huge task of converting the derelict Infant School into an Arts Centre. ... After about ten years as Chairman, I am now on the sidelines exhorting others for an ultra-speedy effort to move mountains. Like John Mortimer, I am 'clinging to the wreckage' hoping to be around for the completion celebrations. I venture to ask everyone ... to contribute something tangible – money, effort or kind – so as to guarantee that our Cranleigh Community Arts Centre will be second to none, truly benefitting the needs of all who wish to enjoy the arts in all its forms."*

Catherine Pike

Catherine had been a Waverley Councillor and sat as an observer on the Board, so knew the Centre quite well. She took over after the two year interregnum of John Dickerson in 1995. She wrote in the same edition of *Vision*,

> *"It was with some trepidation that I agreed to accept the Chairmanship of Cranleigh Arts Centre. I had been debating whether to stand for re-election to Waverley Borough Council, but the offer was the deciding factor. I am therefore very pleased to take over the Chairmanship at such an exciting time when hopefully the 'total vision' for Cranleigh Arts Centre is about to be achieved."*

It was her determination, her knowledge of local councillors and how funding bodies worked, her passion for music, her aesthetic sense and sheer drive that pushed the grant application and rebuilding project through, surrounding herself with the best people for the best outcomes. Like Jack's experience in local government, it seemed that the NHS was just as good a preparation for Catherine in moving mountains. She refused to practise in private medicine seeing public service as the natural thing to do. She was a leader in the research and practical application of medicine for women and was consultant cytologist at St Luke's Cancer Centre, Guildford, making determined and tireless efforts to drive the provision of cervical and breast cancer screening tests for women. She brought this rigour to the Arts Centre. She worked

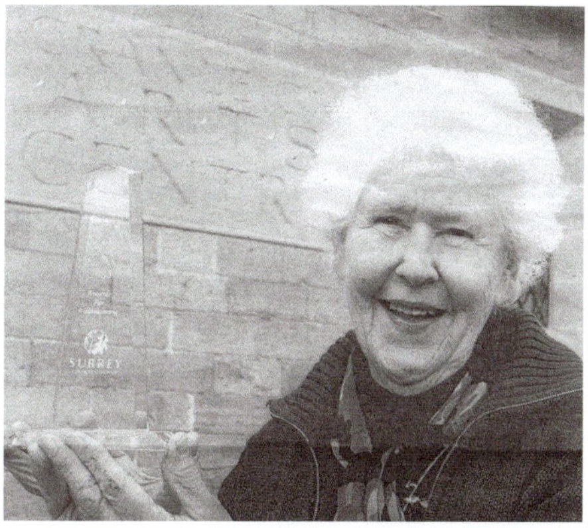

closely with Arthur Gomez, the architect, who remembers her as *"super intelligent. Very, very tactful. She had incredible artistic taste"*. She wanted everything finished to the highest standard possible. Aesthetics mattered to her. Another colleague said, *"Although if she didn't approve of you, you got a sore shoulder as she would prod you with her finger. But she had a heart of gold."* Once she got an idea she wouldn't let go of it. When she decided at the age of 80 to learn Italian, she rented a house in Tuscany with the family for three months to immerse herself in it.

What characterised her most was her interest in people. She would invite staff, and friends of the Arts Centre to her arts and crafts house in Blackheath, which was the love of her life. This even included performers such as Neil Brand and Paul Merton when they appeared at Cranleigh. Age was no barrier and she loved engaging with young people; what were they doing? What did they think? She was also aware of how little money people got paid working in the arts, so valued the staff. She took pleasure in the pleasure others found in discovering the arts.

Like Jack, Catherine also received recognition of her work in 2005 from Surrey County Council with an Award for Volunteering in the category of Living and Working.

As the Mayor, John Savage, wrote to her after the re-opening, *"Cranleigh owes you a great debt"*. She showed great determination in fighting Waverley for the funding for a Centre Manager, with eventual success, so that by 2000 some stability had been achieved. When she died in 2016 her eulogy included a section on her work at Cranleigh Arts, concluding:

"When the arts centre re-opened in 1998 with a bright new building and lots of potential, the challenge for the Board was to create a programme worthy of the building and to staff it. Again, Catherine rose to the challenge and guided the new staff and volunteers through the process of settling down to produce the kind of community arts Cranleigh wanted. You could say that Catherine's Chairmanship was momentous for the Arts Centre. Her relentless focus on the purpose of her task drove her forward – and others with her. She stepped down in 2004 and continued as a volunteer until very recently, her passion and her support for the Centre undimmed."

Rosemary French

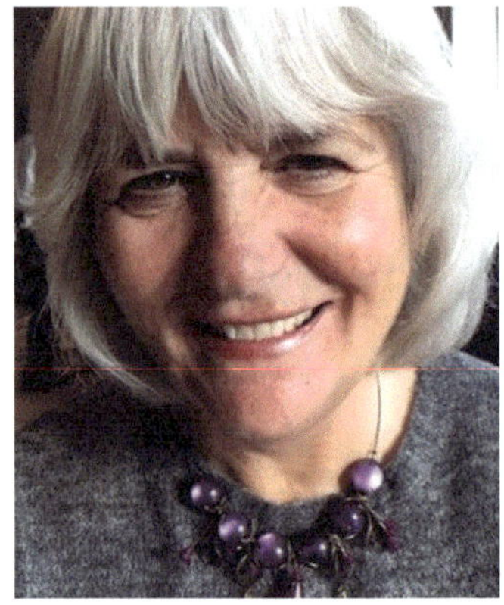

Rosemary, in contrast to Catherine, came in at an ebb point and was swiftly thrown into a crisis, as we have seen. She has said, *"I was sold a bag of nails when I took on the Arts Centre"*. The treasurer was flagging up insolvency and there was complacency that the Arts Council wouldn't let the business fail. Possibly for the first time she brought a sharp practical business focus to the operation. She took some hard decisions in order to avoid the abyss and was not always thanked for it, as her business culture 'clashed with the arts folk'. She made structural and strategic changes which eventually brought the Centre back from the brink, but it was a close call. She focussed on Board responsibilities and brought in more professional expertise, as well as encouraging the partnership with Farnham Maltings and the opportunity to learn from them. She says looking back,

> *"When you rescue someone and you pick them from the water and they're drowning and you put them back on shore, and they're in a bit of a bad state but they're alive. I think that's what I did."*
> *"I cut my teeth at the Arts Centre. It was my first experience of the charity sector."*
> *"But you fall in love with the Arts Centre. I'm proud and glad I was part of it. Cranleigh Arts brought me a whole bunch of good friends."*

She too continued as a volunteer as Duty Manager for a number of years after stepping down as a Trustee and remains a loyal supporter of the programme, particularly films.

Stephen Dennison

Stephen was initially a consultant in the restructuring of 2006/7 but quickly became coopted to the Board, familiar with the Centre as his wife Gina was a regular volunteer. He became Rosemary's Vice-Chair after Nick Morris stood down and was her obvious successor. He was a very supportive mentor to the staff, spending much time counselling the Centre Managers and 'firefighting' where necessary. He continued the process of broadening the expertise of the Trustee appointments and trying to make the business sustainable. There were shocks along the way but he maintained continuity in the face of an increasingly difficult environment. He always stepped up to challenges.

In 2015 Stephen received a bombshell letter from Waverley threatening the termination of the lease as they claimed the building was not being satisfactorily maintained. There were cracks in the kitchen wall and the soft sandstone was crumbling. On the advice of the Rector he got hold of a Guide to Charitable Funding and searched through it. Most building maintenance funders centred on churches but one stood out. The Government had recently established a Landfill tax which took a levy on every tonne disposed of. The waste disposal companies had to set up a Trust to put a percentage of the money back into the communities affected. He got hold of the form and found that you had to be within ten miles of a site. Whipping out an OS map he searched for the nearest: 9.73 miles. He got on the phone to Biffa to ask how this was measured, by road or directly? *"As the crow flies, sir,"* was the answer. Relief. *"You do know the deadline is tomorrow? After that the scheme continues but the catchment will be seven miles."* Panic. Stephen got the form to them by midnight, having worked all day. The next issue was that they needed a contribution of £10,000 in order to provide £45,000. So that had to be found by a donation. It was and the scheme went ahead to carry out the required building repairs.

When it became clear that funding for a designated staff member to manage the volunteers would strengthen the organisation Stephen turned to the Guide again. There he found the Wates Foundation; fortuitously another of his Ewhurst neighbours was Tim Wates, who was able to clarify how to apply successfully for a grant. This achievement was a step change in the management of the Centre's human resources, helped by the fact that the first appointee, Katie Wilson, proved to be particularly effective at it.

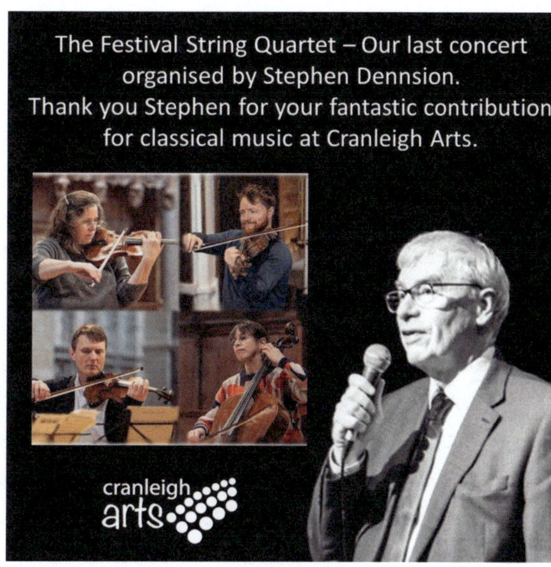

Alongside the celebrity interviews another successful project was his championing of the Classical Music programme, which he built up from almost nothing, by astute sponsorship and partnerships and the acquisition of a new Kawai Shigeru grand piano, to make the facilities the best they could be and the quality outstanding. His personal and financial commitment has been significant over the years. Until he and Gina recently moved away from the area he continued to volunteer, present events, advise and take on marketing projects, bringing his expertise to bear on current issues. It is said of him that, like a stick of rock, if you cut open Stephen you would find 'Cranleigh Arts Centre' running through his core.

Bob Wild

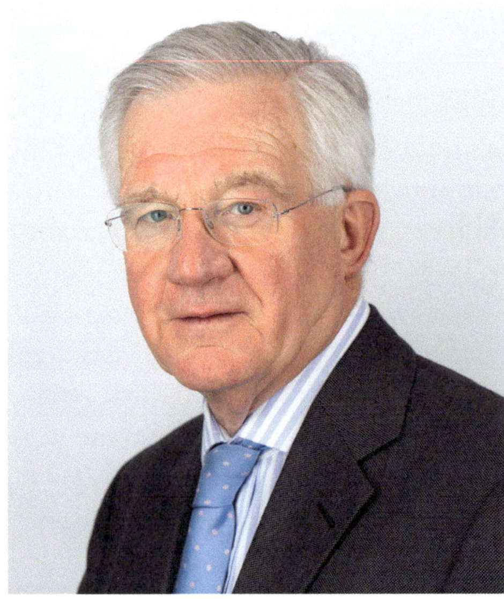

For Bob, as a former banker, it was always going to be about the numbers. He came in as Treasurer, quickly discerned that there were problems, and on becoming Chairman moved to bring fiscal discipline to the organisation. He took the view that Cranleigh Arts might be a charity, but no one owed it a living and if it went bust then it was no good to anyone. He applied all of his training in business and his experience of managing complex organisations to Cranleigh Arts. His tip for good management was to *"get off the back foot and onto the front foot, and for that you need money. Money gives you choices"*. He insisted that the Arts Centre had to be self-sufficient at the operating level and any other income was a bonus. As ten years earlier he found staff costs were rocketing in the pursuit of increased revenue and, like Rosemary French, he took the view that this was unsustainable. So with the support of the Board a restructure created a slimmed down operation. Staff became familiar with his mantras: *"You run it, but just don't do dumb stuff!"*, *"Chairs give stress, they don't take it; if you say you can solve everyone's problems, then all that happens is that you end up with everyone's problems!"* He was keen to give people agency. *"Make sure that people know the mission and then let them get on with it."* *"Chatham House rules"* were invoked for free and frank discussions and his phlegmatic *"the dogs bark, the caravans move on"* reflected his view that nothing was so bad that you had to have a sleepless night over it.

He kept a keen eye on money in and out, making sure that there was no waste. He also took great delight in the programme, attending regularly with his wife Lynne. He ensured the trustees reflected a range of skills and was transparent by calling public meetings to include all stakeholders. As it is a community organisation run largely by volunteers he knew that you had to take people with you. At these meetings he delighted in his PowerPoint spreadsheets and fielded questions well. Only once, faced with a hostile reception to plans to make the Gallery into a bar, did he accept a defeat but was philosophical. He was adept at external relations and bid for S106 money from Waverley which saw internal redevelopment of the building for the first time since 1998. He connected with Waverley at an executive level and showed them how vital Cranleigh Arts was to their arts provision and what could be achieved with their support. Like Jack Wagg, he drew up a broader plan to develop the building further to fit the needs of an expanding Cranleigh, should more money become available in time. By building up reserves to a previously unachievable level he had a war chest which enabled the Centre to weather the storm of Covid when it hit, whereas other comparable arts organisations failed. *"If you make money, you can do stuff. If you don't make money, you can't help anyone."* He also said, *"The Chairmanship is a great responsibility. You are only custodian for a short time and you must hand it over in better shape, or at least no worse."*

Other notable Trustees

Dilys Savedra – ran the Adult Education and was unpaid Centre Manager with Jack Wagg in the very early days.

Rosemary and Chris Dubois

Between them Rosemary and Chris have given 61 years of service to the Arts Centre. Both have served in key roles and made sure that not only has the Centre survived in the difficult years through effective administration, but that the flame of community arts has been kept burning despite the turnover of different Chairs and Managers.

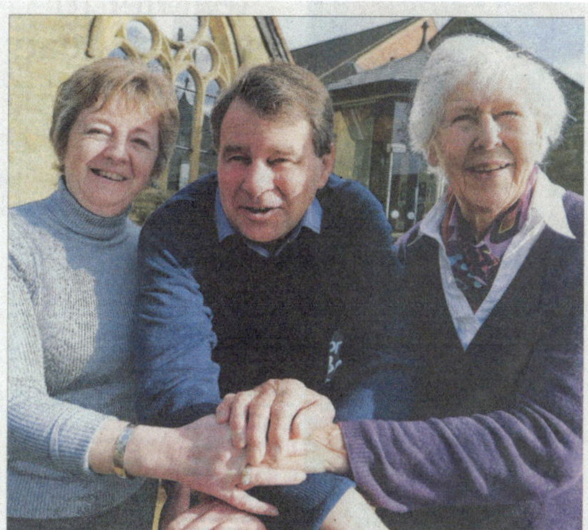

Retiring directors Rosemary Debois, Chris Debois and Catherine Pike.(Ref: 09SA110904)

Rosemary came first to an art class in 1980 and was asked to join the Events Committee in 1983. This involved a bit of fundraising and booking events and she organised theatre trips. When Jack reorganised and brought the programme planning into the Centre's administration she became Centre Manager in 1988. She was for ten years the main person, together with Anne Hull, the Secretary, and Jack Wagg, who kept the Centre open day to day. She did much of the admin, was the key person who liaised with South East Arts, often had to caretake the building and booked much of the programme. She created a vibrant children's offering of theatre, workshops and other events, both in term time and the holidays. She built up relations with adult theatre companies too and pushed street theatre. She stepped in to help organise the art exhibitions and generally was a one-woman wonder. Her tireless commitment to the operation and programming of the Centre and guidance of the staff and volunteers throughout that time was outstanding. Once Catherine had set the path for getting Lottery money she was part of the small team writing the bid and interacting with the key people. This took her into new areas when writing a business plan, managing closure and planning the expanded programme for re-opening. Working with her on the rebuild Arthur Gomez credits her with being *'incredibly supportive'*. Since there was no money initially for a Centre Manager after re-opening she had to cover all the bases, under pressure to succeed, which she said was a steep learning curve until Helen Cundy was loaned by Waverley in the role. Carol Sacha, then Waverley's Arts Officer, says, *"Rosemary needs a fanfare. It was a huge change for her, the expansion. But she knew the public and the politics"*. Helen Cundy remembers her fondly: *"She kept us going. She was tireless, with a passion for quality."* A regular visiting company said, *"Oh yes, Cranleigh Arts Centre, Rosemary Dubois. She always makes us sandwiches"*. In subsequent crises as a Trustee she stepped up again, often teamed with Chrissy Matthews with whom she got on well, to keep the place open, coming in regularly until she retired as a Trustee in 2009.

Chris, whose job meant his time in the beginning was more limited, was co-opted to the Board in 1987 and continued as a Trustee until 2010. He chaired sub-committees, produced reports and analysis, researched the technical requirements of the re-build and after he stood down has been a constant 'senior' volunteer both as a Duty Manager, but more importantly as the guardian of the performance statistics, PRS returns, grant applications and artists' contracts. His strategic approach, considered judgement and his command of data has informed the delivery of the aims of the Centre for the last three decades. Like Rosemary he is a passionate supporter of the art, film and theatre that the Centre provides and he has been a critical friend to the last four Chairmen. As a computer expert he has been digitising much of the record keeping and had a substantial archive which has been added to that which existed at the Centre and has informed this book.

Anne Hull

She was the first employee and served ten years as General Secretary and six years as Board Secretary. She worked many, many hours over what she was paid however and with Rosemary Dubois and Jack Wagg ran the Centre up to 1998. Realising that post-reopening a different structure would be needed she stood down.

Harry Stadler

To get a measure of him a little background will help. Harry was born in Vienna in 1925. In 1934 the Stadler family moved several times following the rise of fascism, ending up in Prague in 1939. In July the two boys, Harry and his brother Robert, were sent to Britain by the Kindertransport rescue mission. His parents were deported from Prague in 1942 moving through a number of camps to end up in Belzec Death Camp where they both perished. His aunt was unable to look after the boys, so they were taken in by the Atkins family in Bromley. They were evangelical Christians and former Salvation Army officers. Before long Harry was playing in the band until he joined the British Army in 1945. The daily household routine was spartan and food scarce due to rationing. Forbidden to speak German they had to pick up English quickly. Unsurprisingly, caught between the Christianity of his 'new' family and the liberal Jewish upbringing of his old, Harry was an agnostic for the rest of his life. As Treasurer he was a rock, firm and always trying to do the best for the Centre. His letters are concise, courteous and well-reasoned when asking for clarification or compromise from Waverley officers over their rent, rates or insurance rises. His control of the budget and spending, especially the complex ins and outs of the Lottery grant's £1.4 million, was meticulous. A stamp dealer by trade he also co-wrote a book on German colonial stamp issues and was a translator and contributor to the Holocaust Education and Archive Research Team. Cranleigh Arts has attracted some remarkable people over the years.

Chrissy Matthews

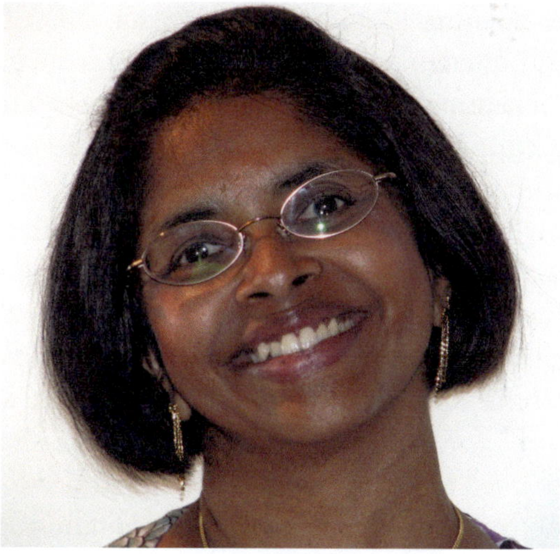

Along with Catherine Pike and the Rosemarys, Dubois and French, Chrissy kept the Arts Centre afloat as it tried to find its course after the rebuilding and then stepped up again in the 2006 crisis. With Chris Dubois she wrote policy documents; she supported the Centre Managers, Mark Wright and Helen Cundy; she found sponsorship and brought in numerous favours. She was able to reach out into the community having been part of the Cranleigh Pageant and to local businesses, having been a founder of the Cranleigh Initiative, an early version of the Chamber of Commerce. She had an analytical mind, always had the data but was also hands on to get things done. She was also committed to making the volunteers more professional. Her husband Mark recalls:

> *"She would never leave a stone unturned. We had a walk up Leith Hill and found there was a lady who baked cakes running a teashop up there. Before long Chrissy had her supplying the Arts Centre and a 'coffee and cake' offer came into being. And she made sure there was a diagram on the fridge door to instruct the volunteers how to cut the cake. Of course then there were only three places in the High Street to get a cup of tea, unlike now."*

She was strong on marketing and worked a lot with Bridget Howland on the development of the Brochure. Bridget is a local artist and graphic designer, whose mother also volunteered at the Centre, who has been responsible for the main marketing product of the Centre for twenty years. Chrissy went on to work with the 'Make a Wish' Foundation, Voluntary Action South West Surrey and was the Senior Manager for volunteers at the Air Ambulance Trust from 2010 to 2013.

From 2001 to 2005 Mark Matthews was the main projectionist and once a week would spend a day doing maintenance with Vaughan. They had both been aircraft engineers so loved to solve the problems regularly thrown up. Although the rebuild had specified a hearing loop, it had not been put in, so they set to and installed it themselves.

Vaughan Mitchell

Vaughan was introduced to the centre by Harry Stadler and the Bridge Club after re-opening. Could he help sort out some of the building problems? His background was in engineering and computing from his work at British Aerospace. Catherine, on hearing he was an engineer, had taken him by the hand on a tour of the building getting his view on everything. For the next eight years or more he was the person who knew how all the machinery worked. His first task was the Air Handling Unit in the Jack Wagg Hall and the software that controlled it. He continued by snagging the other build deficiencies: condensate pipes rusting and leaking, vents upside down, thermostats wrongly set up. He fought with the electricity meter readers. He found cheap ways of doing this and that. He mounted shelves, a projection screen in the Crane Room, blackout curtains and the tab track in the Jack Wagg and partition walls for the back office. There was a shortage of computers and no money. He noticed that some were appearing, thrown out, at the refuse dump. He acquired two or three, refurbished them and brought them into the Centre to use until funds were available for upgrades.

The Volunteers
who are the lifeblood of the organisation

Last, but not least by any measure, is the team of volunteers. In running the Centre the contribution of the Trustees, paid Centre Managers and other salaried staff has been documented in previous chapters, but underpinning all their efforts were the multitude of volunteers who put it all into practice, thousands over the last fifty years. As well as the Chairmen, Patrons and Trustees, there are the front of house staff, the backstage staff, the office staff, the fundraisers, the Friends organisers and the many various art form organisers, who have all put time, energy, money and their expertise into Cranleigh Arts, from their love of what the Arts Centre was trying to do and a passion for wanting everyone to share its vision and opportunities. Appeals for volunteers have usually been well responded to and on occasions special days were organised to recruit volunteers such as the Play a Part Day in October 2003 or coming together with other voluntary organisations in a Community Funding Fair. Support from Voluntary Action South West Surrey has been solid and was enhanced once a Volunteer Coordinator was appointed. In this area, as with most things in the arts, collaboration and communication has supported achievement and integration within the community sector.

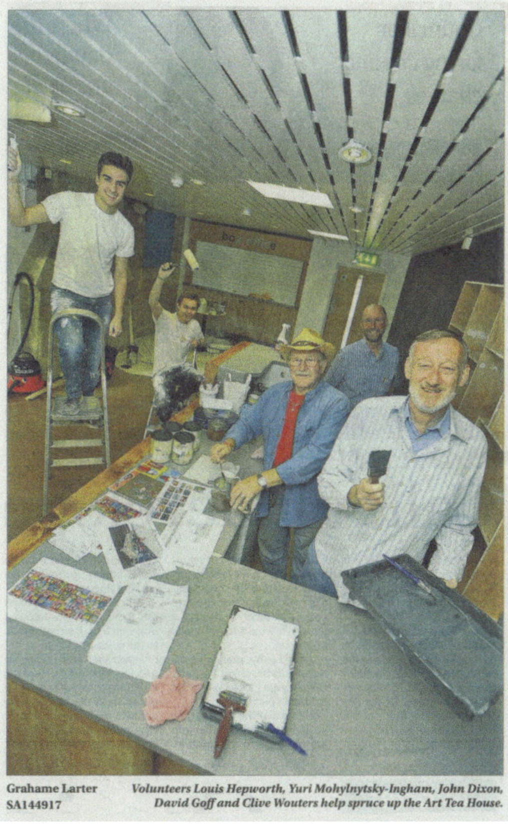

Grahame Larter
SA144917

Volunteers Louis Hepworth, Yuri Mohylnytsky-Ingham, John Dixon, David Goff and Clive Wouters help spruce up the Art Tea House.

What is notable is the regular dedication and commitment of the volunteers, often drawing in the rest of the family. There have been staunch husband and wife pairs, as well as whole families and dedicated individuals from all walks of life. We find this over the years, as with the Dubois, the Horrocks, the Sheltons, the Waggs, the Baverstocks, the Dennisons, the Matthews, the Dales, the Foleys, the Seumes, the Mackies, the Taylors, the Kerbys, the Todmans, and many, many more. Their names are legion and these sample few must represent the many. The majority are retirees who want to use their talents, want to give back to the community or want just to socialise in agreeable surroundings. Week in, week out, they take a regular slot on the tea bar or box office or reception, often for years. The staff know too that in a crisis there is a core of people they can ring at short notice who will rally round. Others may bring a particular skill and help out for a limited period or for a special project.

Technical support has always been at a premium and one example of the calibre of the volunteers is John Dixon (JD). A musician who, for the last twenty-five years, has been the itinerant sound and lighting technician and Mr Odd Job. There isn't a corner of the Centre that he hasn't repaired or refurbished. Whatever the hour cameth the man! Now in his eighties and no longer allowed to go up ladders, he calls in first thing most days to *"see what needs doing"*. His ambition is to die in harness and says that the Arts Centre gives him a reason to go out in the morning. He helped install the CCTV system, the streaming equipment and the cameras and has put up and taken down the rostra and seating more times than he's had hot dinners. In the control box he has been joined by John Coghlan, the current leader of the audio-visual and projection team. He masterminded the installation of the streaming cameras and Cranleigh Arts Online. His predecessor was Bob Foley, a former BBC engineer, who put in the Satellite Streaming equipment. Some touring music and drama bookings bring their own technicians, but two loyal friends of Cranleigh Arts have been 'Captain', a sound engineer, and Leo, a lighting and sound designer, who have expanded the expertise of the team, both adept at rigging and operating and fixing things in emergencies if required.

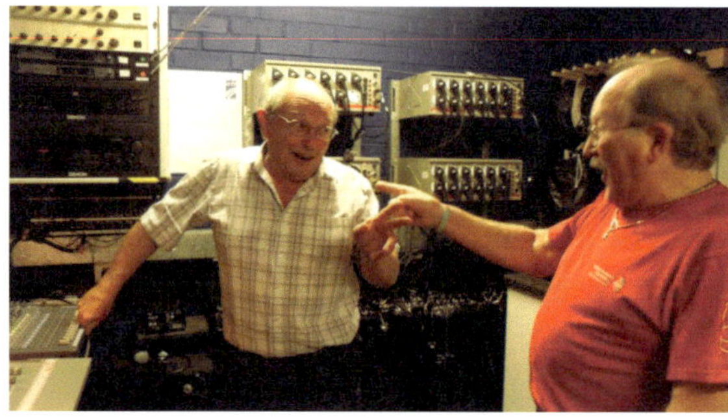

Bob Foley and JD.

The final pieces of the jigsaw

We couldn't open without them too

To complement the work of the few paid staff there has also been a cohort of Duty Managers. They were introduced to relieve some of the burden of the management of the Centre's activities by day and night from the full time paid staff, who could then get on with their allocated responsibilities of programming, marketing or facilities. During the day these are unpaid volunteers, as staff are on hand, but in the evening they have sole charge and paid on a freelance basis. Key members of the team, they are the hosts, guardians, managers and facilitators of all that happens in the building on their watch. A significant responsibility. Some full-time staff, such as Ruth Eastelow and Janet Baverstock, began as DMs and then came onto the payroll as full-timers.

Another paid role, albeit part-time has been the essential 'floor level' administration of the building. If it isn't clean and tidy and set up properly and kept secure then the whole enterprise fails. Often thankless and unrecognised the Centre began by relying on volunteers when they first acquired the building but quickly realised that cleaning at least needed to be paid for. Later, after Dilys and Jack had kept the keys for a while, a paid caretaker was added. Of necessity these were unsocial hourly-paid part-time roles. So on occasions problems were caused by a conflict with other jobs they might have had. George ran the Tuck Shop at Cranleigh School, so had to be up there for certain hours. Jon Edwards drove a bus for the Duke of Kent School so similarly would down tools to do the home run. The cleaners have largely been successful and long serving, although some issues arose that led to one being sacked for taking time off to go to Africa. For a period it was contracted out to a company, but this led to an uneven and inflexible service, so it was brought back in-house recently. An annual summer clean up, deep clean, tidy and repaint by a team of volunteers helps to keep the Centre looking good for its many users.

The common factor for all the volunteers is their pride in Cranleigh Arts. By many it is regarded as the jewel in the crown of Cranleigh. As Bob Wild put it:

> *"What you see here is a legacy. You can see the fingerprints of people that have been here the last forty years. You look around here and you see their fingerprints all over this place. It was made by nobody else, but by Cranleigh. This is what people started off and look where it is today. It is no longer a hobby arts centre; we have created a major responsibility here now."*

Chapter Thirteen

The future for Cranleigh Arts

How might the last fifty years inform the next?

It is said that those who do not learn from the past are doomed to repeat it. That has certainly been the case at times for those involved in the Arts Centre. We have seen that certain problems come up time and again and never seem to get resolved. An existential crisis was avoided twice. As key people come and go 'bright ideas' get recycled with little memory or understanding of why they didn't work last time. Some problems remain out of control of the participants, driven by external factors such as the economic or political climate, but fundamentally the ingredients have always been the space, people and money. When those have been right then the Centre has thrived. Important too has been positive integration with Cranleigh and the people it serves, which has not always been the case, when there has been a perceived disconnect due to inappropriate choices, poor communication or factional interests.

The wider context

Politics, economics and social change

Without a crystal ball the future of the economy is hard to predict. The Arts Centre has weathered the ups and downs of Britain's prosperity over the last fifty years and found a way through somehow. That this has affected policy is undoubted. The current wars and global instability are similar disrupters to the oil crisis, the property crash and Covid previously, that had a profound impact on the country's economic prospects. There is no likelihood of that changing and is something none of us can control. With the election of a Labour Government we may see a more positive attitude to the arts and its future, than under the Tories, although their financial room to manoeuvre may be limited. In the time of Tony Blair the arts were well supported, admittedly at a time of growth rather than a cost of living crisis, with Chris Smith being a long serving and influential Arts Minister, as was Jennie Lee before him. The recent Tory appointments, such as Nadine Dorries, have been a joke in comparison. We can only hope for such inspiration again in the new administration.

At a regional level our local councils have been squeezed, partly by reduced government funding, partly by increased demands for vital social services and, it must be said, some unwise investment choices. Arts spending has been cut completely by some authorities. Should there be a move in our own area for amalgamation or a move to a unitary authority then there might be some advantage, as there was in 1974, in some easing of budgets or reallocation of funds and assets. But for the immediate future their options seem limited.

Demographically we are seeing a shift in the influence of the post-war and baby-boomer generations. Through the second half of the twentieth century they have driven much of the expansion of arts consumption, as more time and money became available. They benefited from consumer-driven economic growth and rising house prices. As they aged they were loyal audience members and sponsors, although their children haven't followed them to be such prolific attendees. When they retired they became the backbone of the volunteer force that sustains many arts organisations. But now they are having health problems, Covid has disrupted their routines, inflation has eaten away their pensions and their children and grandchildren need their time and money. To tackle this, should arts organisations be changing? Is there more flexibility? Are access issues being addressed? Lunchtime and daylight programming of events may encourage attendance, helping them to make the effort to come out. There must also be a push to find the younger audience to replace them. In this Cranleigh is lucky. The expansion of the village with new housing should bring a good proportion of younger people, as in the earlier building boom of the 1960s, which nearly doubled its size. The challenge for Cranleigh Arts is how to engage them, when their attitudes and access to entertainment and their approach to leisure and disposable income is quite different to that of their parents.

Space

How to make the most of the building

The building has a defined footprint, is only leased from Waverley and has probably been expanded as much as it can be. Should it ever be lost and revert to the Council then it would be a prime site for redevelopment into flats, as the Lady Peak Institute behind has been, to realise a considerable sum. But its value, both to Waverley and to Cranleigh, has to be as an Arts Centre. The skill that Jack Wagg and Arthur Gomez showed in their design, was to accommodate the multiple needs of the operation in a group of flexible spaces that interact. Any future change should not compromise that. An example was the proposal to put a Bar into the Gallery. This light-filled space already has to be a dedicated exhibition space for quality art work, much valued by those who use it, as well as an attractive social area serving the Tea Bar and Foyer for events in the Jack Wagg Hall. It is a delicate balance, which if a more profit making Bar were installed, might make more money, but would subjugate the art to scanty wall decoration.

Apart from hireable public space the other two main operational needs have been for storage and for quiet administration. To a degree these have been solved for the moment either by subdivision or clever use of hidden corners. But the ready access to the equipment and furniture used on a regular basis, that doesn't entail great labour to put in place, plus somewhere to store the materials, that may not immediately be used, but must be handy such as for marketing, hospitality and display cabinets and craft materials, all need to be addressed and solved. For the staff quiet access to computers, printers and the possibility of breakout rooms for small confidential or larger team meetings, enables them to do their jobs effectively and efficiently. For good customer service the Duty Manager must be central in the building to see clearly and monitor what is going on; Reception and Box Office must also be central and easily accessible.

So where could any more space be found? The Car Park has long been a problem area. Waverley retained control of it for as long as possible and had concerns that it would not be large enough to serve the Centre. The Parish Church laid claim to it too, eventually conceding that they had no legal right to use it but wanted to continue on historical precedent to use it on a Sunday. The neighbours have found it convenient, as have many other residents of Cranleigh who don't see why they shouldn't use it, a nurse visiting the hospital, someone dropping by the pub opposite after work, all wanting to avoid the pay carparks, despite signs saying that it is for Staff and Hirers of the Arts Centre only. A barrier was tried but was vandalised almost immediately. A polite note on cars or a word from a staff member to persistent offenders has been met with outrage and abuse on occasions. Such pressure may get worse as the Village Way car park is reduced and built on for the new Leisure Centre and the demand for parking inevitably increases. Perhaps the answer is to extend out further at the back, enlarge the Pottery, backstage area, the Box Office administrative area and rear entrance, thus giving more storage, admin and hireable space, and reserve just the minimum parking needed for the disabled, staff and unloading.

Another possibility is to build up. If somehow more seats could be added to the Jack Wagg Hall by another tier then capacity would be increased giving more income for the same overheads. Could the rear flat roofs be built on to extend the second floor? This would be complex and involve structural questions, planning and artistic considerations. This is not something to be undertaken lightly as it could destroy the intimacy, acoustic and comfort of the auditorium, which has been praised by audiences and performers alike. Waverley Planning Department were rigorous about the specification of rooflines and the visual impact on a sensitive historical corner of Cranleigh in 1998 and are likely to be so again.

People

The crucial ingredient

The Centre has been likened to a slot machine. Every few years you pull the handle and if the three key groups of people come up right you are a winner, but if not, then you lose! Those groups are the right Chairman and Board, the right Manager and staff team and the right volunteers giving support in all areas. Sadly, as this record has shown, that doesn't come up very often. A deficit in one relationship, for example a disconnect between the board and the staff, or between the staff and volunteers, has led to tension, overload and breakdown.

Until recently there have largely been long-serving Chairmen who have nurtured and communicated a vision of how the Arts Centre could evolve, survive and thrive. Their qualities can be deduced from their profiles and achievements recorded previously. Most have been hands on, engaged with the grassroots and participants in the daily activities of the Centre. Their leadership came from practical experience of how things worked. They had regular dialogue with the Manager and knew first-hand the stresses and strains of the organisation. Rightly the recruitment of Trustees/Directors has widened from the early days and their tenure limited to a maximum of eight years. However a significant number don't last that long for various reasons. Aside from a change in personal circumstances, despite an interview and induction process there are those who discover that it is not what they expected and head for the door. More difficult for the organisation are those who come in from high powered positions with large and impressive companies. From their great experience they are confident they know just how to solve the problems but are hogtied when they discover that there is no team of people to deliver their solutions – just them. Or their ideas just do not scale down for a small but complex place like Cranleigh Arts. The shift from a largely paid to a largely volunteer work force is another difficult transition for them sometimes. One Chairman likened some trustees to seagulls. *"They fly in, shit on things, then fly away!"* Thankfully not many have done that. The recent rapid turnover of Trustees points to a need for a sharpened selection process, and proper induction and training, so that they can appreciate their role and be prepared for their commitment. Too often it can be identified that the Board has not worked together as a team, partly because meetings are held only every two months or the members have not always been local or are still heavily engaged in their careers. The debate over hands-on or hands-off trustees has gone back and forth but it seems that in a small organisation, provided the roles and responsibilities are clearly delineated and sensitively respected, then practical involvement is inevitable, indeed desirable, if trustees are really to make an informed contribution. From both staff and volunteers the regular feedback has been that the Board is a distant group who are not known to the other teams that work there, who don't appreciate the day to day running of the Centre and whose role is not understood. Better integration and communication are required if they are to effectively support the work of the Centre as well as have governance over the charity.

Paid staff have necessarily operated in a small team, as only few can be afforded. This can be problematic in itself as they need to be compatible. Some difficulties have arisen when there have been clashes of personality or of working style, exacerbated by the pressures of space and time. Young staff have seen the Centre as a training ground and gone on to bigger and better jobs subsequently. We have seen that, as a large, fixed cost, which potentially rises over time, the staff budget has been the target of cuts when times are hard. The level of pay has been discussed earlier and the trade-off identified between full-time versus part-time staff. The former provides possibly greater commitment and oversight, the latter may supply a wider range of skill but have less input. There is the choice too between having fewer well-paid or more less well-paid staff. Here the trade-off is between experienced but probably overstretched employees versus ones learning on the job and keen, but possibly struggling and needing mentoring. Bob Wild tried to get over this by keeping a lower base pay but using annual bonuses to boost salary if profits have been achieved. It seems a necessity to put as much money into the professional staff as possible as they are the core resource and expertise of the organisation.

That there is more work than people to do it is a given. This has been variously because of legislation, the expansion of the level of activities to increase income, higher customer expectations and the diversity of what is required: the delivery of the artistic programme, servicing the needs of the community and the maintenance of the facilities and building. Each new Centre Manager has come in with a 'new broom' and devised a masterplan which, according to their preferences, has targeted restructuring, audiences and marketing, policies and risk, community initiatives or fundraising. The Board have helped by bringing in consultants on occasions, that growing breed of experts spawned largely in the arts by the Lottery and its need for scrutineers. But who had the time (or money) to implement their ambitious schemes? Just to develop a very necessary four year business plan regularly seemed at times a gargantuan effort. As we have seen burnout has been a recurrent fate for those at the Arts Centre and this must be a concern. Pete Allen, arts administrator and creative, commented,

"Arts Centres, and Cranleigh is a perfect example, can be all-consuming for the people

who are running it. And there is never enough money. Some of the greatest and most impressive people I've ever come across working in theatre and venues can be eaten up and spat out by these buildings."

Whether 'artistic' people are more prone to this or their passion gets in the way of their sanity is debateable. Whatever the reason, we are moving into an employment era when a new generation will not do this. A new model must be found that allows people to work smarter, more efficiently or with more support. Technology may help here or more responsibility could be given to volunteers. The holy grail of generating sufficient income or subsidy to afford four full time paid staff, a suggested optimum to run Cranleigh Arts well, has as yet not been found.

Volunteers have already been credited with being the lifeblood of the organisation. However they too can cause problems. Like trustees they may have lots of bright ideas that don't quite fit. They may also decide that their way of doing something is best and do it that way, contrary to Centre practice. Jenny-Anne Dexter recalls early on having to ask a steward not to drink while on duty, much to his outrage. Disputes continue to this day over how to cut the cake and which way up glasses should be put on the shelves. Training is the key and in the past that has at times been poorly delivered and resisted. Ambitions to improve customer service, to make sure procedures are consistent and to conform to statutory regulations, all depend on the volunteers, who are the main interface with the visitors. Volunteers may have to be flattered and cajoled to conform, but most of all, they must be appreciated and communicated with, in order to engage with the Centre's mission as team members, not just as individuals. Some staff have been good at this, but now with a designated Volunteer Coordinator this is front and centre of their role, exemplified by Katie Wilson, the first appointee. When polled the volunteers' main complaints are usually about not knowing what is going on and a lack of connection to the trustees and staff. Newsletters, meetings, training, socials and personal contact can and have addressed this. But they can be resistant to necessary change and, as discussed earlier, are aging. Do they still have the physical and mental efficiency to carry out the tasks? Some rise to the challenge but others bow out. So there is a need in a more competitive climate to keep recruiting volunteers in all roles and hopefully the expanding community of Cranleigh will provide.

Money

Hard to make, easy to lose

If volunteers are the lifeblood of the organisation then money is the lifeblood of the business. The more you can generate then the stronger you are and the better choices you can make. The income streams are many, but some income is held for promoters or hirers where sales have been taken on their behalf. Deals with them vary from splits to a fee, with additional costs to be offset and advances credited. Add VAT and the ticket levy and the final settlement can be complex. Expenditure comes under many headings and those able to authorise it must be limited or it can run out of control. Online transactions must be tallied and cash counted and banked or made up into floats weekly. Keeping track of it all is key. An efficient bookkeeper and an astute Treasurer have some chance of doing this. They need to be the grown-ups in the room. A monthly balance can only be a snapshot. The art is to spot the trend and be able to project the direction of travel. The margin of profit on different activities can vary widely so strategic decisions need to balance out cross-subsidy. Too often the Centre has been on the back foot, reactive to discovering its financial reality, rather than in charge of its own budget to deliver its ambitions.

If sometimes ignorance of the financial reality has been an error, so too has been putting all the eggs in one strategic basket or person. To keep on with something in the hope that it will produce a different outcome is folly and has led to over-commitment for weak returns for which lack of proper scrutiny is to blame.

There is money to be had. The alternative philosophies of business versus subsidy have already been discussed. To get it, in either scenario, you need to create the right relationship with those who have it and get their support for the necessity of the arts. Know your audience and know your funders, be they public or private. Waverley Borough Council have, sometimes reluctantly, always come up with funds in a crisis. Partly because it suits the officers to deliver their arts policy by supporting Cranleigh Arts, and partly because the members have a political interest in rendering help. But as their budget gets squeezed how long can that be the case? One can't cry wolf too often; they will only invest in an organisation that is responsibly run and have needed some convincing on occasions.

Commercially, to get 'bums on seats' you need to give the public what they want. Listen to them. Get them to appreciate the value of Cranleigh Arts in what it offers them, give them a great service and upsell wherever possible, while keeping pricing competitive. In the past the rich data held on customers has been overlooked and not been mined to target marketing sufficiently. That could be exploited much better in the future to communicate with supporters and sell more tickets. Expanding the hires to make the existing space generate more is also key. It does seem in the current climate that making the organisation self-financing at the operational level and using any additional income for capital expenditure, to increase its potential earning capacity, seems the prudent one.

The Community
"This is your Centre"

Cranleigh Arts came into being from a perceived need by sections of the community. Its developing vision was for everyone to work together to provide the best arts opportunities for the community. Its expansion with community money, the Lottery, was celebrated by the community. As a charitable limited company business it has been run for the community by the staff and trustees. So how does this interface operate? Where is the representation, the dialogue, the accountability?

At present the Trustees/Directors are advertised for locally and voted in by Members at the AGM. The Members are a dwindling group who, formally have joined Cranleigh Arts by signing up and accepting a liability of £1. They vote on motions put to them and approve the accounts and annual report sent to the Charity Commission. As such they are the only constituted people holding the management to account. This could be seen as a flaw, leading to a self-appointing oligarchy propped up by a small likeminded group. To overcome this the Articles of Association issue should surely be addressed to broaden access to the members' group and widen community representation in governance.

More Cranleigh residents are involved through being Friends and Volunteers, and Chairmen have been careful over the years to keep them in the loop. They can be vocal in their criticisms at times. Hirers and promoters have also been known to complain to the Chairman if they disapprove of what the staff have done. Waverley too, as a sponsor, receives feedback against the criteria of their support grant and through their elected councillors speaks for the people of Cranleigh with regard to the Centre. Both the Borough and Parish Council still have observers sitting on the Board, although they are non-voting. They too could be seen to represent the community.

Good communication – advertising, marketing, social media, news outlets, word of mouth – all inform and engage the community in the activities of the Centre. That brings about local participation and footfall. But it is still possible to stop someone in the High Street and for them not to know the Arts Centre exists! Involvement with the many different groups that exist in Cranleigh, either as a venue, a sponsor or event promoter, should build partnership and strengthen the connection with them. People must feel a sense of ownership and a love for the building and the organisation that runs it. Only then will it truly be Cranleigh's community arts centre.

Conclusion
Keep on changing, but value what you've got

Because change is constant resilience has been the key. That has usually depended on people and good leadership, but also on financial skills, community support, a welcoming building and a passion to succeed. It has, since the beginning, 'punched above its weight' and enabled so many people to discover what the arts have to offer. That was always the mission. Whoever has been touched by it knows its worth to Cranleigh and because of that, it must be celebrated and handed on. The problems will recur, but maybe, from this record of the corporate memory, past mistakes will not be repeated nor the wheel have to be reinvented.

After fifty years the efforts of so many devotees have created Cranleigh Arts, developed its vision and sustained it through good and bad times. It is a small miracle of what the arts can do for people and what people can do for the arts. They say it takes a village to raise a child – the Arts Centre has been no exception.

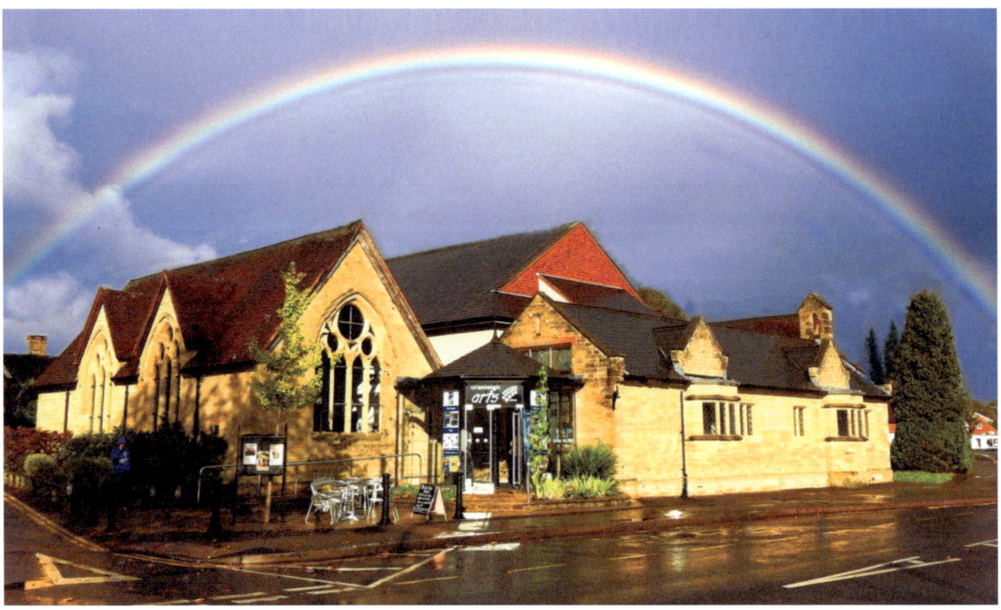

cranleigh arts

To enrich, entertain & inspire our community...

Cranleigh Arts Roll Call

Some of the key players

Chairmen

1974 – 1976	Malcom Beeson
1977	Edgar Odell Foster
1978	Richard Whitehead
1980 – 1993	Jack Wagg
1993 – 1995	John Dickerson
1995 – 2005	Catherine Pike
2005 – 2009	Rosemary French
2010 – 2016	Stephen Dennison
2016 – 2022	Bob Wild
2023	Brian Belcher
2024	Brian Freeston

Treasurers

1974	D Coles
1975	Les Field
1977 – 1985	Reg Lawrence
1986 – 1988	Tony Stevens
1989 – 1999	Harry Stadler
1999	John Pearce
2000 – 2005	Richard Paton
2006 – 2010	Mike Kiernan
2011 – 2015	John Gill
2016	Bob Wild
2017 – 2019	Robert Watkins
2019 – 2022	David Whitaker
2022 – 2023	Brian Belcher/ Charles Hurtley
2024	John Haile

Centre Managers/Artistic Directors/Operations Coordinators

1974 – 1980	*Management Committee*
1980 – 1987	Dilys Savedra
1988 – 1998	Rosemary Dubois
1997	*Closed*
1998 – 1999	Helen Cundy
2000	Mark Wright
2001 – 2005	Helen Cundy
2005 – 2006	Debbie Stubbs
2006 – 2007	*Operations: Derek Sanders*
2007 – 2008	Louise Grundy + Jenny Squire
2009 – 2011	Jenny Squire
2011 – 2013	Jenny-Anne Dexter
2013 – 2017	Kary Backhouse
2017 – 2021	*Operations: Clive Wouters*
2021 – 2024	Sophie Woods
2022 – 2024	*Operations: Jackie Sanctuary*
2024	Paul Scott

Trustees/Directors

This record is for Cranleigh Arts Centre Ltd. Co. at Companies House (not Cranleigh Arts and Leisure Trust) and depended on the Secretary keeping it updated, so may not be complete. It includes some Secretaries in addition to elected members.

Peter	Adams	David	Hitchen	Phil	Rickett
Kavita	Agarwal	Anne	Hull	Ken	Rushton
Kary	Backhouse	John	Hurst	Jackie	Sanctuary
Brian	Belcher	Rob	Kerby	John	Savage
Frederick	Cullingford	Hannah	Kester	George	Scurry
Gordon	Davis	Mike	Kiernan	Henry	Stadler
Stephen	Dennison	Ray	Lambeth	Margaret	Steele
John	Dickerson	Lil	Lambley	Manisha	Thaker
Rosemary	Dubois	Muriel	Longhurst	Anthony	Thould
Chris	Dubois	James	Mainwaring	Anthony	Todd
Brian	Ellis	Chrissie	Matthews	Geoffrey	Tresman
Ruth	Farmer	Danyah	Miller	Sarah	Underhill
Steven	Fowler	Vaughan	Mitchell	Jack	Wagg
Brian	Freeston	Reg	Monk	Robert	Watkins
Rosemary	French	Anita	Morris	Brenda	Weller
Alan	Frogatt	Nicholas	Morris	David	Whitaker
Stephanie	Gallo	Lynne	Murray	Stephen	White
John	Gill	Arthur	Nicholls	Robert	Wild
Geoffrey	Goodfellow	Callum	Paterson	Antonia	Wilson
Roger	Hard	Richard	Paton	Chris	Wilson
Joanne	Hartley	John	Pearce	Alison	Winter
Frances	Haywood	Catherine	Pike	Clive	Wouters
Henry	Hemingway	Simon	Rabinowitz	Arthur	Wren
Caroline	Heslop	Emma	Rafferty		

Sources, acknowledgements and bibliography

Sources

The material for this book has been drawn from the archive of the Arts Centre, which had been boxed and semi-sorted in 2010, but depleted by some over enthusiastic disposal subsequently. There I found Board minutes, press cuttings, letters, memos, accounts, newsletters and much more, including the files of Jack Wagg, Catherine Pike and Harry Stadler. To that was added a substantial number of files from Chris and Rosemary Dubois and from Malcolm Beeson and my own records. My thanks to them and to the Trustees of the Arts Centre for allowing me to access all this wealth of material, but some gaps did remain.

To this were added interviews with the people who had direct experience of events at the time. I must thank the following for talking to me and allowing me to use their memories and insights: Pete Allen, Kary Backhouse, Janet Baverstock, Malcolm Beeson, Jane Bowden, Edwina Burton, Helen Cundy, Gina and Stephen Dennison, Jenny-Anne Dexter, John Dixon (JD), Rosemary and Chris Dubois, Sharon Duggan, Ruth Eastelow, Ruth Farmer, Rosemary French, David Goff, Arthur Gomez, Louise Grundy, Ann and Jon Horrocks, Peter Hunt, Mike Kiernan, Mark Matthews, Vaughan Mitchell, Nick Morris, Sue Palmer-Jones, Callum Paterson, David Pike, Carol Sacha, Linda Salway, Manisha Thaker, Jane Sharpe-Trawber, David Weaver, Bob Wild and Sophie Woods.

Inevitably I have found that 'some recollections may vary' and the Centre folklore did not always align with the written record. Where possible I have sought to triangulate or cross-reference the details. In the end I have tried to give an honest interpretation of what seemed to me to have happened and how and why. I take full and sole responsibility for this and apologise for any errors or omissions made or offence given.

Acknowledgements

The illustrations have come from the Centre's archive and from local newspapers. It has been largely impossible to establish who took them. Those from Cranleigh Arts were probably taken by the Marketing Assistants or Centre Managers over the years, or by other volunteers or contracted photographers, so copyright probably lies with Cranleigh Arts, who have fully supported this book. Personal photos have come from Malcolm Beeson, Rosemary Dubois, Louise Grundy and Mark Matthews. For the Surrey Advertiser and other local newspapers I can credit Alan Golden, Jake Darling, Pete Gardner, Mike Hawley, Janice Jubert, Grahame Larter, Chris Whiteoak and other unnamed staff photographers. I hope that if they spot their work they might be happy to allow republication here retrospectively in the interests of historical record.

I must also thank Peter Holloway, Joy Horn, Bridget Howland for her excellent design and editing skills, Tanya Izzard for the Index, Martin Nelson and his team at Quacks Books and Sue Palmer. They all helped to bring this book to fruition.

Bibliography

Around Cranleigh. Michael Miller. Chalford Publishing Company. 1995

Care, Diligence and Skill. A corporate governance handbook for arts organisations. Scottish Arts Council. 2007

Cranleigh A History. Christopher Budgen. Phillimore. 2008

Cranleigh Life and Times. Muriel Longhurst, Michael Miller, Anne Woodford, Chris Baker. U3A. 1999

Cranleigh Neighbourhood Plan 2016

Reflections From a Village. Frank Swinnerton. Hutchinson. 1969

The Art of Flexibility. Arts Centres in the 1990s. Joy MacKeith & Ruth Glick. Arts Council. 1996

The Economic Importance of the Arts in Britain. John Myerscough. Policy Studies Institute. 1988

Use or Ornament? The social impact of participation in the arts. Francois Matarasso. Comedia. 1997

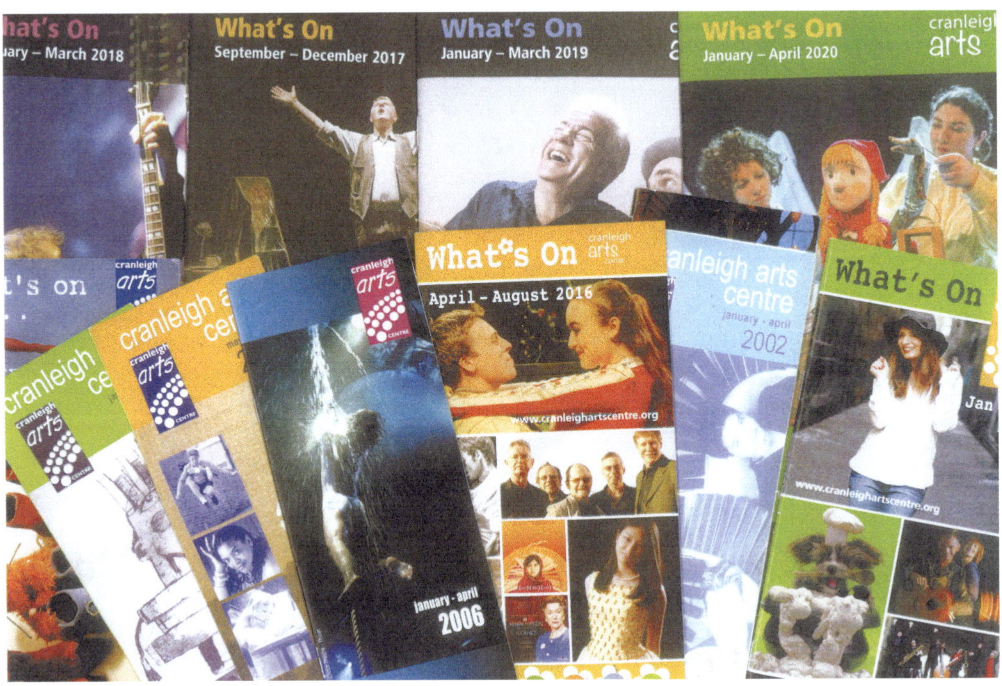

Index

The suffix illus. indicates an illustration, and tab. material in a table.

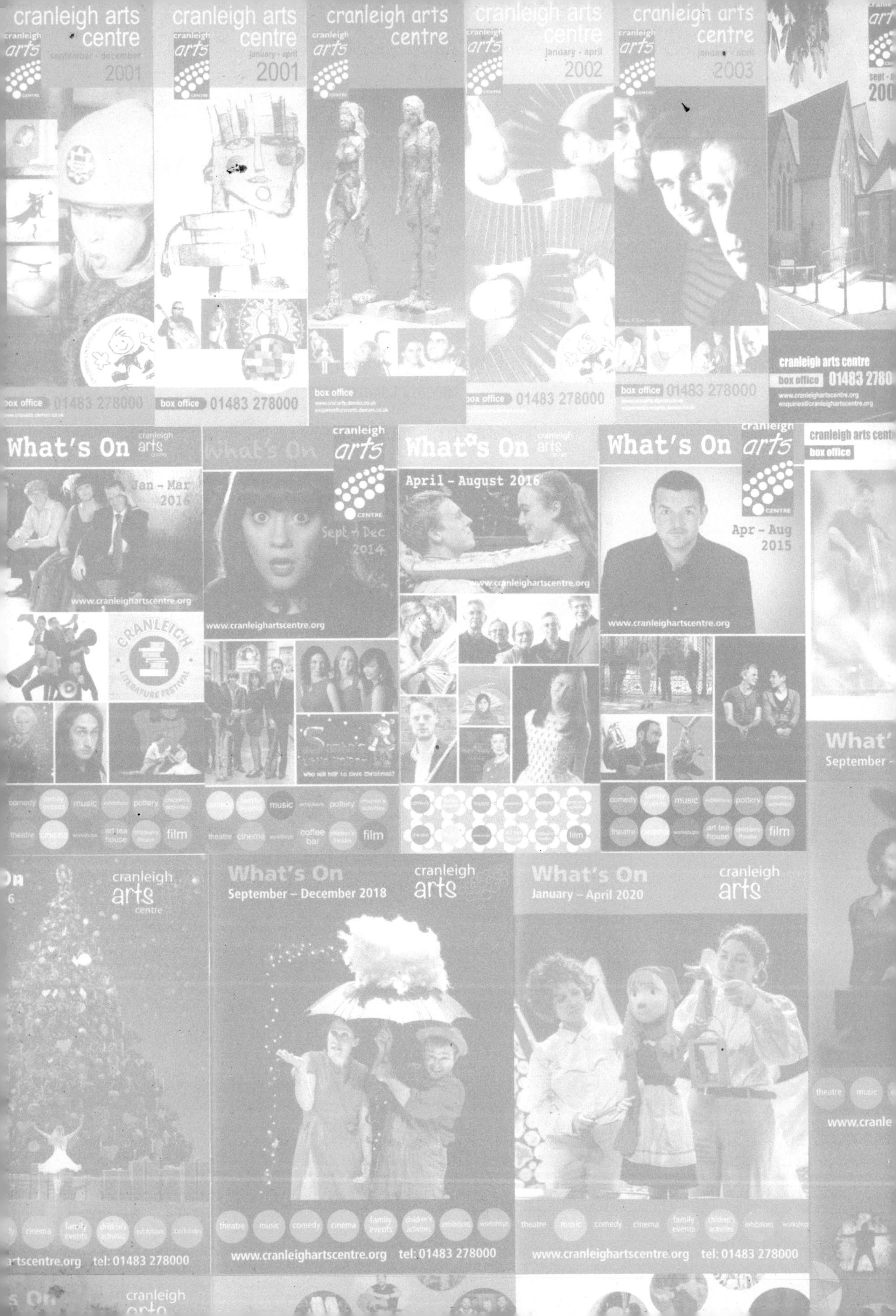

cranleigh arts centre
september - december 2001
box office 01483 278000
cranleigh arts centre
january - april 2001
box office 01483 278000
cranleigh arts centre
box office
cranleigh arts centre
january - april 2002
box office 01483 278000
cranleigh arts centre
january - april 2003
box office 01483 278000
cranleigh arts centre
box office 01483 2780
www.cranleighartscentre.org
enquiries@cranleighartscentre.org
What's On
Jan - Mar 2016
www.cranleighartscentre.org
CRANLEIGH
LITERATURE FESTIVAL
comedy
music
pottery
theatre
cinema
art tea house
film
What's On
cranleigh arts centre
Sept - Dec 2014
www.cranleighartscentre.org
Who will help to save Christmas?
music
pottery
theatre
cinema
coffee bar
film
What's On
April - August 2016
www.cranleighartscentre.org
film
What's On
cranleigh arts centre
Apr - Aug 2015
www.cranleighartscentre.org
comedy
music
pottery
theatre
cinema
art tea house
film
cranleigh arts centre
box office
What's
September -
cranleigh arts centre
cinema
family events
artscentre.org tel: 01483 278000
What's On
September - December 2018
cranleigh arts
theatre
music
comedy
cinema
family events
children's activities
exhibitions
workshops
www.cranleighartscentre.org tel: 01483 278000
What's On
January - April 2020
cranleigh arts
theatre
music
comedy
cinema
family events
children's activities
exhibitions
workshops
www.cranleighartscentre.org tel: 01483 278000
theatre
music
www.cranle
cranleigh